Payment Systems, Banking, and Documentary Transactions

Carolina Academic Press
Law Casebook Series
Advisory Board

❧

Gary J. Simson, Chairman
Dean, Case Western Reserve University School of Law

Raj Bhala
University of Kansas School of Law

John C. Coffee, Jr.
Columbia University Law School

Randall Coyne
University of Oklahoma College of Law

John S. Dzienkowski
University of Texas School of Law

Paul Finkelman
Albany Law School

Robert M. Jarvis
Shepard Broad Law Center
Nova Southeastern University

Vincent R. Johnson
St. Mary's University School of Law

Michael A. Olivas
University of Houston Law Center

Kenneth Port
William Mitchell College of Law

Michael P. Scharf
Case Western Reserve University School of Law

Peter M. Shane
Michael E. Moritz College of Law
The Ohio State University

Emily L. Sherwin
Cornell Law School

John F. Sutton, Jr.
Emeritus, University of Texas School of Law

David B. Wexler
John E. Rogers College of Law
University of Arizona

Payment Systems, Banking, and Documentary Transactions

Problems, Cases, and Comments

SECOND EDITION

Edited by

Dellas W. Lee
EMERITUS PROFESSOR OF LAW
TEXAS TECH UNIVERSITY

and

Timothy R. Zinnecker
PROFESSOR OF LAW
SOUTH TEXAS COLLEGE OF LAW

CAROLINA ACADEMIC PRESS
Durham, North Carolina

Copyright © 2007
Dellas W. Lee and Timothy R. Zinnecker
All Rights Reserved

ISBN 10: 1-59460-429-0
ISBN 13: 978-1-59460-429-4
LCCN 2007928098

Carolina Academic Press
700 Kent Street
Durham, NC 27701
Telephone (919) 489-7486
Fax (919) 493-5668
www.cap-press.com

Printed in the United States of America

To my gracious wife, Mary
— D.L.W.

To Robert and Elaine, my extraordinary and beloved parents
— T.R.Z.

Contents

Preface

Dellas Lee, my co-author and principal draftsman of the first edition, has retired as a professor of law at Texas Tech University. He gave me unfettered discretion in creating this second edition. The fruits of his labor remain throughout this work, which rightfully continues to bear his name.

Like the first edition, this second edition continues to rely heavily on problems as the primary learning tool. Most of the problems found in the first edition remain, with some tweaking here and there. Some new problems have been added. A few cases from the first edition have been deleted, and a handful of new cases have been added. Textual material has been updated where appropriate.

As noted in the first edition, the classroom has served as a working laboratory during the writing of this book. On behalf of Dellas Lee, I extend gratitude to the many students who have offered insightful comments and helpful suggestions, and express appreciation to Carolina Academic Press for being our publisher.

Timothy R. Zinnecker

Introduction

Negotiable instruments have been important to the world of commerce for more than a thousand years, a period during which the right to the payment of money has been conveyed from one person to another by the transfer of a piece of paper. The early development and long importance of negotiable instruments is suggested by the fact that even before the ninth century on the continent of Europe (and probably in England) a right to the payment of money could be merged with and into a piece of paper. That is, the right to the payment of money could be made to depend upon the production of the paper on which the obligation to pay was written.

Negotiable instruments – the most common of which are promissory notes and checks – are still indispensable to the consumer and commercial world, and their end is nowhere in sight. A study conducted for the Federal Reserve System in 2004 revealed that 36.7 billion checks were paid in 2003, having an average value of $1,070 and an aggregate value of $39.3 trillion.[1] But the advent of sophisticated communications technology now permits the majority of noncash payments to be initiated electronically with a debit or credit card, or through an automated clearinghouse (e.g., direct deposits or automatic withdrawals). The same study revealed that 44.5 billion electronic payments originated in the United States in 2003, with an aggregate value of $27.4 trillion and an average value of $617. That trend – more electronic payments and fewer paper-based payments – is expected to continue.

The materials in this textbook cover paper-based and electronic payments and are divided into four parts. In Part I (chapters 1, 2, and 3) our primary focus is on promissory notes, with emphasis on selected provisions of U.C.C. Article 3.[2] In Part II (chapters 4 and 5) we shift our primary focus to drafts and checks, including some banking law and procedure, again focusing attention on selected provisions of U.C.C. Article 3, and adding selected provisions of U.C.C. Article 4. In Part III (chapters 6 and 7), we place the use of notes, drafts, and checks into their commercial context through a study of documents of title under U.C.C. Article 7 and letters of credit under U.C.C. Article 5. Finally, in Part IV (chapters 8, 9, and 10), we explore electronic payment systems, with emphasis on consumer electronic fund transfers under federal law, commercial wire transfers governed by U.C.C. Article 4A, and credit card transactions under federal law.

---

1. See "The 2004 Federal Reserve Payments Study," available at http://www.frbservices.org/Retail/pdf/2004PaymentResearchReport.pdf.

2. Unless otherwise indicated, all U.C.C. citations are to the various Articles as revised through 2006. Citations to former versions of an Article are prefaced with an "F" (e.g., F§ 3-104). A former version of selected Articles can be found in your statutes book.

Payment Systems, Banking, and Documentary Transactions

Part I

Promissory Notes

We begin with promissory notes, although occasionally it will be helpful to make references to drafts and checks for comparison, illustration, and perspective as we proceed. Pedagogically, the sequence of focusing first on promissory notes and then on drafts and checks is desirable for two reasons. First, this permits us to move from the more simple two-party instrument, the promissory note, to the more complex three-party negotiable instruments—drafts and checks. Although the formal differences between notes and drafts are small, the functional differences between these instruments are substantial. First, dealing with the two instruments separately helps to eliminate confusion and encourages more detailed concentration on the nature and financial function of each in its appropriate context. Second, dealing with promissory notes first makes good commercial sense from a functional point of view because in a commercial transaction, whether it be a sale of goods, the purchase of real estate on credit, or a loan, the underlying contract containing the promise to pay the debt will typically be evidenced by a promissory note. But when the note comes due, payments usually will be made by check or draft. Consistent with this commercial sequence, we examine notes before examining checks and drafts.

Although we begin with promissory notes, we will not attempt to cover all of the basic law related to notes before moving on to the other instruments. Rather, we will deal only with the legal problems most frequently encountered when promissory notes are involved. That is, we will focus on those aspects of negotiable instruments law most frequently applied by the courts when promissory notes have been the subject of litigation. We will then do the same with drafts. For example, the formal requisites of negotiability will be discussed in connection with promissory notes, not because formal requisites do not apply to drafts or checks, but because most of the legal problems involving the rules of negotiability have usually arisen in connection with promissory notes.

Chapter 1

The Formal Requisites of Negotiability

The doctrine of negotiability may seem to be unduly formalistic and somewhat nebulous when first encountered. But it becomes more meaningful as we keep in mind the primary purpose of negotiability, which is to promote commerce in a credit economy.

So what is a negotiable instrument, or an "instrument," as defined in Article 3? A negotiable instrument is a contract. But it is a special kind of contract because it has some of the attributes of money. These monetary attributes are a product of negotiability. A negotiable instrument is a piece of paper that contains a promise or an order to pay money to a payee, and if it is in the proper form and transferred in the proper manner, and if the transferee takes the instrument for value and without notice of any problems with it, the transferee becomes a holder in due course and thereby takes the instrument free of most claims and defenses the maker or drawer or any other person may have with respect to the instrument. That is, if a person has a negotiable instrument and if he is a holder in due course, he will take the instrument free of most of the equities and defenses any obligor on the instrument might have against the payee or any other party to the instrument. This rare privilege given to a holder in due course encourages the free flow of such paper and thus promotes commerce.

By contrast, as we know, it is a basic rule of common law that one who takes a contract by assignment takes that paper subject to existing equities and defenses between the original parties. This is a manifestation of the principal of derivative title. A transferee receives the rights of his transferor and no more. That is, the assignee is said to stand in the shoes of the assignor. Therefore if Maker is being sued by Holder who claims to hold a negotiable instrument issued by Maker, Maker should determine whether the instrument is in fact negotiable. If it is not, it is at most a contract obligation to pay, and Holder cannot be a holder in due course and the defenses had by Maker can be raised against Holder. If, however, the instrument is negotiable, Holder may be a holder in due course and thus not be subject to the claims or defenses of Maker.

The implications of using a negotiable instrument, with its monetary attributes, may be further illustrated this way. Suppose Buyer buys goods from Seller and pays for them with *money*. Later Buyer discovers he has a claim or defense against Seller for breach of warranty. Suppose further that in the meantime the money Buyer gave to Seller has passed from the hands of Seller to T, and onward to other parties in the normal course of things. Buyer may have a good claim against Seller to whom Buyer paid his money, but what are Buyer's chances of recovering the money (originally given to Seller) from T or some subsequent party who now holds the money, but with whom Buyer has had no dealings? Without even knowing the law, a layperson would probably expect that legally his chances are nonexistent. This probably is what Buyer would have expected if he had thought the matter through before tendering the money.

So it is with negotiable instruments law. If Buyer had made Seller the beneficiary of a negotiable instrument, whether a promissory note, draft, or check, and the instrument had been passed on to T, and perhaps yet on to another remote party, Buyer may find himself in the same situation as if he had tendered money. That is, Buyer would be obligated to pay the money represented by the instrument, even though he now discovers he has a good defense against Seller — the party to whom he originally gave the instrument. This is because in using a negotiable instrument the parties evidence an intent to simulate the use of money as far as possible.

Since negotiable instruments represent money, or more accurately the obligation to pay money, they are used as payment instruments — to pay debts, the price of goods, and other property. They also play a large role as credit devices in making loans and purchases on credit. As payment and credit instruments they act as a substitute for money while avoiding some of the risks inherent in dealing with money, namely theft, particularly where large amounts of money need to be transferred outside normal banking channels. Negotiable instruments can perform these and still other useful commercial functions largely because of the phenomenon of *negotiability*.

Negotiability is derived largely from the holder in due course doctrine and the merger doctrine which form the basis of the currency and credit attributes of negotiable instruments today. Professor Gilmore made some insightful comments on the origin of these doctrines.

> In putting together their law of negotiable instruments, the courts assumed that the new mercantile currency was a good thing whose use should be encouraged. Two quite simple ideas became the foundation pieces for the whole structure. One was the good faith purchase idea. The stranger who purchased the bill in the market was entitled to do so without inquiry into the facts of the underlying transaction or of previous transfers of the bill and without being affected by them: if he bought the bill for value, in good faith and in the ordinary course of business, he held it free both of underlying contract defenses and of outstanding equities of ownership. The other idea which, the first time you run into it, sounds like nonsense — the legal mind at its worst — was even more basic to the structure and indeed was what gave the completed edifice its pure and almost unearthly beauty. That was the idea that the piece of paper on which the bill was written or printed should be treated as if it — the piece of paper — was itself the claim or debt which it evidenced. This idea came to be known as the doctrine of merger — the debt was merged in the instrument. At one stroke it drastically simplified the law of negotiable instruments, to the benefit of both purchasers and the people required to pay the instruments. Under merger theory the only way of transferring the debt represented by the bill was by physical delivery of the bill itself to the transferee. The courts also worked out an elaborate set of rules on when the transferor was required to endorse, as well as deliver, the bill and on what liabilities to subsequent parties he assumed by endorsing.[1]

From this we see that the obligation to pay and the right to receive payment under a negotiable instrument is a reified right. That is, those rights are embodied in the instrument itself. To obtain those rights a transferee must take the instrument by negotiation.

---

1. Gilmore, "*Formalism and the Law of Negotiable Instruments*," 13 CREIGHTON L. REV. 441, 448–49, reprinted with permission (1979). Copyright © 1979 by Creighton University.

Thus the currency or monetary substitute element comes from two attributes of a negotiable instrument. One is that the obligation to pay and the right to receive payment are merged in the instrument itself. This means that the right to receive payment depends upon having possession of an instrument which contains a promise or order to pay. Basically, that means that only a holder, or one with the rights of a holder, is entitled to enforce the instrument. §3-301. The second element that gives a negotiable instrument the attributes of currency is its cut-off power. A transferee who gives value for an instrument in good faith and without notice of any problems with the instrument may become a holder in due course and thereby take the instrument free of most claims to it and free of most defenses that may be raised by the maker or drawer against the payee. §§3-302, 3-305.

The second reason why negotiable instruments pass like money is that they provide a reliable basis for credit. Transferees are willing to extend credit to makers and drawers of instruments for the very reason that they are a substitute for money, or a right to payment of money. A person who takes an instrument by negotiation becomes a person entitled to enforce the instrument against the obligor. §§3-201, 3-301. Therefore if the maker or drawer is a person of known financial creditworthiness, a transferee of an instrument may be willing to give credit to the maker or drawer in return for an instrument because he knows that it contains the maker's or drawer's obligation to pay on demand or at some stipulated time. Further encouragement comes from the assurance that as a holder in due course he might not be defeated by a future claim to the instrument or by a defense of the maker or drawer, such as a breach of warranty, that the obligor could raise against the payee.

A negotiable instrument also offers the advantage of lowering the cost of credit. This is because an obligation to pay that is embodied in a negotiable instrument is more saleable. It has a greater market value and is more attractive to financial institutions than an obligation embodied in a nonnegotiable contract. This economic advantage of using a negotiable instrument arises from the fact that a negotiable instrument in the hands of a holder in due course reduces the risk of nonpayment. This in turn reduces the administrative costs of those who handle negotiable instruments, who therefore are willing to pay more for them. People who buy or otherwise deal in negotiable instruments can usually determine rather swiftly whether they are dealing with a negotiable instrument by merely perusing the face of the instrument. Thus their administrative costs in handling this paper are reduced accordingly. Consequently, when a bank knows it is buying such a negotiable instrument, it can justifiably charge lower discount rates. However, if a contract is not a negotiable instrument, administrative costs to the bank will be increased by the time and expense involved in determining financial risks, even if the bank should ultimately conclude the risk of nonpayment under the contract is very slight.

A negotiable instrument also offers the holder an advantage in litigation by reducing the procedural and evidentiary obstacles to enforcement. The holder of a negotiable instrument has less to prove, because the law provides certain presumptions in favor of the holder. For example, mere production of the instrument permits the plaintiff to recover unless the defendant proves he has a defense or claim in recoupment. §3-308 OC 1 & 2.

These advantages and consequences associated with a negotiable instrument leads us to the question: Why is a negotiable instrument so easily identifiable, and distinguishable from a nonnegotiable contract? The answer lies in its form. A contract must be in a particular form to qualify as a negotiable instrument. If it meets the legal requirements of §3-104 for the creation of a negotiable instrument, it is negotiable; if it does not, it is not negotiable. The formal requisites of negotiability are specific and limited in number, and whether they exist can usually be determined fairly easily since they must be ascertainable from the face of the instrument alone. Therefore the transferee of an instrument need not review any ancillary writings or search elsewhere to determine whether he will have the advantages of negotiability. He can make that determination by perusing the instrument itself.

The formal requisites of negotiability have evolved from commercial practices of merchants and financial institutions in the ordinary course of business over several centuries. As the commercial world has changed, the formal requisites and other aspects of negotiable instruments law have tried to keep pace. Usually, changes have come in the form of relaxation of what were once rather inflexible form requirements in the earlier history of negotiable instruments law. For example, with respect to the fixed-sum and definite-time requirements, what might be described as a commercial-certainty standard has to some degree overshadowed what was once a mathematical-certainty standard. Notwithstanding such relaxations, interestingly, the formal requisites of negotiability have stood the test of time without much change, which demonstrates that the rules of negotiability are in fact based on good commercial logic and business utility.

The rationale underlying the rules of negotiability is that they aid in determining the present value of an instrument containing a promise or order to pay money in the future.

Article 3 "applies to negotiable instruments." § 3-102(a). The formal requisites of a "negotiable instrument" are stated in § 3-104. The negotiability of an instrument is determined by measuring it against these formal requisites, as illustrated by the following materials.

EMERSON v. ZAGURSKI

531 N.W.2d 237 (Neb. App. Ct. 1995)

Irwin, Judge.

Blake Emerson appeals the judgment of the district court for Douglas County, Nebraska, sustaining the demurrer to her second amended petition and the subsequent dismissal of her lawsuit. Emerson claims that she did state a cause of action that was not barred by the statute of limitations. Because the district court applied the improper statute of limitations, we reverse, and remand for further proceedings.

SECOND AMENDED PETITION

In her second amended petition, Emerson alleges that on or about September 17, 1985, she and Robin M. Zagurski entered into a loan agreement in which she loaned Zagurski $17,000. Emerson alleges that Zagurski failed, neglected, and refused to make payments as called for by the agreement and that the most recent payment was made by Zagurski on January 2, 1987. She alleges that Zagurski acknowledged her liability on the contract and renewed her promise to pay in writing in December 1987. She alleges that a further acknowledgment of liability was contained in a letter dated July 31, 1990, received from Zagurski's legal counsel. Emerson alleges that she made demand upon Zagurski for payment of the debt, although the specific date of the demand is not pled. She also alleges that as a result of Zagurski's failure to pay, she declared the entire debt due. She alleges that as of July 20, 1990, the balance due under the agreement is $23,219.26 plus interest at the rate of 10 percent per year since July 20, 1990. The promissory note between the parties was executed September 17, 1985. It reads, in relevant part, as follows:

For full value received, I promise to pay to L. Blake Emerson ... or her order upon demand the sum of seventeen thousand ($17,000.00) dollars with interest at the rate of ten percent (10%) per annum payable monthly on the 24th day of each and every month until the principal of the within note is fully paid.

PROCEDURAL HISTORY

The original petition in this matter was filed in the district court for Douglas County on December 31, 1992. It alleged that a loan agreement was entered into on September 17, 1985, and that Zagurski had not paid the amounts due and owing. On January 19, 1993, Zagurski filed a demurrer, alleging that the "petition does not state facts sufficient to constitute a cause of action in that it appears from the face of the petition that the alleged cause of action for payment on the demand note is barred by the statute of limitations as set forth in NEB. REV. STAT. §25-205." On February 11, 1993, after arguments were heard, the district court sustained the demurrer and ordered Emerson to file an amended petition within 10 days and to attach the loan agreement mentioned in the original petition.

* * *

ASSIGNMENTS OF ERROR

Emerson makes the following assignments of error: (1) The district court erred in sustaining Zagurski's demurrer, and (2) the district court erred in finding that the letter from Zagurski's counsel to Emerson's counsel did not constitute an acknowledgment of an existing debt or a promise to pay the same.

STANDARD OF REVIEW

Which statute of limitations applies is a question of law that an appellate court must decide independently of the conclusion reached by the trial court. Central States Resources v. First Nat. Bank, 243 Neb. 538, 501 N.W.2d 271 (1993).

DISCUSSION

* * *

In an appellate court's review of a ruling on a general demurrer, the court is required to accept as true all the facts which are well pled and the proper and reasonable inferences of law and fact which may be drawn therefrom, but not the conclusions of the pleader. Ventura v. State, 246 Neb. 116, 517 N.W.2d 368 (1994); Hoffman, supra. The first step in our analysis is to determine the applicable statute of limitations. As a general rule, the limitations period in effect at the time an action is filed governs the action. Schendt v. Dewey, 246 Neb. 573, 520 N.W.2d 541 (1994); Givens v. Anchor Packing, 237 Neb. 565, 466 N.W.2d 771 (1991). Article 3 of the Uniform Commercial Code determines the rights and obligations of parties to negotiable instruments. Neb. U.C.C. §§3-102(a) (Reissue 1992). Neb. U.C.C. §3-118 (Reissue 1992), effective January 1, 1992, provides a 6-year statute of limitations for promissory notes that are negotiable instruments. See Givens, supra (holding that it is competent for the Legislature to change statutes prescribing limitations to actions and that the one in force at the time suit is brought is applicable to the cause of action; however, the Legislature cannot remove a bar or limitation which has already become complete). See, also, Schendt, supra. Emerson's cause of action was not time barred under the applicable statutes prescribing limitations to actions on the effective date of §3-118. See, Neb. U.C.C. §3-122 (Reissue

1980); Neb. Rev. Stat. § 25-205 (Reissue 1989). Therefore, if the promissory note entered into by Emerson and Zagurski is a negotiable instrument, the 6-year statute of limitations provided in the Uniform Commercial Code is applicable. See § 3-118. If the promissory note is not a negotiable instrument, the 5-year statute of limitations for actions on written contracts is applicable. See § 25-205. It appears from the record before us that the district court and the parties applied the 5-year statute of limitations.

The Uniform Commercial Code defines the term "negotiable instrument." An "instrument" is either a "promise," which is a written undertaking to pay money signed by the person undertaking to pay, Neb. U.C.C. § 3-103(a)(9) (Reissue 1992), or an "order," which is a written instruction to pay money signed by the person giving the instruction. § 3-103(a)(6). Neb. U.C.C. § 3-104 (Reissue 1992) provides that an instrument is negotiable if the following requirements are met. First, the promise or order must be unconditional. § 3-104(a). The promise or order is unconditional unless it states an express condition to payment, it is subject to or governed by another writing, or the rights or obligations with respect to the promise or order are stated in another writing. Neb. U.C.C. § 3-106 (Reissue 1992). Second, the amount of money must be "a fixed amount ... with or without interest or other charges described in the promise or order." § 3-104(a). Third, the promise or order must be "payable to bearer or to order." § 3-104(a)(1). This language regarding "payable to bearer or to order" is defined in Neb. U.C.C. § 3-109 (Reissue 1992), which states in part:

(a) A promise or order is payable to bearer if it:

(1) states that it is payable to bearer or to the order of bearer or otherwise indicates that the person in possession of the promise or order is entitled to payment;

(2) does not state a payee; or

(3) states that it is payable to or to the order of cash or otherwise indicates that it is not payable to an identified person.

(b) A promise or order that is not payable to bearer is payable to order if it is payable (i) to the order of an identified person or (ii) to an identified person or order. A promise or order that is payable to order is payable to the identified person.

The fourth requirement for a negotiable instrument is that the promise or order must be payable "on demand or at a definite time." § 3-104(a)(2). A negotiable instrument that is payable on demand may provide for the payment of interest on a specified basis such as monthly or yearly. See Berman v. United States Nat. Bank, 197 Neb. 268, 249 N.W.2d 187 (1976). Fifth, and last, the promise or order may not state "any other undertaking or instruction by the person promising or ordering payment to do any act in addition to the payment of money," with three exceptions that are not relevant to the case before us. § 3-104(a)(3). See, generally, § 3-104, comment 1.

Based upon the properly pled allegations in the second amended petition and its attachments and the applicable law, we conclude that the promissory note in the case before us is a negotiable instrument because it is an unconditional promise made by Zagurski to pay $17,000 plus interest to Emerson or her order upon demand. Therefore, the 6-year statute of limitations in the Uniform Commercial Code is controlling.

* * *

As the promissory note at issue is payable upon demand, the statute of limitations would begin to run after demand for payment was made. See § 3-118(b). If no demand for payment is made, an action to enforce the note is barred if neither principal nor interest on the note has been paid for a continuous period of 10 years. Id.

The second amended petition alleges that demand was made, but does not provide the date on which it was made. As a result, it is not apparent from the face of the petition that the action is time barred. If a particular date of demand were alleged, it could be determined from the face of the petition whether the cause of action was barred by the statute of limitations. As the petition only contains a general allegation of demand, it is not subject to demurrer.

We need not address Emerson's assignments of error regarding whether either the December 1987 letter from Zagurski to Emerson or the July 31, 1990, letter to Emerson's counsel from Zagurski's counsel constituted proper acknowledgment of the debt, tolling the statute of limitations period.

We conclude as a matter of law that the applicable statute of limitations is the 6-year statute of limitations for promissory notes in the Uniform Commercial Code. The district court's judgment sustaining Zagurski's demurrer and holding that Emerson's cause of action was time barred was in error because it applied the incorrect statute of limitations. Therefore, we reverse, and remand for further proceedings.

REVERSED AND REMANDED FOR FURTHER PROCEEDINGS.

A. Writing, Signed by the Maker or Drawer, and Words of Negotiability

Section 3-104 establishes the formal requisites of negotiability. Among other things it requires a writing, signed by the maker or drawer, that includes certain words of negotiability.

1. Writing

Section 3-104(a) requires a "promise or order." Both terms are defined in § 3-103, and each definition requires a writing. Thus there cannot be an oral promissory note or an oral draft or check. The writing requirement is rather easily met because of the broad definition of "written" or "writing" provided in § 1-201(b)(43), which includes "printing, typewriting, or any other intentional reduction to tangible form." This requirement has given the courts little difficulty.

2. Signature

The definitions of "order" and "promise" also require a signature. "Signed," like "writing," is also broadly defined, and "includes using any symbol executed or adopted with present intention to adopt or accept a writing." § 1-201(b)(37). An authentication would include not only a traditional signature, but also a printed signature, a stamp, and even a thumbprint, if so intended. "The question always is whether the symbol was executed or adopted by the party with present intention to adopt or accept the writing." § 1-201 OC 37.

3. Words of Negotiability: "Payable to Bearer or to Order"

Another element of negotiability is bearer or order language. The promise or order must be "*payable to bearer or to order* at the time it is issued or first comes into possession of a holder." § 3-104(a)(1). Words in the instrument indicating it is "payable to bearer or to order" are the words of negotiability. Other words of the same import may be used, providing they are a clear equivalent of "order" or "bearer."

Words of negotiability, "payable to bearer or to order," are traceable to the difficulty the old merchant courts had in our early legal history of recognizing the contractual rights of one who was not himself a party to the contract. That is, in earlier times, in the absence of privity, rights under a contract could not be assigned to a third party without the consent of the obligor. Thus a promise to pay money to Tom Jones could not be enforced by anyone but Tom Jones. This problem ultimately was resolved by merchants making the instrument payable to the *bearer* of the instrument. Thereby the instrument became payable to whomever had possession of it. This meant that the right to enforce a bearer instrument could be transferred by delivery of the instrument alone. The indorsement of the transferor was not required to pass title to the instrument. Although the transfer of the right to payment by delivery of the paper alone was advantageous in the right circumstances, problems would arise when bearer paper fell into the wrong hands, such as a thief or a finder of the instrument, who could pass good title merely by transferring possession. Now problems could arise because rights under bearer paper were too easily transferred. To hedge against this risk merchants began creating *order* paper — making the paper payable "to the payee or his order." These words of negotiability permitted the payee to transfer the instrument to an identified third party, thereby establishing privity between the maker of the instrument and the ultimate holder. Since the indorsement of the payee now would be required as a condition to its transfer, the risk inherent in bearer paper falling into the wrong hands was thereby eliminated.

As a consequence of this historical development, words of negotiability are viewed even today as one of the clearest indications that the parties intended the instrument to be negotiable and form the heart of the negotiable instrument. § 3-104 OC 2.

So today, under Article 3, as at common law, not only do words of negotiability indicate the intent of the parties to create a negotiable instrument, but they also determine how title to the instrument may be negotiated or transferred to future parties. As at common law, an instrument payable to bearer can be negotiated by mere delivery of the instrument to the transferee. However, negotiation or transfer of an instrument payable to the order of an identified person requires the indorsement of the holder plus delivery of the instrument to the transferee in order for the transferee to become a holder. § 3-201 and § 3-109 OC 1.

Section 3-109 elaborates further on what qualifies as "payable to bearer or to order" language.

Problem 1-1

Assuming that *all* of the *other elements* of negotiability are present, would the language in the following hypotheticals satisfy the words of negotiability requirement? (The various elements of negotiability are stated in § 3-104.) That is, focusing *only* on the requirement of words of negotiability (pay "to bearer or to order"), in the following hypotheticals can you find language that would be the equivalent of words of negotiability (pay "to bearer or to order")? To obtain your answers, examine the words and phrases that follow in light of the relevant sections of the Code, including §§ 3-104(a)(1) and OC 2, 3-109, and 1-201(b)(5).

1) "I promise to pay $500 to Tom Jones on March 1, 2008."

2) "I promise to pay to Tom Jones or bearer."

3) "I promise to pay to the order of Tom Jones or bearer."

4) "I hereby order Amy Smith to pay _____." See also §§ 3-115, 3-104(c).

5) "I promise to pay $750 to the order of Account No. 37004683." § 3-110(c) (first sentence).

6) "I.O.U. $500. This document is negotiable."

4. Who Is Entitled to Indorse?

Related to the matter of words of negotiability is the question of *how* an instrument is negotiated. If payable to bearer, an instrument can be negotiated by delivery alone. If payable to an identifiable person, negotiation requires the indorsement of the identified person. §§ 3-201(b), 3-109 OC 1. Section 3-110 sets out the rules for determining who the payee is, and who may indorse the instrument on his behalf when the instrument is payable to an identifiable person or persons, office, or organization. The general rule is that the payee is determined by the intent of the maker or drawer or his representative, whether or not he is authorized.

Problem 1-2

Who is entitled to indorse the instrument in the following cases? See § 3-110(a), (d).

1) "Pay to the order of Tom or Mary Jones."

2) "Pay to the order of Tom and Mary Jones."

3) "Pay to the order of Tom Jones and/or Mary Jones."

4) "Pay to the order of Tom Jones."

a) Suppose the maker intended the payee to be Tom Jones, but not the Tom Jones who indorsed and transferred the instrument.

b) Suppose the maker made the instrument payable to Tom Jones, but he intended to make it out to Perry Jones.

Q: How should Perry Jones indorse an instrument payable to "Tom Jones"? § 3-204(d).

B. Unconditional Promise or Order to Pay

Section 3-104(a) also requires that the promise or order to pay be "unconditional." However, only one or the other is required, depending on the instrument—an unconditional promise in the case of a promissory note, and an unconditional order to pay in the case of a draft.

Problem 1-3

Would any of the following statements in a promissory note make the promise conditional and remove the note from the scope of Article 3? § 3-106.

1) "In consideration of Amber Smith's promise to sell her grand piano to me, I promise to pay $15,000 to the order of Amber Smith."

2) "This negotiable instrument is governed by the credit agreement executed by the maker and the payee on the date hereof."

3) "Notwithstanding any contrary language herein, payment shall not exceed the balance on December 31, 2009, in maker's money market account no. 3456-987 maintained with Gulf Coast Investment Advisors."

4) "The maker and the payee have executed numerous other documents as part of this transaction, including a credit agreement that provides the maker with prepayment rights and the payee with acceleration rights."

Notes

1. The reason for this element is that promissory notes and drafts are designed to represent the right to the payment of money, either on demand or at a definite time. The absence of an unconditional *promise* obviously would defeat this objective in a promissory note because the transferee could not know how to ascertain the weight of the maker's obligation, or even whether the maker would be legally obligated to pay at all. With respect to a draft, the absence of an *order* to pay also would fail to assure a prospective holder that the draft would be paid or accepted when presented. In either case, the obligation to pay would be illusory.

2. There is some flexibility in the words that can be used to satisfy the unconditional promise language. For example, I "undertake" (rather than "promise") to pay, and I "instruct" (rather than "order") you to pay, were sufficient under former Article 3, and it would seem reasonable to assume they also will suffice under current Article 3. § 3-104 OC 1; F§ 3-104 OC 5. Current Article 3 does not appear to change this rule. But an "acknowledgment of an obligation by the obligor is not a promise unless the obligor also undertakes to pay the obligation." § 3-103(a)(12).

1. "Subject to" Language

The promise or order must be unconditional. However, § 3-106 indicates that the instrument may *refer* to a number of things and still contain an unconditional promise or order to pay. Additionally a note may be subject to implied conditions without destroying negotiability.

But if the instrument contains an "express condition to payment," or is "subject to or governed by" another writing, or states that "rights or obligations with respect to the *promise or order* are stated in another writing," then the promise or order is not unconditional and the instrument would not be negotiable. However, mere references to other documents are alright. But what is the difference between a mere reference to another document and a statement that conditions the promise?

TELERECOVERY OF LOUISIANA, INC. v. GAULON
738 So.2d 662 (La. App. Ct. 1999)

Chehardy, Judge.

The primary issue before us is whether a casino patron's markers for gambling debts are enforceable negotiable instruments subject to the penalties imposed by the Nonsufficient Funds Checks statute.

TeleRecovery of Louisiana, Inc. filed suit on December 29, 1995 alleging that Lance D. Gaulon issued two checks to the Belle of Baton Rouge casino, totaling $10,000 and drawn on the First National Bank of Commerce; that payment of the checks had been refused by the drawee as NSF; and that the original creditor had assigned the account to plaintiff. Plaintiff alleged it had made written demand of defendant to no avail. Pursuant to the Nonsufficient Funds Checks statute (La. R.S. 9:2782), plaintiff sought to recover twice the amount of the checks plus service charges, attorney's fees, legal interest and costs.

On February 22, 1996 plaintiff confirmed a default judgment against defendant in the amount of $20,000.00, subject to any credits, with a service charge of $15.00 or 5% of the face amount of each check, whichever is greater, with interest from the date of judicial demand until paid, reasonable attorney's fees in the amount of 25% of the principal and interest, and for all costs.

Defendant filed a rule to set aside the default judgment or, alternatively, for a new trial, contesting the applicability of La. R.S. 9:2782. Defendant argued that the statute was not intended to cover gambling markers and the markers did not constitute checks within the meaning of the statute. Defendant asserted further that the judgment should be set aside because plaintiff had failed to establish a prima facie case. Specifically, defendant argued that plaintiff failed to attach the credit payment agreement on which the markers were predicated and failed to prove that the signature was authentic and that the casino's rights had been assigned to plaintiff.

On April 16, 1996 the trial court denied the motion for new trial as to the principal amount of the judgment in the amount of $10,000.00, plus interest and costs, and the court assessed attorney's fees of $2,000.00. The court granted a new trial, however, on the issue of applicability of the bad check statute.

Defendant appealed, but this Court dismissed his appeal as premature. We ordered the trial court to hold the judgment on the principal amount in abeyance and reserved defendant's appeal rights pending the trial court's determination of the applicability of the NSF check statute....

After remand plaintiff filed a motion for summary judgment on the applicability of La. R.S. 9:2782. The district court ruled in favor of plaintiff, finding that the markers are checks under negotiable instruments law, that the plaintiff had complied with the other requirements of the NSF check statute, and that the plaintiff is entitled to penalties as set forth in La. R.S. 9:2782. On May 21, 1998 the trial court signed a judgment awarding plaintiff $10,000.00 in penalties, together with legal interest from date of judicial demand until paid, attorney's fees of 9.25% of the award and the interest, and all costs. The judgment specified the award was in addition to the amounts awarded in the judgment of April 16, 1996. Defendant appeals.

On appeal defendant asserts the trial court erred in rendering judgment in favor of plaintiff under the NSF check law because gambling markers are unenforceable debts, in granting judgment because the markers in this case are not negotiable instruments, and in granting default judgment because plaintiff produced insufficient evidence to obtain a default judgment.

ENFORCEABILITY OF GAMBLING MARKERS

Defendant asserts that La. C.C. art. 2983 makes gambling debts unenforceable. Article 2983 states, "The law grants no action for the payment of what has been won at gaming or by a bet, except for games tending to promote skill in the use of arms, such as the exercise of the gun and foot, horse and chariot racing."

Our state constitution provides, "Gambling shall be defined by and suppressed by the legislature." La. Const. Art. 12, §6(B). The legislature's right to decide what is gambling that must be suppressed has been upheld by our Supreme Court. Polk v. Edwards, 626 So.2d 1128 (La.1993). Legalized forms of gambling, such as licensed bingo, keno and horseracing, having consistently been held to be exempt from those provisions. Lauer v. Catalanotto, 522 So.2d 656 (La. App. 5 Cir. 1988). Riverboat gaming activities are defined and authorized by statute (La. R.S. 27:41 to 27:113) and are exempted from the statutory definition of gambling in the Louisiana Criminal Code. La. R.S. 14:90(D).

La. R.S. 27:43 authorizes conduct of gaming activities on a riverboat in accordance with provisions of the Louisiana Riverboat Economic Development and Gaming Control Act, "notwithstanding any other provision of law to the contrary." Accordingly, there is no merit to the argument that the debt is unenforceable because incurred in an illegal activity.

ARE THE MARKERS NEGOTIABLE INSTRUMENTS?

Second, defendant contends the bad check law cannot be applied here because the markers are not negotiable instruments. He contends the markers are sui generis and do not fall within the narrow precepts of the bad check law, which must be strictly construed.

La. R.S. 10:3-104 defines "negotiable instrument" as follows, in pertinent part:

> (a) Except as provided in Subsections (c) and (d), "negotiable instrument" means an unconditional promise or order to pay a fixed amount of money * * * * *

Defendant argues the casino markers are conditional because they refer to another document outside the face of the markers and, thus, do not satisfy the requirement of "unconditional promise to pay."

Each marker bears on its face the statement, "I agree to payment according to the terms of the Credit Payment Agreement previously executed by the undersigned." Defendant contends this requires a holder to examine another document to determine rights with respect to payment, making the marker conditional and non-negotiable.

Plaintiff rebuts by arguing that in order to be conditional the instrument must state that it is conditioned by, subject to or governed by another writing, and mere reference to another writing on the face of the instrument does not make it conditional. La. R.S. 10:3-106(a).

La. R.S. 10:3-106(a) provides,

Except as provided in this Section, for the purposes of R.S. 10:3-104(a), a promise or order is unconditional unless it states (i) an express condition to payment, (ii) that the promise or order is subject to or governed by another writing, or (iii) that rights or obligations with respect to the promise or order are stated in another writing. A reference to another writing does not of itself make the promise or order conditional.

Although Louisiana's adoption of the Uniform Commercial Code is recent, the underlying principle in question here has long been part of the law governing negotiable instruments in Louisiana. The issue—the type of reference to another document that makes a promise to pay conditional and an instrument non-negotiable—has seen little litigation in this state, however.

In Newman v. Schwarz, 180 La. 153, 156 So. 206, 207 (1934), the court held that the statement "Rent Note Subject to Terms of Lease Dated May 2, 1927," written in red ink across the face of the note, bore no relation to the unconditional promise of the maker to pay the notes, amounted to "nothing more than a statement of the transaction which gives rise to the notes and which serves to identify them with the transaction," and did not render the note non-negotiable.

In Tyler v. Whitney-Central Trust & Sav. Bank, 157 La. 249, 102 So. 325, 329 (1924), the court concluded that because the expression "as per lease this date" was found in a separate sentence from the promise to pay it bore no relation whatever to the promise. "In fact, the entire sentence in which the reference appears amounts to nothing more than a statement of the transaction which gives rise to the notes and which serves to identify them with the transaction. Such a statement and means of identification do not render the notes nonnegotiable."

We find the following general statement useful:

> (4) Reference to other instruments or agreements. If the note or draft states that it is given "as per" a transaction, "in accordance with" a transaction, or that it "arises out of" a transaction, this does not destroy negotiability, but, if the instrument states that it is "subject to" or "governed by" any other agreement, then negotiability is destroyed. 2 Frederick M. Hart & William F. Willier, Bender's U.C.C. Service, Commercial Paper § 1B.04[3] (1995).

Examining the language at issue in this case, we conclude it does not destroy negotiability of the marker. Its location on the last line of the instrument as well as its use of "according to" simply references another document but does not make payment conditional.

* * *

Problem 1-4

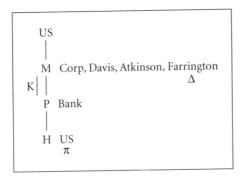

Farrington invested his inheritance in the Davis Aircraft Company, thereby becoming one of its three shareholders (together with Davis and Atkinson). Davis Aircraft borrowed money from a bank. The loan agreement required all three shareholders to indorse the note executed by the company. The loan agreement was signed by Davis and Atkinson but not Farrington, and

Farrington knew nothing about it. However, he did hear that the company had borrowed money, and in due time Davis asked Farrington to sign the back of the promissory note executed by the company in favor of the lending bank. Farrington asked why his signature was needed. Davis told him that the note evidenced a company loan, and the bank insisted on his signature to evidence his knowledge of the loan. He was not told he would incur a legal obligation by signing, and he did not intend to incur any. Farrington then signed on the back under the signatures of Davis and Atkinson. Typed on the face of the note was the following:

Given as security with assigned Government Contracts:

This note evidences a borrowing made under and is subject to the terms of a loan agreement dated Jan. 3, between the undersigned and the payee thereof, and should the market value of the same, in the judgment of the holder or holders hereof, decline, we promise to furnish satisfactory additional collateral on demand.

The note was later transferred to the U.S. who became a holder for value. Davis Aircraft is now insolvent, as are Davis and Atkinson. The U.S. demands payment of the note from Farrington.

1) Is the note negotiable? §§ 3-104, 3-106. (If the note is not negotiable, the U.S. cannot be a holder in due course and could be subject to Farrington's contract defenses. These defenses may be cut off if the note is negotiable and the U.S. is a holder in due course. See § 3-305.)

2) Is Farrington liable on the note?

Q: Can he raise the defense against the U.S. that he was fraudulently induced to sign the note without knowing that he was incurring liability?

Q: But even if the note is not negotiable, are there any facts that should estop Farrington from raising the defense of fraud? Cf. § 1-103(b).

3) Would the note be negotiable if the loan agreement did not condition the promise in the note?

Problem 1-5

"This note is drawn pursuant to the business transaction outlined in a loan agreement of the same date."

Will this clause condition the promise? § 3-106. There is a distinction between merely referring to an extraneous agreement, and incorporating an outside agreement in such a way that it burdens the instrument, i.e., makes it "subject to" the outside agreement. Is this such an incorporation, or a reference? § 3-106(a), (b)(i) and OC 1. Cf. F§ 3-105(1)(b).

Notes

1. Section 3-106 contains an express exception to the incorporation-by-reference rule in the case of a reference to *a mortgage or a security interest*. "A promise or order is not made conditional (i) by a reference to another record for a statement of rights with respect to collateral, prepayment, or acceleration." Since notes are frequently secured by a mortgage or security interest, the rationale is that this exception is a reasonable accommodation of business. Thus even if the language of the note is reasonably construed

to incorporate the terms of the security agreement into the note with respect to "collateral, prepayment, or acceleration," this express exception with respect to mortgages and security agreements in §3-106(b)(i) would prevent the incorporation (notwithstanding that it effectively makes the promise subject to whatever the security agreement said about the collateral, etc.) from destroying the negotiability of the instrument. §3-106(b)(i) and OC 1.

2. Section 3-106 contains another express exception to the necessity of an unconditional promise or order to pay by allowing the maker to limit his obligation to pay "to a particular fund or source." §3-106(b)(ii). That is, by using a particular fund clause the maker makes his obligation conditional upon there being anything in the fund or source. But again, this condition to the promise or order is alright.

By validating the particular fund clause the drafters of current Article 3 made an interesting departure from prior law by repealing the particular fund doctrine. Former Article 3, §3-105(2) provided that "a promise or order is not unconditional if the instrument ... states that it is to be paid only out of a particular fund or source except as provided in this section." But there were numerous exceptions. The drafters of current Article 3 decided to repeal the particular fund doctrine because "[t]here is no cogent reason why the general credit of a legal entity must be pledged to have a negotiable instrument." §3-106 OC 1.

This change will allow greater flexibility in the use of negotiable instruments in commercial transactions. For example, in composition and extension agreements (a convention sometimes used to provide a non-bankruptcy arrangement between creditors and an insolvent debtor—a non-bankruptcy alternative to Chapter 11 of the Bankruptcy Code), one creditor, C-2, may agree to subordinate his claim against the debtor to that of another creditor, C-1. In doing so C-2 thereby conditions his right to payment to whether there will be anything left after C-1 has been paid. If the debtor then formalizes this agreement by making a note promising to pay C-2 after C-1 has received his payment, this is in effect a promise to pay C-2 out of "whatever is left...," and thus it is a promise to pay out of a particular fund. In the past the note would be nonnegotiable. But now such a promise will not condition the maker's undertaking and will be negotiable. §3-106(b)(ii).

This change greatly simplifies this area of the law as a whole and also brings logic into the area, since even a promise to pay out of the entire assets of the debtor is conditional upon whether the debtor will have assets in his estate with which to pay the note—a difference of degree only.

Although payment out of a particular fund is permitted without destroying negotiability, when it comes time for the holder to receive payment, he may find there are no funds in the particular fund. But like all other business risks, this is a risk the prospective transferee of such a note must evaluate for himself.

2. The Effect on the Instrument of Unmentioned Side Agreements

Promissory notes are frequently secured by a security interest or a real estate mortgage. It may not be convenient for the parties to make any reference in the note to the security. What is the effect of such a collateral agreement on the note? Does an unmentioned side agreement condition the order or promise to pay? Does the agreement affect the maker's obligation under the note in any way, or destroy the negotiability of the note?

Problem 1-6

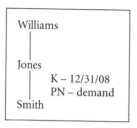

Williams

|

Jones

K – 12/31/08

PN – demand

Smith

Smith executed and delivered a $5,000 negotiable promissory note to Jones. The note was payable on demand. Notwithstanding the demand feature of the note, Smith and Jones agreed in a separate writing (executed contemporaneously with the note) that Jones would not demand payment before December 31, 2008.

1) Jones demands payment from Smith on September 1, 2008. Smith refuses to pay, relying on their agreement. What result? §§ 3-412, 3-117.

2) Assume Jones never demands payment and instead sells the note to Williams in March 2008. Williams demands payment from Smith on September 1, 2008. Smith refuses to pay, relying on the agreement with Jones. What result?

Note

What is the effect of an agreement arising out of the same transaction as the instrument but to which the instrument makes no reference—sometimes referred to as a collateral agreement, or a side agreement? Will it destroy the negotiability of the instrument? The agreement will not affect the negotiability of an instrument if it is otherwise negotiable. As we have seen, negotiability is determined by the terms of the instrument itself. § 3-104. The mere execution of an agreement which purports to qualify the maker's obligations under the note does not become incorporated into the note itself. However, the Code follows the rule that multiple agreements arising out of the same transaction are to be read together in determining the rights of the parties—the rights of the parties to the agreement. § 3-117.

Thus on the one hand "the obligation of a party to an instrument to pay the instrument may be modified, supplemented, or nullified by a separate agreement of the obligor and a person entitled to enforce the instrument, if the instrument is issued ... as part of the same transaction giving rise to the agreement." § 3-117. As between the parties, if the terms of the instrument are qualified by the agreement, the maker will want to raise the agreement as a defense to his obligations, if the agreement contains terms that would benefit him. But whether he will be permitted to do so will depend on the application of the parol evidence rule and other rules regarding merger or integration clauses under local law.

On the other hand, a holder in due course—someone who is unaware of the collateral agreement—takes the instrument free of any conditions that may be in the agreement, whether executed before, after, or contemporaneously with the note. § 3-117 and OC 1, 2.

C. A Fixed Amount of Money

Another element of negotiability is that the unconditional promise must be "to pay a fixed amount of money, with or without interest or other charges described in the promise or order...." § 3-104.

Like the other elements, the requirement of a promise or order to pay "a fixed amount of money" is designed to promote certainty in ascertaining the present value of an instrument payable in the future. Obviously the present value of the instrument cannot be determined unless the amount of the obligation is known. Here we examine what is meant by "a fixed amount of money." Does it mean mathematical certainty?

Section 1-201(b)(24) defines "money" as "a medium of exchange currently authorized or adopted by a domestic or foreign government." Thus "money," for the purposes for the Code, includes foreign currency.

It follows that a promise to pay a certain amount of money in a foreign currency is for "a fixed amount of money," and § 3-107 accommodates promises to pay in foreign currencies.

Problem 1-7

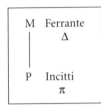

Ferrante executed a promissory note in New Jersey, promising to pay 1,000 Euros to Incitti on June 1. On the due date, Ferrante refused to pay. Incitti commenced an action on the note. Ferrante defended on the ground that the note, containing a promise to pay in a foreign currency, was not for money but for a commodity. Therefore, Ferrante contended that Incitti had failed to state a cause of action because he did not allege any consideration for the note, something that is required in a suit on an ordinary contract, but not in an action on a note.

1) Has Incitti stated a cause of action, i.e., is the note negotiable?

Q: Would your analysis change if Ferrante had promised to pay 1,000 Italian Lire?

2) If you find the note negotiable, may Ferrante pay the note in Euros if he desires? § 3-107.

Q: Conversely, if Ferrante tenders dollars, may Incitti demand Euros?

3) Suppose that instead of Euros, Ferrante had promised to pay "by overhauling the transmission of Incitti's car on demand"? Or, to pay with "50 bales of cotton"? § 1-201(b)(24).

Notes

1. *Interest*: A promise to pay a stated sum of money does not become uncertain merely because it provides for the payment of "interest or other charges described in the promise or order." § 3-104. The interest rate and presumably other finance charges may be "fixed or variable." § 3-112(b). This policy of flexibility would appear to permit a promise to pay in installments, at varying interest and discount rates in varying circumstances, with exchange rates, costs of collection or attorneys fees on default, etc., all of which appear to come within the permissive language of "with or without interest or other charges." § 3-104. Cf. F§ 3-106.

May the interest rate be tied to a formula or rate found outside the four corners of the instrument? See §§ 3-104 and 3-112.

2. *Contradictory Terms of Instrument*: Many instruments describe the amount numerically (e.g., "$100.00") and textually (e.g., "one hundred dollars"). Occasionally the amounts are inconsistent. See, e.g., France v. Ford Motor Credit Co., 913 S.W.2d 770 (Ark. 1996) (drawer prepared check ordering payment of a numerical amount of $8,000.00 and a textual amount of eight dollars). In such a case, words prevail over numbers, and handwritten terms prevail over typewritten terms (which prevail over printed terms). § 3-114.

D. On Demand or At a Definite Time

A negotiable instrument must "be payable on demand or at a definite time." § 3-104(a)(2). This requirement, like the other elements of negotiability, is designed to promote certainty in ascertaining the present value of a negotiable instrument. It is addressed further in § 3-108.

A definite time of payment is required for various reasons. The most obvious is that if an instrument is not payable on demand or at a definite time, the promise to pay is illusory and of undeterminable value. The time of payment also is required in order that the holder may determine when the statute of limitations begins to run. See § 3-118.

KRAJCIR v. EGIDI

712 N.E.2d 917 (Ill. App. Ct. 1999)

Justice Hartman delivered the opinion of the court:

Plaintiff Robert J. Krajcir appeals from the circuit court's orders dismissing count I of his third amended complaint with prejudice and dismissing his fourth amended complaint, with prejudice. Plaintiff had filed suit against defendants Mario R. Egidi (Mario), Dennis R. Egidi (Dennis), Lloyd S. Levine (Lloyd) and Spaulding Associates (Spaulding), an Illinois partnership, seeking to recover the balance due on a contract for the sale of an apartment building to Spaulding Associates and on a promissory note issued in connection with the sale. Krajcir presents as issues on appeal whether the circuit court erred when it dismissed: (1) count I of his verified third amended complaint with prejudice; (2) his verified fourth amended complaint with prejudice; and (3) his action for an equitable seller's lien. The relevant facts follow.

On March 18, 1982, Krajcir and his brother, Richard W. Krajcir (sellers), entered into a written contract to sell the property commonly known as 1944-50 N. Spaulding Avenue, Chicago, Illinois (Spaulding Property) to Spaulding, Lloyd and Mario (purchasers). The contract was signed by plaintiff, as seller, and Lloyd, as a partner on behalf of Spaulding, the purchaser. This original contract between the parties was amended by a letter dated July 9, 1982, from plaintiff and his brother to Lloyd, which altered the payment provisions of the original contract. The copy of the amendatory letter contained in the record is not signed, but its contents are undisputed. It is also undisputed that Dennis is a partner of Spaulding, despite the fact that his name does not appear on the original contract or the amendatory letter.

The original contract provided for the payment of a purchase price in the amount of $350,000 to plaintiff and his brother, in exchange for the Spaulding Property. It specifically provided that "the funds to be paid hereunder are to come out of Project No. 071-35488 when funded by HUD. If said funding is not received by the Purchaser then this contract is null and void."

The July 9, 1982 amendment to the contract stated, among other things, that: "[t]he amount of $10,000.00 [is] to be paid sellers at the time of the initial closing (delivery of the deed); plus, delivery at the same time of a Promissory Note in the principal amount of $110,000.00 payable to sellers and executed by Mario Egidi and [Lloyd S. Levine], individually, as co-makers; the Note shall be due on the date of final endorsement of the subject H.U.D. Loan and will be satisfied in full upon final payout of the proceeds thereof * * *."

* * *

On April 29, 1983, the final endorsement by the United States Department of Housing and Urban Development (H.U.D.) for defendants' Federal Housing Authority Project No. 071-35488 was completed. It was on this date that the $110,000 promissory note paid to the sellers by Mario and Lloyd became due pursuant to the terms of the note.

A payment was subsequently made to plaintiff by check dated March 15, 1984, in the amount of $10,000, drawn on an account of Spaulding, and signed by Lloyd, as partner, and Dennis.... A second payment was made to plaintiff by check dated April 3, 1984, in the amount of $55,000.... On April 22, 1984, Richard W. Krajcir died intestate, leaving plaintiff as his only survivor and heir at law.

On March 3, 1994, plaintiff filed a verified complaint at law against Mario, Dennis, Lloyd and Spaulding, seeking recovery of the unpaid balance of $55,000 on the promissory note, plus interest....

On February 1, 1995, plaintiff filed a verified amended complaint at law, alleging, among other things, that the principal sum of $45,000, plus interest, remained due and owing on the September 15, 1982 promissory note. On June 27, 1995, Dennis and Spaulding filed a combined section 2-619 supplemental motion to dismiss plaintiff's verified amended complaint, alleging that the promissory note was subject to the six-year statute of limitations set forth in section 3-118 of the Uniform Commercial Code (UCC) (810 ILCS 5/3-118 (West 1994) (UCC section 3-118)). They argued that plaintiff's original complaint had been untimely filed, where the statute of limitations had expired on April 29, 1989, six years after the final endorsement by H.U.D., and plaintiff's complaint in this matter was not filed until March 3, 1994.

On August 31, 1995, following a hearing on the preceding day, the circuit court entered an order granting the motion to dismiss pursuant to section 2-619.1 of the Code, based on the expiration of the applicable statute of limitations. It further held that because "this motion is dispositive of this matter as to [Dennis and Spaulding], there is no need to consider the remaining motions to dismiss."

* * *

.... On December 12, 1997, plaintiff moved to vacate the order of dismissal, which the circuit court denied on February 9, 1998. Plaintiff appeals.

I

Plaintiff first contends that the circuit court erred in dismissing, with prejudice, his action on the promissory note alleged in count I of his verified second and third amended complaints, based on its finding that his cause of action on the promissory note was barred by the six-year section 3-118 statute of limitations. 810 ILCS 5/3-118 (West 1994) (section 3-118).

A section 2-619 motion to dismiss (735 ILCS 5/2-619 (West 1996)) is proper if no set of facts may be proven by which the plaintiff can recover. Management Ass'n of Illinois, Inc. v. Board of Regents of Northern Illinois University, 248 Ill.App.3d 599, 606, 188 Ill.Dec. 124, 618 N.E.2d 694 (1993). All well-pleaded facts alleged in the complaint are taken as true for purposes of the motion to dismiss. Conclusions not supported by specific factual allegations are not considered, and where defects do not appear on the face of the pleadings, affidavits may be filed, stating affirmative matters that justify dismissal. Management Ass'n of Illinois, Inc., 248 Ill.App.3d at 606, 188 Ill.Dec. 124, 618 N.E.2d 694.

A

In the present case, plaintiff asserts that his causes of action on the promissory note and the contract are not barred by any statute of limitations. He first argues that section 3-118 is inapplicable to his action on the promissory note and that the 10-year statute of limitations set forth in section 13-206 of the Code (735 ILCS 13-206 (West 1994) (section 13-206)) applies. Plaintiff further contends that uncontroverted, relevant facts alleged in his verified amended complaints establish that payments on the note and contract were made by Dennis and Spaulding within 10 years of the filing of this case, within the terms of section 13-206.

Section 3-118 provides in relevant part:

"(a) Except as provided in subsection (e), an action to enforce the obligation of a party to pay a note payable at a definite time must be commenced within 6 years after the due date or dates stated in the note or, if a due date is accelerated, within 6 years after the accelerated due date." ILCS 5/3-118 (a) (West 1994).

Section 13-206 of the Code states in pertinent part:

"Except as provided in Section 2-725 of the 'Uniform Commercial Code', actions on bonds, promissory notes, bills of exchange, written leases, written contracts, or other evidences of indebtedness in writing, shall be commenced within 10 years next after the cause of action accrued; but if any payment or new promise to pay has been made, in writing, on any bond, note, bill, lease, contract, or other written evidence of indebtedness, within or after the period of 10 years, then an action may be commenced thereon at any time within 10 years after the time of such payment or promise to pay." 735 ILCS 5/13-206 (West 1994).

Section 3-118 of the UCC pertains to negotiable instruments, including negotiable promissory notes; section 13-206 of the Code relates to, among other written evidences of indebtedness, non-negotiable promissory notes and written contracts, with the exception of those that relate to the sale of goods under section 2-725 of the UCC (810 ILCS 5/2-725 (West 1994)). Identification of the applicable statute of limitations turns on whether the promissory note of September 15, 1982, executed by Mario and Lloyd and delivered to plaintiff and his brother, is negotiable.

Section 3-104 defines a negotiable instrument, in part, as follows:

"(a) Except as provided in subsections (c) and (d), 'negotiable instrument' means an unconditional promise or order to pay a fixed amount of money, with or without interest or other charges described in the promise or order, if it:

(1) is payable to bearer or to order at the time it is issued or first comes into possession of a holder;

(2) is payable on demand or at a definite time; * * *." 810 ILCS 5/3-104(a)(1), (2) (West 1994).

The subject promissory note does not comply with the requirement of a negotiable instrument for two reasons: first, in that, although it is payable to specified individuals, it does not contain the words of negotiability, "to order" or "to bearer," as required by section 3-104(a)(1). Second, and perhaps more importantly, the subject note is not "payable on demand or at a definite time," as required by section 3-104(a)(2). Rather, the note states that payment was promised "on the date of final endorsement by the United States Department of Housing and Urban Development Loan on Project No. 071-35488

PM/L8 known as Spaulding Re-Hab." Despite the fact that final endorsement by H.U.D. eventually was made on April 29, 1983, funding by the agency was an uncertainty at the time the note dated September 15, 1982 was executed.

In support of their position that the wording of the note established payment at a definite time, defendants cite cases in which Illinois courts have held that dates of death are considered to be definite, fixed payment dates in promissory notes.

Defendants miss the mark: death is certain; final endorsement by H.U.D. is not. The original contract reveals that the parties recognized this possibility and provided for it. The last two sentences of the three-page hand-written, original contract state:

> "It is further expressly understood and agreed between the parties hereto that the funds to be paid hereunder are to come out of Project No. 071-35488 when funded by HUD. If said funding is not received by the Purchaser then this contract is null and void."

For the foregoing reasons, the promissory note executed by Mario and Lloyd was not a negotiable instrument under Article 3 of the UCC; consequently, section 3-118 of the UCC is not applicable to this case; section 13-206 of the Code does apply.

* * *

Note

How might you redraft the promissory note to create an Article 3 negotiable instrument that accomplishes the parties' intent to tie the payment to the date of HUD's final, but uncertain, indorsement?

1. On Demand

An instrument payable on demand includes an instrument which (1) is expressly payable on demand, (2) is payable at sight or "otherwise indicates that it is payable at the will of the holder," or (3) fails to state any time for payment. § 3-108(a). A check is a demand instrument.

A demand instrument is considered to be due and payable at the moment of issue. Theoretically, a maker could sign a demand note one day and the holder could call the instrument the next day, or even a minute after issue.

2. Definite Time

Section 3-108(b) provides that an instrument payable at a "definite time" includes not only those payable (1) at "a definite ... time after sight," (2) at "a fixed date," and (3) "at a time ... readily ascertainable at the time the promise or order is issued," but also those which are payable at a definite time subject to (4) "prepayment," (5) "acceleration," or (6) "extension."

An instrument made payable on the happening of an event, such as the death of uncle Will, does not qualify as payable at a time "readily ascertainable" merely because the event is certain. However, "payable on Easter Sunday, 2012" would qualify as a definite time even though neither party knew the date at the time the instrument was issued—because it is "readily ascertainable."

A postdated check is a time instrument, as is a draft payable 30 days after sight.

One of the most troublesome problems under pre-Code law was the effect of an acceleration clause on the definite time requirement. An acceleration clause permits the holder of the note to demand payment before the date of maturity, upon the happening of certain specified events. Here we explore the acceleration clause and the policy limits on its validity.

Problem 1-8

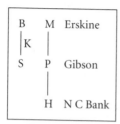

Erskine purchased some mining equipment and executed a promissory note payable to the seller, Gibson, in payment for the balance of the price. The note required payment in installments on the first business day of each calendar month after execution, with a final payment due on August 31, 2010. Gibson discounted the note to National City Bank. The equipment turned out to be defective and Erskine stopped making payments.

The note required payment of $16,529 in installments. The note stated:

> If any installment is not paid when due and/or if the security agreement securing this note is breached in any respect, then this note shall immediately become due at the holder's option without demand or notice.

Then followed a cognovit clause which provided that upon default, the holder would become the attorney for the maker and authorized to confess judgment on the note in favor of the holder without prior notice to, or service of process upon, the maker.

The security agreement referred to in the note contained a statement that "whenever the secured party shall, for any reason, deem said indebtedness insecure, the secured party may, at its option and without notice, elect to treat the balance remaining unpaid on said note immediately due and payable forthwith."

Erskine asserts that the note is not negotiable and, therefore, the bank is subject to Erskine's defenses arising out of the defective equipment. Erskine argues 1) that the acceleration clause in the *note* renders the note uncertain as to time. Further he argues 2) that the acceleration clause in the *security agreement* is incorporated into the note by reference thereby rendering the promise to pay conditional, and 3) that the "insecurity" clause in the security agreement would in any event destroy negotiability.

1) Is the note negotiable? See §§ 3-104(a), 3-108(b), 3-106(b), 1-309.

2) What do you think of Erskine's arguments? Will Erskine have to pay?

3) Does the cognovit clause constitute an undertaking by Erskine that destroys negotiability? See § 3-104(a)(3).

Note

Is a note containing an acceleration clause really payable at a "definite time"? Compare demand instruments with instruments payable at a definite time, subject to acceleration. Is a promissory note payable on demand more certain as to time of payment than a promise to pay on a definite date subject to acceleration on the happening of certain specified events?

Problem 1-9

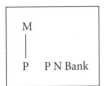

Maker is a beneficiary under his rich uncle Fred's will. Maker cannot wait for uncle Fred to die before sharing in his estate. He requests a loan from Paradise National Bank. As security for the loan he executes a post-obituary note on March 1, 2007, which reads, "I promise to pay $25,000 to Paradise National Bank on the death of uncle Fred. Signed, Maker." Paradise National Bank makes the loan. Uncle Fred dies on January 1, 2008.

1) Does Paradise National Bank hold a negotiable instrument? See § 3-108(b); cf. F§ 3-109(2).

2) How would you draft a post-obituary clause that preserves negotiability?

3) How much will Paradise National Bank be willing to loan Maker for the note?

4) Assume that the noted stated: "I promise to pay $25,000 to the order of Paradise National Bank on July 1, 2007, with the option to extend payment to six weeks after the death of uncle Fred." Uncle Fred dies in 2008. Is the note negotiable?

Notes

1. *Extension clauses*: An extension clause is the converse of an acceleration clause. For example, farmer Clayacre borrows $10,000 from the bank and gives a note in return, "I promise to pay $10,000 to the order of Bank on December 15, 2007, but if my crop yields less than one bale of cotton per acre, I will have the option to extend the time of payment to December 15, 2008." Is the note negotiable?

To understand the rationale underlying the validation of acceleration and extension clauses, we should keep in mind that promissory notes are designed to assure the holder that he will be paid. A note containing an acceleration clause means that the holder may be paid earlier than the maturity date. Although that means the instrument is not mathematically certain as to time of payment, as a matter of policy that is alright because in most instances payment before the maturity date operates to the advantage of the holder and the needs of commerce are not offended by such a clause. Similarly, a clause which permits the time of payment to be extended "at the option of holder" also is valid even though no outside date is specified because it is the holder who negotiable instruments law intends to protect, and if he wants the option to extend the time of payment, that is a business risk and he should be permitted to take it. But if the maker is given the option to extend the time of payment, it is only valid if it is "to a further definite time." § 3-108(b)(iv). Where the maker is given the option to extend, an outside date for maturity is required; otherwise the promise would be illusory.

So we see that the rationale for validating acceleration and extension clauses is not mathematical certainty, but rather commercial certainty.

Since post-obituary notes are neither mathematically nor commercially certain as to maturity, they are not validated by § 3-108. See also F§ 3-109(2). But with the use of an acceleration clause, a valid post-obituary note can be drafted.

2. *Undated, antedated and postdated instruments*: The negotiability of an instrument is not affected by the fact that it is undated, antedated, or postdated. An undated instrument is deemed to be dated as of the date of issue. Nor does postdating a check affect its negotiability. However, § 4-401(c) permits the bank to pay a postdated check before its date, unless notified by the drawer. § 3-113 and F§ 3-114.

The date on an instrument is presumed to be accurate, but this presumption may be rebutted.

3. *Place of Payment*: Although a negotiable instrument must describe a fixed amount of money that is payable either on demand or at a definite time, the negotiable instrument need not indicate a place of payment. The presence or absence, within an instrument, of a place of payment does not affect negotiability. Depending on the language of the instrument, an instrument may be payable at the place stated in the instrument, the address of the drawee or maker stated in the instrument, the place of business of the drawee or maker (and if the drawee or maker has more than one place of business, then any place of business selected by the party enforcing the instrument), or the residence of the drawee or maker. § 3-111.

E. A Negotiable Instrument Must Be a Courier without Luggage

For a negotiable instrument to perform its currency and credit functions efficiently, negotiable instruments must not be cluttered with too many promises, orders, or obligations. Such excess baggage makes it difficult for those dealing with negotiable instruments to determine whether the instrument is negotiable. Accordingly, § 3-104(a)(3) provides that an instrument must "not state any other undertaking or instruction by the person promising or ordering payment to do any act in addition to the payment of money...." This has come to be known as the "courier without luggage" element of negotiability.

Problem 1-10

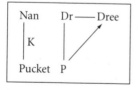

On June 20, Nan and Bob Smith contracted with Pucket Construction Co., who agreed to install some windows and apply some cedar siding on their house. Pucket agreed to do the work for $28 per hour, plus the cost of materials. Pucket completed the project on July 2, and tendered his bill for 46 hours at $28 per hour, plus $700 for materials, for a total cost of $1,988. Unknown to Pucket Construction, the Smiths were keeping track of the hours Pucket spent on the job and their figures showed a total of only 28 hours. Nan made out a check to Pucket for $1,484 (28 hours at $28 per hour, plus $700). On the reverse side, above the place for the signature, Nan typed the following note:

> Your signature evidences full
> satisfaction of your claim:
> X_____

On July 6, Nan mailed the check to Pucket with a letter setting out her figures on the total hours worked by Pucket, and concluding with,

"Accordingly we are enclosing our check for $1,484 in full payment of your bill. Your signature on the check will constitute your agreement that the check is payment in full of your bill.

> Sincerely,
> Nan"

Pucket cashed the check after indorsing it under the "full satisfaction" language as follows:

> "Pucket
> Not satisfactory as full payment.
> $504 (<u>Still</u> due) <u>Bal Due</u>"

1) Is the instrument negotiable?

Q: Does the check contain (i) an unconditional order to pay or (ii) any excess baggage? §§ 3-104(a), 3-311.

2) Pucket wants the other $504. Is he entitled to it? §§ 1-308, 3-311.

Notes

1. *General policy against excess baggage*: The general policy is that an instrument should be as concise as possible and free from clutter, unless otherwise authorized. Thus, if an instrument includes an undertaking or an instruction in addition to a promise or order to pay money, with few exceptions, it will carry too much baggage and be held non-negotiable. § 3-104(a)(3).

2. *Three exceptions*: Section 3-104(a)(3) makes three exceptions to the general limitation that the promise or order must be to pay money and "not state any other undertaking or instruction." That is, there are three promises or orders in addition to the promise or order to pay money that may be made without offending the courier-without-luggage rule. These exceptions, like most of the others, are justified on the ground that although they add baggage to the instrument, the accommodation of business in these three ways is sufficiently desirable to offset any problems that might arise from encumbering the instrument in these ways.

The exceptions are:

"(i) an undertaking or power to give, maintain, or protect collateral to secure payment":

While this language is broad enough to allow a reference to the mortgage or security agreement where statements regarding the undertakings given in connection with the collateral are found, as illustrated in **Problem 1-8**, the language does not appear to be broad enough to allow for the inclusion of the security agreement or mortgage itself in the body of the instrument. That would create too much luggage and be fatal to negotiability. Reference to the collateral is alright, but embodying a security interest in the instrument would appear to go too far, notwithstanding the seemingly permissive, but artful language of § 3-104(a)(3)(i). "The three exceptions stated in § 3-104(a)(3) are based on and are intended to have the same meaning as former Section § 3-112(1)(b), (c), (d), and (e)." § 3-104 OC 1. These subsections were not intended to authorize the incorporation of a security interest in an instrument without destroying its negotiability. See F§ 3-112 OC 1. But some scholars disagree, concluding that a provision which grants a security interest in collateral will not remove the note from the scope of UCC Article 3. See, e.g., 4 William D. Hawkland & Lary Lawrence, Uniform Commercial Code Series § 3-112:5, at 152 (1999); id. at vol. 6, § 3-104:12, at 54 (1999); Sarah Howard Jenkins, Accommodating Spouses: Regulation B and Revised Article 3 — The Suretyship Law Complication, 30 U. Rich. L. Rev. 387, 408–09 (1996).

"(ii) an authorization or power to the holder to confess judgment or realize on or dispose of collateral":

Cognovit notes, as illustrated in **Problem 1-8**, are not popular because of their potential for overreaching and disregard of procedural due process. As a result, confession of judgment clauses in notes are illegal in some states, legal but ineffective or unenforceable in others, and legal and enforceable in a few states. However, even where they are legal they are classified as an "unfair act or practice" and subject to the Federal Trade Commission Act if taken from a consumer in connection with "the extension of credit to consumers." See Federal Trade Commission Credit Practices Regulations, 16 C.F.R. § 444.2(a)(1).

> "(iii) a waiver of the benefit of any law intended for the advantage or protection of an obligor":

Under this exception to the courier-without-luggage rule, an obligor may waive the obligations that normally exist under negotiable instruments law. For example, he could waive his right to have the instrument presented to another potential obligor, such as a surety, as a condition to the maker's or drawer's obligation to pay the instrument, or the obligor could waiver his right to notice of dishonor, as a condition to his obligation to pay, etc. But rights of an obligor arising under consumer-protection laws may be a different matter. A waiver of the obligor's rights in connection with a consumer transaction may be void as a violation of public policy.

F. Contracting Into, and Out of, § 3-104

The conjunctive nature of § 3-104(a) requires the drafting party to satisfy each and every statutory requirement. Whether one, two, or more elements are absent triggers the same result: the writing is not a negotiable instrument, and Article 3 does not apply.

Parties may, intentionally or inadvertently, draft an instrument that is a "negotiable instrument" under § 3-104(a). But one of the interested parties may prefer not to be governed by Article 3. For example, the maker may wish to preserve claims and defenses against a subsequent transferee of the instrument, who otherwise is immune from most claims and defenses if Article 3 applies and the transferee is a holder in due course. Article 3 permits parties to remove themselves from its scope if the instrument (i) is not a check and (ii) at issuance, or first possession by a holder, "contains a conspicuous statement, however expressed, to the effect that the promise or order is not negotiable or is not an instrument governed by this Article." See §§ 3-104(d) and OC 3; 1-201(b)(10) (defining "conspicuous"). But the inverse is not true. Parties worried that a writing may not meet one or more of the elements of § 3-104(a) cannot bootstrap themselves into the definition of "negotiable instrument" by any means other than satisfying the statutory language. Section 1-302(a) provides parties with the freedom to contract, but tinkering with definitions is prohibited. "Thus, private parties cannot make an instrument negotiable within the meaning of Article 3 except as provided in Section 3-104[.]" § 1-302 OC 1.

Chapter 2

The Liability of the Parties to Promissory Notes

When parties place their signatures on an instrument we say they become liable on the instrument. When we say "liable," we are not referring to liability as in the case of a final judgment. Here we use "liable" only to refer to the risk that a party incurs upon signing the instrument. If the party does not have a good defense, ultimately he may indeed be held liable on a final judgment. But until then "liable" only refers to the fact that the signer has entered a contract and thereby has incurred potential liability on the contract. The nature and extent of that liability is dependent upon the capacity in which a party signs, and this in turn is determined by Article 3.

The parties to a promissory note in its most basic form are the maker and payee. If the payee indorses it for the purpose of transferring it to another party, he is an indorser. If a third party signs his name on the note for the purpose of accommmodation or guarantee, he also is an indorser.

The liability of these parties, whether primary or secondary, is well established under the law.

A. The Nature of Primary and Secondary Liability

1. The Maker

A promissory note that is payable on demand requires a demand for payment before the maker becomes obligated to pay. This is not because the maker is not primarily liable; he *is* primarily liable. Demand for payment of a demand note is required for the practical reason that in the absence of a demand, there is no legal obligation on the part of the maker to volunteer payment. Moreover, the maker may require the holder to exhibit the instrument unless the parties have agreed otherwise. §3-501(b)(2).

A note payable at a stated date does not require a demand for payment. Also, presentment and notice of dishonor often are waived by the parties. The expectation is that the maker will send payment to the holder on the date when payment is due. But if the maker fails to pay, the holder then will make a demand upon him. A demand for payment constitutes a "presentment." §3-501(a).

Since dishonor of a note is required as a condition to an action against an indorser (§3-415(a)), and since dishonor often requires presentment (§3-502(a)), as a strategic matter the holder wants unequivocal evidence that a presentment has been made under § 3-501. Thus if there are indorsers on the note, and presentment has not been waived, the holder needs to make a presentment for payment if he wants to preserve his right to sue the indorsers.

Because a maker is primarily liable some special problems exist in connection with the running of the statute of limitations. To appreciate the nature of the problems it may be helpful at the outset to distinguish between when a cause of action begins to accrue and when the statute of limitations begins to run. A cause of action accrues against a party to an instrument when he becomes legally obligated to pay. The rules for the accrual are stated in the various sections setting out the obligations of the parties, such as §§ 3-412, 3-413, 3-414, and 3-415. The time within which an action may be commenced to enforce the accrued obligation is the limitation period, which is governed by the statute of limitations, set out in § 3-118. For example, under § 3-412 the obligation of a maker to pay a demand promissory note arises at the time of issue. Since the maker is primarily liable from the moment of issue, and presentment for payment is not a condition precedent to his liability, the action accrues against the maker as of the time of issue. However, the time when the statute of limitations begins to run on the accrued action against the maker is set out in § 3-118. Section 3-118(b) provides that an action to enforce the obligation of the maker on a demand note must be brought within six years after the demand for payment. If no demand is made, the time for commencing the action is ten years from the time of issue, or ten years from the last payment against principle or interest of the note. (With respect to a note payable at a definite time, an action must be brought within six years after the due date under § 3-118(a).)

The limitation periods for an unaccepted draft, a certified check, a teller's check, a cashier's check, an accepted draft, and actions for conversion and breach of warranty are also set out in § 3-118.

a. Designating the Parties: Who Is the Maker?

Since so much of the business work of the world is done through parties who act in a representative capacity, it is important to have clear rules for determining who is legally bound by a signature affixed to the instrument by an agent or other fiduciary.

i. Notes Made by Agents and Other Representatives

The law of agency generally applies in determining the extent to which principals and agents are bound when their signatures are placed on instruments. Thus an agent may bind his principle, or to use the terminology of the Code, the representative may bind the party represented, either by express, implied, or apparent authority. The applicability of the law of agency is suggested by the first sentence of § 3-402(a) when it says that a represented person is bound to the same extent he would be bound on a simple contract signed by his representative. Section 3-402 is designed to resolve many problems of ambiguity which inevitably arise where negotiable instruments are signed by fiduciaries. For example, when will the representative or agent himself be bound? Suppose the representative does not disclose his representative capacity. Or suppose the original parties did not intend for the representative to be personally bound, but he fails to disclose his representative capacity. Will the representative be personally liable? Will it make a difference if the holder is a holder in due course?

MUNDACA INVESTMENT CORP. v. FEBBA
727 A.2d 990 (N.H. 1999)

Brock, C.J.

The defendants, Doris M. Febba, Thomas G. Scurfield, and Linda L. Kendall, appeal the Superior Court's (Smith, J.) grant of summary judgment in favor of the plaintiff, Mundaca Investment Corporation (Mundaca), holding the defendants personally liable for amounts due on two promissory notes. We reverse and remand.

The defendants served as trustees of the L.T.D. Realty Trust (trust). On July 28, 1987, they purchased two condominium units for the trust. To finance this transaction, the defendants executed two promissory notes, secured by two mortgages, payable to the order of Dartmouth Savings Bank (bank). At the end of both notes below the signature line, the name of each defendant was typewritten beside the preprinted term "Borrower." Following their signatures, each of the defendants handwrote the word "Trustee." While both promissory notes state that they are secured by a mortgage, the trust is not identified on the face of the notes. The trust, however, is identified as the "Borrower" in both mortgages.

On August 19, 1993, Mundaca acquired the two notes from the Federal Deposit Insurance Corporation as receiver for the bank. By letters dated October 28, 1994, Mundaca notified defendants Scurfield and Febba that the two promissory notes were in default. Mundaca foreclosed on the condominium units and filed suit against the defendants individually for the remaining amount due on the notes. Both Mundaca and the defendants moved for summary judgment. The defendants' motion for summary judgment was denied. In granting Mundaca's motion for summary judgment, the trial court ruled that the form of the defendants' signatures—"[defendant's signature], Trustee"—did not show unambiguously that the defendants were signing in a representative capacity. See RSA 382-A:3-402(b) comment 2 (1994). The trial court then ruled that the defendants failed to meet their burden of proving that Dartmouth Savings Bank did not intend to hold them personally liable. See RSA 382-A:3-402(b)(2) (1994). This appeal followed.

On appeal, the defendants argue that reading the notes and mortgages together shows unambiguously that they signed in a representative capacity for the trust as the identified principal, and therefore they are not personally liable under RSA 382-A:3-402(b)(1) (1994). Alternatively, the defendants contend that the trial court erred in granting Mundaca's motion for summary judgment because there was a genuine issue of material fact regarding whether the original parties intended the defendants to be personally liable. See RSA 382-A:3-402(b)(2).

The trial court applied RSA 382-A:3-402 (1994), and the parties do not dispute that this version of the statute governs the defendants' liability. Accordingly, we will assume for purposes of this appeal that this version of the statute applies.... RSA 382-A:3-402 (1994) provides in pertinent part:

(b) If a representative signs the name of the representative to an instrument and the signature is an authorized signature of the represented person, the following rules apply:

(1) If the form of the signature shows unambiguously that the signature is made on behalf of the represented person who is identified in the instrument, the representative is not liable on the instrument.

(2) Subject to subsection (c), if (i) the form of the signature does not show unambiguously that the signature is made in a representative capacity or (ii)

the represented person is not identified in the instrument, the representative is liable on the instrument to a holder in due course that took the instrument without notice that the representative was not intended to be liable on the instrument. With respect to any other person, the representative is liable on the instrument unless the representative proves that the original parties did not intend the representative to be liable on the instrument.

The defendants argue that under RSA 382-A:3-402(b)(1), the handwritten term "Trustee" appearing next to their signatures on the notes shows unambiguously that the signatures were made in a representative capacity. Further, the defendants argue that while the promissory notes did not explicitly identify the trust, the notes and mortgages read together reveal that the term "Borrower" is identified as the trust. Accordingly, the defendants argue that they are not personally liable.

RSA 382-A:3-402(b)(1) requires that the form of the representative's signature show unambiguously that the signature is made on behalf of the represented person who is identified in the instrument. The defendants concede that the instruments in this case are the two promissory notes. The defendants, however, argue that fundamental contract law requires that the notes and mortgages be read together to interpret the contracting parties' intentions. General principles of contract law only apply to negotiable instruments if not displaced by the Uniform Commercial Code. See RSA 382-A:1-103 (1994). Accordingly, we hold that because the represented person, in this case the trust, is not identified in the instrument as required by RSA 382-A:3-402(b)(1), this case falls squarely under RSA 382-A:3-402(b)(2).

Pursuant to RSA 382-A:3-402(b)(2), the defendants could be personally liable in two situations: (1) to a holder in due course who takes the instrument without notice that the defendants did not intend to be personally liable; and (2) to any other party unless the defendants prove that the original parties did not intend them to be personally liable. While the trial court did not address the first situation, it ruled that the defendants failed to meet their burden of proving that the original parties did not intend them to be personally liable. The defendants contend, however, that summary judgment was inappropriate because there was a genuine issue of material fact as to the intent of the original parties. We agree.

"When reviewing a motion for summary judgment, the court must consider the evidence in the light most favorable to the party opposing the motion and take all reasonable inferences from the evidence in that party's favor." Barnsley, 142 N.H. at 723, 720 A.2d at 64 (quotation omitted). "Summary judgment is appropriate when the evidence demonstrates that there is no genuine issue of material fact and that the moving party is entitled to judgment as a matter of law." Grossman v. Murray, 141 N.H. 265, 269, 681 A.2d 90, 93 (1996); see RSA 491:8-a, III (1997).

Our review of the record reveals a disputed issue of material fact as to the intent of the original parties, i.e., Dartmouth Savings Bank and the defendants. While the notes do not explicitly identify the trust as the represented party, the mortgages show that the defendants signed in a representative capacity and identify the trust as the "Borrower." See RSA 382-A:3-402(b)(1). Furthermore, the record contains conflicting affidavits by the defendants and Heidi Postupack, the bank's loan officer who handled this transaction. The defendants' affidavits claim that they intended to sign the notes as representatives of the trust. Conversely, Postupack's affidavit states that she understood that the bank intended the defendants to be personally liable, jointly and severally, on the notes. Considering this evidence in the light most favorable to the defendants, see Barnsley, 142

N.H. at 723, 720 A.2d at 64, we conclude that a genuine issue of material fact exists as to the bank's intent regarding the defendants' personal liability on the notes.

As noted earlier, the trial court did not address whether Mundaca was a holder in due course who took without notice that the defendants did not intend to be personally liable on the notes. See RSA 382-A:3-402(b)(2). Because the record before us is silent on this matter, we leave this issue for the trial court on remand.

The defendants also argue that the mortgages act as a defense to their alleged personal liability on the notes. This argument is without merit. The mortgages only provide a defense to the defendants' alleged personal liability on the notes to the extent that the mortgages modify, supplement, or nullify their obligation on the notes. See RSA 382-A:3-117 (1994). The defendants argue that it is clear that the mortgages modify and supplement the notes. We disagree. What is clear is that the mortgages were issued as collateral for the notes. What is unclear by reading the notes and the mortgages is the identity of the "Borrower." We have already held that the identity of the "Borrower" is a material issue of fact in dispute.

Accordingly, we reverse the grant of summary judgment and remand this case to the trial court for further proceedings consistent with this opinion.

Reversed and remanded.

Problem 2-1

Teal Corporation became indebted to LaPorte & Company for services performed for the corporation. As security for this debt the corporation executed a series of 36 promissory notes with consecutive dates in the following form:

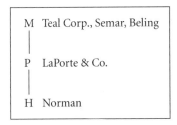

Date: June 5, 2007

One month after date we promise to pay five hundred dollars ($500) to the order of Laporte & Company. Payable at National Bank of Newark.

Teal Corporation
Harold Semar
Christopher Beling

In all the notes "Teal Corporation" was typewritten and the individuals' signatures were in handwriting. Semar was the president of Teal Corporation and Beling was the treasurer. LaPorte & Company negotiated the notes to Norman. The first twenty-one notes were paid, but all subsequent notes were dishonored. Teal Corporation is now insolvent and Semar is nowhere to be found.

1) Norman brings the unpaid notes to you and asks for your advice. What do you tell him? Does your answer depend on whether Norman is a mere holder or a holder in due course? §§ 3-401, 3-402, and 3-412.

Q: In what capacity did Beling sign the notes?

Q: What is the significance of the words "*we* promise"? Cf. § 1-106.

2) What are the policies, social or commercial, that bear upon the solution of this case?

3) Depending on who you think will prevail in this case, how can Norman and Beling protect themselves in this kind of case in the future?

Problem 2-2

Suppose Paul Pratt, principal, employs Adam App as his agent. In the course of App's employment he is authorized to sign promissory notes for Pratt. Assuming App has no intention of being bound personally and that he is authorized to sign for Pratt, who is liable in the following cases? §§ 3-402, 3-117.

a) Paul Pratt by Adam App, Agent
b) Adam App, Agent
c) Paul Pratt
      Adam App
d) Adam App
e) Paul Pratt

Note

Assume Paul Pratt had told Adam App (who is still his agent) that he was not authorized to sign any negotiable instrument in the coming week. It turns out that all of the above signatures occurred during that prohibited week. Are there any signatures on which Pratt would not be bound? See the general laws of agency — apparent authority, ratification, estoppel, etc., for possible application. There may be no change, because apparent authority can override an express prohibition.

ii. Signatures in Ambiguous Circumstances

Whether a person signs on the front or back of an instrument is not conclusive as to the capacity in which he has signed, although the location could be significant in some cases. Rather, his capacity is dependent on the obligation undertaken by the signer. Under the Code indorsers are defined by a process of elimination. Unless "circumstances unambiguously indicate that the signature was for a purpose other than indorsement," the signature is an indorsement. § 3-204(a).

Problem 2-3

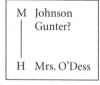

A promissory note states:

John Johnson promises to pay to the order of Mrs. Frank O'Dess five hundred dollars at 7 per cent interest. Due April 11, 2008.

John Johnson [handwritten]
Mike Gunter [handwritten]

1) In what capacity did Mike Gunter sign the note? §§ 3-204(a), (b); 3-103(a)(17).

Q: If Mike Gunter is an indorser, what kind of indorsement did he make? § 3-205.

2) Mrs. O'Dess tells you that John Johnson is her friend and that she would really rather collect from Mike Gunter. What would you advise Mrs. O'Dess? §§ 3-412, 3-415(a).

Q: Will dishonor occur automatically, or must O'Dess take some action? Would your analysis change if the note was payable on demand? § 3-502(a).

3) If Mrs. O'Dess collects from Mike Gunter, what should Mike Gunter do? § 3-412.

2. The Indorser's Liability

An indorser is potentially liable in a transaction involving a negotiable instrument on three theories. (1) He may be liable on his indorsement contract under § 3-415. As we shall see, (2) he may also give certain transfer or presentment warranties in passing on the instrument. And since there is almost always an underlying transaction which gave rise to the negotiable instrument, (3) the indorser may also be liable on the underlying obligation independent of the negotiable instrument. We will explore these three theories of potential liability in order.

The indorser's liability naturally raises the question: What types of indorsements are there? At this juncture we should note that the indorsement contract may be created by any one of several forms of indorsements. For a brief definition of various indorsements, which is all that is needed at this point, see § 3-205, regarding special indorsements, blank indorsements, and anomalous indorsements. We will define and illustrate these indorsements more particularly in connection with the subject of negotiation, for which some form of indorsement is indispensable if the instrument is payable to order, and permissible if the instrument is payable to bearer. For the definition and function of restrictive indorsements, which we will explore later, see § 3-206.

a. Liability on the Indorsement Contract

An indorser normally incurs secondary liability by placing his signature on a negotiable instrument. It follows that there are certain conditions that must be satisfied before the indorser can be held liable on the instrument. These conditions may include some or all of the following: presentment, dishonor, and notice of dishonor. In an international transaction, protest also may be necessary.

An unqualified indorsement of an indorser has the twofold effect of (1) usually conveying title to the instrument to the indorsee, and (2) imposing secondary liability on the indorser. Since the indorser's liability is based on contract, query whether an indorsement accompanied by such words as 'payment guaranteed' would convert the indorser's potential liability from secondary to primary.

If an indorser is held liable on an instrument, to whom is the obligation owed? The obligation is owed to a person entitled to enforce the instrument under § 3-301 and to any subsequent indorser who paid the instrument. § 3-415(a).

What is the extent of an indorser's liability if the terms of the instrument were incomplete at the time of indorsement or have been revised after indorsement? The indorser's liability is measured by the terms of the instrument at the time of indorsement or, if the terms were incomplete upon indorsement, upon completion. § 3-415(a).

Problem 2-4

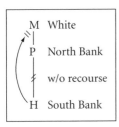

In 2008, White issued two promissory notes payable to the order of North Bank. North Bank indorsed the notes "without recourse" and sold them to South Bank for $3,500. South Bank paid for the notes by crediting North Bank's account maintained at South Bank. Three years previous to this transaction the two banks had orally agreed that neither bank would rely upon its "without recourse" indorsements, but that it would receive back any dishonored instruments and the appropriate account would be debited accordingly. When the two notes came due, White dishonored them. Accordingly, South Bank debited North Bank's account and returned the notes to North Bank pursuant to their agreement. North Bank threatens to sue South Bank if it does not recredit the account.

1) What will North Bank argue? § 3-415(a), (b).

2) Does South Bank have an argument? § 3-117.

3) Will South Bank recredit North Bank's (the indorser's) account? § 1-303.

Note

In view of what is transferred by an unqualified indorsement, consider the impact of a forged indorsement on the conveyance of title. We will take up forged indorsements when we discuss negotiation—the process of transferring an instrument to another in such a manner that the transferee becomes a holder. If a holder of an instrument indorses it in blank and hands it to another, and if the indorsement is genuine and there have been no prior forged indorsements, the transferee becomes a holder and thereby obtains title to the instrument. §§ 3-203, 3-301. If there is a forged indorsement, however, a transferee may not obtain title. But he may have some very substantial rights, depending on the circumstances.

b. Presentment, Dishonor, Notice, and Protest
i. Presentment

We have considered the proposition that a formal presentment or demand is not a condition to a maker's liability on a demand note because a maker is primarily liable on the instrument. However, if no demand is made upon a maker of a demand note, the holder will lose his right to sue upon the note after ten years. If demand for payment is made, the holder then has six years to commence an action to enforce the note. § 3-118(b). Nevertheless, the holder of a demand note must make a demand for payment if he wants to get paid because, by definition, there is no legal obligation on the part of the maker to make payment until a demand for payment has been made. A note payable on a specific date is a different matter. In that case the maker is obligated to send or deliver payment according to agreement. The maker's failure to do so generally triggers a dishonor of the note. § 3-502(a)(3).

By contrast, the liability of an indorser of a demand note is secondary, and presentment or demand upon the maker for payment, dishonor, and notice of dishonor may be conditions to an indorser's liability.

"Presentment" is defined in § 3-501(a) and the rules that follow indicate the ease with which a presentment can be made.

In the case of a demand note, or one payable at a bank, or one which requires presentment by its terms, presentment is a condition precedent to an indorser's liability. §§ 3-415(a), 3-501(a), 3-502(a). If the instrument is payable at a definite time, however, presentment is not a condition to the indorser's liability. § 3-502(a). In that case the maker is obligated to pay on the designated date and if he does not, he has dishonored the note and is automatically liable. § 3-412. Notice of the dishonor to the indorser is required to hold the indorser. §§ 3-415(c), 3-503(a). However, the requirements of presentment and notice of dishonor can be waived, as they frequently are pursuant to language in the note. § 3-504. Such a waiver clause will not destroy negotiability. § 3-104(a)(3)(iii).

Where presentment has not been waived, when must such presentment for payment be made as a condition to indorser's liability? We explore the implications of this condition and related matters in the following problem.

Problem 2-5

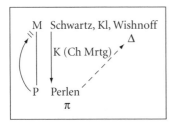

Schwartz Wood Corporation executed a note payable to the order of Perlen for $21,000 dated December 14, 2007, "payable on demand after date." Wishnoff was the third indorser on the note, which had been indorsed by Schwartz (president), Kleefeld (treasurer), and Wishnoff. Repayment of the note was secured by a chattel mortgage given by the maker to Perlen when the note was executed. On April 18, 2009, sixteen months after issue of the note, Perlen presented the note and made demand for payment. It was dishonored. Perlen gave notice of dishonor to Wishnoff a week later and he refused to pay. Perlen then commenced an action against Wishnoff on the note.

1) To whom did Perlen present the note for payment? § 3-501.

Q: Did Perlen give timely notice of dishonor to Wishnoff? § 3-503(c).

2) Wishnoff, an indorser, argues that Perlen, a holder, failed to make a timely presentment of the note, that a lapse of sixteen months on a demand note is too long to expect an indorser to stand willing to pay if the maker does not, and that his obligation is therefore discharged. Is Wishnoff right, or is he liable? §§ 3-415(a), (c); 3-502(a); 3-503.

3) Must a holder make presentment within a certain period of time (such as "within a reasonable time after its issue" as under the Negotiable Instruments Law [the forerunner to U.C.C. Article 3], or "within a reasonable time after such party becomes liable thereon" as under F§ 3-503(1)(e)) in order to then charge a secondary party such as an indorser? See §§ 3-415, 3-501. Cf. F§ 3-503(1)(e).

Q: Should the statute require an outside time for presentment for the benefit of the indorser?

ii. Dishonor and Notice of Dishonor

Closely related to the condition of presentment are two other conditions to an indorser's liability, namely dishonor and notice of dishonor. Proper presentment may be, but is not always, a condition precedent to dishonor. A demand promissory note is dishonored if the maker fails to pay it after it has been presented for payment. § 3-502(a)(1). But a time note is dishonored if it is not paid on the day it becomes payable; no presentment is required. § 3-502(a)(3).

Problem 2-6

Ben's new house cost $60,000. He made a $3,000 down payment and borrowed $57,000 from Bank of America. The bank took a note from Ben for $57,000 and a deed of trust on the property to secure the note. Later, Ben sold the house to C who paid $3,500 for

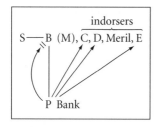

Ben's equity. A year later C sold the house to D, who thereafter sold it to C.C. Meril. Notwithstanding a declining economy Meril prospered, sold the house to E, and bought another in Pebble Creek. C, D, Meril, and E had signed their names in succession on the back of the original note at the time each assumed the obligations under the original deed of trust in favor of Bank of America. Hard times got worse and E defaulted on the loan when the unpaid balance was $50,000. Bank of America sold the house at a foreclosure sale for $40,000 and then demanded payment of the balance from Ben on June 1, 2007. Ben failed to pay, and Bank of America mailed notices of dishonor by certified mail (return receipt requested) to each of the indorsers on June 5. No addresses appeared on the note. Their addresses were obtained from a list in the Bank's files. On this list was type-written the name of "C.C. Meril," followed by "V.P. Westn. Portland Cement Co., 2277 W. 23rd St., Pebble Creek" in pencil. All the indorsers except Meril received their notice. His letter was returned on June 15 marked "Unclaimed, return to sender." Meril's letter was addressed to 2277 W. 23rd St., Pebble Creek, as per the penciled note in the file, which the Bank erroneously assumed was Meril's home address. In fact his home address was 490 W. 40th, Pebble Creek. When addressing the letters, bank employees had consulted the telephone directory, but Meril's residence address did not appear in the current telephone directory. However, his address was in the current city directory, which the bank employees did not consult. The Portland Cement address in the file did show Meril's correct business address and his position with the company.

1) Is Meril liable on the note?

Q: What is the consequence of lack of notice of dishonor to an indorser? §§ 3-415(a), (c); 3-503(a), (b).

2) If notice is mailed, must the letter be received by the indorser, or even sent to the correct address? Consider §§ 1-201(b)(36), 1-202(d). Cf. F§ 3-508(4).

Notes

1. What is necessary for a valid notice of dishonor? How, when, and by whom? See § 3-503(b), (c).

For parties other than banks, the general rule is that "notice of dishonor must be given within 30 days following the day on which dishonor occurs." With respect to an instrument taken for collection by a bank, "notice of dishonor must be given (i) by the bank before midnight of the next banking day following the banking day on which the bank receives notice of dishonor of the instrument...." Rephrased, banks must give notice before the "midnight deadline" as defined in § 4-104(a)(10). Any other holder of an instrument has 30 days to give notice of dishonor. § 3-503(c).

2. *Protest*: Before leaving the conditions to secondary liability, it would be well to take note of a very useful evidentiary device that is provided for in § 3-505(b): protest. Protest is the equivalent of notice of presentment and dishonor, but in notarized form, which was required by F§ 3-501(3) in the case of a draft drawn or payable outside the United States. Protest is no longer mandatory in overseas transactions but it is *permitted* by § 3-505, not only in foreign transactions but also in the case of domestic instruments. Section 3-505(b) provides that "a protest is a certificate of dishonor made under the hand and seal of a United States consul or vice consul, or a notary public or other person au-

thorized to administer oaths by the law of the place where dishonor occurs.... The protest may also certify that notice of dishonor has been given to some or all parties." Since a protest is in the nature of an affidavit and is presumptive evidence that presentment and notice of dishonor have occurred, it is probably the easiest way to establish these facts and should be used routinely where practical.

Problem 2-7

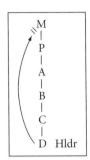

M gives a note for $1,000 to P who indorses it to A, who indorses it to B, who indorses it to C, who indorses it to D. The note comes due, D demands payment from M, and M refuses to pay. D does not know where A, B, or C are, so he gives timely notice of dishonor only to P. P knows where A is and gives timely notice to A.

1) Can D sue P or A even though D took the note from C? §§ 3-415(a), 3-301.

2) Can A avoid liability to D because A received notice of dishonor from P, not D? § 3-503(b).

3) Why might P want to give notice to A? §§ 3-415(a), (c); 3-503(a).

iii. Waiver or Excused Presentment and Notice of Dishonor

Section 3-504 recites the circumstances under which these conditions precedent are entirely excused. They include express waiver on the instrument, impossibility of payment, etc.

Problem 2-8

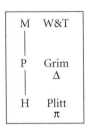

Walton & Taylor, a partnership, executed a promissory note for $6,150 in favor of Grim, the bookkeeper and tax advisor to the partnership. The note was payable in five installments of $1,230. Grim indorsed the note to Plitt. When the first installment came due the maker's first check for $1,230 was returned marked "account closed." Grim and Plitt therefore assumed the other four installments would not be paid either. But fortunately the maker did scrape up enough money to pay the first installment. When the second installment came due the maker managed to pay $530 of it, and through the persuasions of Grim, the maker obtained the consent of Plitt to give it more time to pay the remainder in return for a bonus of $70. Grim also persuaded Plitt to give time extensions on the subsequent installments in return for an additional 10% bonus to Plitt from the maker. Unfortunately the maker was not able to carry through on its promises and the remaining installments were not paid. Two months later, Plitt commenced an action against Grim for the balance on the note. Grim defended on the ground that no presentment had been made or notice of dishonor given with respect to the balance, and therefore he was discharged from liability.

1) What is Grim's capacity on the note?

2) Were the conditions to his liability satisfied? §§ 3-415(a), (c); 3-502(a); 3-503(a).

3) Does Plitt have an argument? §§ 3-503(a); 3-504(a), (b).

B. Who Is a PETE?

The phrase "person entitled to enforce" appears in Article 3 over three dozen times, suggesting that mastering its meaning is critical to understanding Article 3. The phrase has already appeared in many statutes that we have examined, including §§ 3-412 and 3-415(a). The following materials examine the parameters of "PETE" status under § 3-301.

Problem 2-9

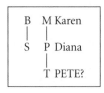

Karen buys a used piano from her sister, Diana, for $4,000. Karen cannot pay cash, but Diana is willing to take a $4,000 note that bears interest. Karen executes a $4,000 promissory note. Consider the following scenarios.

Scenario #1: Karen places the executed note, which is payable to bearer, on her kitchen table. The note is stolen by Thief. Is Thief a PETE? §§ 3-301, 1-201(b)(21), 3-305(c) (second sentence).

Scenario #2: Same as #1, except the note is payable to the order of Diana.

Scenario #3: Karen delivers the executed note, which is payable to bearer, to Diana. Diana then sells and delivers the note to Brad. Diana never indorsed the note. Is Brad a PETE? §§ 3-301, 1-201(b)(21).

Scenario #4: Same as #3, except the note is payable to the order of Diana. Is Brad a PETE? §§ 3-301, 1-201(b)(21), 3-203. Assume that Karen has a warranty claim against Diana because the piano is defective in some way. Does Brad care whether he can qualify as a PETE on his own, rather than by asserting the rights of his transferor? §§ 3-308 and OC 2; 3-203 OC 2. Does Brad have the right to insist on Diana's indorsement? § 3-203(c). Does Brad prefer a blank indorsement (e.g., "Diana") or a special indorsement (e.g., "Pay to Brad; Diana")? Could Brad convert Diana's blank indorsement to a special indorsement without her consent? § 3-205(c).

Scenario #5: Karen delivers the executed note, which is payable to bearer, to Diana. Thief steals the note from Diana. Diana never indorsed the note. Is Thief a PETE? Is Diana a PETE? §§ 3-301, 3-309(a). Should Karen be concerned that she may be forced to pay twice? §§ 3-309(b), 3-305(c).

Scenario #6: Karen delivers the executed note, which is payable to bearer, to Diana. Diana loses the unindorsed note. Later, she sells her property rights in the lost note to Brad. Is Brad a PETE, even though he never possessed the note? §§ 3-301, 3-309(a).

C. Accommodation Parties

1. Suretyship Law

Another subject relevant to the signature liability of parties is that of accommodation law. The law of accommodation contemplates a tripartite situation—a creditor, a primary obligor, and a secondary obligor or surety.

As the Official Comments to F§ 3-415 indicate, the rules governing the rights and duties of accommodation parties are based on the law of suretyship. The law of accommodation in current Article 3 (§§ 3-419 and 3-605) is substantially consistent with this proposition.

FLOOR v. MELVIN
283 N.E.2d 303 (Ill. App. Ct. 1972)

Appeal from the Circuit Court of LaSalle County.

ALLOY, J.

The action in the present case was instituted by Marjorie Irene Floor in the Circuit Court of LaSalle County to recover money alleged to be due on a promissory note. On motion of defendant Mildred B. Melvin, executrix of the estate of Charles W. Melvin, deceased, an order was entered dismissing the claim for failure to state a cause of action. Claimant, Marjorie Irene Floor, seeks reversal of the order on the theory that the deceased Charles W. Melvin was a guarantor of payment.

On April 14, 1959, Melco, Inc., an Illinois corporation, acting through its president, Charles W. Melvin, made and issued its negotiable promissory note in the principal amount of $12,000.00, payable to the order of Marjorie Irene Floor. On the back of the note the following language appears:

> "For and in consideration of funds advanced herein to Melco, Inc., we irrevocably guarantee Marjorie Irene Floor against loss by reason of non-payment of this note."

The signature of Charles W. Melvin, as well as others, appeared below such statement.

The complaint of plaintiff in this case does not allege prosecution of her claim to judgment as against the principal obligor on the note and it, also, does not allege the insolvency of the obligor, Melco, Inc. The only issue, therefore, before the court is whether, with respect to the undertaking on the back of the note, plaintiff is required to prosecute her claim against the maker of the note as a pre-condition to making a valid claim as against the estate of Charles W. Melvin.

Under the negotiable instruments act applicable, Illinois Revised Statutes, Ch. 26, § 3-416 [R§ 3-419] the subsections which are pertinent to the issue in this case read as follows:

> "(1) 'Payment guaranteed' or equivalent words added to a signature mean that the signer engages that if the instrument is not paid when due he will pay it according to its tenor without resort by the holder to any other party.

> "(2) 'Collection guaranteed' or equivalent words added to a signature mean that the signer engages that if the instrument is not paid when due he will pay it according to its tenor, but only after the holder has reduced his claim against the maker or acceptor to judgment and execution has been returned unsatisfied, or after the maker or acceptor has become insolvent or it is otherwise apparent that it is useless to proceed against him.

> "(3) Words of guaranty which do not otherwise specify guarantee payment."

The quoted subsection in the portion marked as "(1)" codifies the rule of several Illinois cases including Beebe v. Kirkpatrick, 321 Ill. 612, 152 N.E. 539, and Weger v. Robinson Nash Motor Co., 340 Ill. 81, 172 N.E. 7. In the Weger case referred to, the guaranty contract which had been executed, read (at page 85):

"We, the undersigned directors and stockholders of the Robinson Nash Motor Company, do hereby guarantee the *payment of notes* of said company given the Robinson State Bank of Robinson, Illinois, and hereby agree to be personally liable therefor and to all the conditions and requirements written in said notes ..." (emphasis ours)

The court in construing said language said, at page 90:

"A contract guaranteeing the payment of a note is an absolute contract, and by it the guarantor undertakes for a valuable consideration to pay the debt at maturity if the principal debtor fails to do so, and upon it, if the debt is not paid at maturity, the guarantor may be sued at once. Guarantors must be regarded as original promisors, who bound themselves to pay the notes when they matured, and their duty was, on their maturity, to go to the holder and take them up, and their liability was not to depend upon the prosecution of suit against the maker."

In Beebe v. Kirkpatrick, 321 Ill. 612, the question was with respect to construction of the words "I hereby guarantee this loan". In support of its holding that the cited language was absolute in nature, the Supreme Court stated (at page 616):

"In this State contracts of guaranty of negotiable instruments are of two kinds: contracts guaranteeing the collection of the notes, and contracts guaranteeing the payment of the notes. A contract guaranteeing the collection of a note or debt is conditional in its character, and the guarantor thereby undertakes to pay the debt upon condition that the owner thereof shall make use of the ordinary legal means to collect it from the debtor with diligence but without avail. A contract guaranteeing the payment of a note or a debt is an absolute contract, and by it the guarantor undertakes, for a valuable consideration, to pay the debt at maturity if the principal debtor fails to do so, and upon it, if the debt is not paid at maturity, the guarantor may be sued at once."

Other cases, such as Dillman v. Nadelhoffer, 160 Ill. 121, treat the language of subsection (2) referring to "collection guaranteed". In the Dillman case the language before the court was "for a valuable consideration we do hereby guarantee the collection of the within note at its maturity ..." (at page 124). In construing this language, the Supreme Court stated that "the guaranty is not a guaranty of the payment of the note, but a guaranty of the collection of the note." The court stated (at page 125) that a contract guaranteeing the collection of a note or debt is conditional in its character and the guarantor thereby undertakes to pay the debt, "upon condition that the owner thereof shall make use of the ordinary legal means to collect it from the principal debtor with diligence and without avail".

In the cause before us, the primary contention made by plaintiff is that the language of defendant's guarantee presents an absolute undertaking and is, therefore, a guarantee of payment within purview of subsection (1) of the statute in question. In support of that contention, Beebe v. Kirkpatrick, 321 Ill. 612, 152 N.E. 539, Hance v. Miller, 21 Ill. 636, and Empire Sec. Co. v. Berry, 211 Ill. App 278, are cited as authority. We have indicated that in the Beebe case, the court found that the language "I hereby guarantee this loan" presented a guarantee of payment and not collection. The Hance case involved construction of language which read "For value received I guarantee payment of the within note at maturity". Consistently, the court had no difficulty in construing that language to be a guarantee of payment. In the Berry case, the guarantor had agreed to pay the note if the maker did not "retire" it at maturity. The court found that the word "retire" as used in the context meant "pay" and, therefore, that the guarantee was of payment and not of collection.

The language involved in each of the cases referred to by plaintiff is clearly in conformity with the law in Illinois regarding guaranty contracts. We believe, however, that plaintiff draws an erroneous analogy between guarantees appearing in those cases and that which we have under consideration in the cause before us. In our opinion, the terms of the guarantee in the instant case are made conditional upon collection of the note. While it is true that the word "collection" has not been used, in our view the guarantee as against "loss" is in effect a guarantee of collection rather than payment. At least one case of another jurisdiction, Michelin Tire Co. v. Cutter, 240 P. 895 (Ore. 1925), involved language similar to that in the instant case. There the defendant agreed to indemnify plaintiff against "any loss on account of any monies" which a certain party may owe from time to time. The court had no difficulty in concluding that the guarantee involved was of collection and not of payment in that case.

A distinction is sought to be made by plaintiff in the instant case to the effect that Michelin Tire Co. v. Cutter, supra, to which we have referred, cannot be considered in this case, in that the court in the Oregon case was not involved with the question of guarantee of payment of collection on a negotiable instrument. The argument is substantially that construction of language of a guaranty contract will change depending on the substance or form of the underlying agreement. We do not agree with such contention. A guaranty contract must be construed in like manner with other guaranty contracts notwithstanding that its execution is of a negotiable instrument or a non-negotiable instrument. Words rendering a guaranty conditional must have similar effect whether the obligation which is being guaranteed arose out of a simple contract or an obligation negotiable in form. We see no basis in law for the distinction which plaintiff has suggested.

While we agree with plaintiff that decisions of another state would not overrule the law of Illinois, we believe that decisions of courts of the respective states, where relevant, should be examined for such value as Illinois courts may find in them when out-of-state courts have construed certain language and Illinois courts have not. Parties to an appeal in fact have an obligation, when no Illinois authority is in point, to cite existing appropriate authority from other jurisdictions when available (Kelley v. Kelley, 317 Ill. 104).

A final contention made by plaintiff is that subsection "(3)" of the Illinois statute quoted earlier in our opinion to the effect that where words of guaranty do not otherwise specify, the guarantee [is] of payment could be controlling in such case. We cannot agree with such analysis since it is apparent that the use of subsection "(3)" is limited to instances where no conditional language of the type we find in the present case has been used.

We, therefore, conclude that it is apparent that the instant guarantee is one of collection and not of payment. Since plaintiff does not allege that her claim was prosecuted to judgment and execution thereon returned unsatisfied or that the maker was insolvent, she has not complied with §3-416(2) [R§3-419(d)] of the Uniform Commercial Code (Illinois Revised Statutes, Ch. 26). The trial court's dismissal of the action was, therefore, proper, and should be affirmed.

Affirmed.

Note

Would a court reach the same conclusion under the current statute? See §3-419(d), (e).

2. The Accommodation Contract

A suretyship or accommodation relationship may be described as the relationship which exists when two parties, one for the accommodation of the other, are under an obligation to a third party, and as between the two parties the accommodated party (the principal obligor) rather than the surety (the secondary obligor) ought to perform. See, e.g., Restatement Third, Suretyship and Guaranty § 1. Or to use the words of Article 3, "An accommodation party is a person who signs an instrument to benefit the accommodated party either by signing at the time value is obtained by the accommodated party or later, and who is not a direct beneficiary of the value obtained." § 3-419, OC 1. The usual accommodation relationship arises as a result of the accommodation party signing a note as a co-maker or anomalous indorser. *Id.*

VENAGLIA v. KROPINAK

35 U.C.C. Rep.Serv.2d 556 (N.M. Ct. App. 1998)

HARTZ, Chief Judge.

The Appellants, Frank Venaglia, Ann P. Venaglia, and Roy J. Venaglia (the Venaglias), sued Roy M. Kropinak on his guarantee of a $68,000 promissory note from Downtown Business Center, Inc. (DBC) to the Venaglias. On cross-motions for summary judgment the district court granted Kropinak's motion and denied the Venaglias'. The Venaglias appeal, asking that we set aside the summary judgment against them and order the district court to enter summary judgment in their favor. This appeal requires us to examine suretyship defenses under the Uniform Commercial Code (the UCC) and the common law, and the relationship between these two sources of law. We hold that the record before us will not sustain a summary judgment for either party. We therefore reverse the summary judgment and remand for further proceedings.

I. BACKGROUND

On August 3, 1992 DBC entered into a purchase agreement to buy from the Venaglias a commercial property (the Property) in downtown Albuquerque. The negotiated price was $470,000, with $90,000 cash due at closing and the $380,000 balance payable under a standard form real estate contract. Although there is some dispute regarding precisely what documents were executed by the time the transaction closed, it is not contested that (1) on November 19, 1992 DBC entered into a real estate contract (the Real Estate Contract) to purchase the Property from the Venaglias for $460,000, (2) the contract acknowledged the receipt of a $90,000 cash down payment, and (3) $68,000 of the down payment was in the form of a promissory note (the Promissory Note) dated October 30, 1992.... The note was signed by Robert J. Doucette as president of DBC. Immediately beneath Doucette's signature was the heading "GUARANTORS (individually)," under which were the signatures of William W. Anderson, Kropinak, and Doucette. No collateral secured the note.

DBC defaulted on the Promissory Note in October 1993. When the guarantors failed to pay, the Venaglias sued DBC, Anderson, and Kropinak. Pursuant to a stipulated order, the Venaglias obtained judgment against all three defendants in the amount of $48,727.91 on August 29, 1994. (As will be explained below, the judgment against Kropinak was later set aside.)

In the meantime DBC had continued to make some payments under the Real Estate Contract. But in August 1994 DBC failed to make any payments and the Venaglias terminated the contract effective September 19, 1994. On October 11, 1994 the Venaglias entered into an Agreement of Compromise and Mutual Release (the Settlement Agreement) with DBC, signed on behalf of DBC by its then president Ron Perea. Under the agreement DBC relinquished the Property to the Venaglias and the parties mutually released any potential claims against one another.... Nine days after the date of the Settlement Agreement, the Venaglias entered into an agreement to sell the Property to Suzanne Dutcher for $425,000, an agreement that was consummated by a real estate contract dated November 28, 1994. The $425,000 sum would apparently have been more than enough to pay off all the principal and interest that DBC owed on the Real Estate Contract and the Promissory Note.

On March 31, 1995 Kropinak moved to set aside the August 1994 stipulated judgment against him on his guarantee. He contended that he had never retained the attorney who purportedly represented him in the proceedings. After a hearing the district court granted the requested relief.

Once the judgment against him was set aside, Kropinak filed an answer to the claim, the parties conducted discovery, and Kropinak and the Venaglias each filed motions for summary judgment. The motions for summary judgment focused on the validity of defenses raised by Kropinak. On July 3, 1996 the district court granted summary judgment to Kropinak, ruling that all his defenses were meritorious.

We disagree with that ruling. Most of Kropinak's defenses fail as a matter of law. And the one defense with possible legal merit did not entitle him to summary judgment; issues of fact remain with respect to the extent, if any, to which that defense entitles him to relief.

Kropinak's potentially meritorious defense is his claim that he is fully discharged from his guarantee because the Settlement Agreement between the Venaglias and DBC prejudiced his rights as a guarantor. The gist of his assertion of prejudice is as follows: Although the Settlement Agreement explicitly states that "DBC acknowledges that it has 'equity' in the [P]roperty," DBC relinquished all its rights in the Property to the Venaglias. This left DBC with no assets whatsoever. Thus, if Kropinak were to pay off the Promissory Note in accordance with his guaranty, he would not be able to obtain any reimbursement from DBC. The unfairness of this result is apparent from the fact that a few days after execution of the Settlement Agreement, the Venaglias entered into a contract to sell the Property for a sum that exceeded what DBC owed on the Real Estate Contract and the Promissory Note. In other words, one could say that DBC's "equity" in the Property prior to the Settlement Agreement (the value of the Property less the amount owed on the Real Estate Contract) exceeded the amount owed on the Promissory Note. Hence, if DBC had obtained full value for its interest in the Property, it could have paid off the note guaranteed by Kropinak.

We hold that this defense finds support in Section 44 of the recently adopted Restatement (Third) of Suretyship and Guaranty (1996) (the Restatement), which states that a guarantor is discharged to the extent that the payee impairs the guarantor's recourse against the payor. Rather than citing to the just-published Restatement, however, Kropinak attempted in district court to fit the above argument into more familiar legal pigeonholes. He contended: (1) Pursuant to NMSA 1978, Section 55-3-605(b)(1992), Kropinak was discharged because the Settlement Agreement destroyed his right of recourse against DBC, whose only asset was its interest in the Property. (2) Under the common law of guarantees, the Venaglias' release of DBC discharged Kropinak from his obligation as a guarantor. (3) The Venaglias are not entitled to recover against Kropinak because they did not suffer any damages from the default on the Promissory Note, when one considers the payments made on the Real Estate Contract, the payments on the note, and the proceeds of the Dutcher sale. (4) Kropinak's guaranty was discharged under Section 55-3-605(d) because the release of DBC materially modified his obligation as guarantor.

In the remainder of the opinion we first explain why we reject these four contentions. We then discuss Section 44 and explain why it is not preempted in this case by the provisions of the Uniform Commercial Code governing negotiable instruments. Applying Section 44, we hold that the present record will not support summary judgment for either party.

II. DISCUSSION

There are two principal sources of law governing the rights and duties of the parties with respect to a guarantee of a promissory note. One is Article 3 of the Uniform Commercial Code, codified in New Mexico at NMSA 1978, Sections 55-3-101 to -605 (1992). (In the New Mexico statutes the numbering is identical to that in Article 3 of the UCC, except that the New Mexico chapter number—55—precedes the UCC number.)

The other is the common law. For authoritative guidance on the common law we look to the Restatement. Our notice for oral argument in this case advised counsel to be prepared to discuss the applicability of the provisions of the Restatement to the facts presented here.

To begin our analysis, we observe that Kropinak is an accommodation party with respect to the Promissory Note. As stated in Section 55-3-419(a):

> If an instrument is issued for value given for the benefit of a party to the instrument ("accommodated party") and another party to the instrument ("accommodation party") signs the instrument for the purpose of incurring liability on the instrument without being a direct beneficiary of the value given for the instrument, the instrument is signed by the accommodation party "for accommodation."

Section 55-3-419(c) states in pertinent part:

> A person signing an instrument is presumed to be an accommodation party and there is notice that the instrument is signed for accommodation if the signature ... is accompanied by words indicating that the signer is acting as surety or guarantor with respect to the obligation of another party to the instrument.

Kropinak meets the definition of Section 55-3-419(a) because it is undisputed that Kropinak signed the Promissory Note, that the purpose of the note was to enable DBC (the promisor on the note) to enter into the Real Estate Contract with the Venaglias, and that Kropinak did not benefit directly from the transaction, see § 55-3-419 official cmt. 1 (employee or shareholder of corporation is "indirect" beneficiary of loan to corporation). Also, the presumption of Section 55-3-419(c) applies because Kropinak's signature appears under the heading "GUARANTORS (individually)." It is worth noting that if the guarantee signed by Kropinak had been a document separate from the Promissory Note, then Kropinak would not have been an accommodation party because he would not have been a "party to the instrument" and he would not have "sign[ed] the instrument." In that event Article 3 would not apply, and the suretyship relationship would be governed by the common law....

To recognize that Kropinak is an accommodation party under Article 3 of the UCC is not, however, to say that the common law (and hence the Restatement) is of no interest. The UCC itself states:

Unless displaced by the particular provisions of this act [the New Mexico UCC], the principles of law and equity, including the law merchant and the law relative to capacity to contract, principal and agent, estoppel, fraud, misrepresentation, duress, coercion, mistake, bankruptcy or other validating or invalidating cause, shall supplement its provisions.

NMSA 1978, §55-1-103 (1961). More directly in point, specific relevant sections of Article 3 explicitly incorporate, at least in part, the common law with respect to contract defenses. See §55-3-305(a)(2) (obligation to pay negotiable instrument may be subject to defenses available with respect to obligation to pay under a simple contract); §55-3-601(a) (obligation to pay negotiable instrument may be discharged by act or agreement that would discharge obligation to pay under a simple contract). As we shall see, some aspects of the common law of suretyship are not superseded by Article 3 and may provide relief to Kropinak.

[The court's discussion of alleged defenses appears below, following **Problem 2-13**.]

Problem 2-10

```
Max Zall, Sarah Z, Lyons
B   M                    Δ

  |
  |K
  |
S    P   Callery, Lyons?
         π
         |
         |
    H   Mont Bank
```

Max Zall, a building contractor, became indebted to Callery, a building supply dealer that frequently borrowed funds against its customers' paper at Monticello Bank. Callery demanded payment for materials supplied to Zall, but Zall was unable to pay. Callery then requested Zall to execute a promissory note with satisfactory indorsements to enable Callery to discount the note at the bank. Zall executed a promissory note for $7,000 payable to the order of Callery. The note was indorsed by Zall's wife, Sarah. Zall then requested Lyons to indorse the note. Lyons then asked Callery why he wanted Lyons to indorse. Callery told Lyons that he had a lot of paper with the bank, that the bank would not be satisfied with just the names of Zall and his wife, and that Zall would like to have Lyons' indorsement to help the Zalls out. Lyons then indorsed the note. Callery then discounted the note to Monticello Bank. At maturity Max Zall dishonored the note and the bank gave notice of dishonor to Callery, who paid it and took possession. Callery then gave timely notice of dishonor to Lyons and demanded payment from him. Lyons had received no consideration for his indorsement. The bank would not have discounted the note for Callery without Lyons' signature.

1) What status does Lyons occupy on the instrument? §§3-419(a), (b); 3-103(a)(17).

Q: What kind of indorsement did Lyons make? §3-205.

2) Who is the accommodated party? §§3-419(a), 3-303(a)(3); PEB Commentary #11 (Discussion of Issue #1).

Q: Does Lyons care who the accommodated party is? §3-419(f).

3) Is Lyons liable to Callery? §§3-415(a), 3-419(f).

Note

The accommodation relationship can sometimes ease the conditions (e.g., presentment and notice of dishonor) that a holder must satisfy as a prerequisite to suing the parties. That is, the conditions precedent to secondary liability of an accommodated party may be entirely excused.

To illustrate further how the rights of an accommodation maker or indorser may differ under suretyship law, consider the following problem.

Problem 2-11

```
PD                    S
M Ben/Dad ──K-3── Dad/Ben
   │
   │K-1
   │          K-2
P  │
Bank
C
```

Ben wants to borrow $2,500 from the bank but has no collateral. The bank agrees to make the loan if Ben will execute a demand note, also signed by his father. Dad agrees, after telling Ben, "I want it understood between you and me that the bank is coming after you first, not me."

1) Ben signs the front of the note, and Dad signs the back of the note. In what capacity did Dad sign the note? What is the nature of his liability?

2) Suppose Dad signed the front of the note and Ben signed on the back. A year later the bank calls Dad but does not demand payment. Dad says, "This is Ben's obligation and he ought to pay it. I will not pay." Must the bank make a demand for payment on Dad and give notice of dishonor to Ben as a condition to Ben's liability? §§ 3-415(c); 3-502(a)(1), (e); 3-503(a); 3-504(a), (b).

3. The Accommodation Party's Affirmative Rights

As we have seen, an accommodation party is "obligated to pay in the capacity in which the accommodation party signs." § 3-419(b). That is, he is merely a maker or an indorser so far as the holder is concerned. However, the accommodation party has certain affirmative rights which make his status as a surety very important in the right circumstances. These affirmative rights are *reimbursement, subrogation, contribution, and exoneration.* See § 3-419(f) (reimbursement from the accommodated party); §§ 3-419(f), 3-103(d), and 1-103(b) (subrogation to the holder's rights against the accommodated party); § 3-116 (contribution from another accommodation party); and §§ 3-419(f) and 1-103(b) (exoneration by the accommodated party).

More than one accommodation party may execute a negotiable instrument, creating either a co-suretyship relationship or a sub-suretyship relationship. In the former, each surety accommodates the principal obligor, is known as a co-surety, and enjoys a right of contribution against each other co-surety. In the latter, a surety accommodates another surety. The accommodating surety is a sub-surety and has a right of reimbursement against the accommodated surety.

Problem 2-12

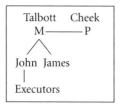

On April 7, Talbott, John, and James executed a note for $16,000, payable to Cheek or order, 120 days after date. Talbott was the principal on the note, and John and James were co-sureties. Talbott died in July, entirely insolvent. Cheek began pressing the co-sureties for payment on the note, so James paid $16,000. John then died, also insolvent, but leaving sufficient assets to pay 50 cents on the dollar for his debts. James tendered to John's executors proof of his $16,000 payment to Cheek and requested payment from John's estate.

1) How does Cheek view John, James, and Talbott? § 3-412.

2) How do John and James view their relationship with Talbott? §§ 3-419, 3-116.

3) James argues that he is entitled to be subrogated to Cheek's rights under the note. John's executors argue that James is limited to contribution. Should the amount paid to James be calculated by applying the principle of contribution, subrogation, or reimbursement? What is the rationale for your choice? § 3-116 (contribution), § 3-419 (subrogation), § 3-419 (reimbursement).

4) How much should James be paid?

5) Would your answer change if John's estate was paying 75 cents on the dollar?

Notes

1. The principle of *exoneration* provides that if the principal debtor fails to perform at maturity, the surety may institute a suit in equity to compel him to pay. The rationale is that the surety is entitled to have the debtor pay the obligation so that the surety will not have to pay. This equitable doctrine is available to an accommodation party via U.C.C. § 1-103(b) and § 3-419(f).

Thus in **Problem 2-11**, if Dad knew that Ben had come into a large sum of money and was about to spend it all on an around-the-world trip, leaving nothing to honor his debts, Dad could bring a suit in equity and obtain a decree that Ben must pay the debt on which Dad was a surety. If Ben still refused to pay, Dad would not be relieved of his liability on the note, but Dad would be entitled to whatever equitable remedy may be suitable in the circumstances, such as an injunction, appointment of a receiver, or equitable garnishment. § 1-103(b) and § 3-419(f).

2. Conversely, under the judicial doctrine of *Pain v. Packard*, 13 Johns. 174 (S.C. N.Y. 1816), or what is sometimes referred to as the doctrine of "reverse exoneration," the surety may request the holder to demand payment when the note is due, and if the holder fails to act within a reasonable time the surety will be released from liability.

Problem 2-13

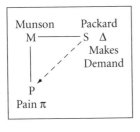

Munson and Packard executed a demand note for $1,000. Packard signed as surety for Munson. Munson's financial affairs became shaky, but while he was still solvent Packard called on the holder, Pain, to proceed immediately to collect the money owing on the note, averring that if he did not do so Packard would suffer the loss. Pain delayed action until Munson was insolvent and then commenced an action on the note against Packard.

1) What result under the doctrine of *Pain v. Packard*?

2) Does this doctrine preclude the holder from moving directly against the surety at maturity without joining the principal?

3) Earlier we noted that under § 3-419(b) an accommodation party also is liable on the instrument "in the capacity in which the accommodation party signs." To what extent is

that rule qualified by a statute such as the following? May the surety be sued separately in his capacity as maker or indorser under this statute?

17.001. Suit on Contract With Several Obligors or Parties Conditionally Liable:

(a) Except as provided by this section, the acceptor of a bill of exchange or a principal obligor on a contract may be sued alone or jointly with another liable party, but a judgment may not be rendered against a party not primarily liable [surety] unless judgment is also rendered against the principal obligor.

(b) The assignor, endorser, guarantor, or surety on a contract or the drawer of an accepted bill may be sued without suing the maker, acceptor, or other principal obligor, or a suit against the principal obligor may be discontinued, if the principal obligor:

(1) is a nonresident or resides in a place where he cannot be reached by the ordinary process of law;

(2) resides in a place that is unknown and cannot be ascertained by the use of reasonable diligence;

(3) is dead; or

(4) is actually or notoriously insolvent.

(Texas Civil Practices and Remedies Code 17.001; and see Texas Rules of Civil Procedure 31.)

Note

Virtually all jurisdictions have a statute that requires a creditor with a judgment against both a principal and surety to satisfy his judgment against the principal before going after the surety.

Compare the sequence where the surety guarantees collection rather than payment under § 3-419(d). In this case the holder must exhaust his remedies against the principal debtor before looking to the surety. However, if he guarantees payment, the surety becomes absolutely liable and the holder may go directly against him. He has waived his rights to presentment, notice of dishonor, etc., by assuming primary liability.

4. The Accommodation Party's Defenses

After the accommodation party has signed the instrument, a creditor may revise the terms of the instrument or take (or fail to take) other action that may discharge part or all of the accommodation party's liability. The following materials explore the contours of the discharge rules of § 3-605.

VENAGLIA v. KROPINAK
35 U.C.C. Rep.Serv.2d 556 (N.M. Ct. App. 1998)

[See previous discussion of facts preceding **Problem 2-10.**]

We now turn to Kropinak's proffered defenses.

A. Kropinak Was Not Discharged Under Section 55-3-605(b).

Section 55-3-605 addresses the discharge of accommodation parties. Subsection (b) states:

> Discharge ... of the obligation of a party to pay an instrument does not discharge the obligation of an ... accommodation party having a right of recourse against the discharged party.

Relying on this language, Kropinak argues essentially as follows: (1) By saying that discharge of another party does not discharge an accommodation party who has a right of recourse against the discharged party, the statute implies that the accommodation party is discharged if the accommodation party does not have a right of recourse against the discharged party. (2) Kropinak has no right of recourse against DBC because DBC no longer has any assets; its sole asset was an interest in the Property, and DBC relinquished that interest to the Venaglias in the Settlement Agreement. (3) Therefore, the discharge of DBC also discharges Kropinak.

We reject this argument. The second premise in the syllogism is flawed; Kropinak does have a right of recourse against DBC. (We therefore need not determine the validity of the first premise.) Kropinak fails to distinguish between (a) the right of recourse against a party and (b) the economic value of that right. One can have a right of recourse against a destitute person. The right may not be worth anything, but it exists.

Here, Kropinak has a right of recourse against DBC to the extent that he makes payment on the Promissory Note. This right of recourse is explicitly provided by Article 3 of the UCC. Section 55-3-419(e) states:

> An accommodation party who pays the instrument is entitled to reimbursement from the accommodated party and is entitled to enforce the instrument against the accommodated party. An accommodated party who pays the instrument has no right of recourse against, and is not entitled to contribution from, an accommodation party.

Although in some, perhaps most, contexts a "worthless" right should be treated as no right at all, such treatment is inappropriate when dealing with accommodation parties. After all, the purpose of procuring an accommodation party is to have a source of payment if the accommodated party is unable to pay in full. For example, Section 55-3-305(d) provides that an accommodation party can assert against the payee any defense that the accommodated party could assert "except the defenses of discharge in insolvency proceedings, infancy, and lack of legal capacity." When the accommodated party cannot pay in full, the promisee should be able to collect everything possible from the accommodated party and then proceed against the accommodation party. Collecting from the accommodated party can often be facilitated by the promisee's release of the accommodated party in return for the accommodated party's paying what it can. In general, the accommodation party should have no complaints about such a settlement agreement between the promisee and the accommodated party because it knew that the promisee would look to it if the accommodated party encountered financial difficulty. The accommodation party should not be entitled to relief on the ground that the accommodated party has no assets from which the accommodation party can obtain recourse, because it is precisely the potential of such financial straits of the accommodated party that created the utility of having the accommodation party guarantee the note.

The history of Section 55-3-605(b) makes clear its application in the present circumstances. Under the previous version of Article 3, the promisee could release the accommodated party without releasing the accommodation party only if it obtained the consent of the accommodation party or expressly reserved its rights against the accommodation party when it released the accommodated party. See NMSA 1978, § 55-3-606(1)(a) (1961). As stated in official comment 3 to Section 55-3-605, the current version of Article 3 abolishes the reservation-of-rights doctrine. The comment explains:

> As a practical matter, Bank [the promisee] will not gratuitously release Borrower [the accommodated party]. Discharge of Borrower normally would be part of a settlement with Borrower if Borrower is insolvent or in financial difficulty. If Borrower is unable to pay all creditors, it may be prudent for Bank to take partial payment, but Borrower will normally insist on a release of the obligation. If Bank takes $3,000 and releases Borrower from the $10,000 debt, Accommodation Party is not injured. To the extent of the payment Accommodation Party's obligation to Bank is reduced. The release of Borrower by Bank does not affect the right of Accommodation Party to obtain reimbursement from Borrower if Accommodation Party pays Bank. Section 3-419(e). Subsection (b) is designed to allow a creditor to settle with the principal debtor without risk of losing rights against sureties. Settlement is in the interest of sureties as well as the creditor....
>
> Subsection (b) changes the law stated in former Section 3-606 [repealed] but the change relates largely to formalities rather than substance. Under former Section 3-606 [repealed], Bank could settle with and release Borrower without releasing Accommodation Party, but to accomplish that result Bank had to either obtain the consent of Accommodation Party or make an express reservation of rights against Accommodation Party at the time it released Borrower. The reservation of rights was made in the agreement between Bank and Borrower by which the release of Borrower was made. There was no requirement in former Section 3-606 [repealed] that any notice be given to Accommodation Party. The reservation of rights doctrine is abolished in Section 3-605 [55-3-605 NMSA 1978] with respect to rights on instruments.

A recent revision to Section 3-305 official comment 5 (which does not appear in New Mexico Statutes Annotated) reinforces our conclusion:

> As explained in Comment 3 to Section 3-605, discharge of the accommodated party is normally part of a settlement under which the holder of a note accepts partial payment from an accommodated party who is financially unable to pay the entire amount of the note. If the holder then brings an action against the accommodation party to recover the remaining unpaid amount of the note, the accommodation party cannot use Section 3-305(d) to nullify Section 3-605(b) by asserting the discharge of the accommodated party as a defense....

In short, Section 55-3-605(b) is not intended to protect an accommodation party from a settlement in which the promisee discharges the accommodated party in return for paying all that it can on the note. The accommodation party should expect to be obligated to pay to the extent that the accommodated party does not have the resources to pay. (We note, however, that aspects of the settlement agreement other than the release of the accommodated party may provide a source of relief to the accommodation party. That issue will be addressed in the discussion below of Restatement Section 44.)

B. The Common Law of Guarantees.

* * *

C. Full Payment of the Debt.

* * *

D. Material Modification Under Section 55-3-605(d).

Kropinak's fourth defense is that he is discharged under Section 55-3-605(d) because of a material modification to his obligation. Section 55-3-605(d) states:

> If a person entitled to enforce an instrument agrees, with or without consideration, to a material modification of the obligation of a party other than an extension of the due date [which is addressed in Section 55-3-605(c)], the modification discharges the obligation of an indorser or accommodation party having a right of recourse against the person whose obligation is modified to the extent the modification causes loss to the indorser or accommodation party with respect to the right of recourse. The loss suffered by the indorser or accommodation party as a result of the modification is equal to the amount of the right of recourse unless the person enforcing the instrument proves that no loss was caused by the modification or that the loss caused by the modification was an amount less than the amount of the right of recourse.

Kropinak contends that his obligation was modified by the Settlement Agreement because the agreement provided for DBC to deliver to the Venaglias its only asset, the Property, and abandon all claims with respect to the Property. As a result, Kropinak would not be able to recover any reimbursement from DBC.

In our view, however, Kropinak interprets "the obligation of a party" too broadly. The obligation referred to in Section 55-3-605(d) is the set of duties of the principal obligor set forth in the instrument itself. See § 55-3-605 official cmt. 5. The primary duties would be to make certain payments at certain dates. Typical material modifications would be increases in the amount due or in the interest rate, or changes in covenants binding the obligor (such as restrictions on incurring other debt). See UCC § 3-605 rev. official cmt. 5, 2 U.L.A., supra, at 51-52; cf. Restatement § 41 (addressing material modifications of underlying obligation in general suretyship context).

Here, the only instrument on which Kropinak was obligated was the Promissory Note. There was no change in the terms set forth in the note, except for the discharge of DBC, which is governed by Section 55-3-605(b), as discussed above. To be sure, Kropinak's exposure—his risk of loss—may have increased as a result of the Settlement Agreement, but his obligation remained the same. We observe that Section 55-3-605(e) specifically addresses increases in exposure resulting from impairment of collateral. If Section 55-3-605(d) intended "modification of the obligation" to encompass increases in exposure under the obligation, we would expect it to contain a cross-reference to Section 55-3-605(e), so that the beginning of Section 55-3-605(d) would read: "If a person entitled to enforce an instrument agrees ... to a material modification of the obligation of a party other than an extension of the due date or an impairment of collateral...." We conclude that here there was no "material modification of the obligation" within the meaning of Section 55-3-605(d).

E. Impairment of Recourse.

Although we reject Kropinak's contention that he is entitled to relief under Section 55-3-605(d), his argument in support of that contention captures a common-law defense that may assist him. His answer brief states:

> The [Settlement Agreement] directly caused a loss to Mr. Kropinak in his right of recourse against DBC, which owned no assets of value after execution of the [Settlement Agreement].... Because DBC waived all rights and claims to the Property and delivered possession of the Property back to [the Venaglias], along with all the accrued equity in the Property, Mr. Kropinak cannot obtain payment from DBC. Thus, the unauthorized modification has effectively caused the loss of Mr. Kropinak's right of recourse against DBC.

We have already explained our rejection of the contentions that there was a modification of the obligation and that Kropinak was deprived of his right of recourse, but the real thrust of what he is saying is that his right of recourse was impaired by the Settlement Agreement. The essence of Kropinak's argument is that the manner in which the Venaglias dealt with DBC eliminated his ability to obtain any reimbursement from DBC as the accommodated party. One might infer from the price at which Dutcher purchased the Property from the Venaglias that DBC had a significant equity interest in the Property when DBC relinquished its interest and claims with respect to the Property to the Venaglias shortly before the Dutcher transaction. If so, Kropinak may have been able to use that equity to obtain reimbursement from DBC for whatever Kropinak had to pay on his guarantee to the Venaglias.

Restatement Section 44, entitled "Other Impairment of Recourse," states:

> If ... the obligee impairs ... the principal obligor's duty to reimburse..., or the secondary obligor's right of restitution ... or subrogation..., the secondary obligor is discharged from its duties pursuant to the secondary obligation to the extent that such impairment would otherwise cause the secondary obligor a loss.

In other words, if the Venaglias impaired DBC's ability to repay Kropinak for whatever Kropinak had to pay on his guarantee to the Venaglias, Kropinak is discharged to that extent on his guarantee. We adopt this provision of the Restatement. Although the case law on the general subject of impairment of recourse appears to be limited almost entirely to discharges based on actions that are addressed in other specific sections of the Restatement—release of the underlying obligation (Section 39), extensions of time (Section 40), modification of the underlying obligation (Section 41), impairment of collateral (Section 42), and delay in enforcement (Section 43)—the proposition set forth in Section 44 captures the principle underlying the more-specific propositions set forth in those sections. Section 44 can be viewed as the general proposition exemplified by the preceding sections or as a catch-all. See Annual Meeting The American Law Institute, 70 A.L.I. Proc. 179 (1993) (Reporter for Restatement describes draft section later numbered as Section 44 as "residual clause" that "recognizes that ... one cannot think of all the possible ways that the obligee and the principal obligor could get together to impair the recourse of the secondary obligor"); Peter A. Alces, The Law of Suretyship and Guaranty § 7.03 (1996). Either way, we find Section 44 to be sound policy, firmly grounded in common-law traditions reflected in other sections of the Restatement. At oral argument Kropinak relied in part on Section 44.

There remains the question, however, whether Restatement Section 44 applies to an accommodation party on a negotiable instrument. In other words, does Article 3 of the UCC preclude this defense?

We think not. Two provisions of Article 3 indicate that common-law defenses not specifically excluded by the article are available to an obligor on a negotiable instrument. Section 55-3-305(a)(2) states:

> Except as stated in Subsection (b) [relating to holders in due course], the right to enforce the obligation of a party to pay an instrument is subject to the following:
>
> ....
>
> (2) a defense of the obligor stated in another section of this article or a defense of the obligor that would be available if the person entitled to enforce the instrument were enforcing a right to payment under a simple contract....

In other words, an obligor has a defense (except to holders in due course) on a negotiable instrument if the defense would be available with respect to a contract (other than a negotiable instrument) to pay money. Cf. Ellen A. Peters, Suretyship Under Article 3 of the Uniform Commercial Code, 77 Yale L.J. 833, 875 n. 167 (1968) (former UCC § 3-306(c) [Section 55-3-306(c) (1961)] leaves a role to the common law of the individual states in determining what suretyship defenses bind holders who are not holders in due course).

Similarly, Section 55-3-601 states:

> (a) The obligation of a party to pay the instrument is discharged as stated in this article or by an act or agreement with the party which would discharge an obligation to pay money under a simple contract.
>
> (b) Discharge of the obligation of a party is not effective against a person acquiring rights of a holder in due course of the instrument without notice of the discharge.

A straightforward reading of Section 55-3-601(a) is that Article 3—which includes Section 55-3-605—does not set forth the only grounds on which accommodation parties can be discharged from their obligation to pay on an instrument. To be sure, Section 55-3-605 would prevail over any conflicting common law; for example, Subsection (b) of Section 55-3-605 would override otherwise applicable common law regarding the obligation of an accommodation party when the accommodated party is discharged, and Subsections (c), (d), and (e) may modify common-law burdens of persuasion and the extent of the discharge resulting from extension of a due date, modification to the obligation, or impairment of the value of collateral. See Restatement §§ 39, 40, 41, 42. But Section 55-3-605 does not on its face, particularly in light of Section 55-3-601, preclude additional defenses that do not contradict the terms of Section 55-3-605. Thus, it would appear that Kropinak's obligation to the Venaglias (who are not holders in due course) could be discharged by the common-law contract defense set forth in Restatement Section 44.

A fourth section of Article 3, however, gives us pause. Section 55-3-419(c), which has already been quoted in part, states in full:

> A person signing an instrument is presumed to be an accommodation party and there is notice that the instrument is signed for accommodation if the signature is an anomalous indorsement or is accompanied by words indicating that the signer is acting as surety or guarantor with respect to the obligation of another party to the instrument. Except as provided in Section 55-3-605 NMSA 1978, the obligation of an accommodation party to pay the instrument is not affected by the fact that the person enforcing the obligation had notice when the instrument was taken by that person that the accommodation party signed the instrument for accommodation.

What is the effect of the second sentence of this subsection? One could read it as saying that Section 55-3-605 provides the exclusive grounds upon which an accommodation party may be discharged. One could reason as follows: (1) An accommodation party who signs a promissory note is liable as a maker if the obligee has no notice that the accommodation party has signed the note in that capacity; in other words, an accommodation party has no suretyship defense unless the obligee has notice. (2) Under the second sentence of Section 55-3-419(c), the fact that the obligee is on notice that the signer is an accommodation party has no effect other than what is provided in Section 55-3-605. (3) Therefore, any purported suretyship defense not set forth in Section 55-3-605 must be unavailable.

Nevertheless, we hold that Section 55-3-419(c) does not limit suretyship defenses to those set forth in Section 55-3-605. Several considerations lead us to this conclusion. First, the language of Section 55-3-419(c) would be a rather obtuse way of stating the relatively straightforward proposition that Section 55-3-605 provides the exclusive grounds of discharge for accommodation parties. If such were the drafters' intent, one would expect a less circuitous expression of the proposition.

Second, Section 55-3-419(c) states that "notice" does not affect the accommodation party's obligation except as stated in Section 55-3-605. It says nothing about available defenses when there is not just notice, but actual knowledge. Significantly, Section 55-3-605 distinguishes between "notice" and "knowledge." Section 55-3-605(h) states:

> An accommodation party is not discharged under Subsection (c), (d), or (e) unless the person entitled to enforce the instrument knows of the accommodation or has notice under Section 55-3-419(c) NMSA 1978 that the instrument was signed for accommodation.

One can infer that Section 55-3-419(c) does not restrict discharges requiring knowledge of the promisee to those set forth in Section 55-3-605. Section 55-3-605 would thus be the exclusive source for discharge only to the extent that notice alone is a sufficient predicate for the discharge.

Third, we must keep in mind the purposes of Article 3.[3] Its chief purpose is greasing the wheels of commerce by establishing clear, practical rules governing negotiable instruments, so that subsequent parties (after the negotiation) know their rights. See Peters, supra, at 861–79. Article 3 advances the "policies of unclogged negotiability and inquiry-free transfer [of negotiable paper]." Id. at 877. Although Article 3 says much that also governs the relationship between the original parties, we should not presume that the Uniform Commercial Code attempts to occupy that field to the exclusion of the common law. See § 55-3-103. Consequently, we are unwilling to infer from the oblique language of Section 55-3-419(c) that the only suretyship defenses that can be raised against the original promisee are those set forth in Section 55-3-605. Recognition here of the suretyship defense set forth in Restatement Section 44 should not impede transactions in negotiable in-

---

3. We also note, but do not rely on, another consideration that could support our conclusion. Section 55-3-305 may not be restricted by Section 55-3-605 in the same manner that Section 55-3-601 is. Section 55-3-305 permits "defenses" available to a party to a simple contract, whereas Section 55-3-601 and 55-3-605 speak in terms of "discharge" of an obligation. Professor (later Justice) Peters suggested that there is a difference between a discharge and other defenses. See Peters, supra, at 874-75; William D. Hawkland, Commercial Paper 132 (2d ed. 1979) ("[A] discharge clearly is only a personal defense that is cut off by a holder in due course."). Consequently, perhaps a suretyship defense under common law may be recognized between the original parties even though Article 3 establishes the exclusive grounds for a discharge.

struments. We note that holders in due course are not bound by defenses or discharges of which they lack knowledge. See § 55-3-305(b), § 55-3-601(b). We need not address what suretyship defenses might be available against subsequent holders who are not holders in due course.

In sum, we conclude that Kropinak may be entitled to relief, in whole or in part, from his obligation on his guarantee if the Settlement Agreement between DBC and the Venaglias impaired his right of recourse against DBC. Whether such impairment occurred, however, is an unresolved issue of fact. Although the sale price for the Property in the real estate contract between the Venaglias and Dutcher is evidence that the Settlement Agreement between the Venaglias and DBC impaired Kropinak's right of recourse, it is hardly conclusive. The practicalities of the situation were not addressed in the district court, primarily because each side adopted an all-or-nothing position. Kropinak contended in essence that any impairment would provide him with a complete discharge, whereas the Venaglias argued that there was no basis at all for a discharge. On remand the district court will need to determine precisely what was owed under the Real Estate Contract and how much, if at all, the Settlement Agreement in fact prejudiced Kropinak.

III. CONCLUSION

We hold that the district court erred in granting Kropinak summary judgment. Additionally, we conclude that the existence of material factual issues precludes the award of summary judgment to the Venaglias. We remand for further proceedings consistent with this opinion.

IT IS SO ORDERED.

Note

Would the court's analysis be affected by the 2002 amendments to Article 3, particularly § 3-605(a)?

Problem 2-14

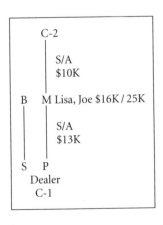

Lisa buys a new car on credit from Dealer. Lisa executes a $20,000 promissory note that is co-signed by her father, Joe. To secure repayment of the purchase price, Dealer retains an enforceable security interest in the car. Lisa subsequently defaults on the note at a time when she owes $13,000. Evidence reveals that Dealer failed to perfect its security interest in the car, which is now encumbered by a perfected security interest in favor of Smith. (Lisa granted Smith's security interest three months after granting Dealer's security interest. Lisa owes $10,000 to Smith.) The car has a fair market value of $16,000. After Lisa refuses to pay Dealer, Dealer demands payment of $13,000 from Joe.

1) Dealer decides to sue Joe before liquidating its security interest. How much must Joe pay? §§ 3-605(d); 9-322(a)(2).

2) Would your answer change if the car had a fair market value of $25,000?

3) Assume that the note stated: "Each of the undersigned waives all suretyship defenses, including, without limitation, any defense arising from Dealer's impairment of the collateral." How would this affect your analysis? § 3-605(f).

4) Assume that Dealer did not impair the collateral. When Lisa defaults, Lisa and Dealer agree to modify the terms of the note by extending the maturity date by one year in exchange for an interest rate increase of 2%. These changes are made without Joe's knowledge or consent. Lisa again defaults on the extended maturity date and refuses to pay the amount owed. Dealer demands payment from Joe. How much must Joe pay? §§ 3-605(b), (c), (h); 3-412.

5) Assume the car is defective in some manner, giving Lisa a valid warranty claim against Dealer. May Joe assert this defense against Dealer when Dealer demands payment from Joe? § 3-305(d).

6) May Joe assert his discharge defenses under § 3-605 if Dealer has negotiated the promissory note to Finance Company, a holder in due course? § 3-601(b).

D. Warranties

We are still exploring the liability of parties to a negotiable instrument. Another theory on which an indorser, or other party, may be bound is on the implied warranties of Articles 3 and 4. These are in addition to the indorsement contract. In the case of instruments, warranty liability is not a product of contract but of statute. Statutory warranties are provided in various Articles of the U.C.C.: Article 2 (Sale of Goods); Article 3 (Negotiable Instruments); Article 4 (Banking); Article 7 (Documents of Title); and Article 8 (Securities). Relevant federal warranty law also appears in Regulation J (12 C.F.R. § 210.5(a), § 210.6(b)) and Regulation CC (12 C.F.R. § 229.34). Of course the federal regulations preempt state law, but since state law is substantially similar to relevant federal law, we will focus primarily on the warranties of Articles 3 and 4.

There are two types of warranties provided by Article 3—transfer warranties and presentment warranties. If an indorser, or even a person who does not indorse, makes a "transfer" (as distinct from a "presentment for payment or acceptance") for consideration, he gives the transfer warranties listed in § 3-416 (cf. § 4-207). "Transfer" is defined in § 3-203. If a person presents a draft, check, or note for payment or acceptance, he gives the presentment warranties as provided by § 3-417 (cf. § 4-208).

The purpose of warranty liability is to assure the transferee that he gets what he is paying for—primarily good title to an instrument and the assurance that it is as valid in all respects as it appears to be. An additional purpose, in the case of presentment warranties, is to assure the payor that he is paying the right person and that the person making presentment has a right to be paid on the instrument. The warranties are implied by law. Breach leads to strict liability.

These warranty purposes are achieved with respect to "transfers" of instruments through § 3-416, which provides that a transferor gives six warranties: (1) that he is entitled to enforce the instrument under § 3-301; (2) that his, and at the time of transfer every other, signature is authentic and authorized; (3) that the instrument has not been altered under § 3-407; (4) that no defense or claim in recoupment is good against him; (5) that he has no knowledge of any insolvency proceedings against the maker; and (6) that with respect to a remotely-created consumer item, the person on whose account the item is drawn authorized the amount. In looking at this list of warranties the question naturally arises, what protection do warranties give the transferee that he does not get under the indorsement contract? Rephrased, what is the difference between the indorsement contract and the warranty contract? The following problems suggest answers to these questions.

Most of §3-417 on presentment warranties applies to unaccepted drafts, which include common checks. Only one presentment warranty is given by a person who presents a promissory note for payment, namely that he is "a person entitled to enforce the instrument or authorized to obtain payment." §3-417(d)(1). This warranty, and no other, also is given by a person who presents a dishonored draft "for payment to the drawer or an indorser." Since the rest of the presentment warranties of §3-417 are not given by a person who receives payment of a note, we will reserve our discussion of those warranties until Part II on drafts and checks.

1. Who Gives Transfer Warranties and to Whom Do They Run?

Another relevant question is to whom do the transfer warranties run, and against whom may they be imposed. Section 3-416 answers these two questions in the following words: "A person who transfers an instrument for consideration warrants to the transferee, and if the transfer is by indorsement, to any subsequent transferee...." Any person who transfers the instrument gives the warranties to his immediate transferee whether or not he indorses it, but if he indorses the instrument he gives the warranties to all subsequent transferees.

2. Disclaimer of Warranties

Under current Article 3, the drafters have provided that the transfer warranties may be disclaimed, but unlike former Article 3, the right to disclaim warranties is denied in the case of a check. "Transfer warranties may be disclaimed with respect to any instrument except a check. Between the immediate parties disclaimer may be made by agreement. In the case of an indorser, disclaimer of transferor's liability, to be effective, must appear in the indorsement with words such as 'without warranties' or some other specific reference to warranties." §3-416 OC 5.

What would be the impact of an indorsement "without recourse" on the warranties of §3-416?

Problem 2-15

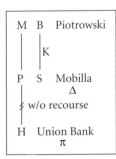

Mobilla, a used car dealer, forged the name of Piotrowski (as maker) to a promissory note (payable to Mobilla), secured by a security interest in an automobile (probably nonexistent), and then asked Union Bank to discount the paper, which it did. Mobilla indorsed the note over to the bank "without recourse" and assigned the security interest to the bank. The security agreement stated "that the above instrument is genuine, and in all respects what it purports to be." The note also contained a clause providing for attorney's fees for collection. When payment was not made on the maturity date, the bank contacted Piotrowski. He denied executing the note and being any part of the transaction. Mobilla claims that the documents were signed by Piotrowski's authorized agent. The bank commenced an action against Mobilla, alleging breach of an express warranty of genuineness and breach of implied warranties of genuineness. Mobilla argues 1) that he is not liable because he indorsed the note "without recourse," and 2) that the provision for attorney's fees as damages is not effective against an indorser without recourse.

1) What does Mobilla warrant under the express warranty: "the above instrument is genuine, and in all respects what it purports to be"?

2) Did Mobilla make the statutory warranties in § 3-416?

Q: Did Mobilla receive any consideration?

Q: Was the movement of the note from Mobilla to Union Bank a "transfer of the instrument"? § 3-203(a).

Q: Who was the issuer of the note? §§ 3-105(c), 3-403(a).

3) Did Mobilla breach the warranty in (a)(1)? § 3-301.

Q: Was Mobilla a holder? § 1-201(b)(21).

4) Did Mobilla breach any of the other five warranties?

5) Did Mobilla effectively disclaim liability for any warranty breach by indorsing "without recourse"? §§ 3-415(b); 3-416(c) and OC 5.

6) What damages may Union Bank recover under § 3-416?

Q: Will damages include attorney's fees?

7) Is there another capacity in which Mobilla could have been sued? §§ 3-403(a), 3-412.

Note

As you will note from reading § 3-416(a), there is no warranty of good title as under former § 3-417(2)(a). Former § 3-417(2)(a) provides that a transferor warrants to his transferee that he "has a good title to the instrument or is authorized to obtain payment or acceptance on behalf of one who has a good title and the transfer is otherwise rightful." What is the effect of this change? Does it mean that a transferor is no longer in breach of warranty if he transfers an instrument to which he does not have good title? No, but the reasons for breach are a little different.

Suppose, for example, that a promissory note payable to bearer is stolen and then transferred to a person without knowledge of the theft, but with knowledge that the note is overdue. The transferee is not a holder in due course but he is a holder. Under former law the warranty of title is broken. If the note is then dishonored or if the true owner surfaces and claims the note, as he rightfully could as against the holder, the holder can then sue his transferor and all previous indorsers for breach of the warranty of title, thereby, in theory, passing the loss back to the thief.

Under current Article 3, suppose the same situation: M gives a note to P, payable to bearer. The note is stolen by T and given to A after it is overdue, who indorses to B "without recourse," who indorses to C "without recourse." None of the transferees are holders in due course because the note is overdue when transferred to A. C threatens to sue M, and P intervenes and successfully takes the note away from C, as P can do since equities of ownership are enforceable against a holder. C cannot sue B or A on the indorsement contract, but can he sue B, A, and T for breach of any of the transfer warranties in §3-416(a)?

Yes, under §3-416(a)(4). The transferors warrant that "the instrument is not subject to a defense or claim in recoupment of any party which can be asserted against the warrantor." Add to this the second sentence of §3-305(c), which precludes enforcement of an instrument that has been lost or stolen if the person seeking to enforce it is not a holder in due course. In view of this, M has the defense of theft against T and can raise the same defense against A and B because they are not holders in due course, having taken an overdue instrument. Thus T, A, and B are in breach of the §3-416(a)(4) transfer warranty.

C, the holder, is able to recover against B, A, and T for breach of the warranty that the instrument is not subject to a defense. This analysis ultimately shifts the loss to the party who dealt with the thief, which is one of the traditional purposes of warranty law. So we see that the holder is as well off under §3-416(a)(4) as if he had received a warranty of title under former law.

3. Measure of Damages

Section 3-416(b) provides the measure of damages for breach of warranty. The amount of damages for breach is "an amount equal to the loss suffered as a result of the breach, but not more than the amount of the instrument plus expenses and loss of interest incurred as a result of the breach." Under this test, the measure of damages is the difference between the value of the instrument at the time of transfer and the value the instrument would have had if there had been no breach. Under this test, is the measure of damages always the face amount of the instrument?

Problem 2-16

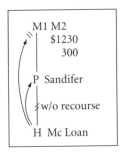

Roscoe Charles and his wife, Gladys, purportedly issued a note for $1,230 to Sandifer. Sandifer transferred the note to McNaghten Loan Co. in payment for some land. Sandifer indorsed the note "without recourse," followed by the statement that the "note is bonified with genuine signatures and given for a valuable consideration." It turned out that the signature of Gladys Charles had been forged by her husband. There was a conflict of evidence as to whether Sandifer knew Roscoe had forged his wife's signature. When Sandifer transferred the note to McNaghten Loan, Roscoe and Gladys were insolvent and owned assets worth only $300. Under state law, without a valid signature of Mrs. Charles on the note, their assets were entirely exempt from seizure by creditors. McNaghten Loan presented the note for payment to Roscoe and Gladys, but they declined to pay. McNaghten Loan gave timely notice of dishonor to Sandifer.

1) On what theory will McNaghten Loan seek to hold Sandifer liable?

    Q: Is it relevant that Sandifer may have known of the forgery?

2) Of what effect is "without recourse"?

3) What damages, if any, will the holder recover for breach of warranty? §3-416; cf. §1-305(a).

Q: What amount would McNaghten Loan have recovered from Roscoe and Gladys if Gladys's signature had been authentic? Rephrased, how much was Sandifer warranting? §3-416; cf. §1-305(a).

4) How much would McNaghten Loan recover from Sandifer if Sandifer had not qualified his indorsement?

E. The Underlying Contract

The third theory on which a party may be liable in a transaction involving a negotiable instrument is liability on the underlying obligation.

Typically negotiable instruments arise from underlying transactions. That is, the obligor gives a negotiable instrument, rather than money, in payment of the debt created by the underlying transaction. However, unless the instrument is a certified check or a cashier's check or the like, the parties usually do not assume that the giving of a negotiable instrument pays the underlying obligation. They understand that it is the honoring of the instrument in due course that will discharge the debt. They are aware of the possibility that the instrument might not be paid. They probably are not aware that, until dishonor, their rights on the underlying obligation are temporarily suspended. That is, their rights on the underlying obligation are temporarily merged in the instrument until dishonor. But most recipients of an instrument are optimistic about its future payment, and in the vast majority of cases they are not disappointed.

The provisions of Article 3 are consistent with this general understanding of the parties. The inference to be drawn from §3-310(a) is that if the parties do not use a certified or cashier's check or the like, the giving of a negotiable instrument is only conditional payment. Subsection (b) lays out the rules on the suspension of rights on the underlying obligation. It also sets out the impact on the underlying obligation of discharge of the parties to the instrument. We explore these rules through the following problem.

Problem 2-17

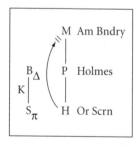

Orange Screen sold some screens to Holmes for $2,000. Holmes had in his possession a note for $1,500 from American Bindery dated May 4, 2007, payable to Holmes in four months. Holmes indorsed the note in blank and gave it to Orange Screen as partial payment for the screens. Orange Screen presented the note for payment when due, September 4, 2007, but it was not paid. On January 11, 2008, Orange Screen demanded payment of the price for the screens from Holmes.

1) What contract was Orange Screen trying to enforce when it demanded payment of the price from Holmes?

2) How much is Holmes obligated to pay Orange Screen on (a) the $1,500 note (§ 3-415) and (b) the $2,000 sales contract (§ 3-310(b))?

3) Suppose that shortly after receiving the note, Orange Screen's president learned of the legal effect of taking the note on the underlying obligation (i.e., that he could not sue on the underlying obligation until the note came due in four months, and the need for presentment, dishonor, and notice). He then became angry, burned the note, and sent a bill to Holmes, demanding immediate payment of $2,000. Is Orange Screen out of luck? §§ 3-310, 3-309.

Chapter 3

Defenses to Liability

As we approach the subjects of defense to liability and holder in due course status, it will be helpful to put these subjects in perspective.

We have recognized that an instrument is a specialized contract, and we have considered the contract liability of various parties to an instrument, limiting our discussion primarily to promissory notes. We also have observed that all parties to an instrument are liable to a "person entitled to enforce the instrument," defined in § 3-301.

Here we note that an instrument is not only a contract, but also a species of property, with all of the usual incidents of property. "Although transfer of an instrument might mean in a particular case that title to the instrument passes to the transferee, that result does not follow in all cases. The right to enforce an instrument and ownership of the instrument are two different concepts." § 3-203 OC 1.

The quantum of rights a person may have in any particular piece of property can be large or small. This is true with respect to instruments. For example, a person can use an instrument for some purposes and still not own it. This gradation of rights with respect to an instrument is manifested in Article 3 when it provides for the "transfer" of an instrument "for the purpose of giving to the person receiving delivery the right to enforce the instrument." § 3-203(a). An instrument can be transferred so that the transferee gets *the right to enforce* it without acquiring *title* to the instrument or even becoming a *holder*. Or he might become a holder and a person entitled to enforce the instrument (§ 3-301), but still not have title.

While matters of title and property rights in an instrument may be determined by the law of property and not Article 3, ultimately we will see that the primary reasons for splitting the incidents of property in this way are for the protection of property rights and the promotion of commerce. We begin to see this as we observe that when an instrument is transferred it is usually transferred by negotiation (§ 3-201), in which case the transferee becomes a holder as well as a person entitled to enforce the instrument. And usually the negotiation of the instrument will carry with it all of the property rights to the instrument, so that the transferee will also acquire title, as well as the status of holder, and thus be a person entitled to enforce the instrument. Here we will explore the relevance of each of these levels of property rights in connection with defenses to liability and again in Part II on Drafts and Checks.

Whether a person is entitled to enforce an instrument, or whether an obligor on an instrument may effectively raise a defense against a holder of the instrument depends upon several factors: (1) the nature of the defense — whether real or personal (§ 3-305), (2) the status of the party — whether he is a holder, or a person with the rights of a holder, or a holder in due course (§ 3-301), and (3) whether the maker or holder was negligent with respect to the transaction or whether some other legal theory may be relevant, such as estoppel. The relevance of each of these elements is explored here.

A. Holder in Due Course

A person cannot be a holder in due course unless he is first a holder. And unless a person receives the instrument from the issuer (§ 3-105), a person cannot be a holder unless he takes the instrument by negotiation.

1. Negotiation: § 3-201

Negotiation refers to the transfer process. "'Negotiation' means a transfer of possession, whether voluntary or involuntary, of an instrument by a person other than the issuer to a person who thereby becomes its holder." § 3-201(a). The "issuer" is the maker or drawer who first delivers the instrument. § 3-105(a). Thus a transfer of possession of a note by the maker to the payee is not technically within the definition of negotiation in § 3-201. However, by definition an issuer can confer holder status on a transferee by giving him possession of either a bearer or order instrument. § 1-201(b)(21).

A "transfer" requisite for negotiation may be either voluntary or involuntary. Thus a theft of an instrument may result in a transfer for purposes of negotiation, and the thief could thereby become a holder (and a PETE) if the other elements of negotiation are met. §§ 3-201, 3-301. "Transfer," as used here (to refer to an element of negotiation) is to be distinguished from the definition of "transfer" as it is used to define a person to whom an instrument is transferred, other than by negotiation, for the purpose of giving him the right to enforce the instrument. § 3-203. In the latter instance the transfer must be voluntary. In this sense, taking an instrument by negotiation is a step beyond taking by mere transfer. That is, in some instances a person who has taken by negotiation will find that he has more rights than one who has taken only by transfer. § 3-203(a).

Nevertheless, whether a person takes by negotiation or only by transfer, he may become "a person entitled to enforce" the instrument under § 3-301 if the instrument is "delivered by a person other than its issuer for the purpose of giving to the person receiving delivery the right to enforce the instrument." § 3-203.

If the instrument is in bearer form, the instrument is negotiated by mere transfer of possession. If the instrument is in order form, or payable to an identified person, it is negotiated by indorsement plus transfer of possession. § 3-201(b).

Since negotiation of *order paper* requires an indorsement, and since indorsements, though not required for negotiation of *bearer paper*, are frequently put on bearer paper in the course of transfer, the definition of indorsement and the types and effects of various indorsements are relevant to a discussion of the subject of negotiation, and so we make incidental reference to them here. See § 3-204. The Code recognizes seven indorsements: qualified, unqualified, special, blank, anomalous, restrictive, and nonrestrictive. §§ 3-415, 3-205, 3-206. To be complete, an indorsement must tell us (1) the method to be used in making a subsequent negotiation, (2) the nature of the interest to be transferred, and (3) the nature of the liability of the indorser—whether qualified or unqualified.

We will explore these indorsements and what they reveal in connection with the problems that follow.

a. Holder: § 1-201(b)(21)

Fundamentally, only a holder is entitled to enforce an instrument, or a person who derives his rights through a holder. § 3-301. A holder is a person to whom an instrument has been issued or negotiated. § 3-201 OC 1.

As we know, "negotiation" means "a transfer of possession, whether voluntary or involuntary, of an instrument by a person other than the issuer to a person who thereby becomes its holder." § 3-201. If an instrument is payable to bearer, all that is required for a person to become a holder is to obtain possession. It does not matter how he obtains possession. If an instrument is payable to the order of an identified person, a person can become a holder only if he obtains possession and the instrument is either issued to the possessor or indorsed in blank or to the possessor by the person to whose order it was payable. If indorsements are missing, the person in possession of the instrument cannot become a holder until he obtains the missing indorsements. Until that time, the instrument is payable only to the first identified person who has not yet indorsed the instrument.

A holder is a person to whom an instrument has been negotiated or issued. As we have noted, "issue" means "the first delivery of an instrument by the maker or drawer, whether to a holder or nonholder, for the purpose of giving rights on the instrument to any person." § 3-105(a). The Code defines a holder as "the person in possession of a negotiable instrument that is payable either to bearer or to an identified person that is the person in possession." § 1-201(b)(21)(A). Or to put it more simply, a holder is a person in possession of an instrument, whether in bearer or order form, which contains a promise or order that runs to him. Still more simply, a holder is a person in possession of an instrument which is payable to him or to bearer.

As we know, in the normal course of business transactions the transfer of an instrument usually results in the transfer of title to the instrument as well. This is because parties who negotiate an instrument also usually have title to the instrument and intend to transfer title as well as possession. Under prior law a valid or effective indorsement by the payee, or a special indorsee where called for, was indispensable to the passage of good title to the instrument. Under current law, since title and right to enforce are separate concepts, an agreement to sell the instrument can transfer title even without an effective indorsement. In that case, the absence of an effective indorsement will preclude the right to enforce the instrument, even though the transferee has title. It follows that where there is no intent to transfer title, a forgery of the payee's name or of a special indorsee's name will not only break the chain of title, but also render the instrument unenforceable, regardless of how skillful the forgery. It also follows that there can be no holder following such forgery, and therefore no holder in due course. So although Article 3 does not determine property rights per se, by limiting the capacity of those who can transfer rights to instruments to those who take from persons entitled to enforce, property rights in the instrument are protected and sometimes determined thereby. § 3-306.

Problem 3-1

Brad
|
Grace

Scenario #1: Brad executes a promissory note payable to bearer and delivers it to Grace. Has the instrument been issued under § 3-105, negotiated under § 3-201, and/or transferred under § 3-203?

Brad
|
Grace
|
Thief

Scenario #2: Brad executes a promissory note payable to bearer and delivers it to Grace. Thief steals the unindorsed note from Grace. Is the movement of the note from Grace to Thief a negotiation under §3-201 and/or a transfer under §3-203? Would your analysis change if Grace had placed her special indorsement on the note prior to the theft?

Scenario #3: Brad executes a promissory note payable to the order of Grace. Brad delivers the note to Tom, Grace's brother, with instructions to deliver the note to Grace. Has the note been issued? Is Tom a PETE?

Scenario #4: Brad executes a promissory note payable to bearer and leaves it on his kitchen table. Thief steals the note. Has the instrument been issued or negotiated? Is Brad an issuer? Is Thief a holder?

Scenario #5: Same as #4, except Thief delivers the instrument to Grace. Has the note been issued yet? Is Brad an issuer yet? Has the note been negotiated yet? Is Grace a PETE?

b. Holder in Due Course Defined: §3-302

Holder in due course status is material primarily when defenses to or claims against the instrument are made by the maker, drawer, or a third party. If the person entitled to enforce the instrument is not a holder in due course, he may still assert his claim on the instrument and enforce it *subject to* any competing claim and any defense. It is only when a party asserts a claim or defense to which a holder will be subject that the distinction between a holder and holder in due course becomes material.

For a holder to be a holder in due course, he must meet the elements set out in §3-302. Forgery, alteration, irregularity, or incompleteness with respect to the instrument do not of themselves preclude holder in due course status. But evidence of any of these deficiencies will preclude holder in due course status if there is evidence of any of them on the face of the instrument sufficient to "call into question its authenticity." "'Authenticity' is used to make it clear that the irregularity or incompleteness must indicate that the instrument may not be what it purports to be." OC 1. It is not any irregularity or incompleteness, etc.—the deficiency must be apparent, and it must be sufficient to "call into question" the authenticity of the instrument. If such irregularity or incompleteness is found to be "apparent," the holder in effect has taken it with notice of a possible claim or defense and he cannot be a holder in due course.

In addition to the instrument appearing to be authentic, a holder in due course must take the instrument (i) for value, (ii) in good faith, (iii) without notice it was overdue, dishonored, forged, or altered, and (iv) without notice of any claim described in §3-306 or defense or claim in recoupment described in §3-305(a).

Because a negotiable instrument in the hands of a holder in due course is clothed with currency attributes, equity or justice requires that a holder who is given the advantages of a holder in due course must satisfy all of these conditions. As we observed at the beginning of these materials, one of the consequences of negotiability is the favored status of a holder in due course, who is permitted to take an instrument free of all claims to the instruments and also free of most defenses that a maker or drawer would otherwise be permitted to raise against him. This favored status would be unfair and would not promote commerce unless the holder has met these conditions.

i. Value: § 3-303

"Value" is another term of art defined in Article 3, and it differs from consideration. Consideration is defined as "any consideration sufficient to support a simple contract." § 3-303(b). The consequence of a lack or failure of consideration is that a maker or drawer will have a personal defense good against a holder of an instrument. However, the absence of "value" will prevent the holder from becoming a holder in due course, even though consideration has been given. Thus, "value" implies more than consideration, although the giving of value will constitute consideration. § 3-303(b).

The moment value is given is a critical time in determining whether a holder is a holder in due course. For a holder to be a holder in due course, normally value must be given before the holder learns of any claim or defense that otherwise would disqualify him as a holder in due course.

Problem 3-2

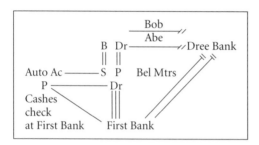

Honest John, doing business as Belmont Motors, represented in a vehicle contract that the car was "without question, good for at least another 50,000 miles." Honest John sold the car to Abe for $5,000 on March 1, and the same day deposited Abe's check in his account with First Bank. On March 2, John sold a car to Bob for $5,000, making a similar representation, and on the same day deposited Bob's check with First Bank. On March 3, Honest John bought two more cars from Auto Auction to replenish his inventory and gave Auto Auction his check for $5,000 in payment. Auto Auction went to First Bank and presented the check for payment the same day. First Bank paid the check as a public relations gesture, although it was not technically obligated to do so since neither of the checks of Abe or Bob had cleared, and Belmont Motors had no other money in its account. As it turned out the cars sold to Abe and Bob stopped running before they made it home. Accordingly, Abe and Bob went to their respective banks and withdrew the money they had on deposit to pay for the cars. In due time their checks were returned to First Bank marked "not sufficient funds." Honest John of Belmont Motors is now insolvent. First Bank seeks to recover its loss from Abe and Bob on the two checks issued by them.

1) With respect to the two checks issued by Abe and Bob, is First Bank a PETE?

2) In what capacity may Abe and Bob be sued? §§ 3-103(a)(5), 3-104(f), 3-414(b).

3) What defense to payment will Abe and Bob raise?

4) Is this a defense that is good against a holder in due course? § 3-305(b).

5) Is First Bank a holder in due course? § 3-302(a).

   Q: Did First Bank give value? §§ 3-303; 4-211; 4-210(a), (b).

6) On which of the two checks would you advise First Bank to sue, the one given by Abe or Bob? § 4-210(b).

7) Who has the burden of proof regarding due course status? § 3-308(b).

8) Assume that Auto Auction had presented two checks for $2,500 each (instead of a single check for $5,000), and at least a day passed between presentment of each check. Can

something happen during this passage of time that would impair First Bank's ability to assert HDC status?

Note

Why is an unperformed promise not value? See § 3-303 OC 2.

Problem 3-3

On June 1, BizCorp issued and delivered a $40,000 promissory note to Furniture Dealer as payment for office furniture to be delivered in the near future. Shortly thereafter, Furniture Dealer discounted the note to Finance Company for $32,000. Finance Company agreed to pay $24,000 upon receipt of the note and orally promised to pay the $8,000 balance in three months. After buying the note but before making the $8,000 payment, Finance Company discovered that BizCorp has an enforceable personal defense against Furniture Dealer – no furniture has been delivered. Subsequently, Finance Company presented the $40,000 note to BizCorp for payment. At that time, the furniture still had not been delivered and Finance Company had not yet made the $8,000 payment to Furniture Dealer.

1) How much can Finance Company recover from BizCorp? § 3-302(d).

2) Would your analysis change if, at presentment, Finance Company had made the $8,000 payment to Furniture Dealer (but payment was made after learning of BizCorp's personal defense, which still exists at presentment)?

3) Would your analysis change if the promise by Finance Company to pay $8,000 to Furniture Dealer was not an oral promise but instead was evidenced by an Article 3 promissory note? § 3-303.

Problem 3-4

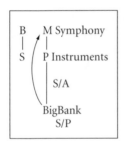

The Uptown Symphony issued and delivered a $75,000 promissory note to Musical Instruments, Inc., as payment for several orchestral instruments.Musical Instruments granted a security interest in the promissory note to BigBank to secure repayment of a $65,000 loan. Musical Instruments indorsed the note and delivered it to BigBank in accordance with relevant provisions of U.C.C. Article 9. After Musical Instruments defaulted on the $65,000 loan from BigBank (having paid only $40,000), BigBank presented the note to the Symphony for payment on the due date. Unknown to BigBank, the Symphony has a personal defense that is enforceable against Musical Instruments.

1) How much can BigBank recover from the Symphony? § 3-302(e).

2) Assume the same facts except Musical Instruments sold the $75,000 note to Finance Company, a holder in due course, who used the promissory note as collateral for a $65,000 loan from BigBank. After Finance Company defaulted on the $65,000 loan from BigBank (having paid only $35,000), BigBank presented the note to the Symphony for payment on the due date. Unknown to BigBank, the Symphony has a personal defense

that is enforceable against Musical Instruments. How much can BigBank recover from the Symphony?

ii. Good Faith: § 1-201

The courts have had difficulty with the element of good faith. Over the years they have applied a number of tests for determining whether the holder has taken the instrument in good faith. These various tests have been known as the "commercial reasonableness," "red lights," "prudent man," and "white heart" tests. Article 1 defines good faith as "honesty in fact and the observance of reasonable commercial standards of fair dealing." § 1-201(b)(20).

MAINE FAMILY FEDERAL CREDIT UNION v. SUN LIFE ASSURANCE COMPANY OF CANADA
727 A.2d 335 (Maine 1999)

SAUFLEY, J.

We are called upon here to address the concept of "holder in due course" as defined by recent amendments to the negotiable instruments provisions of the Maine Uniform Commercial Code. We conclude that, pursuant to those amendments, the Superior Court (Cumberland County, Calkins, J.) did not err when it entered a judgment based on the jury's finding that the Maine Family Federal Credit Union was not a holder in due course. Because we find, however, that Sun Life Assurance Company was not entitled to raise a third party's defense of fraud to its liability as drawer of the instruments, we vacate that portion of the judgment entered in favor of Sun Life and against the Credit Union.

I. Facts

Daniel, Joel, and Claire Guerrette are the adult children of Elden Guerrette, who died on September 24, 1995. Before his death, Elden had purchased a life insurance policy from Sun Life Assurance Company of Canada, through Sun Life's agent, Steven Hall, and had named his children as his beneficiaries. Upon his death, Sun Life issued three checks, each in the amount of $40,759.35, to each of Elden's children. The checks were drawn on Sun Life's account at Chase Manhattan Bank in Syracuse, New York. The checks were given to Hall for delivery to the Guerrettes.

The parties have stipulated that Hall and an associate, Paul Richard, then fraudulently induced the Guerrettes to indorse the checks in blank and to transfer them to Hall and Richard, purportedly to be invested in "HER, Inc.," a corporation formed by Hall and Richard. Hall took the checks from the Guerrettes and turned them over to Richard, who deposited them in his account at the Credit Union on October 26, 1995. The Credit Union immediately made the funds available to Richard.

The Guerrettes quickly regretted having negotiated their checks to Hall and Richard, and they contacted Sun Life the next day to request that Sun Life stop payment on the checks. Sun Life immediately ordered Chase Manhattan to stop payment on the checks. Thus, when the checks were ultimately presented to Chase Manhattan for payment, Chase refused to pay the checks, and they were returned to the Credit Union.

The Credit Union received notice that the checks had been dishonored on November 3, 1995, the sixth business day following their deposit. By that time, however, Richard had withdrawn from his account all of the funds represented by the three checks. The

Credit Union was able to recover almost $80,000 from Richard, but there remained an unpaid balance of $42,366.56, the amount now in controversy.

The Credit Union filed a complaint against Sun Life alleging that Sun Life was liable as drawer of the instruments, and that Sun Life had been unjustly enriched at the Credit Union's expense. Although it could have done so, the Credit Union did not originally seek any recovery from the Guerrettes. Sun Life, however, filed a third-party complaint against Daniel Guerrette and Paul Richard, whose signatures appeared on the back of one of the checks. The Credit Union then filed a cross-claim against third-party defendants Guerrette and Richard, alleging that they were liable as indorsers of the checks, and Daniel Guerrette filed cross-claims against the Credit Union and against Sun Life. Finally, Sun Life eventually filed third-party complaints against Joel and Claire Guerrette.

The Credit Union moved for summary judgment. The Superior Court held, as a matter of law, that Daniel Guerrette had raised a "claim of a property or possessory right in the instrument or its proceeds," 11 M.R.S.A. § 3-1306 (1995), and therefore that Sun Life was entitled to assert that claim as a "defense" against the Credit Union. See 11 M.R.S.A. § 3-1305(3) (1995).[9] The court found, however, that a genuine issue of material fact remained as to whether the Credit Union had acted in "good faith" when it gave value for the checks — a fact relevant to determining whether the Credit Union was a holder in due course. See 11 M.R.S.A. § 3-1302(1)(b)(ii) (1995). Accordingly, the court denied the Credit Union's motion for summary judgment, and the matter proceeded to trial.

At trial, the only issue presented to the jury was whether the Credit Union had acted in "good faith" when it gave value for the checks, thus entitling it to holder in due course status. At the close of evidence, the Credit Union made a motion for a judgment as a matter of law, which the Superior Court denied. The jury found that the Credit Union had not acted in good faith and therefore was not a holder in due course. Therefore, the Superior Court entered judgment in favor of Sun Life, Daniel, Joel, and Claire, and against the Credit Union. The court denied the Credit Union's renewed motion for judgment as a matter of law and motion to amend the judgment, and the Credit Union filed this appeal.

II. Obligations of the Parties

At the heart of the controversy in this case is the allocation of responsibility for the loss of the unpaid $42,366.56, given the fact that Paul Richard and Steven Hall, the real wrongdoers, appear to be unable to pay. Maine, like the other forty-nine states, has adopted the Uniform Commercial Code. Under the Maine U.C.C., Articles 3-A and 4 deal with "Negotiable Instruments" and "Bank Deposits and Collections." See 11 M.R.S.A. §§ 3-1101, 4-101 (1995). It is these statutes that govern the parties' dispute.

Pursuant to Article 4 of the Maine U.C.C., the Credit Union, as a depositary bank, is a "holder" of the instruments, see 11 M.R.S.A. § 4-205(1) (1995),[12] making it a "person

---

9. Section 3-1305(3) provides, in part:

> ... [I]n an action to enforce the obligation of a party to pay the instrument, the obligor may not assert against the person entitled to enforce the instrument a defense, claim in recoupment or claim to the instrument (section 3-1306) of another person, but the other person's claim to the instrument may be asserted by the obligor if the other person is joined in the action and personally asserts the claim against the person entitled to enforce the instrument.

11 M.R.S.A. § 3-1305(3).

12. 11 M.R.S.A. § 4-205(1) provides that a depositary bank becomes a holder of an item if the item was deposited by a customer who was also a holder. The Credit Union's customer, Paul Richard, became a holder of the checks when Daniel, Joel, and Claire indorsed them in blank and transferred

entitled to enforce" the instrument under Article 3-A. See 11 M.R.S.A. § 3-1301(1) (1995). Upon producing an instrument containing the valid signature of a party liable on the instrument, a person entitled to enforce the instrument is entitled to payment, unless the party liable proves a defense or claim in recoupment, see 11 M.R.S.A. § 3-1308(2) (1995), or a possessory claim to the instrument itself. See 11 M.R.S.A. § 3-1306.

Because their signatures appear on the backs of the checks, Daniel, Joel, and Claire are "indorsers" of the checks. See 11 M.R.S.A. § 3-1204(1), (2) (1995). As indorsers, they are obligated to pay the amounts due on each dishonored instrument "[a]ccording to the terms of [each] instrument at the time it was indorsed." 11 M.R.S.A. § 3-1415(1)(a) (1995). This obligation is owed "to a person entitled to enforce the instrument or to a subsequent indorser who paid the instrument under this section." Id.

As drawer of the checks, Sun Life is obligated to pay each dishonored instrument "[a]ccording to its terms at the time it was issued." 11 M.R.S.A. § 3-1414(2)(a) (1995). Again, this obligation is owed to a person entitled to enforce the instrument or to an indorser who paid the draft under section 3-1415. See 11 M.R.S.A. § 3-1414(2) (1995). Chase Manhattan, as drawee of these checks, was not obligated to accept them for payment, see 11 M.R.S.A. § 3-1408 (1995), and therefore has not been made a party to this action.

Unless the Credit Union is a holder in due course, its right to enforce the obligations of the drawer and indorsers of the instruments is subject to a variety of defenses, including all those defenses available "if the person entitled to enforce the instrument[s] were enforcing a right to payment under a simple contract." See 11 M.R.S.A. § 3-1305(1)(b) (1995). In addition, its right to enforce is subject to any claims in recoupment, see 11 M.R.S.A. § 3-1305(1)(c) (1995), or claims to the instruments themselves. See 11 M.R.S.A. § 3-1306. If, however, the Credit Union establishes that it is a "holder in due course," it is subject to only those few defenses listed in section 3-1305(1)(a). See 11 M.R.S.A. § 3-1305(2) (1995). None of those specific defenses is applicable here. Thus, the Credit Union argues that because it is entitled as a matter of law to holder in due course status, it is entitled to enforce the instruments against the Guerrettes and Sun Life.

III. Holder in Due Course
A. Burden of Proof and Standard of Review

A holder in due course is a holder who takes an instrument in good faith, for value, and without notice of any claims or defenses. See 11 M.R.S.A. § 3-1302(1) (1995). Once the persons who may be liable on the instruments have raised a recognized defense to that liability, the burden is on the holder to prove by a preponderance of the evidence that it is a holder in due course. See New Bedford Inst. for Sav. v. Gildroy, 36 Mass.App.Ct. 647, 634 N.E.2d 920, 925 (1994). If it fails in that proof, the persons otherwise liable on the instruments may avoid liability if they prove a defense, claim in recoupment, or possessory claim to the instrument. See 11 M.R.S.A. §§ 3-1305(1)(b), 3-1308(2).

The issue of whether a party is a holder in due course is usually one of fact, although "where the facts are undisputed and conclusive, [a court] can determine ... holder in due course status as a matter of law." See Triffin v. Dillabough, 552 Pa. 550, 716 A.2d 605, 611 (1998). In this case, the Superior Court declined to decide the holder in due

---

them to Richard and Hall. See 11 M.R.S.A. § 3-1201(1) (1995) ("'Negotiation' means a transfer of possession, whether voluntary or involuntary, of an instrument by a person other than the issuer to a person who thereby becomes its holder."); 11 M.R.S.A. § 3-1202(1)(b) (1995) ("Negotiation is effective even if obtained ... [b]y fraud.").

course issue as a matter of law, and submitted the question to the jury. The jury found that the Credit Union was not a holder in due course, implicitly because the Credit Union did not act in good faith.

The Credit Union argues that the court erred in failing to find, as a matter of law, that it was a holder in due course. "We review the denial of a motion for judgment as a matter of law 'to determine if any reasonable view of the evidence and those inferences that are justifiably drawn from that evidence supports the jury verdict.'" Larochelle v. Cyr, 707 A.2d 799 (quoting Davis v. Currier, 704 A.2d 1207). The question before us, therefore, is whether any reasonable view of the evidence, along with any justifiable inferences therefrom, can possibly support the jury's conclusion that the Credit Union did not act in good faith and therefore was not a holder in due course. Alternatively stated, the question is whether the evidence compelled a finding that the Credit Union was a holder in due course. If there is any rational basis for the jury's verdict, we must affirm the judgment.

B. Good Faith

We therefore turn to the definition of "good faith" contained in Article 3-A of the Maine U.C.C.[15] In 1990, the National Conference of Commissioners on Uniform State Law recommended substantial changes in the U.C.C. The Maine Legislature responded to those recommendations in 1993 by repealing the entirety of Article 3 and enacting a new version entitled Article 3-A, which contains a new definition of "good faith." While the previous version of the good faith definition only required holder to prove that it acted with "honesty in fact," the new definition provides:

> "Good faith" means honesty in fact *and the observance of reasonable commercial standards of fair dealing.*

11 M.R.S.A. § 3-1103(1)(d) (1995) (emphasis added). Because the tests are presented in the conjunctive, a holder must now satisfy both a subjective and an objective test of "good faith."

1. Honesty in Fact

Prior to the changes adopted by the Legislature in 1993, the holder in due course doctrine turned on a subjective standard of good faith and was often referred to as the "pure heart and empty head" standard. See M.B.W. Sinclair, Codification of Negotiable Instruments Law: A Tale of Reiterated Anachronism, 21 U. Tol. L. Rev. 625, 654 (1990); see also Seinfeld v. Commercial Bank & Trust Co., 405 So.2d 1039, 1042 (Fla.Dist.Ct.App.1981) (noting that the U.C.C. "seem[s] to protect the objectively stupid so long as he is subjectively pure at heart"). That standard merely required a holder to take an instrument with "honesty in fact" to become a holder in due course.

Courts interpreting this language have routinely declared banks to be holders in due course, notwithstanding the failures of these banks to investigate or hold otherwise negotiable instruments, when they took the instruments with no knowledge of any defects,

---

15. We reject the Credit Union's argument that the good faith element of holder in due course status was not intended to encompass the giving of value for the check. Unless the depositary bank has given value, it cannot become a holder in due course, and its conduct is not scrutinized for compliance with section 3-1302. To determine whether a holder is a holder in due course, the factfinder must determine whether the holder acted with good faith when it took the checks and gave value for them.

defenses, or stop payment orders. See, e.g., UAW-CIO Local # 31 Credit Union v. Royal Ins. Co., 594 S.W.2d 276, 279 (Mo.1980) (en banc); Bank of New York v. Asati, Inc., 15 UCC Rep.Serv.2d (CBC) 521 (N.Y.Sup.Ct. 1991). This approach has been understood to promote the negotiability of instruments, particularly checks, in the stream of commerce. Rejecting a contrary approach, one court put it bluntly:

> The requirement urged by defendant would bring the banking system to a grinding halt. A stop payment order issued by the drawer to the drawee which is unknown to the paying-collecting bank cannot fasten upon the paying bank any legal disability; particularly it cannot reduce the status of the collecting bank to a mere assignee of the instrument or a holder of a non-negotiable instrument, or a mere holder of a negotiable instrument.

Mellon Bank, N.A. v. Donegal Mutual Ins. Co., 29 UCC Rep.Serv. (CBC) 912 (Pa. Ct. C.P. Alleghany County 1980).

Although courts were often urged to engraft an objective reasonableness standard onto the concept of "honesty in fact," most refused to do so. Their refusals recognized that: "[T]he check is the major method for transfer of funds in commercial practice. The maker, payee, and endorsers of a check naturally expect it will be rapidly negotiated and collected.... The wheels of commerce would grind to a halt [if an objective standard were adopted]." Bowling Green, Inc. v. State St. Bank & Trust, 425 F.2d 81, 85 (1st Cir.1970).

Moreover, under the purely subjective standard, a bank was not expected to require the presence of offsetting collected funds in the customers' account in order to give value on newly deposited checks: "A bank's permitting its customers to draw against uncollected funds does not negate its good faith." Asati, Inc., 15 UCC Rep.Serv.2d at 521....

Application of the "honesty in fact" standard to the Credit Union's conduct here demonstrates these principles at work. It is undisputed that the Credit Union had no knowledge that Richard obtained the Sun Life checks by fraud. Nor was the Credit Union aware that a stop payment order had been placed on the Sun Life checks. The Credit Union expeditiously gave value on the checks, having no knowledge that they would be dishonored. In essence the Credit Union acted as banks have, for years, been allowed to act without risk to holder in due course status. The Credit Union acted with honesty in fact.

Thus, had the matter at bar been decided before the Legislature's addition of the objective component of "good faith," there can be little question that the Credit Union would have been determined to have been a holder in due course. Because it took the instruments without notice of any possible dishonor, defect, fraud, or illegality, it could have given value immediately and yet have been assured of holder in due course status.... Today, however, something more than mere subjective good faith is required of a holder in due course.

2. Reasonable Commercial Standards of Fair Dealing

We turn then to the objective prong of the good faith analysis.

The addition of the language requiring the holder to prove conduct meeting "reasonable commercial standards of fair dealing" signals a significant change in the definition of a holder in due course. While there has been little time for the development of a body of law interpreting this new objective requirement, there can be no mistaking the fact that a holder may no longer act with a pure heart and an empty head and still obtain holder in due course status. The pure heart of the holder must now be accompanied by reasoning that assures conduct comporting with reasonable commercial standards of fair dealing.

The addition of the objective element represents not so much a new concept in the doctrinal development of holder in due course status, but rather a return, in part, to an earlier approach to the doctrine. See James J. White & Robert S. Summers, Uniform Commercial Code §14-6, at 628–29 (3d ed. 1988) (discussing the objective test of good faith in England, first applied by the King's Bench in Gill v. Cubitt, 3 B & C 466, 107 Eng.Rep. 806 (K.B. 1824)). The concept of an objective component of good faith has been part of the discussion regarding the holder in due course doctrine since the first enactment of the U.C.C. See id. (noting that "[t]he good faith requirement has been the source of a continuing and ancient dispute"). The early drafters debated the need and wisdom of including such an objective component and ultimately determined not to include it in the definition of good faith because of its potential for freezing commercial practices. See Sinclair, supra, at 653–54 (noting, in particular, the objection by the banking industry to the addition of an objective good faith component). The "new" element of good faith requiring the holder to act according to reasonable commercial standards of fair dealing is actually a more narrow version of the "reasonable person" standard considered and rejected by the drafters of the 1962 Code.

The new objective standard, however, is not a model of drafting clarity. Although use of the word "reasonable" in the objective portion of the good faith test may evoke concepts of negligence, the drafters attempted to distinguish the concept of "fair" dealing from concepts of "careful" dealing:

> Although fair dealing is a broad term that must be defined in context, it is clear that it is concerned with the fairness of conduct rather than the care with which an act is performed. Failure to exercise ordinary care in conducting a transaction is an entirely different concept than failure to deal fairly in conducting the transaction.

U.C.C. §3-103 cmt. 4 (1991).

Unfortunately, the ease with which the distinction between "fair dealing" and "careful dealing" was set forth in the comments to the U.C.C. revisions belies the difficulty in applying these concepts to the facts of any particular case, or in conveying them to a jury. The difficulty is exacerbated by the lack of definition of the term "fair dealing" in the U.C.C. The most obvious question arising from the use of the term "fair" is: fairness to whom? Transactions involving negotiable instruments have traditionally required the detailed level of control and definition of roles set out in the U.C.C. precisely because there are so many parties who may be involved in a single transaction. If a holder is required to act "fairly," regarding all parties, it must engage in an almost impossible balancing of rights and interests. Accordingly, the drafters limited the requirement of fair dealing to conduct that is reasonable in the commercial context of the transaction at issue. In other words, the holder must act in a way that is fair according to commercial standards that are themselves reasonable.

The factfinder must therefore determine, first, whether the conduct of the holder comported with industry or "commercial" standards applicable to the transaction and, second, whether those standards were reasonable standards intended to result in fair dealing. Each of those determinations must be made in the context of the specific transaction at hand. If the factfinder's conclusion on each point is "yes," the holder will be determined to have acted in good faith even if, in the individual transaction at issue, the result appears unreasonable. Thus a holder may be accorded holder in due course status where it acts pursuant to those reasonable commercial standards of fair dealing — even if it is negligent — but may lose that status, even where it complies with commercial standards, if those standards are not reasonably related to achieving fair dealing.

Therefore the jury's task here was to decide whether the Credit Union observed the banking industries' commercial standards relating to the giving of value on uncollected funds, and, if so, whether those standards are reasonably designed to result in fair dealing.

The evidence produced by the Credit Union in support of its position that it acted in accordance with objective good faith included the following:

> The Credit Union's internal policy was to make provisional credit available immediately upon the deposit of a check by one of its members. In certain circumstances — where the check was for a large amount and where it was drawn on an out-of-state bank — its policy allowed for a hold to be placed on the uncollected funds for up to nine days. The Credit Union's general written policy on this issue was reviewed annually — and had always been approved — by the National Credit Union Administration, the federal agency charged with the duty of regulating federal credit unions. See 12 U.S.C.A. § 1752a (Law. Coop. 1996). In addition, the policy complied with applicable banking laws, including Regulation CC. See 12 C.F.R. §§ 229.12(c), 229.13(b) (1998).

The Credit Union also presented evidence that neither Regulation CC nor the Credit Union's internal policy required it to hold the checks or to investigate the genesis of checks before extending provisional credit. It asserted that it acted exactly as its policy and the law allowed when it immediately extended provisional credit on these checks, despite the fact that they were drawn for relatively large amounts on an out-of-state bank.[22] Finally, the Credit Union presented expert testimony that most credit unions in Maine follow similar policies.

In urging the jury to find that the Credit Union had not acted in good faith, Sun Life and the Guerrettes argued that the Credit Union's conduct did not comport with reasonable commercial standards of fair dealing when it allowed its member access to provisional credit on checks totalling over $120,000 drawn on an out-of-state bank without either: (1) further investigation to assure that the deposited checks would be paid by the bank upon which they were drawn, or (2) holding the instruments to allow any irregularities to come to light.

The applicable federal regulations provide the outside limit on the Credit Union's ability to hold the checks. Although the limit on allowable holds established by law is evidence to be considered by the jury, it does not itself establish [a] reasonable commercial standard of fair dealing. The factfinder must consider all of the facts relevant to the transaction. The amount of the checks and the location of the payor bank, however, are relevant facts that a bank, observing reasonable commercial standards of fair dealing, takes into account when deciding whether to place such a hold on the account. The jury was entitled to consider that, under Regulation CC, when a check in an amount greater than $5,000 is deposited, or when a check is payable by a nonlocal bank, a credit union is permitted to withhold provisional credit for longer periods of time than it is allowed in other circumstances. See 12 C.F.R. § 229.13(b), (h) (1998). Therefore, the size of the check and the location of the payor bank are, under the objective standard of good faith, factors which a jury may also consider when deciding whether a depositary bank is a holder in due course.

---

22. The Credit Union could also have withheld provisional credit under the law and its own internal policy if there were other reasons to doubt the validity of the checks. See 12 C.F.R. § 229.13(e) (1998).

The Credit Union's President admitted the risks inherent in the Credit Union's policy and admitted that it would not have been difficult to place a hold on these funds for the few days that it would normally take for the payor bank to pay the checks. He conceded that the amount of the checks were relatively large, that they were drawn on an out-of-state bank, and that these circumstances "could have" presented the Credit Union with cause to place a hold on the account. He also testified to his understanding that some commercial banks followed a policy of holding nonlocal checks for three business days before giving provisional credit.[23] Moreover, the Credit Union had no written policy explicitly guiding its staff regarding the placing of a hold on uncollected funds. Rather, the decision on whether to place a temporary hold on an account was left to the "comfort level" of the teller accepting the deposit. There was no dispute that the amount of the three checks far exceeded the $5,000 threshold for a discretionary hold established by the Credit Union's own policy.

On these facts the jury could rationally have concluded that the reasonable commercial standard of fair dealing would require the placing of a hold on the uncollected funds for a reasonable period of time and that, in giving value under these circumstances, the Credit Union did not act according to commercial standards that were reasonably structured to result in fair dealing.

We recognize that the Legislature's addition of an objective standard of conduct in this area of law may well have the effect of slowing the "wheels of commerce." As one commentator noted:

> Historically, it was always argued that if negotiable instruments were to be usefully negotiable a subsequent holder should not have to investigate the transaction giving rise to the paper. The paramount necessity of negotiability has dominated thinking and legislation on negotiable instruments law. Drafts and promissory notes, it has been believed, must be able to change hands freely, without investigation beyond the face of the instrument, and with no greater requirement than the indorsement of the holder.

Sinclair, supra, at 630 (footnotes omitted). Notwithstanding society's oftcited need for certainty and speed in commercial transactions, however, the Legislature necessarily must have concluded that the addition of the objective requirement to the definition of "good faith" serves an important goal. The paramount necessity of unquestioned negotiability has given way, at least in part, to the desire for reasonable commercial fairness in negotiable transactions.

IV. Effect of Fraud Defense
A. The Guerrettes

Having failed to persuade the jury that it was a holder in due course, the Credit Union is subject to any defense of the Guerrettes or Sun Life "that would be available if the person entitled to enforce the instrument were enforcing a right to payment under a simple contract," 11 M.R.S.A. § 3-1305(1)(b), or any "claim of a property or possessory right in the instrument or its proceeds." 11 M.R.S.A. § 3-1306. Generally, fraud, such as that perpetrated by Paul Richard and Steven Hall, may be the basis for both a valid defense, see Silber v. Muschel, 190 A.D.2d 727, 593 N.Y.S.2d 306, 307 (1993), and a valid claim to the instrument itself. See generally Bowling Green, Inc. v. State St.

---

23. There was evidence that, on the second business day after he deposited the checks, Paul Richard notified the Credit Union that there may have been a problem with his deposit.

Bank & Trust Co., 307 F.Supp. 648, 651–52 (D.Mass. 1969), aff'd, 425 F.2d 81 (1st Cir. 1970).

Fraud is an affirmative defense to a contract. See M.R. Civ. P. 8(c). To prevail on their fraud defense, the Guerrettes were required to prove, by clear and convincing evidence, that a fraudulent or material misrepresentation induced them to transfer the proceeds of their father's life insurance policy, in the form of the Sun Life checks, to Steven Hall and Paul Richard. In addition, they were required to prove they were justified in relying on the fraudulent misrepresentation. See Kuperman v. Eiras, 586 A.2d 1260, 1261 (Me. 1991). The parties' stipulation that Hall and Richard fraudulently induced the Guerrettes to invest the checks in their company, HER, Inc., is sufficient to satisfy the Guerrettes' burden on this issue. The Guerrettes are not liable to the Credit Union for their indorsement of the Sun Life checks.

B. Sun Life

Sun Life, however, may not raise the fraud as a defense to its liability on the instrument. Section 3-1305(3) provides generally that:

> in an action to enforce the obligation of a party to pay [an] instrument, the obligor may not assert against the person entitled to enforce the instrument a defense, claim in recoupment or claim to the instrument (section 3-1306) of another person.

11 M.R.S.A. §3-1305(3). Accordingly, a defense to liability on an instrument—such as fraud in the underlying transaction—raised by one party to an action may not be raised by another party to the action as its own defense to liability. Section 3-1305(3) provides, however, that "the other person's claim to the instrument may be asserted by the obligor if the other person is joined in the action and personally asserts the claim against the person entitled to enforce the instrument." Id. Therefore, only if the Guerrettes have made a claim to the instrument and are parties to the proceeding may Sun Life assert the fraud in defense of its own liability. See 11 M.R.S.A. 3-1305(3); First Nat'l Bank of Nocona v. Duncan Sav. & Loan Ass'n, 656 F.Supp. 358, 366 (W.D.Okla. 1987), aff'd, 957 F.2d 775 (10th Cir. 1992).

The Guerrettes, however, made no claim that they were entitled to possession of the instruments held by the Credit Union.[25] Instead, they merely argued that they were not liable as indorsers of the checks held by the Credit Union as a result of the fraud. The issue of fraud was therefore raised by the Guerrettes as a defense to their liability as indorsers of the instruments. See Louis Falcigno Enters., Inc. v. Massachusetts Bank & Trust Co., 14 Mass.App.Ct. 92, 436 N.E.2d 993, 993–94 (1982). The Superior Court erred when it held that the issue of fraud had been raised as a "claim to the instruments."

Therefore, Sun Life may not raise the fraud against the Guerrettes as a defense to its own liability. Because Sun Life raises no other relevant defenses, it is liable to the Credit Union as the drawer of the instruments, see 11 M.R.S.A. §3-1414(2)(a), and we vacate that portion of the Superior Court's judgment finding that Sun Life was not liable to the Credit Union.

The entry is:

Judgment in favor of Daniel, Joel, and Claire Guerrette and against Maine Family Federal Credit Union affirmed. Judgment in favor of Sun Life Assurance Company of Canada and against Maine Family Federal Credit Union vacated and remanded for further proceedings consistent with the opinion herein.

---

25. The Guerrettes were issued new checks for the same amounts by Sun Life after Sun Life stopped payment on the original instruments.

Notes

1. Did the court confuse "good faith" with "ordinary care"? See § 3-103 OC 4.

2. Did the court erroneously conclude that Sun Life could not assert the third-party fraud defense? Did Sun Life not become subrogated to that defense when it issued replacement checks?

3. Presumably the Guerrettes did not assert a claim to the three checks (or proceeds therefrom) because Sun Life had issued replacement checks. Ironically, Sun Life's decision to issue the replacement checks worked against it. In the absence of any replacement checks, the Guerrettes may have asserted a "claim" to the three checks (or proceeds therefrom) under § 3-202 (negotiation may be rescinded, giving third parties a claim to the checks under § 3-306). And then, § 3-305(c) would have permitted Sun Life to assert the same claim if the Guerrettes were joined in the action.

4. In *Mid Wisconsin Bank v. Forsgard Trading, Inc.*, 608 N.W.2d 830 (Wis. Ct. App. 2003), Lakeshore Truck and Equipment Sales issued an $18,500 check, drawn on its account at a Michigan bank, to Forsgard Trading on May 7, 2001. Forsgard Trading deposited the check into its checking account at Mid Wisconsin Bank on May 8. Mid Wisconsin Bank gave immediate credit for the check. Forsgard's account had been overdrawn on twenty-four previous occasions, but each time Forsgard deposited additional funds when contacted by Mid Wisconsin Bank. Lakeshore Trucking issued a stop-payment order on the check on May 8. When Mid Wisconsin Bank learned of the stop-payment order on May 16, it deducted $18,500 from Forsgard's account, creating a negative balance. Later, Mid Wisconsin Bank sued several parties, including Lakeshore Trucking as the drawer, contending that its status as a holder in due course entitled it to recovery. Lakeshore Trucking conceded that Mid Wisconsin Bank took the $18,500 check with honesty in fact, but argued that Mid Wisconsin Bank failed to observe reasonable commercial standards of fair dealing and therefore did not take the check in good faith. Specifically, Lakeshore Trucking argued that "reasonable commercial standards of fair dealing should have led Mid Wisconsin to place a hold on the check instead of giving immediate credit" because the owner of Forsgard Trading "was a foreign citizen [from Sweden], the check was drawn on an out-of-state account, the check was for greater than $5,000, and Forsgard's account had been overdrawn many times in the past." Id. at 833. The Wisconsin appellate court affirmed the trial court's decision to grant summary judgment in favor of Mid Wisconsin Bank after reviewing the applicable banking agreement and case law from Wisconsin and elsewhere (but never citing *Maine Family Federal Credit Union*). "These cases teach that extending immediate credit is not contrary to reasonable commercial standards of fair dealing. Moreover, it does not matter whether, as here, the account had been overdrawn previously. Mid Wisconsin's policy is to place holds on checks when it has reasonable doubt about the check based on the depositor's history. Here there was no reasonable doubt. Whenever Forsgard had been overdrawn previously, it always deposited funds to cover the overdraft when the bank alerted it to the problem. Mid Wisconsin had no reason to suspect there would be any problem if immediate credit was extended for this check. Consequently, we conclude that Mid Wisconsin observed reasonable commercial standards of fair dealing and therefore was a holder in due course." Id.

5. In *Buckeye Check Cashing, Inc. v. Camp*, 825 N.E.2d 644 (Ohio Ct. App. 2005), Sheth issued a check for $1,300 to Camp as payment for services to be rendered by October 15. The check was postdated to October 15. Camp negotiated the check to Buckeye Check Cashing on October 13. Buckeye deposited the check into its account on October 14, without knowledge that Sheth was placing a stop payment order on the check

on the same day. The stop payment order was timely, so the drawee dishonored the check. Buckeye's attempt to recover the amount of the check from Sheth was unsuccessful, prompting Buckeye to initiate a lawsuit against Sheth (and Camp). The trial court held in favor of Buckeye after concluding that Buckeye took the check as a holder in due course. On appeal, Sheth argued that Buckeye failed to take the check in good faith because its decision to cash a postdated check was not commercially reasonable. The appellate court agreed with Sheth, offering the following thoughts:

> Under a purely subjective "honesty in fact" analysis, it is clear that Buckeye accepted the check from Camp in good faith and would therefore achieve holder-in-due-course status. When the objective prong of the good faith test is applied, however, we find that Buckeye did not conduct itself in a commercially reasonable manner. While not going so far as to say that cashing a postdated check prevents a holder from obtaining holder-in-due-course status in every instance, the presentation of a postdated check should put the check cashing entity on notice that the check might not be good. Buckeye accepted the postdated check at its own peril. Some attempt at verification should be made before a check-cashing business cashes a postdated check. Such a failure to act does not constitute taking an instrument in good faith under the current objective test of "reasonable commercial standards" enunciated in [§ 3-302].

> We conclude that in deciding to amend the good faith requirement to include an objective component of "reasonable commercial standards," the Ohio legislature intended to place a duty on the holders of certain instruments to act in a responsible manner in order to obtain holder-in-due-course status. When Buckeye decided to cash the postdated check presented by Camp, it did so without making any attempt to verify its validity. This court in no way seeks to curtail the free negotiability of commercial instruments. However, the nature of certain instruments, such as the postdated check in this case, renders it necessary for appellee Buckeye to take minimal steps to protect its interests. That was not done. Buckeye was put on notice that the check was not good until October 15, 2003. "Good faith," as it is defined in the UCC and the Ohio Revised Code, requires that a holder demonstrate not only honesty in fact but also that the holder act in a commercially reasonable manner. Without taking any steps to discover whether the postdated check issued by Sheth was valid, Buckeye failed to act in a commercially reasonable manner and therefore was not a holder in due course.

Id. at 647. Do you agree? Did Buckeye fail to act in a commercially reasonable manner? Or did Buckeye merely fail to exercise ordinary care?

Problem 3-5

M B Calvetti

K

P S Un Al

w/o

HDC? NJ Mtg

On June 14, United Aluminum contracted with Mr. and Mrs. Calvetti to install aluminum siding on their home. The contract price was $26,000, with a 2% cash discount. The Calvettis agreed to sign a blank note in return for the promise of United's representative that it would hold the note pending the Calvettis' determination as to whether or not to pay cash and pending their acceptance of the workmanship. United completed the instrument with a date of June 15, an amount of $26,000, payable on demand,

and sold the instrument to New Jersey Mortgage on June 16, for $19,000. United indorsed the note "without recourse" and assigned the contract to New Jersey Mortgage, as it had done with approximately 2,000 other notes over the previous five years. The transferee took the note and contract with knowledge that the contract had not yet been performed. By the time United had done about half the job, the Calvettis concluded that the workmanship was unsatisfactory. The Calvettis told United to stop the installation, which it did. New Jersey Mortgage demanded payment of the note from the Calvettis.

1) Is New Jersey Mortgage a holder in due course? § 3-302.

Q: What elements are most in doubt?

2) What test of good faith does the Code adopt? Is New Jersey Mortgage obligated to inquire into the circumstances out of which the note arose? § 1-201(b)(20).

3) What is the significance of knowledge of the executory contract? F§ 3-304(4)(b).

4) Will it be easier for the Calvettis to establish a lack of good faith or to establish notice of a defense? § 1-202(a).

5) If New Jersey Mortgage took the note in bad faith or with knowledge of a defense, what rights will it have against the Calvettis? § 3-305(a), (b).

iii. Without Notice — Overdue, Dishonored, Default

Another due course element is that the holder must take the instrument "without notice that the instrument is overdue or has been dishonored...." § 3-302(a)(2)(iii). Section 1-202(a) defines notice. Section 3-304 determines when an instrument is overdue. The general rule is that an instrument is overdue the day after it is payable. Then come the refinements. For example, "[w]hether a demand note is stale may vary a great deal depending on the facts of the particular case." § 3-304 OC 1.

Problem 3-6

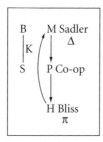

On January 2, 2007, California Co-operative Producers (CCP) sold some bonds bearing 8% interest to Sadler on the representation that they were redeemable in six months for $11,000 plus interest, but that they would be even more valuable as a long-term investment. In payment for the bonds, Sadler executed a note in favor of CCP for $10,000 plus interest at 2% above the prime rate, payable in ten annual installments. When the redemption date for the bonds arrived, Sadler presented them to the obligor and was told they were redeemable for only $2,000. Therefore when the first installment on his note to CCP came due on January 2, 2008, Sadler refused to pay it. On April 17, 2008, CCP negotiated the note to Bliss as payment of a debt CCP owed to him. When the second annual installment came due on January 2, 2009, Bliss notified Sadler that he, Bliss, now held the note, but Sadler refused to pay. Meanwhile, CCP had become insolvent. Bliss commenced an action against Sadler on the note.

1) Is Bliss a holder in due course? §§ 3-302(a), 3-304, 3-303(a), 1-202(a).

2) Assume that the first nine annual payments are "interest only" payments, with a balloon payment of principal (together with accrued and unpaid interest) due at maturity in ten years. Assume that Sadler had missed the first annual "interest only" payment. Would your analysis change?

3) Suppose CCP was not insolvent, making it an attractive source of recovery. On what two statutory grounds might CCP be liable?

iv. *Without Notice of Claims or Defenses*

Problem 3-7

Fazzari was engaged in business in New York. One of his employees, John Wade, came to his home and asked Fazzari to sign a paper which he needed for income tax purposes. Although Fazzari was unable to read or write English, he signed the paper. It turned out to be a promissory note in the amount of $400, dated December 17, 2008, payable at First Bank, the bank where Fazzari had his account. At the time, Fazzari's wife and daughter were home and his wife was able to read English, but he did not request her to read the instrument. Fazzari knew that he had paid Wade $500 in wages, but he signed a purported statement of wages in the amount of $400. When Fazzari learned that what he signed might have been a note, he consulted a lawyer who advised him to notify all the banks in the county and advise them not to accept it. On January 4, 2009, Fazzari went to First Bank and orally informed the cashier, Gilbert, that he "had been tricked," that he did not intend to sign the note, and he instructed the cashier not to "cash a note" for John Wade, and "not to give him any money under my name." The cashier told him "not to worry," and Fazzari departed. On April 10, 2009, the note was negotiated to First Bank by Doane, a customer of the bank and an indorsee of Wade. Doane indorsed the instrument in blank, and Gilbert, the cashier, paid $400 to Doane with a cashier's check, having forgotten his conversation with Fazzari.

1) Is First Bank a holder in due course?

2) What arguments will Fazzari raise? §§ 3-302(a); 3-305(a), (b); 1-202(a).

3) But does the bank have notice of a defense as a matter of law? § 1-202(a).

4) What significance should be placed on Gilbert's statement, "not to worry"? § 1-103(b).

5) On which defenses will Fazzari prevail?

6) Would any of the analysis change if Doane was a holder in due course? § 3-203(b).

B. Judicial and Legislative Qualifications to Negotiability in Consumer Transactions

As we have seen, the essence of negotiability is the merging of the right to payment into a piece of paper that can be transferred to another free of defenses. This freedom has been progressively diminished. During the past fifty years judicial and statutory developments have narrowed the field of application of the holder in due course doctrine. That is, courts and legislatures have attacked the concept of negotiability as a means of consumer protection.

The courts have done this by allowing consumers to raise defenses they have against the payee (seller or lender) also against a subsequent holder asserting holder-in-due-course status. Various reasons have been advanced in support of this approach. The most prominent is that in consumer transactions the subsequent holder (often a financial institution) is too closely connected with the underlying transaction to qualify as a holder in due course. The courts have reached this conclusion by saying that the holder is so involved in the activities of the payee that he could not take with good faith, or that he had notice of problems with the instrument. Or they have concluded that the payee and the transferee financial institution are so closely connected that they are really a single entity, or that the seller is acting as the agent or representative of the bank, that legally they are the same entity, and that the holder therefore failed to take the instrument in good faith and without notice of claims and defenses.

State legislatures have done the same thing, but irrespective of close connection, by enacting statutes which forbid the use of negotiable notes in consumer transactions, or render consumer notes nonnegotiable. The Uniform Consumer Credit Code (UCCC) is an example of such state legislation.

Federal law has likewise attacked negotiability by providing that it is "an unfair or deceptive act or practice" to fail to insert a statement preserving the maker's or drawer's defenses in all consumer credit contracts. Federal Trade Commission Holder-in-Due-Course Regulations, 16 C.F.R. §433.2.

DE LA FUENTE v. HOME SAVINGS ASS'N
669 S.W.2d 137 (Tex. Civ. App. 1984)

KENNEDY, J. This is an appeal from a suit on a note brought by appellee, Home Savings, against appellants, Pedro and Paula de la Fuente. The transaction underlying the note was the sale of materials and services for the installation of aluminum siding for the de la Fuentes' home. We reverse and render judgment for appellants.

Trial was to the court, and findings of fact and conclusions of law were filed. The court's finding of fact are summarized as follows. In late April or early May of 1978, Roberto Gonzales, a representative of Aluminum Industries, Inc., visited the de la Fuente home to sell them aluminum siding. As a result, on May 3, 1978, the de la Fuentes executed, in their residence, a number of documents, including a contract and promissory note for improvements to their home. The contract granted a first lien on appellants' home. The total contract amount was $9,138.24, with 96 monthly installments of $95.19 and an annual percentage rate of 12%. The contract included a trust deed to Aluminum Industries which granted a first lien on the de la Fuentes' residence. Aluminum Industries, Inc. is no longer in existence.

Appellants, by their fourth, sixth and seventh points of error, complain of violations of the Texas Consumer Credit Code, TEX. REV. CIV. STAT. ANN. art. 5069, et seq. (Vernon 1971).

By their fourth point of error, appellants assert that the trial court erred in concluding that the lien taken in the transaction was not unlawful and, therefore, there was no violation of the Texas Consumer Credit Code. The version of art. 5069-6.05 of the Texas Consumer Credit Code in effect on May 3, 1978 read:

Art. 6.05 Prohibited Provisions

No retail installment contract ... shall: (7) Provide for or grant a first lien upon real estate to secure such obligation, except, (a) such lien as is created by law upon the recording of an abstract of judgment or (b) such lien as is provided for or granted by a contract or series of contracts for the sale or construction

and sale of a structure to be used as a residence so long as the time price differential does not exceed an annual percentage rate of 10 percent.

Act of May 4, 1977; ch. 104, § 1, 1977 Tex. Gen. Laws, Local and Spec. 212, amended by
Act of May 8, 1981, ch. 111, § 18, 1981 Tex. Gen. Laws, Local and Spec. 284. See TEX.
REV. CIV. STAT. ANN. art. 5069-6.05 (Vernon Supp. 1984).

The trial court, in the findings of fact, found that the contract for Labor and Materials and Trust Deed granted a first lien on appellants' residence. We agree. See Jim Walter
Homes v. Chapa, 614 S.W.2d 838 (Tex. Civ. App. - Corpus Christi 1981, writ ref'd n.r.e.).
The contract and Trust Deed clearly grant a lien, and both the credit report filled out by
Robert Gonzalez, the salesman, and the undisputed testimony of Pedro de la Fuente show
that there was no lien on the appellants' home at the time of the transaction. However,
even if we did not agree with this finding, it was not challenged and is binding upon the
appellate court. Texas Real Estate Commission v. Hood, 617 S.W.2d 838 (Tex. Civ. App.
- Eastland 1981, writ ref'd n.r.e.). The retail installment contract signed by the de la
Fuentes is in violation of the Texas Consumer Credit Code, art. 5069-6.05 in that the
contract provided for a first lien on the de la Fuentes' home. See Anguiano v. Jim Walter Homes, Inc., 561 S.W.2d 249 (Tex. Civ. App. - San Antonio 1978, writ ref'd n.r.e.).

Appellee asserts that, even if the contract is in violation of the Credit Code, appellee
is not liable because of its status as a holder in due course under TEX. BUS. & COM.
CODE ANN. § 3.302 [R§ 3-302] (Vernon 1968). The trial court found in its conclusions
of law both that appellee, as an assignee of the contract, is derivatively liable for all claims
against the contract and that appellee is not liable to appellants on the counterclaim because of its status as a holder in due course of appellants' note. We agree that an obligor
may assert against the assignee the defenses he could have asserted against the assignor.
York v. McNutt, 16 Tex. 13, 14 (1856); Glass v. Carpenter, 330 S.W.2d 530 (Tex. Civ.
App. - San Antonio 1959, writ ref'd n.r.e.); 7 Tex.Jur.2d Assignments § 52 (1980); J. Cala-
mari & J. Perillo, Contracts § 269 (1970). However, we disagree that appellee was entitled to the protection of a holder is due course of a negotiable instrument, because (1)
the holder is due course doctrine has been abolished in consumer credit transactions by
FTC regulations; and, (2) the appellee did not conform to the notice requirements of the
Texas Credit Code so as to cut off the rights of action and defenses of the buyer. The note
in question contained a notice in bold face type which reads in part:

NOTICE

ANY HOLDER OF THIS CONSUMER CREDIT CONTRACT IS SUBJECT TO
ALL CLAIMS AND DEFENSES WHICH THE DEBTOR COULD ASSERT
AGAINST THE SELLER OF GOODS OR SERVICES OBTAINED PURSUANT
HERETO OR WITH THE PROCEEDS HEREOF....

This FTC Rule, subjecting the holder of the note to the claims and defenses of the debtor,
is in direct conflict with the doctrine of the holder in due course. The Federal Courts
have stated, without so holding, that the effect of this FTC Rule is to abolish the holder
in due course doctrine. Federal Trade Commission v. Winters National Bank & Trust Co.,
601 F.2d 395, 397 (6th Cir. 1979). National Automobile Dealers Association v. Federal
Trade Commission, 421 F. Supp. 31, 33 (M.D.La. 1976). See also J. White and R. Summers, Uniform Commercial Code § 14.8 (2d Ed. 1980).

* * *

The FTC, in its Statement of Basis and Purpose, specifically named the holder in
due course doctrine as the evil addressed by 16 C.F.R. § 433.2. "[A] consumer's duty

to pay for goods and services must not be separated from a seller's duty to perform as promised ..." 40 Fed. Reg. 53,506, 53,523 (November 18, 1975). The FTC intended the Rule to compel creditors to either absorb the cost of the seller's misconduct or return them to sellers. 40 F.R. at 53,523. The FTC "reach[ed] a determination that it constitutes an unfair and deceptive practice to use contractual boiler plate to separate a buyer's duty to pay from a seller's duty to perform." 40 F.R. at 53,524. The effect of this rule is to "give the courts the authority to examine the equities in an underlying sale, and it will prevent sellers from foreclosing judicial review of their conduct. Seller *and creditors* will be responsible for seller misconduct." 40 F.R. at 53,524 (emphasis added). It was clearly the intention of the FTC Rule to have the holder of the paper bear the losses occasioned by the actions of the seller; therefore, the benefits of the holder in due course doctrine under TEX. BUS. & COM. CODE ANN. § 3.302 are not available when the notice required by the FTC in 16 C.F.R. § 433.2 is placed on a consumer credit contract.

In addition, the holder of a note subject to the Credit Code has an independent duty to ensure that the retail installment contract conforms to the statutory requirements of the Credit Code. Art. 5069-6.07 of the Credit Code provides in part:

> No right of action or defense of a buyer arising out of a retail installment transaction which would be cut off by negotiation, shall be cut off by negotiation of the retail installment contract or retail charge agreement to any third party unless such holder acquires the contract relying in good faith upon a certificate of completion or certificate of satisfaction, if required by the provisions of Article 6.06; and *such holder gives notice of the negotiation to the buyer* as provided in this Article, and within thirty days of the mailing of such notice receives no written notice from the buyer of any facts giving rise to any claim or defense of the buyer. (Emphasis added.)

See TEX. REV. CIV. STAT. ANN. art. 5069-8.01 (Vernon Supp. 1984); Horn v. Nationwide Financial Corp., 574 S.W.2d 218 (Tex. Civ. App. - San Antonio 1978, writ ref'd n.r.e.) (interpreting art. 5069-7.07(b) to impose this duty).

We find that appellee is liable under the Texas Consumer Credit Code as a "person who violates this Subtitle ... by (ii) committing any act or practice prohibited by this Subtitle...." TEX. REV. CIV. STAT. ANN. art. 5069-8.01(b) (Vernon Supp. 1984). Appellee is therefore liable to appellant under art. 5069-8.01(b) for an amount equal to twice the time price differential or interest contracted for, charged, or received but not to exceed $4,000 in a transaction in which the amount financed is in excess of $5,000 and reasonable attorneys' fees fixed by the court. Appellants' fourth point of error is sustained.

* * *

We REVERSE the judgment of the trial court and RENDER judgment that appellee take nothing and that the contract, the subject of this suit, is null and void and that appellants recover against appellee, Home Savings, in the amount of $4,000 plus attorney's fees of $3,500 as found by the trial court. Costs are adjudged against appellee.

FORD MOTOR CREDIT COMPANY v. MORGAN
536 N.E.2d 587 (Mass. Supreme Ct. 1989)

O'CONNOR, Justice.

The defendants, Rose and William Morgan, appeal from a judgment denying them recovery on their counterclaims in an action brought by the plaintiff, Ford Motor

Credit Company (Ford Credit), to recover amounts due on an automobile instalment contract and to recover possession of the automobile covered thereby. We affirm the judgment.

The trial judge's findings of fact made in conjunction with Ford Credit's complaint and two counts of the counterclaim may be summarized as follows. On June 27, 1978, the Morgans purchased a new 1978 Mercury Zephyr automobile from Neponset Lincoln Mercury, Inc. (dealer). The Morgans had made several visits to the dealer who assured them that the automobile was reliable and economical. In order to finance their purchase through Ford Credit, the Morgans signed a "Massachusetts Automobile Retail Instalment Contract," a standard printed form contract prepared by Ford Credit. Printed in capital letters at the bottom of the first page of the form was the following statement:

> "NOTICE[:] ANY HOLDER OF THIS CONSUMER CREDIT CONTRACT IS SUBJECT TO ALL CLAIMS AND DEFENSES WHICH THE DEBTOR COULD ASSERT AGAINST THE SELLER OF GOODS OR SERVICES OBTAINED PURSUANT HERETO OR WITH THE PROCEEDS HEREOF. RECOVERY HEREUNDER BY THE DEBTOR SHALL NOT EXCEED AMOUNTS PAID BY THE DEBTOR HEREUNDER."

Section 19 of the contract requires purchasers to procure and maintain insurance on the vehicle at their own expense, "for so long as any amount remains unpaid" under the contract.

Ford Credit financed the automobile for $3,833. Payment was to be in thirty-six consecutive monthly instalments of $137.13 each. On July 11, 1978, a certificate of title was issued to Rose Morgan listing Ford Credit as first lienholder. The Morgans drove the automobile for approximately eighteen months, for a distance of over 11,500 miles. During this time, they experienced several problems with the automobile, such as water leaking into the trunk, a faulty head gasket, rust, hood misalignment, and loss of shine. Their greatest complaint was that, when left unattended, the transmission would shift from "park" to "reverse," and would have to be shifted back to "park" before the vehicle could be started.

During the Fall of 1979, the Morgans began having financial difficulty, and missed their monthly automobile payments for November and December. Before January 1, 1980, William Morgan rented a garage in which he concealed the automobile. He removed the battery and removed or deflated the tires. He also failed to renew his insurance for 1980. In January, Ford Credit notified the Morgans that they were in default on the credit contract and requested that the default be cured by February 6, 1980. The Morgans made no further payments. To that time, they had made fifteen of their monthly payments totalling $2,056.95. The Morgans continued to hide their automobile for approximately two months after the court issued a surrender order. As a result, William Morgan received what the trial judge termed a "well earned" contempt judgment, which Morgan subsequently purged by surrendering the vehicle. The court later authorized Ford Credit to sell the vehicle. William Morgan successfully moved to delay the sale of the vehicle pending inspection, examination, and testing. By the time it was inspected, it had been extensively vandalized and was a total loss. The loss was not recoverable due to the Morgans' failure to obtain insurance for 1980.

Ford Credit sought recovery of $2,628.87 plus costs and attorney's fees. The Morgans counterclaimed in three counts, each of which is predicated on the theory, which we reject, that as assignee of the contract, Ford Credit stands fully in the same position as the assignor-dealer, and thus, any wrongful acts of the dealer are fully attributable to, and may provide the basis of affirmative recovery from, Ford Credit. The first count alleged the dealer's fraud and deceit in making false representations to the Morgans on which they relied. The second count alleged a G.L. c. 93A, §2 (1986 ed.), violation for unfair and deceptive practices. The third count was for the dealer's breach of express and implied warranties of merchantability and fitness for a particular purpose. The Morgans sought $7,061.68 in damages on each of the counts, and damages treble that amount under counts I and II.

Count I, except for damages, was submitted to a jury on special questions. The jury found that the dealer knowingly made false representations to the Morgans, on which the Morgans relied. Thereafter, the judge heard the complaint and counts II and III of the counterclaim without jury. The judge determined that the jury's special verdict provided the Morgans with a valid defense against Ford Credit's collection claim, but that the Morgans were not entitled to damages on any count of their counterclaim. The judge entered judgment for the Morgans on Ford Credit's complaint, and for Ford Credit on each of the counterclaims. The Morgans appealed to the Appeals Court, claiming that the judge erred in allowing their counterclaims to be used only defensively to extinguish Ford Credit's claim for the balance due on the credit contract. They also contend that the jury should have been permitted to assess damages as to counts I and III. We transferred the case to this court on our own initiative.

The Morgans' first contention is that the explicit language of the notice provision contained in the contract, which subjects holders to all "claims and defenses which the debtor could assert against the seller" permits them to recover affirmatively from Ford Credit for the dealer's wrongdoing. As the Morgans acknowledge, that notice provision is mandated by a Federal Trade Commission (FTC) rule which provides that it is an unfair or deceptive act or practice to take or receive a consumer credit contract which fails to include that provision. 16 C.F.R. §433.2 (1978). Therefore, we look to the FTC's purpose in enacting the rule as a guide to our interpretation of the contract provision.

The rule was designed to preserve the consumer's claims and defenses by cutting off the creditor's rights as a holder in due course. Federal Trade Commission, Preservation of Consumers' Claims and Defenses, Final Regulation, Proposed Amendment and Statement of Basis and Purpose, 40 Fed. Reg. 53505, 53524 (Nov. 18, 1975) (to be codified at 16 C.F.R. §433). See Thomas v. Ford Motor Credit Co., 48 Md. App. 617, 622, 429 A.2d 277 (1981). Under the holder in due course principle, which would apply were it not for the contract provision mandated by the FTC rule, the creditor could "assert his right to be paid by the consumer despite misrepresentation, breach of warranty or contract, or even fraud on the part of the seller, and despite the fact that the consumer's debt was generated by the sale." 40 Fed. Reg. at 53507. Thus, "[being] prevented from asserting the seller's breach of warranty or failure to perform against the assignee of the consumer's instrument, the consumer [would lose] his most effective weapon—nonpayment." Id. at 53509. Eliminating holder in due course status prevents the assignee from demanding further payment when there has been assignor wrongdoing, and rearms the consumer with the "weapon" of nonpayment.[3]

---

3. Merely raising a valid claim does not fully insulate the consumer from payments due if the value of the claim is less than payments outstanding. "Laymen, particularly automobile dealers, are wont to complain that under the rule any microscopic defect in the goods will give the buyer a right to quit paying, return the goods, and demand his money back. This is not an accurate statement of the law.... [M]ost defects in the underlying transaction do not give the buyer the right to stop paying entirely." White & Summers, supra at 729–730. However, in the present case, Ford Credit does not contest the judge's determination that the Morgans may raise their valid claim for fraud and deceit against the dealer as a complete defense to further payment.

The FTC anticipated that in addition to nonpayment, affirmative recovery, that is, a judgment for damages against the assignee-creditor, would be available in limited circumstances. Thus, in its statement of policy and purpose, the FTC spelled out the avenues of relief under the rule as follows: "[A] consumer can (1) defend a creditor suit for payment of an obligation by raising a valid claim against a seller as a set-off, and (2) maintain an affirmative action against a creditor who has received payments for a return of monies paid on account." 40 Fed. Reg. at 53524. However, the FTC made clear that "[t]he latter alternative will only be available where a seller's breach is so substantial that a court is persuaded that rescission and restitution are justified. The most typical example of such a case would involve non-delivery, where delivery was scheduled after the date payments to a creditor commenced." Id. The FTC re-emphasized this point in stating, "[c]onsumers will not be in a position to obtain an affirmative recovery from a creditor, unless they have actually commenced payments and received little or nothing of value from the seller. In a case of non-delivery, total failure of performance, or the like, we believe the consumer is entitled to a refund of monies paid on account." Id. at 53527. Finally, the FTC anticipated that the rule would enable the courts to weigh the equities in the underlying sale, and "remain the final arbiters of equities between a seller and a consumer." Id. at 53524. Thus, the function of the rule is to allow consumers to stop payments, and, in limited circumstances, not present here, where equity requires, to provide for a return of monies paid. The FTC did not intend that the rule would, as a matter of course, entitle a consumer to a full refund of monies paid on account.[4] It follows, of course, that there is no merit to the Morgans' assertions that the contractual language allows them affirmative recovery even beyond the amount they paid in. To expose a creditor to further affirmative liability would not only contravene the intention of the FTC, but would "place the creditor in the position of an absolute insurer or guarantor of the seller's performance." Home Sav. Ass'n v. Guerra, 733 S.W.2d 134, 136 (Tex.1987). Michelin Tires (Canada) Ltd. v. First Nat'l Bank, 666 F.2d 673, 679–680 (1st Cir.1981). This we decline to do.

The Morgans do not quarrel with the judge's conclusion that, in the circumstances, they had no right to rescind the sale. Further, they do not argue that they received little or nothing of value from the dealer. We do not imply that such an argument would have been appropriate. However, absent such a showing, and absent any support for the argument that the language in the contract should receive any interpretation other than the one the FTC intended it to have, the Morgans' contention that the language mandated by 16 C.F.R. § 433.2, affords them a right to affirmative recovery is without merit.[5]

---

4. The cases addressing affirmative recovery go no further than to hold that affirmative recovery is available up to the amounts paid in by the debtor. None has addressed the question whether a showing of rescission and restitution is a necessary precedent to such recovery. In each of the cases, it is arguable that the goods received were valueless. Home Sav. Ass'n v. Guerra, 733 S.W.2d 134 (Tex.1987) (rock siding installed crumbled). Thomas v. Ford Motor Credit Co., 48 Md. App. 617, 429 A.2d 277 (1981) (car argued to be "valueless"). Hempstead Bank v. Babcock, 115 Misc.2d 97, 453 N.Y.S.2d 557 (N.Y.Sup.Ct.1982) (solar heating system "never worked"). Tinker v. DeMaria Porsche Audi, Inc., 459 So.2d 487 (Fla. App.1984) (car "totally inoperable").

5. We do not hold that a consumer may only assert his rights defensively in response to a claim initiated by an assignee for balance due on the contract. This would be in clear contravention of the FTC's intention. 40 Fed. Reg. at 53526. Eachen v. Scott Hous. Syss., Inc., 630 F.Supp. 162, 164–165 (M.D. Ala.1986). "Under such circumstances the financier may elect not to sue, in the hopes that the threat of an unfavorable credit report may move the consumer to pay." 40 Fed. Reg. at 53527. Therefore, it is clear that the account debtor may initiate suit to enforce his right, however limited it may be, to discontinue credit payments. See Eachen, supra at 164–165; Tinker v. DeMaria Porsche Audi, Inc., supra at 492–493.

* * *

We conclude that in the circumstances of this case, the judge was correct in ruling that the Morgans were not entitled to affirmative recovery against Ford Credit. Thus, error, if any, that may have occurred in reference to counts II and III of the counterclaim was harmless. The Morgans were entitled to no more than a judgment in their favor on Ford Credit's original claim as ordered by the judge.

Judgment affirmed.

Notes

1. The implications of the close-connection doctrine are suggested by such questions as:

1) What might be the significance of the 2,000 past dealings between United and New Jersey Mortgage in **Problem 3-5**? § 3-302(a)(2)(ii) — re good faith.

2) Would it be significant if evidence revealed that New Jersey Mortgage had investigated the credit of the Calvettis before United contracted with them? § 3-302(a)(2)(v). Where such facts are found, the courts have tended to find the holder of the note to be too closely connected with the payee to be considered a holder in due course.

3) What would be the impact of the FTC HDC Regulation on **Problem 3-5**? You will find this regulation in the statutory supplement. Also see §§ 3-106(d), 3-302(g), and 3-305(e).

In Chapter 1, we noted that the major advantage of negotiability is the power it gives a holder in due course to cut off certain defenses a maker or drawer may have against certain other parties, such as a seller of goods for which the instrument was given in payment. Earlier in this chapter, we noted that the HDC doctrine is material primarily when defenses to or claims against the instrument are made by the maker, drawer, or a third party. Now we note that the De La Fuente court holds that the "holder in due course doctrine has been abolished in consumer credit transactions by FTC regulations...." Thus the FTC HDC Regulation not only effectively destroys the HDC doctrine, but it also goes a long way to functionally destroy negotiability, if not technically. However, for the sake of preserving the application of Article 3 to such consumer transactions, § 3-106(d) provides that such language as in the FTC HDC Regulation does not render a promise or order associated therewith conditional for purposes of § 3-104, so that an instrument bearing such language remains negotiable, at least in a technical sense.

2. With the advent of the FTC HDC Regulation, coupled with § 3-106(d), the courts no longer have to rely on the closely connected rationale for finding that the transferee is not a holder in due course in consumer transactions. This does not mean the too closely connected doctrine will be irrelevant. Courts may still apply this rationale in non-consumer transactions in appropriate cases. That is, although commercial transactions are not subject to the FTC HDC Regulation, the courts might still come to the conclusion that the transferee is not a holder in due course because it was too closely connected with the transferor in the underlying transaction.

3. Abolition of the holder in due course advantages in consumer transactions has been criticized as being unduly paternalistic and economically inefficient. Paternalism destroys self-reliance. Economic inefficiency is evidenced by the fact that destroying holder in due course advantages in consumer transactions has only increased the cost of goods and services by spreading the risks of consumer financing to all consumers, while depriving consumers of the option to buy at a cheaper price by waiving their de-

fenses if they choose to do so. Destruction of holder in due course cut-off power will be reflected in the higher discount rates the dealer will encounter at the bank. It is an economic certainty that this increase will be passed on to the consumer. In view of this it has been argued that it would be more desirable to allow a consumer a choice in these matters—a choice either to waive his defenses and pay a lower price, or to retain his defenses and pay a higher price.

C. Successors to Holders in Due Course— The Shelter Doctrine

Problem 3-8

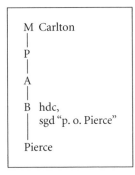

On June 1, Carlton was fraudulently induced by P to give a note for $7,000 payable in one month after date. P negotiated the note by special indorsement to A, who negotiated it by special indorsement and sold it to B on June 20. On July 5, B wrote "pay to the order of Pierce," followed by his signature, and then sold the note to Pierce.

1) Is Pierce a PETE? § 3-301.

2) Will Carlton assert a defense? Is it good against a holder in due course? §§ 3-305(a), (b).

3) Is Pierce a holder in due course? §§ 3-302(a), 3-304(b), 1-202(a).

4) Was B a holder in due course?

5) Can Pierce assert B's rights? § 3-203(b). What is the purpose of such a result? § 3-203 OC 2.

6) Suppose B never indorsed the instrument before giving it to Pierce. Is Pierce a PETE? Does Pierce have the rights of a holder in due course?

7) Suppose P reacquired the note from Pierce. Is P a PETE? Does P have the rights of a holder in due course?

D. Real and Personal Defenses

Although § 3-305 does not use the terms "real" and "personal" to describe defenses, traditionally these terms have been used by lawyers and judges to explain the rights and obligations of parties to instruments. The terms remain useful, as suggested by the fact that they appear in the official comments.

Real defenses are generally available when the instrument lacks legal validity from its beginning. Personal defenses do not deny the legal validity of the instrument at its inception, but assert that the promise or order is void or voidable because of circumstances related to the transaction out of which the instrument arose.

Real defenses are those which are available against holders in due course, whereas personal defenses are not. A PETE that is not a holder in due course (e.g., a mere holder) is subject to both real and personal defenses. § 3-305.

A holder establishes a prima facie right to payment by producing the instrument, if he proves that he is a person entitled to enforce the instrument. His prima facie case is rebutted, however, if evidence of a defense or claim in recoupment is proved by the obligor. The holder then loses unless he proves that he is a holder in due course. § 3-308.

Problem 3-9

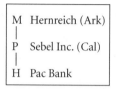

Hernreich, who operated a jewelry store in Arkansas, executed a promissory note for $10,600, payable in three months, in favor of Sebel, a wholesale jewelry company in California. Sebel had not registered to do business in Arkansas, and therefore was not legally qualified to conduct business in that state. Sebel discounted the note to Pacific Bank, an Arkansas bank which was duly authorized to do business in that state. Thereafter the principal owner of Sebel died, and the corporation was dissolved. The note came due and Pacific Bank demanded payment. Hernreich refused to pay.

The statute requiring registration stated: "Any foreign corporation which shall fail to comply with this act shall be subject to a fine of not less than $1,000, and any foreign corporation which shall fail to file its articles of incorporation cannot make any contract in the State which can be enforced by it either in law or in equity."

1) What is Pacific Bank's status?

2) Does Hernreich have a good defense? Is it real or personal? § 3-305.

3) If Sebel had not dissolved, on what theories might Pacific Bank recover from Sebel?

Problem 3-10

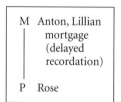

Rose loaned $100,000 to Anton Homsey to be used in his business. To induce Rose to make the loan, Anton persuaded his wife, Lillian, to sign the note as co-maker. Rose was aware that Lillian received no consideration for her signature. The note was secured by a mortgage (signed by both Anton and Lillian) on real estate in which Anton and Lillian had a joint interest. Anton delivered the note and mortgage to Rose. Without Lillian's knowledge, Anton requested Rose not to record the mortgage. Rose acquiesced and did not record the mortgage until September, after learning that Anton had run into financial difficulty. Rose failed to properly record the mortgage, and it was held to be defective, thereby rendering the mortgage unenforceable against a bona fide purchaser, such as a bankruptcy trustee, who took the property free of Rose's lien. Anton was adjudicated a bankrupt in December and received a discharge.

1) What is Anton's liability to Rose? § 3-305.

Q: Is Rose a holder or a holder in due course?

2) What is the capacity in which Lillian signed the note? §§ 3-419, 3-412.

3) Is Lillian liable on the note? §§ 3-412, 3-116, 3-419(f), 3-605(d).

Q: How is the extent of the impairment measured?

4) Assume that the loan was not secured by real estate or any other collateral. Can Lillian avoid co-maker liability by asserting Anton's defense of bankruptcy discharge? § 3-305(d).

Problem 3-11

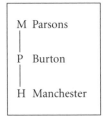

Parsons raised Arabian horses and became indebted to Burton for breeding fees. On September 22, 2007, Parsons executed a note to Burton for $10,000 payable in 18 months. On November 1, 2007, Burton negotiated the note to Manchester. Burton never informed Parsons of the negotiation. On June 3, 2008, Parsons sold and delivered some colts to Burton for $11,000 and received a letter from Burton acknowledging receipt of the colts and promising to send Parsons his canceled note in full payment of his debt, plus the balance owing for the colts. Manchester demands payment of the note on the maturity date.

Parsons argues that he paid the note by delivering the horses to Burton and is therefore discharged. Does he have a good defense? §§ 3-601; 3-602(a), (b), (d).

Problem 3-12

P pulls a knife on M, a wealthy man, and demands that M put his signature on a note in favor of P in the amount of $1 million payable on demand. M does so. P negotiates the note to Stock Broker for stock worth $900,000. P then sells the stock and flees the country. Stock Broker demands payment of the note from M.

1) What result?

2) Instead of a knife, P tells M that he will give photographs of M's extramarital affair to the tabloids if he does not sign the note. M signs. What result?

E. Claims of Ownership and Conversion

Arguments over instruments generally fall in one of two categories: (1) claims of ownership, and (2) defenses to liability. We have observed that a valid defense may preclude liability on the instrument. By contrast, rights of ownership are affirmative assertions of legal or equitable interests in the instrument itself. We have also observed that property rights in and rights to enforce an instrument are separable, and property rights may be determined by property law outside of Article 3. However, in some instances property rights are determined by Article 3. Here we will examine what protection is given to a third party who asserts a property right against a holder or a holder in due course.

Problem 3-13

City Bank issued a note for $10,000 to Finney or bearer, payable on demand. Finney mailed it to Bernard. Thief extracted the letter from the mail and used the note to buy a

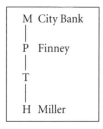

boat worth $9,800 from Miller, who knew nothing about the theft. Finney learned of the theft and notified City Bank to stop payment, which it did. Miller presented the note for payment. The bank requested possession of the note but Miller said, "I will give you the note if you will pay it, but in the meantime I will exhibit it to you," which he did. The bank refused to pay it.

1) What is the status of Miller?

2) What if Finney asserts his right ("claim") to the instrument against Miller? §§ 3-306, 3-203 OC 1.

3) Is the bank liable to Miller? §§ 3-305(c), 3-306, 3-301, 3-412.

4) Suppose Miller had handed the instrument to the bank who then refused to pay it and refused to give it back. Is the bank liable to Miller? §§ 3-309, 3-420(a).

5) Suppose the bank had ignored the stop payment request and paid the note. Will it have to pay twice if Finney demands payment? §§ 3-301(iii), 3-309, 3-602(a).

6) Assume the note was a time note and overdue. Miller calls the bank and asks the clerk if the note is okay. The clerk replies affirmatively, never mentioning that the note has been stolen and is subject to a stop payment request. Miller then buys the note from Thief. May Miller enforce the note when the bank raises the defense of theft? §§ 3-305(c), 1-103(b).

Notes

1. *Jus Tertii*: Jus Tertii refers to defenses of third parties. In an action to enforce an instrument against an obligor, the obligor is generally not allowed to raise the defenses of third parties. However, there are a few exceptions, mainly to protect a party against double payment (for example, where the instrument has been lost or stolen). The principle is found in some degree in § 3-305(c) and (d).

2. If the instrument had been a check drawn by Finney on City Bank, rather than a note, the bank-customer contract may cause the stop payment notice to have very different legal consequences, as we will see in Part II, Drafts and Checks.

F. Claims in Recoupment

An obligor that asserts a claim in recoupment against a PETE is not denying liability per se. Instead, the obligor is contending that its liability under the terms of the instrument should be reduced by damages or out-of-pocket expenses that the obligor has incurred. The following problem explores the merits of such a claim.

Problem 3-14

Lisa executed a $3,000 promissory note payable to the order of Dealer to evidence Lisa's purchase of a piano from Dealer. On delivery, Dealer damaged Lisa's studio, requiring Lisa to pay $400 to a contractor for repairs.

Two weeks later, Lisa agreed to give piano lessons to several of Dealer's students in exchange for Dealer's agreement to pay Lisa a fixed hourly rate.

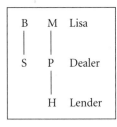

Later, Dealer negotiated the promissory note to Lender, who demanded payment of $3,000 from Lisa on the due date. At that time, Dealer owed Lisa $250 for piano lessons.

1) How much must Lisa pay to Lender if Lender (a) is not a holder in due course, (b) is a holder in due course? §§ 3-305(a)(3), (b).

2) Would your analysis change if Dealer caused damages of $3,300 on delivery?

Part II

Drafts and Checks

Most of the principles we have covered thus far in relation to promissory notes also are fully applicable to drafts and checks. For this reason it is unnecessary to reiterate them here, but you will recognize some familiar terrain as we proceed.

A. Formal Differences

The draft and check are quite different in form from the promissory note. In theory an instrument can be created that looks like both a draft and a note, in which case the holder is free to treat it as either (§ 3-104(e)), but in practice the two are quite different in form. As we have seen, unless accommodation parties are involved, in its original condition a note is a two-party instrument containing an unconditional promise of the maker to pay to the bearer or to the order of the payee. In substance, a cashier's check is also a two-party instrument because the drawer and drawee are usually the same entity. Nevertheless a cashier's check is classified as a draft by the Code. § 3-104(g). Drafts and checks, at their inception, are initially three-party instruments containing an order of a drawer upon a drawee to pay the bearer or to the order of the payee. A draft drawn by a bank on another bank is a teller's check, sometimes called a bank draft. § 3-104(h). A draft drawn on a bank and payable on demand is a check. § 3-104(f).

B. Functional Differences

The draft is the most versatile negotiable instrument because it is frequently used as a means of (1) credit, (2) payment, or (3) transmitting funds.

A draft is used as a *credit* instrument, for example, when a seller draws a time draft on a buyer as a means of collecting the price. However, if it is payable at sight (i.e., on demand), it is a non-credit instrument. In these examples the object of the instrument is collection of the price and the instrument is drawn and issued by the seller — the creditor.

A draft is used as a *payment* device when the buyer draws a draft on his bank in favor of the seller in payment of the price. In this instance the draft is issued by the debtor, and if the draft is payable on demand, it is a common check. A check also can be used as a credit instrument. A post-dated check is an example. But the promissory note is the most common credit instrument, and the check is the most common payment instrument.

A draft may also be used for the purpose of *transmitting funds*, as when a traveler wants to transfer money to a bank in a foreign country so it will be there when he arrives. In this instance the traveler buys a draft (a bank draft or teller's check) drawn on the foreign bank. When he presents it to the foreign bank he will receive his money.

Because checks and drafts are three-party instruments, to be comprehensive we will consider the rights and duties of the parties arising out of each of these three relationships. First we will examine the drawer-drawee relationship, then the holder's relationship to the drawer, and finally the legal problems arising out of the holder's relationship with the drawee. We have already dealt with the relationship between indorsers, but this subject inevitably comes up again here and there, and thereby provides further insight into the liability of the parties. We will also put these matters in context by taking notice of the Federal Reserve System and the check collection process as we go along.

Chapter 4

Rights and Duties under the Drawer-Drawee Relationship

When a draft or check leaves the drawer's hands, there is no legal relationship between the drawer and drawee, unless the parties have previously entered a contract which establishes a legal relationship. That is, the mere drawing of a check or draft on another party does not of itself impose any legal obligation on the drawee to honor the check or draft. But typically the drawer has had some previous dealings with the drawee so that by understanding or contract the drawee is obligated to honor the draft.

So when drafts or checks are drawn, there is usually some preexisting duty to honor them. For example, a sales contract may provide that the seller may draw a draft on a buyer to collect the price. But the obligations arising out of the contract and the obligation arising out of the draft are separate. Thus, even though the drawee (buyer) is obligated to the drawer (seller) to pay the draft pursuant to the contract, the drawee (buyer) will not be liable on the draft to the payee (e.g., a bank) unless the drawee (buyer) "accepts" it. §§ 3-408, 3-409(a).

A. Non-Bank Drawees

NORTON v. KNAPP
19 N.W. 867 (Iowa 1884)

SEEVERS, J. Because of the statements contained in an amended abstract we are required to set out the petition as follows:

"That the plaintiffs sold and delivered to the defendant, about February 17, 1882, a certain flaxseed-cleaner mill, at the agreed price of eighty dollars, no part of which had been paid, and that the same was then due.

"That on or about April, 1882, plaintiffs drew a sight draft on defendant for the agreed price of said mill, which was in words and figures as follows:

$80   La Crosse, Wis., April 18, 1882

At sight pay to the order of Exchange Bank of Nora Springs, Iowa, eighty dollars, value received, and charge the same to the account of Norton & Keeler.

To Miles Knapp, Nora Springs, Ia.

Which was accepted by said Miles Knapp in written words and figures on the back thereof, as follows: "Kiss my foot. Miles Knapp." Also alleging "that said draft was still the property of plaintiff, due and unpaid, and claiming judgment for eighty dollars, interest, and costs."

To the foregoing petition the defendant demurred, on the ground "that the draft set out in the petition does not show a legal acceptance." The demurrer was overruled, and the defendant answered, denying the allegations of the petition, and pleaded a special defense as to the flaxseed cleaner. The plaintiffs withdrew or dismissed "so much of their cause of action as was based on the sale of the flaxseed-cleaning machine, leaving the draft as their sole cause of action." A jury was impaneled to try the issue joined, and the plaintiff offered in evidence the draft, as above set out; to which the defendant objected, on the ground that it had not been accepted by him. This objection was sustained, and the jury, under the direction of the court, found for the defendant, and judgment was rendered on the verdict. The amount in controversy being less than $100, the court has certified certain questions upon which the opinion of this court is desired. In substance, two of them are whether the words "kiss my foot," on the back of the draft, signed by the drawee, is a legal and valid acceptance; and whether such acceptance can be introduced in evidence without showing it was the intention to accept the draft. The rule upon this subject is thus stated in 1 Pars. Bills & Notes, 282: "If a bill is presented to a drawee for the purpose of obtaining his acceptance, and he does anything to or with it which does not distinctly indicate that he will not accept it, he is held to be an acceptor, for he has the power, and it is his duty, to put this question beyond all possibility of doubt."

Counsel for the defendant insist that it was held in Spear v. Pratt, 2 Hill, 582, that the words "I will not accept this bill," signed by the defendant, constituted a valid acceptance. As we understand the case, the defendant's name was written "across the face of the bill," and this was held to be a sufficient acceptance, on the ground that the request to accept had not been negatived.

The rule we understand to be, if the drawee does anything with or to the bill, or writes thereon anything, which does not clearly negative an intention to accept, then he can or will be charged as an acceptor. The question, then, is, what construction should be placed on the words "kiss my foot," written on the bill and signed by him? They cannot be rejected as surplusage. Such language is not ordinarily used in business circles or polite society. But by their use the defendant meant either to accept or refuse to accept the bill. It cannot be he meant the former; therefore, it must be the latter. It seems quite clear to us that the defendant intended, by the use of the contemptuous and vulgar words above stated, to give emphasis to his intention not to accept or have anything to do with the bill or with the plaintiff. We understand the words, in common parlance, to mean and express contempt for the person to whom the words are addressed, and when used as a reply to a request, they imply, and are understood to mean, a decided, unqualified, and contemptuous refusal to comply with such request. In such sense they were undoubtedly used when the defendant was requested to accept the bill. The question asked upon this point must be answered in the negative. Whether parol evidence is admissible to show the intent of the defendant, we have no occasion to determine, because no such evidence was offered, and our rule is not to determine mere abstract propositions.

* * *

Affirmed.

B. Banks as Drawees, the Federal Reserve System, and Check Collection

In dealing with drafts and checks we will inevitably be discussing the activities of banks and banking law. This will take us into Article 4, which contains the law on bank deposits and collections. At the outset it will therefore be helpful to take note of some basic terminology. For example, the drawer's bank, which is referred to in Article 3 as the drawee bank, is known as the payor bank under Article 4. The bank in which the payee deposits the item for collection is the depositary bank. When the depositary bank forwards the item, it becomes a collecting bank. The bank that presents the item for payment is the presenting bank. The transmitting banks between the depositary bank and the payor bank are known as intermediary banks. See § 4-105.

As a background for our discussion of drafts and checks, a brief sketch of the Federal Reserve collection process may also be helpful at this point. The Federal Reserve Bank was established by federal law to regulate banking. Banks that are members of the Federal Reserve banking system (i.e., all banks chartered under federal law, together with state-chartered banks that opt into the system) must keep a certain percentage of their deposits—known as a "reserve"—on deposit with the Federal Reserve Bank. Nonmember banks will usually clear their items through banks that are members. There are twelve Federal Reserve districts throughout the nation. Although not all drafts are collected through the Federal Reserve system, most of them are if they have to travel outside a given city for collection. That is, virtually all checks are collected through this system unless the drawee (payor) bank and the depositary bank are the same bank ("on us" items), or the check is drawn on another bank in the same city.

In order to permit electronic processing of checks, almost all checks are preprinted with a row of numerals and symbols along the bottom of the check that are read by machines. This machine-readable printing is known as Magnetic Ink Character Recognition (MICR) encoding, which was first used in the late 1950's. The first nine digits are a routing field. The first two digits represent the Federal Reserve district in which the drawee-payor bank is located. (For example, "02" represents the second district, headquartered in New York City, and "11" represents the eleventh district, headquartered in Dallas.) The third digit indicates the Federal Reserve office within the district that serves the drawee-payor bank. (A "1" represents the main office; any other number represents a branch office.) The fourth digit represents the processing center to which the check should be routed. The fifth through eighth digits identify the drawee-payor bank. And the ninth digit is a number generated by an algorithm that the check processing system uses to check the legitimacy of the previous eight digits and to guard against MICR fraud. (Occasionally the MICR line is mutilated or otherwise unreadable, preventing electronic processing. In that instance the nine-digit routing field can be created by using the fractional numbers that appear in the upper right area of the check and the check will be manually processed.)

Two other pre-printed MICR-encoded fields appear on the bottom of a check: the drawer's bank account number and check number. One MICR-encoded field—the amount—does not appear on a check until after it is issued. Usually the amount is encoded by the depositary bank, although a payee that receives a significant number of checks (e.g., a utility company or a retailer) may encode the amount. A party that encodes the amount warrants the accuracy of the information encoded. § 4-209(a), (c). Occasionally the party makes an encoding mistake. See, e.g., Cabelka v. Herring National Bank, 56 U.C.C. Rep. Serv. 2d 952 (N.D. Tex. 2005) ($37,500 check erroneously encoded for $375.00); U.S. Bank, N.A. v. First Security Bank, N.A., 44 U.C.C. Rep. Serv. 2d 1088 (D. Utah 2001) ($23,000 check erroneously encoded for $223,000); France v. Ford Motor Credit Company, 913 S.W.2d 770 (Ark. 1996) ($8,506.19 check erroneously encoded for $506.19).

There are two basic check collection processes: check forwarding, and check truncation. Under the traditional collection process, the check itself is forwarded to the payor bank for payment, a process that can be inefficient and costly. Check truncation, of comparatively recent origin, contemplates that at some point in the check clearing process the original check will cease to travel and parties will forward information electronically. A potential roadblock to widespread electronic check processing is that banks are required to transfer, present, and return the original check, absent contrary agreement. §§ 4-209 and 4-110. To overcome this roadblock, Congress enacted the Check Clearing for the 21st Century Act in October 2003. The Act, popularly known as "Check 21," became effective in October 2004 and is codified at 15 U.S.C. §§ 5001-5018 and implemented through Regulation CC, 12 C.F.R. pt. 229 (subpart D). Check 21 permits (but does not require) banks to create so-called "substitute checks," a paper reproduction of both sides of the original check. When the substitute check is accompanied by specific warranties, the substitute check becomes — and must be accepted by all parties as — the legal equivalent of the original check. This feature of legal equivalence should encourage increased electronic check processing.[1]

To illustrate the check collection process, suppose Buyer, located in Houston, pays for goods purchased from Seller, located in Dallas, with a check drawn on Paradise National Bank in Houston. Seller deposits the check in its account at Lone Star Bank in Dallas, which gives Seller provisional credit (provisional settlement). Provisional settlement means that although Seller may not draw upon the credit as a matter of right immediately, out of courtesy Lone Star Bank (the depositary bank) may allow Seller to do so, depending on the circumstances, and conditional upon a right of charge back if the check is dishonored—i.e., returned "NSF" (commonly understood to mean the drawer's account balance is insufficient to pay the check). §§ 4-104(a)(11); 4-214(a). The depositary bank is not required to give a provisional settlement at the time of deposit, but frequently it does. § 4-201(a). Lone Star Bank sends the check to its check processing agent (which may be the Federal Reserve Bank's district office in Dallas or some other entity). Items moving through the collection process are generally carried by special courier, although the mail, express, and the like are available alternatives, depending on the circumstances. § 4-204 OC 2. The check processing agent then will send the check, directly or indirectly, to Paradise National Bank's check processing agent (which may be the same agent used by Lone Star Bank, the Houston branch office of the Federal Reserve Bank, or some other entity), or to Paradise National Bank itself. As the check moves along the collection chain, each subsequent collecting bank also will typically give provisional credit or provisional settlement to its transferor, and in return the transferor gives certain warranties to the transferee bank. §§ 4-205, 4-207, 4-209. Each bank has until its midnight deadline (defined under § 4-104(a)(10) as midnight of the banking day after the banking day on which the collecting bank receives the check) to pass the item on to the next collecting bank in the chain. § 4-202(a)(1), (b).

---

1. For an extensive analysis of Check 21 prepared by the Board of Governors of the Federal Reserve System, visit http://www.federalreserve.gov/BoardDocs/Press/bcreg/2003/20031222/attachment.pdf.

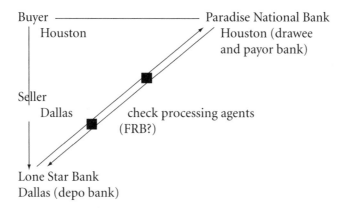

Buyer ————————————— Paradise National Bank
| Houston   Houston (drawee
| and payor bank)

Seller
Dallas   check processing agents
| (FRB?)
|
Lone Star Bank
Dallas (depo bank)

When the check is finally presented to Paradise National Bank (the drawee and payor bank) for payment, Paradise National Bank has until its midnight deadline to decide whether it will pay the check. §4-302(a). If it decides to pay the check, final payment will firm up the provisional credits all along the collection chain, and when Lone Star Bank "has had a reasonable time to receive return of the item and the item has not been received within that time," the provisional credit becomes final and Seller is entitled to draw on the funds as of right. §4-215(e). (On the other hand, if the check is dishonored, Paradise National Bank must return the item or send notice of dishonor directly or indirectly to Lone Star Bank (§4-302(a)), and Lone Star Bank will charge back the amount of this check against Seller's account (§4-214(a)).) So we see that final payment and final settlement are terms of art.

More specifically, final payment in effect refers to the time when Buyer loses control of the funds in its account in any of the three ways mentioned in §4-215(a) (payment in cash, settlement without a right to revoke, and provisional settlement followed by a failure to revoke in time), not just to the moment when Paradise National Bank remits the funds to Seller (e.g., pays in cash). Of course final payment does include payment in cash to Seller, such as in over-the-counter transactions. But final payment may occur before the funds are remitted. For example, if Paradise National Bank gives provisional settlement, such as by posting the item when the item comes in, but then fails to revoke the settlement before the expiration of its midnight deadline, final payment will have occurred. §4-215(a)(3). And concurrently, final settlement will have been made. §4-215(c). Therefore if Paradise National Bank has given provisional settlement and later decides that it is not going to pay the item, it must return the check or give notice of dishonor before the expiration of its midnight deadline; otherwise the lapse of time will convert the provisional settlement into a final payment and hence final settlement. Once final payment has occurred in any of the ways mentioned in §4-215(a), even if it turns out that the check is not properly payable, Paradise National Bank becomes accountable for payment of the item and must at some point remit the funds. §§4-301, 4-302.

Final settlement refers to the collection process under which all of the provisional credits or settlements are firmed up by final payment, starting with the provisional credit or settlement given by the payor bank all the way back to the depositary bank. Thus final payment simultaneously triggers final settlement. To use the clearest examples, this happens when cash is sent, or when credit is given by a Federal Reserve Bank. Or, if a remittance draft has been used in the collection chain, such as a cashier's check or a teller's check, final settlement occurs when the remittance draft has been paid, thereby firming up the provisional credits all the way back to the depositary bank. § 4-213.

Federal law also has an impact on the check collection process. In 1987 Congress enacted The Expedited Funds Availability Act (EFAA), 12 U.S.C. §§ 4001–4010, and it became effective in 1988. The EFAA regulates the "float" and, as illustrated by **Problem 5-10**, also regulates how soon banks are required to make money available to their customers following deposits. As might be expected, banks are required to make money available more quickly following cash deposits than they are if the customer deposits checks. But because banks are given limited time before they are required to allow their customers to draw upon check deposits, banks are compelled to speed up the collection process. The EFAA is implemented by a regulation promulgated by the Federal Reserve Board called Regulation CC, 12 C.F.R. pt. 229, which also went into effect in 1988. An additional federal source is Regulation J, 12 C.F.R. pt. 210. Subpart A "governs the collection of checks and other cash and noncash items and the handling of returned checks by Federal Reserve Banks." 12 C.F.R. § 210.1.

As we take notice of further banking practice, we will also define and discuss various other concepts and terms of art encountered in banking law, such as "banking day," "midnight deadline," "final payment," "final settlement," etc. §§ 4-104, 4-215.

BLAKE v. WOODFORD BANK & TRUST CO.

555 S.W.2d 589 (Ky. Ct. App. 1977)

PARK, J. This case involves the liability of the appellee and cross-appellant, Woodford Bank and Trust Company, on two checks drawn on the Woodford Bank and Trust Company and payable to the order of the appellant and cross-appellee, Wayne Blake. Following a trial without a jury, the Woodford Circuit Court found that the bank was excused from meeting its "midnight deadline" with respect to the two checks. Blake appeals from the judgment of the circuit court dismissing his complaint. The bank cross appeals from that portion of the circuit court's opinion relating to the extent of the bank's liability on the two checks if it should be determined that the bank was excused from meeting its midnight deadline.

Basic Facts

The basic facts are not in dispute. On December 6, 1973, Blake deposited a check in the amount of $16,449.84 to his account at the Morristown Bank, of Morristown, Ohio. This check was payable to Blake's order and was drawn on the K & K Farm Account at the Woodford Bank and Trust Company. The check was dated December 3, 1973.

On December 19, 1973, Blake deposited a second check in the amount of $11,200.00 to his account in the Morristown Bank. The second check was also drawn on the K & K Farm Account at the Woodford Bank and Trust Company and made payable to Blake's order. The second check was dated December 17, 1973.

When Blake deposited the second check on December 19, he was informed by the Morristown Bank that the first check had been dishonored and returned because of insufficient funds. Blake instructed the Morristown Bank to re-present the first check along with the second check. Blake was a cattle trader, and the two checks represented the purchase price for cattle sold by Blake to James Knight who maintained the K & K Farm Account. Blake testified that he had been doing business with Knight for several years. On other occasions, checks had been returned for insufficient funds but had been paid when re-presented.

The two checks were forwarded for collection through the Cincinnati Branch of the Federal Reserve Bank of Cleveland. From the Federal Reserve Bank, the two checks were delivered to the Woodford Bank and Trust Company by means of the Purolator Courier Corp. The checks arrived at the Woodford Bank and Trust Company on Monday, December 24, 1973, shortly before the opening of the bank for business. The next day, Christmas, was not a banking day. The two checks were returned by the Woodford Bank and Trust Company to the Cincinnati Branch of the Federal Reserve Bank by means of Purolator on Thursday, December 27, 1973.

The two checks were received by the bank on Monday, December 24. The next banking day was Wednesday, December 26. Thus, the bank's "midnight deadline" was midnight on Wednesday, December 26. KRS 355.4-104(1)(h) [R§4-104(a)(10)]. As the bank retained the two checks beyond its midnight deadline, Blake asserts that the bank is "accountable" for the amount of the two checks under KRS 355.4-302(a) [R§4-302(a)(1)].

History of Payor Bank's Liability for Retaining Check

Under the Uniform Negotiable Instruments Law a payor bank was not liable to the holder of a check drawn on the bank until the bank had accepted or certified the check. Ewing v. Citizens National Bank, 162 Ky. 551, 172 S.W. 955 (1915); W. Britton, Bills and Notes § 169 (1943). Because of the payor bank's basic nonliability on a check, it was essential that some time limit be placed upon the right of the payor bank to dishonor a check when presented for payment. If a payor bank could hold a check indefinitely without incurring liability, the entire process of collection and payment of checks would be intolerably slow. To avoid this problem, a majority of courts construing § 136 and § 137 of the Uniform Negotiable Instruments Law held that a payor bank was deemed to have accepted a check if it held the check for 24 hours after the check was presented for payment. Britton, op. cit. § 179. Thus, in a majority of jurisdictions, the payor bank had only 24 hours to determine whether to pay a check or return it. However, in Kentucky and a few other jurisdictions, the courts held that § 136 and § 137 of the Uniform Negotiable Instruments Law applied only to checks which were presented for acceptance. In Kentucky Title Savings Bank and Trust Company v. Dunavan, 205 Ky. 801, 266 S.W. 667 (1924), the Court of Appeals held that § 136 and § 137 of the Uniform Negotiable Instruments Law had no application to a check which was presented for payment. Consequently, the payor bank would be liable on the check only if it held the check "for an unreasonable length of time" and could thus be deemed to have converted the check.

In order to bring uniformity to the check collection process, the Bank Collection Code was proposed by the American Bankers' Association. The Bank Collection Code was adopted by Kentucky in 1930. Under § 3 of the Bank Collection Code, a payor bank could give provisional credit when a check was received, and the credit could be revoked at any time before the end of that business day. The payor bank became liable on the check if it retained the item beyond the end of the business day received. 1930 Kentucky Acts, ch. 13, § 3 (former KRS 357.030).

Banks had only a few hours to determine whether a check should be returned because of insufficient funds. Banks were required to "dribble post checks" by sorting and sending the checks to the appropriate bookkeepers as the checks were received. This led to an uneven workload during the course of a business day. At times, the bookkeeping personnel might have nothing to do while at other times they would be required to process a very large number of checks in a very short time. H. Bailey, The Law of Bank Checks (Brady on Bank Checks) § 10.4 (4th ed. 1969). Because of the increasingly large number of checks processed each day and the shortage of qualified bank personnel during World

War II, it became impossible for banks to determine whether a check was "good" in only 24 hours. The banks were forced to resort to the procedure of "paying" for a check on the day it was presented without posting it to the customer's account until the following day. See First National Bank of Elwood v. Universal C.I.T. Credit Corporation, 132 Ind. App. 353, 170 N.E.2d 238, at 244 (1960). To meet this situation, the American Banking Association proposed a Model Deferred Posting Statute. The Model Deferred Posting Statute was not adopted in Kentucky until 1956. 1956 Kentucky Acts, ch. 47 (former KRS 357.125).

Under the Model Deferred Posting statute, a payor bank could give provisional credit for a check on the business day it was received, and the credit could be revoked at any time before midnight of the bank's next business day following receipt. A provisional credit was revoked "by returning the item, or if the item is held for protest or at the time is lost or is not in the possession of the bank, by giving written notice of dishonor, nonpayment, or revocation; provided that such item or notice is dispatched in the mails or by other expeditious means not later than midnight of the bank's next business day after the item was received." 1956 Kentucky Acts, ch. 47, §1(1) (former KRS 357.125). If the payor bank failed to take advantage of the provisions of the deferred posting statute by revoking the provisional credit and returning the check within the time and in the manner provided by the act, the payor bank was deemed to have paid the check and was liable thereon to the holder. First National Bank of Elwood v. Universal C.I.T. Credit Corporation, supra.

The Model Deferred Posting Statute was the basis for the provisions of the Uniform Commercial Code. Under §4.301(1) [R§4-301(a)] of the Uniform Commercial Code (UCC), a payor bank may revoke a provisional "settlement" if it does so before its "midnight deadline" which is midnight of the next banking day following the banking day on which it received the check. Under the Model Deferred Posting Statute, the payor bank's liability for failing to meet its midnight deadline was to be inferred rather than being spelled out in the statute. Under UCC §4.302, the payor bank's liability for missing its midnight deadline is explicit. If the payor bank misses its midnight deadline, the bank is "accountable" for the face amount of the check. See Farmers Cooperative Livestock Market v. Second National Bank, Ky, 427 S.W.2d 247 (1968).

Like the Model Deferred Posting Statute, the Uniform Commercial Code seeks to decrease, rather than increase, the risk of liability to payor banks. By permitting deferred posting, the Uniform Commercial Code extends the time within which a payor bank must determine whether it will pay a check drawn on the bank. Unlike the Bank Collection Code or the Uniform Negotiable Instruments Law as construed by most courts, the Uniform Commercial Code does not require the payor bank to act on the day of receipt or within 24 hours of receipt of a check. The payor bank is granted until midnight of the next business day following the business day on which it received the check.

Excuse For Failing To Meet Midnight Deadline

UCC §4-108(2) [R§4-109(b)] [KRS 355.4-108(2)] provides:

> "Delay by a ... payor bank beyond time limits prescribed or permitted by this Act ... is excused if caused by interruption of communications facilities, suspension of payments by another bank, war, emergency conditions or other circumstances beyond the control of the bank provided it exercises such diligence as the circumstances require."

The circuit court found that the bank's failure to return the two checks by its midnight deadline was excused under the provisions of UCC §4-108.

The circuit court dictated its findings of fact into the record:

"From all of the evidence that was presented in this case, it would appear that there was no intentional action on the bank to hold these checks beyond the normal course of business as an accommodation to its customer. In fact, the uncontroverted testimony of the bank officers was to the contrary. To say that the bank failed, through certain procedures, to return the checks by the midnight deadline does not, in the mind of this Court, imply or establish an intentional act on the part of the bank.

* * *

"In this instance we have the Christmas Holiday, which causes in the bank, as in all businesses, certain emergency and overloaded situations. This is not unique to the banking industry; but is true of virtually every business in a Christian society, in which the holiday of Christmas is observed as the major holiday of the year. Special considerations are always given to employees as well as customers of these banking institutions.

"... On the Christmas Holiday, two machines were broken down for periods of time during this critical day in question. There was an absence of a regular bookkeeper."

Under CR 52.01, these findings of fact cannot be set aside by this court unless they are clearly erroneous. The foregoing findings are supported by the record, and are not questioned by Blake on the appeal.

After making findings of fact, the circuit court dictated the following conclusions into the record:

"... The entire cumulative effect of what happened would constitute diligence on the part of the bank, as circumstances required.

"It is the opinion of the court and it is the finding of the court that the circumstances described by the banking officers, the standards of banking care, as described by expert witnesses, would bring the bank within 4-108(2), and the court therefore, finds as a fact that there were circumstances here beyond the control of the bank, and that it exercised such diligence as those circumstances required."

When the circuit court concluded "that there were circumstances here beyond the control of the bank, and that it exercised such diligence as those circumstances required," the circuit court was doing no more than repeating the words of the statute. This court must determine whether the circuit court's findings of fact support these conclusions.

Before turning to the facts presented in this case, it is appropriate to discuss the only two cases involving the application of UCC §4-108 to a payor bank's midnight deadline. In Sun River Cattle Co. v. Miners Bank of Montana, 164 Mont. 237, 521 P.2d 679, 14 UCC Rep. 1004 (1974), the payor bank utilized a computer in the adjacent town of Great Falls to process its checks. The checks were picked up at the Miners Bank by a armored car between 5:00 p.m. and 6:00 p.m. on the date of receipt. The checks would normally reach the computer center at Great Falls around 10:30 p.m. Ordinarily the checks would have been processed by 11:30 p.m., returned to the Miners Bank by 8:00 a.m. the next morning. The checks in question were received by the Miners Bank on May 11. On that day, the armored car broke down, and the checks did not reach the computer center at Great Falls until 1:30 a.m. the next morning, May 12. On that morning, the computer malfunctioned and the checks were not returned to the Miners Bank until 2:30 p.m. on May 12. There was no testimony as to what actually happened to the checks after they were received by the Miners Bank on the afternoon of May 12, but the Miners Bank failed to return the checks by midnight of May 12. The trial court held that the failure of the Miners Bank to meet its midnight deadline was excused by the provisions of UCC §4-108(2). The Montana Supreme Court reversed, holding that the Miners Bank had failed to show the degree of diligence required under the circumstances. The Montana court pointed out that the Miners Bank had more than the normal interest in the activities in the account upon which the checks were drawn, and that due diligence could not be shown merely by following ordinary operating procedures.

In Port City State Bank v. American National Bank, 486 F.2d 196, 13 UCC Rep. 423 (10th Cir. 1973), the payor bank, American National, was changing from machine posting to computer processing of its checks commencing Monday, December 1, 1969. Two checks were in dispute. The first check arrived at American National on Friday, November 28, 1969. As Monday was the next banking day, the midnight deadline for the first check was December 1. The second check arrived on Tuesday, December 2, 1969, and the midnight deadline for that check was Wednesday, December 3. American National's new computer developed a "memory error" which rendered it unusable at 10:00 a.m. on December 1, the first day of computer operations. The computer manufacturer assured the bank that repairs would not take "too long." Unfortunately repairs and testing were not completed until the early hours of Tuesday, December 2. In the meantime, American National attempted to utilize an identical computer in a bank some two and a half hours away. Processing commenced at the other bank at 11:30 p.m. on December 1, and continued through the night. Although work proceeded to the point of "capturing" all of the items on discs, the backup computer was required by its owner, and the American National personnel returned to the bank to complete the printing of the trial balances. Another memory error developed in the new computer which again rendered the computer unusable. No further use could be made of American National's computer until a new memory module was installed on Thursday, December 4. The trial court held that the computer breakdown constituted a condition beyond the control of American National and that the bank had exercised due diligence. On appeal, the United States Court of Appeals affirmed, holding that the findings of the district court were not clearly erroneous.

* * *

The basic facts found by the circuit court can be summarized as follows: a) the bank had no intention of holding the checks beyond the midnight deadline in order to accommodate its customer; b) there was an increased volume of checks to be handled by reason of the Christmas Holiday; c) two posting machines were broken down for a period of time on December 26; d) one regular bookkeeper was absent because of illness. Standing alone, the bank's intention not to favor its customer by retaining an item beyond the midnight deadline would not justify the application of §4-108(2). The application of the exemption statute necessarily will turn upon the findings relating to heavy volume, machine breakdown, and absence of a bookkeeper.

The bank's president testified that 4,200 to 4,600 checks were processed on a normal day. Because the bank was closed for Christmas on Tuesday, the bank was required to process 6,995 checks on December 26. The bank had four posting machines. On the morning of December 26, two of the machines were temporarily inoperable. One of the machines required two and one half hours to repair. The second machine was repaired in one and one half hours. As the bank had four bookkeepers, the machine breakdown required the bookkeepers to take turns using the posting machines for a time in the morning. One of the four bookkeepers who regularly operated the posting machines was absent because of illness on December 26. This bookkeeper was replaced by the head book-keeper who had experience on the posting machines, although he was not as proficient as a regular posting machine operator.

Because of the cumulative effect of the heavy volume, machine breakdown and absence of a regular bookkeeper, the bank claims it was unable to process the two checks in time to deliver them to the courier from Purolator for return to the Federal Reserve Bank on December 26. As the bank's president testified:

> "Because we couldn't get them ready for the Purolator carrier to pick them up by 4:00 and we tried to get all our work down there to him by 4:00, for him to pick up and these two checks were still being processed in our book-keeping department and it was impossible for those to get into returns for that day."

The increased volume of items to be processed the day after Christmas was clearly foreseeable. The breakdown of the posting machines was not an unusual occurrence, although it was unusual to have two machines broken down at the same time. In any event, it should have been foreseeable to the responsible officers of the bank that the book-keepers would be delayed in completing posting of the checks on December 26. Nevertheless, the undisputed evidence establishes that no arrangements of any kind were made for return of "bad" items which might be discovered by the bookkeepers after the departure of the Purolator courier. The two checks in question were in fact determined by Mrs. Stratton to be "bad" on December 26. The checks were not returned because the regular employee responsible for handling "bad" checks had left for the day, and Mrs. Stratton had no instruction to cover the situation.

Even though the bank missed returning the two checks by the Purolator courier, it was still possible for the bank to have returned the checks by its midnight deadline. Under UCC § 4-301(4)(b) [R§ 4-301(d)(2)] an item is returned when it is "sent" to the bank's transferor, in this case the Federal Reserve Bank. Under UCC § 1-201(38) an item is "sent" when it is deposited in the mail. 1 R. Anderson, Uniform Commercial Code § 1-201 pp. 118-119 (2d ed. 1970). Thus, the bank could have returned the two checks before the midnight deadline by the simple procedure of depositing the two checks in the mail, properly addressed to the Cincinnati branch of the Federal Reserve Bank.

This court concludes that circumstances beyond the control of the bank did not prevent it from returning the two checks in question before its midnight deadline on December 26. The circumstances causing delay in the bookkeeping department were foreseeable. On December 26, the bank actually discovered that the checks were "bad," but the responsible employees and officers had left the bank without leaving any instructions to the bookkeepers. The circuit court erred in holding that the bank was excused under § 4-108 from meeting its midnight deadline. The facts found by the circuit court do not support its conclusion that the circumstances in the case were beyond the control of the bank.

* * *

CONCLUSION

The judgment of the circuit court on the appeal is reversed with directions to enter judgment in favor of Blake for the face amount of the two checks, less a credit for any amounts which Blake may have recovered from Knight. The judgment on the cross-appeal is affirmed. All concur.

C. The Contract of Deposit and Damages for Wrongful Dishonor

We have observed that when a draft is drawn there is usually a preexisting duty on the part of the drawee to accept or pay the draft when presented. A pervasive example of this prior contractual duty is the basic checking account. The usual understanding between the customer and the bank is that the bank is contractually obligated to pay the checks if the customer has money in its account to cover them. Also relevant to this understanding is the properly payable rule: "An item is properly payable if it is authorized by the customer and is in accordance with any agreement between the customer and bank." § 4-401. But what happens if the drawer has money in his account and the bank fails to honor his check when it arrives? We explore the implications of that question here.

Problem 4-1

Weaver bought a tire from Tire Shop, paying with her check for $62.68 drawn on American Savings. Weaver's checking account had sufficient funds to pay the check. Upon presentment, American Savings refused to pay the check and marked on its face "account closed." American Savings timely returned the marked check to Tire Shop, which then swore out a warrant for Weaver's arrest. She was thereafter arrested, charged with petty theft, and temporarily confined. As a result Weaver became ill and her reputation was damaged. Weaver sues American Savings.

1) What must Weaver prove in order to recover damages? §§ 4-402(a), (b); 4-401(a); 4-104(a)(5); 4-105(3).

2) Will Weaver rely on a tort, or contract, theory to recover damages in view of the "proximately caused" language?

3) What will be the validity of the bank's argument that Tire Shop (an intervening cause) and not the bank was the proximate cause of Weaver's arrest?

4) What is the measure of actual and consequential damages? §§ 1-305(a), 4-103(e), 4-402(b).

Q: How much will Mrs. Weaver be awarded?

5) Suppose the check was issued by a well-known merchant to Tire Shop as payment for maintenance of the merchant's vehicles. How would that effect the type of consequential damages? Are damages presumed? § 4-402 OC 1.

D. The Bank's Right to Charge the Drawer's Account: The Properly Payable Rule

At common law, by virtue of the customer-bank contract, the bank was permitted to charge the customer's account only to the extent it had complied with his order to pay out money. Section 4-401 continues this principle by providing that a bank "may charge against the account of a customer an item that is properly payable from the account." The question is, when is a check "properly payable from the account"? We now turn our attention to that question for the remainder of our discussion of the drawer-drawee relationship.

1. Conditional Orders

An order to pay may be conditioned by the terms of the instrument. Of course the instrument would not be negotiable if the order is conditional, but the bank is obliged to heed the condition in any event.

Problem 4-2

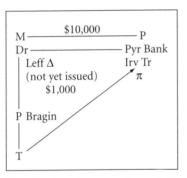

Leff borrowed $10,000 from Irving Trust and as security gave Irving Trust a promissory note to his own order and indorsed by him to Irving Trust. Leff paid $6,000 and then defaulted. In the meantime Leff had made out and signed a check to Bragin for $1,000 drawn on his account with Irving Trust. The check contained the following note in the bottom left corner:

> "Void unless and until title to premises 402-14 Liberty Street, Camden, New Jersey, is taken by Joe Leff."

The check had not yet been delivered to Bragin when Bragin stole it, and ultimately Irving Trust paid it. In due course Leff did obtain title to 402-14 Liberty Street. Irving Trust commenced suit against Leff for the $4,000 balance on the note, without credit for the $1,000 check the bank had paid from Leff's account.

1) What is the relevance of the conditional note on the check? §§ 3-104(a), 3-102.

2) What is the relevance of the fact that Leff never notified the bank about the theft? § 1-103(b).

3) How should the case be resolved? § 4-401.

4) How might the bank protect itself against conditional orders in the future? § 4-103(a).

2. Post-dated Checks, Stale Checks, and Overdrafts

Some old cases followed the rule that the payor bank could not properly charge its customer's account on a check which created an overdraft. Nor could it charge an account after payment of a stale check. What do Articles 3 and 4 do to these rules?

Problem 4-3

On December 14, 2007, Woodward delivered to Hunt a $600 check dated January 14, 2008, and drawn on Lancaster Bank. On January 13, 2008, Woodward gave a letter containing $600 to Zell, an airline flight attendant, instructing her to deliver it that evening to Hunt who was in Philadelphia, and to take up the check and return it to Woodward.

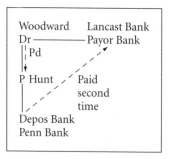

Zell met Hunt in Philadelphia, tendered the letter, and asked for the check. Hunt put his hand in his pocket and said he had left it at home. He said he would give it to Woodward the next week. Hunt did not return the check. Instead, he deposited the check into his account at Penn Bank on January 16, 2008. On January 19, 2008, the check was presented to Lancaster Bank for payment. The bank paid it and charged the amount to Woodward's account which had only $13.86 in it at the time of payment. Later, Lancaster Bank notified Woodward that his check had been paid and demanded reimbursement for the overdraft. Woodward refused to pay.

1) How would you describe the check given to Hunt? § 3-113.

2) What economic function did it perform?

3) Can the payor bank rightly charge Woodward's account? §§ 3-302, 3-304, 1-103(b), 3-305.

4) Who bears the loss, if there is a loss, when an overdue check is paid? § 4-404.

5) Who bears the burden of an overdraft? § 4-401.

6) Suppose the check had been presented for payment a week after it was given to Hunt, i.e., on December 21, 2007, and that the bank had paid it. Woodward, not knowing of the payment, then sends the money to Hunt. Who bears the loss? § 3-113(a).

Problem 4-4

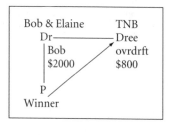

Bob and Elaine Smith maintain a joint checking account at Texas National Bank (TNB). Last week, Bob attended his weekly poker game. Bob's luck hit an all-time low, and he lost over $2,000. To pay his losses he wrote a $2,000 check to the winner. TNB paid the check on presentment, even though payment created an $800 overdraft.

1) Can TNB recover the overdraft from Elaine? § 4-401(b).

2) Assume that TNB's standard deposit account agreement contains the following provision: "If the account is a joint account, each joint owner is responsible for repaying any overdraft, whether or not that joint owner signed the item(s) that created the overdraft or benefitted in any way from payment of the item(s)." Is the provision enforceable? § 4-103(a).

Problem 4-5

After a storm damaged his roof, Steve hired a contractor to repair the damage. The contractor did so and presented a bill for $480. Steve paid with a check that was postdated by a week. Steve told the contractor that he had adequate funds in his account but asked the contractor not to deposit the check prior to the date on the check because payment might trigger a $50 service charge if his balance fell below a certain amount. Sure enough, the contractor immediately deposited the check. Two weeks later, when Steve received his monthly bank statement, he learned that the bank had

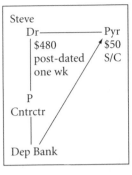

paid the $480 check before the date on the check. Because this premature payment caused Steve's balance to fall below the minimum balance, the statement reflected a $50 service charge.

1) Can Steve recover the $50 service fee from his bank? § 4-401(c).

2) What action might Steve have taken to avoid paying the fee?

3) Assume that Steve's deposit account agreement includes the following provision: "Customer agrees not to issue any post-dated checks. Bank incurs no liability for paying any postdated checks." Is this provision enforceable? § 4-103(a).

3. Order in Which Items May Be Charged

Problem 4-6

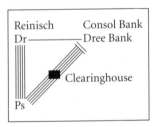

Reinisch, a merchant in Philadelphia, had an account with Consolidated Bank. On the morning of September 4, the account balanace was $3,280.12. On that day the bank was presented with seventeen checks drawn by Reinisch in the aggregate amount of $6,640.45. The largest was $750 and the smallest was $50. The bank declined to pay any of them. Later that day, Reinisch arrived at the bank with a deposit of $4,800. The bank refused to receive the deposit and asked Reinisch to close his account. Reinisch unsuccessfully tried to persuade the bank to reconsider its earlier decision. On September 5, he closed his account and consulted his lawyer.

1) What advice should the lawyer give to Reinisch? §§ 4-303(b); 4-402(a), (b).

2) Is the bank legally obligated to pay until all the funds are gone?

3) In what order would you recommend the checks be paid? What are the alternatives?

4) Suppose there had been only one check drawn by Reinisch for $6,640.45, and that the bank had already decided to return it NSF before Reinisch arrived with the balance needed to pay the check. Would that change the result? § 4-402(c).

Problem 4-7

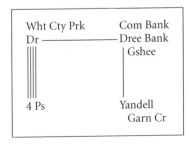

White City Amusement Park had $8,200 in an account with Commerce Bank on July 29, a Friday, and the last business day of the month. On that day the bank received four of White City's checks in the aggregate amount of $7,998.75. These checks came in after 2:00 p.m., which was the bank's cutoff hour. Since these checks had come in after 2:00 p.m., and too late to be posted that day, the posting (i.e., debiting of White City's account) was done at 10:00 a.m.

on Monday, August 1, which was the next business day, but the bank took no further action with respect to the checks. Previously Yandell had commenced suit against White City to collect a $9,000 debt, and he subsequently obtained a writ of garnishment (attachment). On Monday, August 1, at 2:15 p.m., the writ of garnishment was served on the bank, naming White City as the primary debtor and the bank as trustee of all funds held for White City. At that moment, the account balance was insufficient to pay the four checks and Yandell.

Who will prevail—the four payees, or the garnishment creditor?

1) Putting Yandell aside for a moment, how long would Commerce Bank have to decide whether it will pay or dishonor the four checks? §§ 3-502, 4-301. What is meant by "banking day," "midnight deadline," and "settle"? § 4-104(a)(3), (10), (11). See also §§ 4-213 (medium and time of settlement); 4-215 (final payment); 4-108 (time of receipt).

Q: Has the payor bank (Commerce Bank) settled for the checks?

Q: What was the "banking day of receipt"?

Q: What was the "midnight deadline"?

Q: What is "final payment"?

2) Now consider the rights of the garnishment creditor. How would you characterize the competing parties on the facts of the problem? § 4-303.

3) What is the priority rule that resolves this conflict? § 4-303.

4) Has the bank settled for the items as mentioned in § 4-303(a)(3)? § 4-104(a)(11).

5) Does the bank have a "right to revoke the settlement under statute, clearing-house rules, or agreement" as mentioned in § 4-303(a)(3)? §§ 4-108, 4-301, 4-215 OC 4.

Q: Has the bank "made *final payment*" as defined in § 4-215(a)? That is, the items were not "paid ... in cash," but was there a settlement "*without having a right to revoke the settlement under statute, clearing-house rule, or agreement*"?

6) Who will prevail? § 4-303.

Notes

1. In a case where "the bank settles for the item...," §§ 4-215 and 4-301 become relevant. Under § 4-301(a) a provisional settlement may be revoked before the bank's midnight deadline. Thus in a case like **Problem 4-7**, where the bank has settled for an item, the creditor might prevail since the garnishment writ arrived at the bank before the midnight deadline. Depending on the form of bank settlement, under the garnishment mandate the bank may be required to return the checks unpaid and freeze whatever credit the drawer has pending the outcome of the garnishment suit.

2. *The Four Legals*: Banks have traditionally worried that circumstances may arise in the course of business that will impose liability on them or otherwise deprive them of legal rights they would have if adequately forewarned. These fears are in connection with the four following events or rights: (1) stop payment orders, (2) judicial process against a customer's account (e.g., a garnishment or attachment order), (3) death of a customer without notice to the bank, or any other event of which knowledge could have far-reaching consequences, such as knowledge of insolvency proceedings, and (4) the loss of a right of set-off of the drawee-bank's claims against the customer's account. These areas of concern are known as "the four legals." They are set out in § 4-303. The above prob-

lem illustrates the relationship between time of payment of an item and the efficacy of a writ of garnishment on a customer's account. Each of the other four legals will be illustrated as we continue.

4. Forgeries, Fictitious Payees, Impostors, and Alterations

Since the payor bank is permitted to charge the drawer's account only when his instructions have been followed, logically there would be no right to charge where payment was pursuant to a forged signature of the drawer or the forged indorsement of the payee, because the instructions were not from the drawer (forged drawer's signature) or were to pay to the order of the payee (forged indorsement). This is the general rule, but there are exceptions.

VICTORY CLOTHING CO. v. WACHOVIA BANK, N.A.
59 U.C.C. Rep. Serv. 2d 376 (1st Jud. Dist. Pa. 2006)

ABRAMSON, J.

Background:

This is a subrogation action brought by the insurance carrier for plaintiff Victory Clothing, Inc., d/b/a Torre Clothing ("Victory") to recover funds paid to Victory under an insurance policy. This matter arises out of thefts from Victory's commercial checking account by its office manager and bookkeeper, Jeanette Lunny ("Lunny"). Lunny was employed by Victory for approximately twenty-four (24) years until she resigned in May 2003. From August 2001 through May 2003, Lunny deposited approximately two hundred (200) checks drawn on Victory's corporate account totaling $188,273.00 into her personal checking account at defendant Wachovia Bank, N.A. ("Wachovia"). Lunny's scheme called for engaging in "double forgeries" (discussed *infra*). Lunny would prepare the checks in the company's computer system, and make the checks payable to known vendors of Victory (e.g., Adidas, Sean John), to whom no money was actually owed. The checks were for dollar amounts that were consistent with the legitimate checks to those vendors. She would then forge the signature of Victory's owner, Mark Rosenfeld ("Rosenfeld"), on the front of the check, and then forge the indorsement of the unintended payee (Victory's various vendors) on the reverse side of the check. The unauthorized checks were drawn on Victory's bank account at Hudson Bank (the "drawee bank" or "payor bank"). After forging the indorsement of the payee, Lunny either indorsed the check with her name followed by her account number, or referenced her account number following the forged indorsement. She then deposited the funds into her personal bank account at Wachovia (the "depositary bank" or "collecting bank").

At the time of the fraud by Lunny, Wachovia's policies and regulations regarding the acceptance of checks for deposit provided that "checks payable to a non-personal payee can be deposited ONLY into a non-personal account with the same name." (Emphasis in original).

Rosenfeld reviewed the bank statements from Hudson Bank on a monthly basis. However, among other observable irregularities, he failed to detect that Lunny had forged his signature on approximately two hundred (200) checks. Nor did he have a procedure to match checks to invoices.

In its Complaint, Victory asserted a claim against Wachovia pursuant to the Pennsylvania Commercial Code, 13 Pa.C.S. §§ 3405 and 3406. A bench trial was held on September 21, 2005. At trial, Victory asserted a claim solely under 13 Pa.C.S. § 3405.... Section 3405 of the Pennsylvania Commercial Code states, in relevant part:

§ 3405. Employer's responsibility for fraudulent indorsement by employee

(b) RIGHTS AND LIABILITIES. – For the purpose of determining the rights and liabilities of a person who, in good faith, pays an instrument or takes it for value or for collection, if an employer entrusted an employee with responsibility with respect to the instrument and the employee or a person acting in concert with the employee makes a fraudulent indorsement of the instrument, the indorsement is effective as the indorsement of the person to whom the instrument is payable if it is made in the name of that person. If the person paying the instrument or taking it for value or for collection fails to exercise ordinary care in paying or taking the instrument and that failure substantially contributes to loss resulting from the fraud, the person bearing the loss may recover from the person failing to exercise ordinary care to the extent the failure to exercise ordinary care contributed to the loss.

In essence, Victory contends that Wachovia's actions in accepting the checks payable to various businesses for deposit into Lunny's personal account were commercially unreasonable, contrary to Wachovia's own internal rules and regulations, and exhibited a want of ordinary care....

Discussion:
I. Double Forgeries

As stated *supra*, this case involves a double forgery situation. This matter presents a question of first impression in the Pennsylvania state courts, namely how should the loss be allocated in double forgery situations. A double forgery occurs when the negotiable instrument contains both a forged maker's signature and a forged indorsement. The Uniform Commercial Code ("UCC" or "Code") addresses the allocation of liability in cases where either the maker's signature is forged or where the indorsement of the payee or holder is forged.... However, the drafters of the UCC failed to specifically address the allocation of liability in double forgery situations.... Consequently, the courts have been left to determine how liability should be allocated in a double forgery case.

The seminal case on double forgeries is *Perini Corp. v. First National Bank*, 553 F.2d 398 (5th Cir.1977). The facts of *Perini* can be summarized as follows:

Perini Corp. maintained checking accounts with two New York banks, and drew against these accounts using preprinted checks signed by a facsimile signature machine. Seventeen preprinted checks were stolen, run through the machine and made out to the order of Quisenberry Contracting Co. and Southern Contracting Co., both fictitious firms. A man calling himself Jesse D. Quisenberry opened accounts in the names of these payees at First National Bank, deposited the stolen checks in these accounts [by indorsing them in a personal capacity, signing simply "Jesse D. Quisenberry"] and later withdrew almost all of the credit in both accounts.

When Perini discovered the fraud, Quisenberry was long gone. Worse still, Perini had filed a facsimile specimen with its two banks and agreed to hold them harmless if checks purporting to bear the facsimile signature were honored. Perini was left with recourse against First National Bank only. First National Bank found itself in a bind, because Quisenberry had indorsed the checks to the fictitious companies in his *personal* capacity, yet First National Bank offered no resistance to this practice. The checks therefore presented an unusual combination of circumstances: they bore undoubtedly forged drawer's signatures, but also bore indorsements that could also be characterized as forged.

See White & Summers, Uniform Commercial Code, § 16-4 at 585 (5th ed., West 2000).

In its analysis of how to treat a double forgery case, the Court in *Perini* examined the loss allocation principles applied by the Code in cases of single forgeries. The Court observed that in cases where only the maker's signature was forged, liability generally rested with the drawee bank; however, in cases where there was only a forged indorsement, the drawee bank could generally "pass liability back through the collection chain to the party who took from the forger [usually the depositary bank] and, of course, to the forger himself if available." *Perini*, 553 F.2d at 403, 405.

The traditional rationale for placing liability on the drawee bank in cases of checks bearing only a forged maker's signature is that the drawee bank is in the best position to recognize the maker's signature (its customer), and therefore is in the best position to discover the forgery. Id. at 405. A less fictional rationalization for this rule is that the UCC drafters believed that "it is highly desirable to end the transaction on an instrument when it is paid rather than reopen and upset a series of commercial transactions at a later date when the forgery is discovered." Id. In contrast, the rationale for placing liability on the depositary bank in cases of checks bearing a forged indorsement is that the depositary bank is in the best position to detect the false indorsement, such as by verifying the identification of the person making the deposit. Id. at 405, 406. However, the Court recognized that this superior ability by the depositary bank to detect a forged indorsement may be reduced in the case of a double forgery:

> Someone forging a check will likely draw the check to a payee whose identity he can readily assume, such as himself or a fictitious person. In such circumstances the party who first takes the check may well have no particular opportunity to detect any impropriety in the indorsement.

Id. at 406. The Court then emphasized the Code's commitment to finality, and concluded that a check bearing a double forgery should be treated as a check bearing only a forged maker's signature. Thus, the Court held that in double forgery situations, liability should fall on the drawee bank.

In addition to the finality principle, there is a separate, but related, reason for the rule announced in *Perini*. This rationale, known as the "loss causation principle," can be explained as follows:

> In a double forgery situation a check was never validly drawn to a payee entitled to payment, and hence, no true payee can appear with a claim against the drawer or drawee. Neither the drawer or drawee, therefore, can be said to have suffered a loss attributable to the forged indorsement, but rather the loss results from the drawee having paid the check over the forged drawer's signature where no payment was ever intended.

See Travelers Indemnity Co., 895 F.Supp. at 748, citing National Credit, 771 F.2d at 157-58; Perini, 553 F.2d at 414-15. Thus, under this reasoning, double forgeries should be treated as if they only bear a forged drawer's signature because the forged indorsement was not the cause of the drawer's loss. See National Credit, 771 F.2d at 159. In other words, "whatever negligence caused the collecting bank to pay the forger over the forged indorsement, such negligence cannot be regarded as the cause of the customer's loss. Loss accrued only when the customer's account was debited by the drawee bank, not when the forger collected on his indorsement." See Brighton, Inc. v. Colonial First National Bank, 176 N.J. Super. 101, 116, 422 A.2d 433, 440 (N.J. Super. Ct. App. Div.1980), aff'd, 86 N.J. 259, 430 A.2d 902 (N.J.1981).

Numerous jurisdictions have since adopted the *Perini* holding and have treated double forgery cases, for loss allocation purposes, as cases bearing only the forged maker's signature....

II. The Effect of the UCC Revisions

In 1990, new revisions to Articles 3 and 4 of the UCC were implemented (the "revisions").... The new revisions made a major change in the area of double forgeries.... Before the revisions, the case law was uniform in treating a double forgery case as a forged drawer's signature case, with the loss falling on the drawee bank (as outlined above).... The revisions, however, changed this rule by shifting to a comparative fault approach.... Under the revised version of the UCC, the loss in double forgery cases is allocated between the depositary and drawee banks based on the extent that each contributed to the loss.... Thus, under the revised Code, a depositary bank may not necessarily escape liability in double forgery situations, as they did under the prior law....

Specifically, revised § 3-405 of the UCC, entitled "Employer's Responsibility for Fraudulent Indorsement by Employee," introduced the concept of comparative fault as between the employer of the dishonest employee/embezzler and the bank(s). This is the section under which Victory sued Wachovia. Section 3-405(b) states, in relevant part:

> If the person paying the instrument or taking it for value or for collection fails to exercise ordinary care in paying or taking the instrument and that failure substantially contributes to loss resulting from the fraud, the person bearing the loss may recover from the person failing to exercise ordinary care to the extent the failure to exercise ordinary care contributed to the loss.

Wachovia argues that this section is applicable only in cases of forged indorsements, and not in double forgery situations. However, at least one court has found that the new revisions have made section 3-405 apply to double forgery situations. The case of *Gina Chin & Associates, Inc. v. First Union Bank*, 256 Va. 59, 500 S.E.2d 516 (Va.1998), involved a double forgery scheme where an employee of the Gina Chin company (the "company") forged the signature of one of the company's officers on a number of checks that were made payable to the company's suppliers. Id. at 61, 500 S.E.2d 516. The employee then forged the indorsements of the payees, and deposited the checks into her own account at First Union Bank ("First Union"). Id. The drawee banks then paid the checks and debited a total of $270,488.72 from the company's account. Id. The company sued First Union (the depositary bank) under revised sections 3-404 and 3-405. Id. The company alleged that First Union was negligent in accepting the forged checks for payment, and that the acceptance of the forged checks was in contravention of established banking standards. Id. at 63, 500 S.E.2d 516. First Union argued that the company did not have a cause of action against it under those sections because those sections only applied to forged indorsements, and not to double forgery situations. Id. at 61, 500 S.E.2d 516. The Virginia Supreme Court rejected this argument and held that sections 3-404 and 3-405 may be used by a drawer against the depositary bank in double forgery situations. Id. The Court stated:

The revisions to [§§ 3-404 and 3-405] changed the previous law by allowing "the person bearing the loss" to seek recovery for a loss caused by the negligence of any person paying the instrument or taking it for value based on comparative negligence principles. The concept of comparative negligence introduced in the revised sections reflects a determination that all participants in the process have a duty to exercise ordinary care in the drawing and handling of instruments and that the failure to exercise that duty will result in liability to the person sustaining the loss. Nothing in the statutory language indicates that, where the signature of the drawer is forged, the drawer cannot qualify as a "person bearing the loss" or that the drawer is otherwise precluded from seeking recovery from a depositary bank under these sections. In the absence of any specific exclusion, we conclude that the sections are applicable in double forgery situations.

Id. at 62, 500 S.E.2d 516. Accordingly, the Court determined that the company was not precluded from asserting a cause of action against First Union under sections 3-404 and 3-405. Id. at 63, 500 S.E.2d 516.

The Court finds the reasoning of *Gina Chin & Associates* persuasive and holds that, under the revised Code, a drawer is not precluded from seeking recovery from a depositary bank in a double forgery situation under section 3-405. Therefore, Victory can maintain its cause of action against Wachovia under 13 Pa.C.S. § 3405.

III. The Fictitious Payee Rule

Lunny made the fraudulent checks payable to actual vendors of Victory with the intention that the vendors not get paid. Wachovia therefore argues that Victory's action against it should be barred by the fictitious payee rule under [§ 3404].... Section 3404 of the Pennsylvania Commercial Code states, in relevant part:

§ 3404. Impostors; fictitious payees

(b) FICTITIOUS PAYEE. – If a person whose intent determines to whom an instrument is payable (section 3110(a) or (b)) does not intend the person identified as payee to have any interest in the instrument or the person identified as payee of an instrument is a fictitious person, the following rules apply until the instrument is negotiated by special indorsement:

(1) Any person in possession of the instrument is its holder.

(2) An indorsement by any person in the name of the payee stated in the instrument is effective as the indorsement of the payee in favor of a person who, in good faith, pays the instrument or takes it for value or for collection.

The fictitious payee rule applies when a dishonest employee writes checks to a company's actual vendors, but intends that the vendors never receive the money; instead, the employee forges the names of the payees and deposits the checks at another bank.... Under section 3-404(b) of the UCC, the indorsement is deemed to be "effective" since the employee did not intend for the payees to receive payment.... The theory under the rule is that since the indorsement is "effective," the drawee bank was justified in debiting the company's account.... Therefore, the loss should fall on the company whose employee committed the fraud....

Revised UCC § 3-404 changed the prior law by introducing a comparative fault principle.... Subsection (d) of 3-404 provides that if the person taking the checks fails to exercise ordinary care, "the person bearing the loss may recover from the person failing to exercise ordinary care to the extent the failure to exercise ordinary care contributed to the loss." Therefore, "although the fictitious payee rule makes the indorsement 'effective,' the corporate drawer can shift the loss to any negligent bank, to the extent that the bank's negligence substantially contributed to the loss." ... Under the revised Code, the drawer now has the right to sue the depository bank directly based on the bank's negligence.... Under the Old Code, the fictitious payee rule was a "jackpot" defense for depository banks because most courts held that the depository bank's own negligence was irrelevant.... However, under revised UCC §§ 3-404 and 3-405, the fictitious payee defense triggers principles of comparative fault, so a depository bank's own negligence may be considered by the trier of fact....

Under the revised UCC, a double forgery situation would still be treated as a fictitious payee situation under Section 3-404(b).... Comparative fault would again come into play as between the drawer, drawee bank, and depository bank.... The liability of either the drawer or drawee bank could be shifted upstream to the depository bank where the dishonest employee opened his or her account.... This result under the revised Code "differs sharply from the result under the old Code, where double forgery cases were treated as forged drawer's signature cases, with the depository bank escaping liability based on the finality of payment principle and the notion that the forged indorsement was irrelevant because of the fictitious payee rule." ... Therefore, based on the foregoing reasons, the fictitious payee defense does not help Wachovia in this case.

IV. Allocation of Liability

As stated *supra*, comparative negligence applies in this case because of the revisions in the Code. In determining the liability of the parties, the Court has considered, *inter alia*, the following factors:

• At the time of the fraud by Lunny, Wachovia's policies and regulations regarding the acceptance of checks for deposit provided that "checks payable to a non-personal payee can be deposited ONLY into a non-personal account with the same name." (Emphasis in original)....

• Approximately two hundred (200) checks drawn on Victory's corporate account were deposited into Lunny's personal account at Wachovia....

• The first twenty-three (23) fraudulent checks were made payable to entities that were not readily distinguishable as businesses, such as "Sean John." ... The check dated December 17, 2001 was the first fraudulent check made payable to a payee that was clearly a business, specifically "Beverly Hills Shoes, Inc." ...

• In 2001, Victory had approximately seventeen (17) employees, including Lunny....

• Lunny had been a bookkeeper for Victory from approximately 1982 until she resigned in May 2003.... Rosenfeld never had any problems with Lunny's bookkeeping before she resigned....

• Lunny exercised primary control over Victory's bank accounts....

• Between 2001 and 2003, the checks that were generated to make payments to Victory's vendors were all computerized checks generated by Lunny. No other Victory employee, other than Lunny, knew how to generate the computerized checks, including Rosenfeld....

• The fraudulent checks were made payable to known vendors of Victory in amounts that were consistent with previous legitimate checks to those vendors....

• After forging the indorsement of the payee, Lunny either indorsed the check with her name followed by her account number, or referenced her account number following the forged indorsement.... All of the checks that were misappropriated had the same exact account number, which was shown on the back side of the checks....

• About ten (10) out of approximately three hundred (300) checks each month were forged by Lunny and deposited into her personal account.

• Rosenfeld reviewed his bank statements from Hudson Bank on a monthly basis.

• Rosenfeld received copies of Victory's cancelled checks from Hudson Bank on a monthly basis. However, the copies of the cancelled checks were not in their normal size; instead, they were smaller, with six checks (front and back side) on each page....

• The forged indorsements were written out in longhand, i.e. Lunny's own handwriting, rather than a corporate stamped signature....

• Victory did not match its invoices for each check at the end of each month.

• An outside accounting firm performed quarterly reviews of Victory's bookkeeping records, and then met with Rosenfeld.... This review was not designed to pick up fraud or misappropriation....

Based on the foregoing, the Court finds that Victory and Wachovia are comparatively negligent. With regard to Wachovia's negligence, it is clear that Wachovia was negligent in violating its own rules in repeatedly depositing corporate checks into Lunny's personal account at Wachovia. Standard commercial bank procedures dictate that a check made payable to a business be accepted only into a business checking account with the same title as the business.... Had a single teller at Wachovia followed Wachovia's rules, the fraud would have been detected as early as December 17, 2001, when the first fraudulently created non-personal payee check was presented for deposit into Lunny's personal checking account.... Instead, Wachovia permitted another one hundred and seventy-six (176) checks to be deposited into Lunny's account after December 17, 2001.... The Court finds that Wachovia failed to exercise ordinary care, and that failure substantially contributed to Victory's loss resulting from the fraud.[3] Therefore, the Court concludes that Wachovia is seventy (70) percent liable for Victory's loss.

Victory, on the other hand, was also negligent in its supervision of Lunny, and for not discovering the fraud for almost a two-year period. Rosenfeld received copies of the cancelled checks, albeit smaller in size, on a monthly basis from Hudson Bank. The copies of the checks displayed both the front and back of the checks.... Rosenfeld was negligent in not recognizing his own forged signature on the front of the checks, as well as not spotting his own bookkeeper's name and/or account number on the back of the checks (which appeared far too many times and on various "payees" checks to be seen as regular by a non-negligent business owner).

Further, there were inadequate checks and balances in Victory's record keeping process. For example, Victory could have ensured that it had an adequate segregation of duties, meaning that more than one person would be involved in any control activity.... Here, Lunny exercised primary control over Victory's bank accounts. Another

---

3. Official Comment 4 to UCC § 3-405 states: "Failure to exercise ordinary care is to be determined in the context of all the facts relating to the bank's conduct with respect to the bank's collection of the check. If the trier of fact finds that there was such a failure and that the failure substantially contributed to loss, it could find the depositary bank liable to the extent the failure contributed to the loss." "Ordinary care" is defined as the "observance of reasonable commercial standards, prevailing in the area in which the person is located with respect to the business in which the person is engaged." See UCC § 3-103(9).

Victory employee, or Rosenfeld himself, could have reviewed Lunny's work. In addition, Victory could have increased the amount of authorization that was needed to perform certain transactions.... For example, any check that was over a threshold monetary amount would have to be authorized by more than one individual.... This would ensure an additional control on checks that were larger in amounts. Furthermore, Victory did not match its invoices for each check at the end of each month.... When any check was created by Victory's computer system, the value of the check was automatically assigned to a general ledger account before the check could be printed.... The values in the general ledger account could have been reconciled at the end of each month with the actual checks and invoices.... This would not have been overly burdensome or costly because Victory already had the computer system that could do this in place. Based on the foregoing, the Court concludes that Victory is also thirty (30) percent liable for the loss.

CONCLUSION

For all the foregoing reasons, the Court finds that Wachovia is 70% liable and Victory is 30% liable for the $188,273.00 loss. Therefore, Victory Clothing Company, Inc. is awarded $131,791.10. The Court will enter a contemporaneous Order consistent with this Opinion.

JUDGMENT

AND NOW this 21st day of March, 2006, the Court finds in favor of plaintiff Victory Clothing Company, Inc. and against defendant Wachovia Bank, N.A in the amount of $188,273.00, less thirty (30) percent of that amount based on plaintiff Victory Clothing Company Inc.'s comparative negligence, as set forth in the Court's contemporaneously filed Opinion. Therefore, plaintiff Victory Clothing Company, Inc. is awarded $131,791.10.

Note

The opinion cites and discusses *Gina Chin & Associates, Inc. v. First Union Bank*, a case that appears after **Problem 4-13**.

SCHRIER BROTHERS v. GOLUB

56 U.C.C. Rep. Serv. 2d 317 (3rd Cir. 2005)

RENDELL, Circuit Judge.

Appellee/Plaintiff Schrier Brothers, a division of Bunzel Distribution Northeast, LLC, brought this action against Appellant/Defendant Hudson United Bank ('HUB') and other Defendants seeking damages for the conversion of six checks payable to Schrier Brothers by its former employee Harvey Golub. Golub, a salesperson, fraudulently indorsed checks collected from his customers and deposited them in his own commercial account with HUB. The District Court granted summary judgment to Schrier Brothers. On appeal, HUB's principal argument is that the District Court erred in its ruling because Golub was an employee with 'responsibility' over the checks within the meaning of N.J. Stat. Ann. § 12A:3-405 (corresponding to Uniform Commercial Code § 3-405) and, therefore, the loss may fall on Schrier Brothers.

The District Court had jurisdiction pursuant to 28 U.S.C. § 1334(b), as this case was related to Golub's bankruptcy proceeding. We have jurisdiction over this appeal of a final judgment and order by the District Court pursuant to 28 U.S.C. § 1291. Because we believe the District Court erred in concluding that Golub was not an employee entrusted with responsibility with respect to the checks under N.J. Stat. Ann. § 12A:3-405, we will reverse and remand.

I.

The facts of this case are relatively straightforward. Harvey Golub worked as a salesperson for Schrier Brothers, a wholesaler of paper products and janitorial supplies. Golub's responsibilities included locating new potential customers and servicing existing customers by going to their places of business, taking orders, and selling new products. Schrier Brothers' customers typically paid for orders by mailing a check to the company's 'lockbox,' where bookkeeping staff would receive and process payments. Customers could, however, also tender payment by check or cash to salespersons, like Golub, or to the drivers who delivered orders. When drivers accepted payments, they were instructed to bring them back to the office, as drivers would typically leave from and return to the office each day. When salespersons accepted payments, however, they were instructed to send them directly to the lockbox by express mail, as salespersons did not necessarily return to the office each day. For cash payments, salespersons were instructed to obtain and mail a money order to the lockbox, rather than sending cash. Payment to salespersons and drivers was not encouraged by Schrier Brothers, but the company offered this alternative form of payment as an accommodation to its customers, and this method of payment was favorable with and frequently used by Schrier Brothers' 'street business' customers, e.g., smaller retailers, as opposed to its larger distributor or wholesale customers.

In November 2001, Golub received six checks from customers, made payable to Schrier Brothers, totaling $121,614.43. Instead of mailing the checks directly to the lockbox, Golub deposited them in an account maintained by a company he owned, H & H Food Brokers, at HUB. Golub indorsed each check with the words 'Schrier Brothers Inc' or 'Schrier Brothers' and the account number of his H & H account. HUB accepted the checks for deposit, deposited them into the H & H account, and sometime following HUB's acceptance, the drawee banks made payment to HUB for the face amounts of the checks.

Since the fraud was exposed, Golub has reimbursed Schrier Brothers in the amount of $18,895.67; Schrier Brothers now seeks to recover the remaining $102,718.76. The action was originally brought in the Superior Court of New Jersey for fraud and conversion against Golub, negligence and conversion against the drawee banks, and fraud, negligence, and conversion against HUB. Eventually the action was removed to federal court.

The District Court granted summary judgment for Schrier Brothers on its claims against HUB and dismissed the complaint with prejudice as against the drawee banks. Interpreting N.J. Stat. Ann. § 12A:3-405, the District Court concluded that Golub did not have 'responsibility' for the checks because he had limited access to them and was "merely authorized ... to forward customers' checks to the company lockbox," but did not have "continuing access to the checks needed to cover [his] tracks." (Dist. Ct. Op. at 6.) The District Court reasoned that because "Golub simply had access to the checks, not responsibility for them[,] Section 3-405 does not shift the loss to Schrier Brothers," and HUB is liable for conversion of the checks. (Id.) The District Court dismissed the claims against the drawee banks because Schrier Brothers had made an equivocal suggestion that it would consider dismissal absent evidence of negligence or other improper conduct and indeed failed to adduce such evidence.

II.

We exercise plenary review over the District Court's grant of summary judgment, applying the same test as the District Court.... To affirm the grant of summary judgment, we must be convinced that there is no genuine issue as to any material fact and that the moving party is entitled to a judgment as a matter of law when the facts are viewed in the light most favorable to the non-moving party. Fed.R.Civ.P. 56(c).

III.

A. 'Responsibility'

Under N.J. Stat. Ann. § 12A:3-420(a), "[a]n instrument is ... converted if it is taken by transfer, other than a negotiation, from a person not entitled to enforce the instrument or a bank makes or obtains payment with respect to the instrument for a person not entitled to enforce the instrument or receive payment." Under the normal operation of this Section, the bank bears the risk of loss when it makes or obtains payment on a fraudulently indorsed check. However, N.J. Stat. Ann. § 12A:3-405 will shift the burden of the loss to the named payee of a fraudulently indorsed check when the bank has acted in good faith and the indorsement is made by an employee of the payee entrusted with 'responsibility' for the check. 'Responsibility' is defined under the same section as follows:

> "Responsibility" with respect to instruments means authority to: sign or indorse instruments on behalf of the employer; process instruments received by the employer for bookkeeping purposes, for deposit to an account, or for other disposition; prepare or process instruments for issue in the name of the employer; supply information determining the names or addresses of payees of instruments to be issued in the name of the employer; control the disposition of instruments to be issued in the name of the employer; or act otherwise with respect to instruments in a responsible capacity. "Responsibility" does not include authority that merely allows an employee to have access to instruments or blank or incomplete instrument forms that are being stored or transported or are part of incoming or outgoing mail, or similar access.

N.J. Stat. Ann. § 12A:3-405(a)(3).

It is undisputed that Golub was an employee of Schrier Brothers and that he fraudulently indorsed the checks. If Golub was an employee entrusted with responsibility for the checks under Section 12A:3-405(a)(3), then Schrier Brothers may bear the loss of the fraud, depending on whether HUB acted in good faith and exercised ordinary care. If he was not an employee with responsibility, then HUB bears the loss under Section 12A:3-420.

In *Menichini v. Grant*, we commented on the "newly enacted" but yet-to-take-effect revision of UCC Article 3 under Pennsylvania law and opined that revised Section 3-405 "generally denies an employer the ability to externalize the costs of employee embezzlement, virtually creating a bright line making fraudulent indorsements effective against the employer when employees who have 'responsibility with respect to instruments' forge indorsements." 995 F.2d 1224, 1233 (3d Cir.1993).... This principle justified placing on the employer rather than the bank the burden of the loss of the fraud committed by an employee of a legal support services firm who singly had the responsibilities of bookkeeping and receiving payments without supervision or any control mechanisms.... A number of state courts construing UCC Section 3-405 have come to conclusions consistent with this interpretation....

The statute gives little direction as to the limits of "responsibility," and even the "catch all" phrase at the end of the relevant section circles back to the concept of "responsible capacity." The courts have not really defined "responsible" except to say that certain fact patterns do or do not fit within its bounds. We, too, are left to examine the facts and determine how we view Golub's responsibility as it relates to the checks and monies entrusted to him in the course of his job.

Here, as noted above, Golub was authorized to accept payments from customers, both by check and in cash, and he was instructed to send anything he accepted to Schrier Brothers' lockbox by express mail. Although Golub was not authorized to indorse any of the checks he accepted on behalf of Schrier Brothers, he had more than just occasional or fortuitous access to them. Schrier Brothers expressly authorized him, and indeed all its salespersons, to accept payments whenever customers tendered them. Regardless of the reasoning behind this policy or the company's apparent preference for its customers to pay by sending a check directly to its lockbox, the fact remains that Golub regularly accepted payments, especially in the company's street business, at the customer's discretion and under circumstances where Schrier Brothers would have no way of monitoring when a payment had been made until it was received in the lockbox or, in the case of the converted checks, until no check had been received in the lockbox after a customer's payment term expired. Additionally, with respect to cash payments, Golub was entrusted with obtaining and mailing money orders; this presented a clear opportunity for hard-to-detect defalcation. As such, we disagree with the District Court's conclusion that Schrier Brothers "merely authorized [Golub] to forward customers' checks to the lockbox," and, therefore, that he had access to the checks, but not responsibility for them. (Dist. Ct. Op. at 6.) The regularity and authorization of Golub's practice of accepting checks coupled with the relative lack of control Schrier Brothers exercised over this practice leads us to conclude that Golub acted "in a responsible capacity" with respect to the checks, and, consequently, that Golub was an employee entrusted with "responsibility" with respect to the checks....

Further, we note that our conclusion is consistent with the policy underlying the shifting of the burden of the loss under this Section. Truly, this is a case where, as the UCC commentary explains, "the employer is in a far better position to avoid the loss by care in choosing employees, in supervising them, and in adopting other measures to prevent forged indorsements on instruments payable to the employer." UCC § 3-405 cmt. 1. The risk of loss, therefore, "should fall on the employer rather than the bank that takes the check or pays it, if the bank was not negligent in the transaction." Id.

B. HUB's Good Faith and Deviation from the Standard of Ordinary Care

A bank may only invoke the protection of N.J. Stat. Ann. § 12A:3-405(b) if it "pays the instrument or takes it for collection" in "good faith." Because the District Court determined that Golub did not have responsibility with respect to the checks, it did not reach the issue of HUB's good faith.

Additionally, under N.J. Stat. Ann. § 12A:3-405(b), once it has been determined that the bank acted in good faith and that the employee had been entrusted with responsibility with respect to the fraudulently indorsed checks, the employer must bear the loss unless it can prove that the bank "fail[ed] to exercise ordinary care in paying or taking the instrument and that failure substantially contribute[d] to loss resulting from the fraud." Upon such a showing, 'the person bearing the loss may recover from the person failing to exercise ordinary care to the extent the failure to exercise ordinary care contributed to the loss." N.J. Stat. Ann. § 12A:3-405(b). Because the District Court determined that Golub did not have responsibility with respect to the checks, it did not reach the issue of HUB's negligence.

Consequently, in light of our contrary conclusion on the issue of responsibility, we will remand this case to the District Court for a determination as to whether HUB acted in good faith and, if so, exercised ordinary care.

IV.

For the foregoing reasons, we will REVERSE the District Court's judgment and RE-MAND for further proceedings consistent with this opinion.

Problem 4-8

Security Bank (drawee)
|
Grocery store, bar, Security Bank branch
 (cashed by Green)
|
Employees (former)
 Green (forged indorsements)
|
Edgington (drawer)
 Green (payroll clerk, submits
 time sheets for former employees)

Edgington was in the oil business and had an account with Security Bank. His payroll clerk, Green, was responsible for collecting time sheets of employees, preparing payroll checks, submitting them to Edgington for signature, and then turning them over to the foreman for distribution to the employees. If an employee was absent Green would hold the check and the employee would pick it up the next day. At the end of the month Green took the canceled checks and statement and forwarded them to the accountant at the refinery. Upon investigating excessive expenditures from petty cash in the office, Edgington discovered Green had been forging payee indorsements and keeping the money. Beginning in May 2006, shortly after being hired, Green began naming former employees as payees and also preparing fictitious time sheets for them. After the checks were signed by Edgington, Green would indorse the names of the payees. Then he would take the checks to a local grocery store, a bar, and sometimes a branch of Security Bank, indorse his own name in pencil, and cash them. When the checks were returned with the statement, Green would erase his indorsement, in some cases not completely. By the time Edgington discovered the scam in June of 2008, the loss amounted to about $70,000.

1) Who will bear the loss? §§ 4-401(a), 3-404, 3-405, 3-406.

Q: Has Edgington, Green's employer, "entrusted an employee (Green) with responsibility"?

Q: What is the effect of a fraudulent indorsement by a responsible employee?

Q: What is the rationale?

Q: Does § 3-406 resolve this problem?

Q: Why does § 3-404(b) not resolve this problem?

Q: Would § 3-404(b) apply if Green and Edgington had co-signed the checks?

2) Suppose Green never indorsed any of the checks but deposited them into accounts that he had opened in the names of the payees. Does § 3-405 apply?

3) Suppose Green had not indorsed the instruments in his own name. Instead he posed as the payee and indorsed the payee's name. Because of its negligence in not asking for identification when Green cashed checks at its branch, Security Bank was required to re-credit Edgington's account. § 3-405(b) (last sentence). On what theories might Green be liable to Security Bank? §§ 3-403(c); 3-415(a); 3-416(a) and 3-203 OC 1 (third paragraph); 3-417(a), (b).

TITLE INSURANCE CO. OF MINNESOTA v. COMERICA BANK – CALIFORNIA

24 U.C.C. Rep. Serv. 2d 584 (Cal. Ct. App. 1994)

MIHARA, Associate Justice.

At issue in this appeal is the applicability and scope of the "impostor rule," which makes an indorsed check effective if the drawer was induced to issue the check by an impersonator of the payee.... Plaintiff Title Insurance Company of Minnesota contends the trial court erroneously applied this rule in sustaining the demurrer of the drawee bank, respondent Comerica Bank-California ("Bank"), to plaintiff's complaint for negligence. We agree that the impostor rule is not applicable under the circumstances presented, and accordingly reverse the judgment of dismissal.

Allegations of the Complaint

A general demurrer presents the same question to the appellate court as to the trial court—namely, whether the plaintiff has alleged sufficient facts in the complaint to justify relief on any legal theory.... Accordingly, in reviewing an order sustaining a demurrer, we assume the truth of all material facts properly pleaded in the complaint and determine whether it states any valid claim entitling the plaintiff to relief.... In light of this established principle of review, we summarize the facts as alleged in plaintiff's first amended complaint.

Plaintiff is the assignee of the interests of First National Mortgage Company ("FNMC"), who made two equity loans to Helen Nastor ("Helen"), secured by deeds of trust. Plaintiff issued a policy of land title insurance for each of these loans.

On September 22, 1988, FNMC issued a check payable to Helen in the amount of $58,659.29, the proceeds of the first loan. FNMC gave the check to Helen's son, Rudy Nastor ("Rudy"), for delivery to Helen. That day, someone impersonating Helen indorsed the check and presented it to Bank, where FNMC held an account. Bank paid the impersonator the full amount of the check.

On December 29, 1988, FNMC made a second loan to Helen in the amount of $108,300. Part of the proceeds of this loan were used to pay off the first loan. The remainder was issued to Rudy in the form of a check made payable to him.

When FNMC failed to receive payment on the $108,300 loan, it initiated nonjudicial foreclosure proceedings against Helen's property. On October 17, 1989, Helen's attorney informed FNMC that its deed of trust on the property was invalid because it had been executed by Rudy using a forged power of attorney. Helen thereafter testified by deposition that she had not executed the power of attorney, nor had she indorsed or presented the check to Bank for payment.

FNMC made a claim for payment under the second title insurance policy, and plaintiff paid FNMC $108,300. Plaintiff, acting as subrogee and assignee with respect to FNMC's claim, then sued Bank for negligence, seeking recovery of the $108,000. According to the first amended complaint, Bank had a duty "to establish and practice such procedures and business practices as are or may be reasonably necessary and effective to avoid a breach of any of the duties of care owed by BANK ... to the depositors and customers of BANK ... including therein a duty to immediately inform customers such as FNMC when impostors and/or forgers attempt to cash a check drawn on such customers' accounts with BANK." Bank breached this duty, plaintiff alleged, by failing to ensure "that only properly indorsed and presented checks of its depositors [were] paid." Had Bank "caught" the impostor trying to cash the check payable to Helen, it would have informed FNMC of the attempt, and FNMC would have discovered the forged power of attorney before it made the second loan.

Applicability of the Impostor Rule

Bank's demurrer is based entirely on the asserted applicability of the impostor rule, which, according to Bank, interposes an "absolute defense" against plaintiff's allegations of negligence. Bank relies on the current provisions of section 3404, subdivision (a) (hereafter, "section 3404(a)"), which makes an indorsement by any person effective if an impostor had induced the issuance of the instrument to either the impostor or "a person acting in concert with the impostor." In this case, argues Bank, Rudy was acting in concert with the impostor (the impersonator of Helen), who presented the check to Bank for payment.

Plaintiff responds that section 3404(a) is not applicable, because it was not enacted until 1992, after the events alleged in the complaint. Instead, plaintiff maintains, this case is controlled by former section 3405, subdivision (1)(a) (hereafter, "former section 3405(1)(a)"). The expression of the rule in the latter statute is substantially the same as that of the current provisions, but excluded from its reach are false representations of agency. Because Rudy obtained the check from FNMC by falsely representing that he was authorized to act as Helen's agent, plaintiff argues the transaction at issue is outside the scope of the impostor rule.

We agree with plaintiff that former section 3405(1)(a) governs the disposition of this case, since the events at issue took place in 1988, while that statute was still in effect. Former section 3405(1)(a) provided: "An indorsement by any person in the name of a named payee is effective if (a) An impostor by use of the mails or otherwise has induced the maker or drawer to issue the instrument to him or his confederate in the name of the payee...."

This section does not protect Bank from liability under the circumstances presented. As one California court explained prior to the enactment of former section 3405, the impostor rule is applicable only when the issuance of the check has been accomplished through *impersonation* of the payee: "[W]here a check is delivered to an impostor as payee and the drawer believes that the impostor is the person upon whose endorsement it will be paid, the endorsement by such impostor in the name which he is using to impersonate another is not a forgery.... The soundness of the rule obtains in the fact that the money has actually been paid to the person for whom it was really intended. Because another person might bear the very name assumed by the impostor and might have some contractual relationships with the impostor does not subject to a loss the drawee bank when it has paid the check to the person intended as the payee." (Schweitzer v. Bank of America (1941) 42 Cal.App.2d 536, 540, 109 P.2d 441....)

The reasoning of the *Schweitzer* court directs our analysis in the present case. If FNMC (the drawer) had been induced *by an impostor* of Helen to issue the check either to Rudy or to the impostor, then the indorsement would be considered effective as to FNMC under the impostor rule. The rationale for this result is that Bank has paid the person whom FNMC intended to receive the money. When viewed under principles of negligence or estoppel, the outcome of this scenario would be the same: the risk of loss would be shifted to the drawer of the instrument (FNMC), who was in a better position to detect the fraud....

This case presents different facts, however. Here, FNMC made the check payable to the true Helen, not to an impostor representing herself as Helen. FNMC intended that Helen herself – not a person it believed to be Helen – indorse the check and receive the proceeds. There is no question that FNMC intended to deal solely with Helen. The rationale underlying the protection of the impostor rule thus does not apply here.

A person's false representation that he or she is an agent of the payee is not sufficient. Uniform Commercial Code Comment 2 to former section 3405 notes: "'Impostor' refers to impersonation, and does not extend to a false representation that the party is the authorized agent of the payee. The maker or drawer who takes the precaution of making the instrument payable to the principal is entitled to have his indorsement." (See Uniform Com. Code com., 23B West's Ann.Com.Code (1964 ed.) § 3405, p. 287.) Here, Rudy obtained issuance of the check to Helen not by impersonating her, but by falsely representing that he was authorized to act on her behalf. Although clearly fraudulent, this conduct does not constitute impersonation and thus cannot be considered an inducement to issue the instrument within the meaning of former section 3405(1)(a).

Bank's emphasis on the asserted fact that Rudy was acting in concert with Helen's impostor is of no consequence. To invoke the protection of former section 3405(1)(a) Bank would have to point to facts showing that *by impersonation* the impostor induced FNMC to issue the check either to her or to Rudy, her confederate. The complaint alleges no such facts, however. The only impersonation that took place was in the presentation of the check to Bank.

Some courts have found impersonation where the payee's signature is forged on the very documents required to obtain the money. In Minster State Bank v. Baybank Middlesex (1993) 414 Mass. 831, 611 N.E.2d 200, 202, for example, the husband engaged in imposture "by the use of mails or otherwise" by forging his wife's name to a promissory note.... Fidelity & D.Co. of Md. v. Manufacturers Han. Tr. Co. (1970) 63 Misc.2d 960, 313 N.Y.S.2d 823 involved a forgery of a depositor's signature on a withdrawal order, resulting in the issuance of two checks against the depositor's account. Similarly, the court in Intelogic v. Merchants Nat. Bank, supra, 626 N.E.2d 839, 846, considered whether the forgery of a payee's signature directly induced the drawer to issue checks under a purported lease-back agreement.

In the case before us, however, there is no allegation that Rudy forged Helen's signature on the loan documents themselves. Instead, Rudy forged Helen's signature on a power of attorney, which enabled him only to represent himself as Helen's agent. Thereafter, he used that agency status to obtain the loan from FNMC, ostensibly on Helen's behalf. Thus, even assuming that forgery of a payee's signature on loan documents constitutes an imposture, that scenario did not occur here. Rudy's act of forgery was not an impersonation but only a misrepresentation of his authority to do business on behalf of Helen.

The result is no different even under section 3404(a), the current version of the rule. The only significant change in this section is its recognition that the impostor may pretend to be either the payee or the payee's agent. As the Uniform Commercial Code Comment to the revised law notes, "Under former Section 3-405(1)(a), if Impostor impersonated Smith and induced the drawer to draw a check to the order of Smith, Impostor could negotiate the check. If Impostor impersonated Smith, the president of Smith Corporation, and the check was payable to the order of Smith Corporation, the section did not apply.... Section 3-404(a) gives Impostor the power to negotiate the check in both cases." (See Uniform Com.Code com., 23B West's Ann.Com.Code (1964 pocket supp.) § 3404, p. 60.) This comment makes it clear that impersonation is still required to invoke the impostor rule, whether the perpetrator of the deception pretends to be the principal or the agent. Misrepresentation of the perpetrator's agency status does not suffice....

We must conclude, therefore, that the impostor rule is inapplicable under these circumstances. By correctly identifying himself as Rudy but falsely representing himself to be Helen's agent Rudy did not engage in the impersonation required by the impostor rule, as expressed both in former section 3405, which was applicable at the time of the transactions at issue, and in its contemporary form, section 3404(a). The impersonation by Helen's impostor cannot be said to have induced FNMC to issue the check, since it took place only afterward, when the impostor presented the check to Bank.

Bank does not challenge the legal sufficiency of the complaint in any respect other than the asserted bar of the impostor rule.... Accordingly, we hold that the trial court incorrectly sustained Bank's demurrer based on the application of the impostor rule.

* * *

Disposition

The judgment of dismissal is reversed. The trial court shall enter a new order overruling the demurrer to the first amended complaint and directing Bank to answer. Plaintiff is entitled to costs on appeal.

Problem 4-9

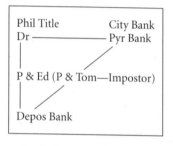

Edmund and Paula Jezemski were married, but living apart. Paula needed some money so she applied to Philadelphia Title to borrow $15,000. Philadelphia Title agreed to lend the money in return for a mortgage on the Jezemskis' house. At closing, Paula appeared with Tom, whom she introduced to the title company's employees as her husband Edmund. Tom and Paula both signed the requisite documents in the names of Edmund and Paula Jezemski. Philadelphia Title then gave them a check for $15,000 drawn on City Bank, who paid the check and debited Philadelphia Title's account. Sometime later when Edmund Jezemski tried to sell the property he discovered the mortgage and instituted a suit to cancel the mortgage. Philadelphia Title joined City Bank as a third-party defendant. The mortgage was canceled. Philadelphia Title asks the court to compel City Bank to recredit its account for $15,000 because the check was not properly payable.

How should City Bank respond? §§ 3-404, 3-406.

Problem 4-10

In which of the following situations does the imposter rule of § 3-404(a) apply?

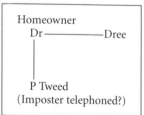

Scenario #1: Homeowner receives a telephone call from "Harris Tweed, the county tax assessor." Tweed informs Homeowner that she is behind on her property taxes. Tweed suggests that Homeowner mail a check as soon as possible to avoid the assessment of a property tax lien. Homeowner complies, mailing the check (payable to the order of "Harris Tweed, County Tax Assessor") to an address supplied by Tweed. Later, after the drawee has paid the check, Homeowner discovers that the telephone call was not from Harris Tweed or anyone associated with the county tax assessor's office. The recipient of the check had forged the payee's indorsement.

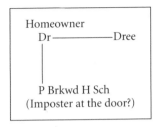

Scenario #2: Homeowner answers a knock on her door. "Hi, I'm Julie Abrams, the head soccer coach at Brookwood High School. I'm going door to door collecting donations so our soccer team can travel to Denver to defend its title in a national tournament. Your donation is tax deductible. Would you please help us out?" Homeowner gives Julie a check payable to the order of Brookwood High School. Several months after drawee has paid the check, Homeowner contacts Brookwood High School for a receipt (for tax purposes). Homeowner is informed that Brookwood High School does not have a soccer team, and no one named Julie Abrams is employed by Brookwood High School. Julie Abrams had forged the payee's indorsement.

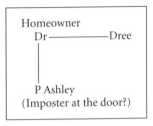

Scenario #3: Homeowner receives a telephone call from her lawyer on the morning of December 30, informing her that she owes $300 for services rendered. The lawyer expresses interest in being paid no later than December 31. When Homeowner informs the lawyer that her car is in the shop for extensive repairs, the lawyer volunteers to send his paralegal, Ashley McGregor, to Homeowner's house to pick up a check later that day or tomorrow. Homeowner agrees, and prepares a check payable to the order of her lawyer. Around noon on December 30, Homeowner answers a knock on her door. "Hi. I'm Ashley, from the lawyer's office. I'm here to pick up your check." "Great. Here's the check. Thanks for driving out." The next afternoon, the real Ashley McGregor stops by Homeowner's house to pick up the check. Homeowner immediately contacts the drawee, placing a stop payment order on the check. The drawee informs Homeowner that the check (bearing the lawyer's forged indorsement) was paid, in cash, around 4:30 p.m. on December 30.

Problem 4-11

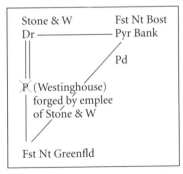

Stone & Webster Corporation was indebted to Westinghouse Corporation for $64,755 for goods and services furnished by Westinghouse. To pay this debt, on January 5, April 1, and May 1, 2007, Stone & Webster drew three checks in favor of Westinghouse on the First National Bank of Boston (FNBB). But before the checks were mailed to Westinghouse an employee of Stone & Webster forged the indorsement of Westinghouse. At the employee's request, First National Bank of Greenfield (FNBG) cashed the checks. The employee used the money for his own purposes. FNBG sent the checks to FNBB who paid them and debited Stone & Webster's account for $64,755. The checks were indorsed by typewriter,

For Deposit Only
Westinghouse Electric Corporation
Mr. O.C. Costine, Treasury Representative

followed by a signature in pen, "O.C. Costine." Then followed the rubber-stamped indorsement on all three checks,

Pay to the order of any bank, banker or trust co. prior indorsements guaranteed. The First National Bank of Greenfield.

Stone & Webster discovered the forgeries on February 1, 2008.

1) As between Stone & Webster and FNBB, who will bear the loss? §§ 4-401, 3-406.

Q: Why do neither § 3-404 nor § 3-405 apply?

2) Can Stone & Webster bring a conversion action against FNBG? § 3-420(a).

3) Can Westinghouse bring a conversion action against FNBG?

Q: Can Westinghouse demand payment of the underlying obligation? § 3-310(b).

4) Can FNBB recover any of its loss from FNBG or the employee? § 4-208(a) (or § 3-417(a)).

Q: What is the applicable statute of limitations on the action? §§ 4-111, 3-118.

5) Can FNBG recover any of its loss from the employee? § 4-207(a) (or § 3-416(a)).

HSBC BANK USA v. F & M BANK NORTHERN VIRGINIA
246 F.3d 335 (4th Cir. 2001)

HAMILTON, Senior Circuit Judge:

On or about March 31, 1999, Donald Lynch purchased a check (the Check) from Allied Irish Bank (AIB) in Ireland. The Check was made payable to Advance Marketing and Investment Inc. (AMI) in the amount of US$250.00, which was hand written as "Two Hundred Fifty" on the center line of the Check (with "US Dollars" hand written on the line below), (i.e., the written portion of the Check), and "US$250.00" hand written on the upper right-hand side of the Check (i.e., the numerical portion of the Check). The manner in which AIB made out the Check left just less than one-half inch of open space in the numerical portion and one inch of open space in the written portion.

The drawee/payor on the Check was Marine Midland Bank, now known as HSBC Bank USA (HSBC). Prior to the Check's deposit into AMI's account at F & M Bank Northern Virginia (F & M), the amount of the Check was altered from $250.00 to $250,000.00 by adding three zeros and changing the period to a comma in the numerical portion of the check and adding the letters "Thoud" in the written portion. The alteration was unauthorized, and the Check was endorsed "A.M.I., Inc."

F & M presented the Check for payment to HSBC. In so doing, F & M warranted, pursuant to Virginia Code § 8.4-207.2(a)(2), that the Check "had not been altered." Va. Code Ann. § 8.4-207.2(a)(2) (Cum. Supp. 2000) [§ 4-208(a)(2)]. HSBC honored the Check as presented and paid $250,000.00 to F & M, and debited AIB's account for that amount.

HSBC was subsequently advised by AIB of the Check's unauthorized alteration. HSBC then recredited AIB's account for the amount of the unauthorized alteration and brought the present diversity action against F & M in the United States District Court for the Eastern District of Virginia. Among other claims not relevant to the present appeal, F & M [authors' note: should be HSBC] alleged a claim for breach of presentment warranty pursuant to Uniform Commercial Code § 4-207(1)(c) and (2)(c) [§ 4-208(a)(1), (2)].

Using the Virginia Commercial Code as the substantive law governing HSBC's breach of presentment warranty claim, on July 12, 2000, the district court conducted a bench trial on the claim.[4] F & M asserted as an affirmative defense that by leaving the open spaces as it did in the numerical and written portions of the Check, AIB failed to exercise ordinary care in preparing the Check, which failure substantially contributed to the unauthorized alteration of the Check.[5] The only evidence F & M actually submitted in support of its affirmative defense was the Check itself.

The district court found that HSBC had established all elements of its breach of presentment warranty claim under Virginia Commercial Code §8.4-207.2(a)(2) [§4-208(a)(2)]. The district court also found that AIB had exercised ordinary care in preparing the Check. In this last regard, the district court stated:

> I have examined this check. And, of course, there does have [sic] to be sufficient writing on a check that there is not an open space so someone can fill it in for additional amounts and alter the check.
>
> But regardless of what you do about writing in zero, zero over 100 and then put a line in, which is, I guess, the standard way to do it—I don't know that if I looked at all the checks in this country that I would know the standard. It is the way I have always done it. There is still some kind of an open space regardless of what you do.
>
> And so, the test has got to be is that line sufficiently filled so that someone cannot come along and add into that writing in a way that just alters the check so that it will go through unnoticed.
>
> That certainly wasn't done on this check. This check was substantially written across the line. As a matter of fact, it was written far enough along the line that you could not write the word "thousand" in. It had to be scrawled up in the manner in which it was.
>
> And I just[,] looking at this check[,] and the way it is made out, I can't find that the preparer was negligent or participated in the alteration of it.

---

4. The parties agreed that Virginia's Commercial Code governed HSBC's breach of presentment warranty claim. The applicable provision of Virginia's Commercial Code provides as follows:

> (a) If an unaccepted draft is presented to the drawee for payment or acceptance and the drawee pays or accepts the draft, (i) the person obtaining payment or acceptance, at the time of presentment, and (ii) a previous transferor of the draft, at the time of transfer, warrant to the drawee that pays or accepts the draft in good faith that: ... (2) the draft has not been altered....

Va. Code Ann. §8.4-207.2(a)(2) (Cum. Supp. 2000) [§4-208(a)(2)].

5. F & M asserted its affirmative defense pursuant to Virginia Commercial Code §8.4-207.2(c), which provides, in relevant part, as follows:

> If a drawee asserts a claim for breach of warranty under subsection (a) based on ... an alteration of the draft, the warrantor may defend by proving that ... the drawer is precluded under [Virginia Commercial Code] §8.3A-406 ... from asserting against the drawee the ... alteration.

Va. Code Ann. §8.4-207.2(c) [§4-208(c)]. To restate this section using the names of the actual parties in this case, the section provides that F & M, the warrantor, can defend against the warranty claim of HSBC, the drawee, by proving that AIB, the drawer, is precluded under Virginia Commercial Code §8.3A-406 from asserting the unauthorized alteration of the Check against HSBC. Of relevance in this appeal, AIB is precluded from asserting the unauthorized alteration of the Check against HSBC under Virginia Commercial Code §8.3A-406(a), if AIB failed to exercise ordinary care in preparing the check and such failure substantially contributed to the unauthorized alteration of the Check. Va. Code Ann. §8.3A-406(a). Notably, the question of whether AIB failed to exercise ordinary care in preparing the Check is a question to be answered by the trier of fact. Va. Code Ann. §8.3A-406 cmt. 1 (Cum. Supp. 2000).

There was sufficient writing there that any alteration that was made was obvious. And I can't find negligence in that regard.

(J.A. 242).

Subsequently, on July 31, 2000, the district court entered an order stating that for the reasons stated from the bench, judgment should be entered in favor of HSBC in the amount of $249,750.00, plus interest at the rate of 9% from April 13, 1999 to the date of the entry of judgment. The docket sheet reflects that such judgment was entered on July 31, 2000. F & M noted a timely appeal.

On appeal, F & M contends the district court's factual finding that AIB exercised ordinary care in preparing the Check is clearly erroneous. F & M seeks reversal of the judgment in favor of HSBC solely upon this basis. For the reasons stated below, we affirm.

I.

F & M concedes that if the district court's factual finding that AIB exercised ordinary care in preparing the Check is not clearly erroneous, it cannot successfully rely upon its affirmative defense to HSBC's breach of presentment warranty claim and, therefore, the judgment in favor of HSBC should be affirmed. Fed.R.Civ.P. 52(a) (providing that a district court's finding of fact shall not be set aside unless clearly erroneous). We now turn to consider whether the district court's factual finding that AIB exercised ordinary care in preparing the Check is clearly erroneous.

The "foremost" general principle governing the exercise of our appellate power to overturn factual findings of a district court "is that '[a] finding is "clearly erroneous" when although there is evidence to support it, the reviewing court on the entire evidence is left with the definite and firm conviction that a mistake has been committed.'" Anderson v. City of Bessemer City, 105 S.Ct. 1504 (1985) (quoting United States v. United States Gypsum Co., 68 S.Ct. 525 (1948)). Accordingly, "[i]f the district court's account of the evidence is plausible in light of the record viewed in its entirety, [we] may not reverse it even though convinced that had [we] been sitting as the trier of fact, [we] would have weighed the evidence differently." Id. 105 S.Ct. 1504.

The only evidence submitted by F & M in support of its burden of proving that AIB failed to exercise ordinary care in making out the Check was the Check itself. The district court physically examined the Check, including the just less than one-half inch of open space in the numerical portion of the Check and the one inch of open space in the written portion of the Check. Based upon this physical examination, the district court found that AIB had filled in the open spaces in the numerical and written portions of the check sufficiently such that "any alteration that was made was obvious." (J.A. 242). Accordingly, the district court found that AIB had exercised ordinary care in making out the Check.

After reviewing a copy of the Check contained in the joint appendix (the sole evidence on this issue presented below), we are not left with a definite and firm conviction that the district court's finding that AIB exercised ordinary care in making out the Check is wrong, mistaken, or implausible. Indeed, we see sound logic in the district court's rationale that if the written portion of the Check contained enough writing such that the Check's alteration could only be accomplished with the "scrawled up," abbreviated form of the word "thousand," i.e. "Thoud," ordinary care was exercised in making out the Check. (J.A. 242). In short, we hold that the district court's factual finding that AIB exercised ordinary care in making out the check is not clearly erroneous.

We also note that F & M's reliance upon the following comment to Virginia Commercial Code § 8.3A-406 is misplaced:

> 3. The following cases illustrate the kind of conduct that can be the basis of a preclusion under Section 3-406(a): ... Case # 3. A company writes a check for $10. The figure "10" and the word "ten" are typewritten in the appropriate spaces on the check form. A large blank space is left after the figure and the word. The payee of the check, using a typewriter with a type face similar to that used on the check, writes the word "thousand" after the word "ten" and a comma and three zeros after the figure "10." The drawee bank in good faith pays $10,000 when the check is presented for payment and debits the account of the drawer in that amount. The trier of fact could find that the drawer failed to exercise ordinary care in writing the check and that the failure substantially contributed to the alteration. In that case the drawer is precluded from asserting the alteration against the drawee if the check was paid in good faith.

Va. Code Ann. § 8.3A-406, cmt. 3 (Cum. Supp. 2000) (emphasis added). This illustration is easily distinguishable from the facts of the present case. First, the illustration involves typewritten preparation of a check. The small nature of typewritten characters obviously would take up much less space than the handwriting involved in the present case. Furthermore, the actual number of words and numbers typed on the check that is discussed in the commentary prior to alteration is significantly less than the number of words and numbers AIB hand wrote on the Check prior to its alteration.

Because the district court's finding that AIB exercised ordinary care in making out the Check is not clearly erroneous, we affirm the judgment in favor of HSBC.

Problem 4-12

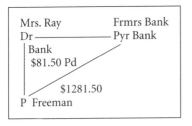

Freeman, posing as a serviceman for an electric utility company, called on Mrs. Ray, an elderly woman living alone. Once inside, he examined several wall plug outlets and then told Mrs. Ray he would return after lunch and finish the job. In the meantime he said he would need a check for $81.50 for the services rendered. He offered to fill out the check for her. She was feeling nervous about him being there and allowed him to do so to "get rid of him" as quickly as she could. He wrote the check with considerable space after the dollar sign: $_____81.50, leaving the rest of the check blank except for Mrs. Ray's signature. After leaving the house he completed the check by writing (i) the numbers "12" between the dollar sign and the "$_____81.50" as follows: $__1281.50, (ii) "one thousand two hundred eighty-one and 50/100", (iii) the current date, and (iv) his name on the payee line. Freeman cashed the check and disappeared. Mrs. Ray demanded that her bank recredit her account for the altered amount.

1) How would you characterize this instrument? §§ 3-115, 3-407.

2) Did Mrs. Ray exercise ordinary care? If so, of what relevance is that? §§ 3-103(a)(9), 3-406(a), 4-401(a).

3) As between Mrs. Ray and her bank, who will bear the loss? §§ 3-115(b); 3-407(b), (c); 4-401(d); 3-414(b).

Problem 4-13

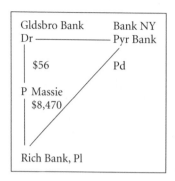

Massie periodically requested teller's checks from Goldsboro Bank in small amounts for payment of purchases from sellers who refused to take personal checks. On one occasion, Goldsboro Bank issued a $56 teller's check to Massie, payable to his order and drawn on Bank of New York (BONY). Using advanced technology, Massie then skillfully changed the amount from $56 to $8,470.50. Massie then purchased a cashier's check for $8,470.50 from Richmond Bank, who sent the altered draft to BONY. BONY paid the altered draft and debited Goldsboro's account. Goldsboro Bank demands that BONY restore Goldsboro's account to its original position.

1) What will Goldsboro Bank argue? §§ 3-407, 4-401.

2) What is the relevance of Goldsboro Bank's argument that even if Goldsboro Bank was negligent in issuing the draft, Massie's crime broke the chain of causation and BONY should bear the loss? § 3-406 OC 2.

3) If Goldsboro Bank is negligent, what will be its counter-argument? §§ 3-406(b), 3-103(a)(9).

4) Decide the case.

5) If Goldsboro Bank can shift some or all of the loss to BONY, can BONY recover its loss from Richmond Bank or Massie? § 4-208(a) (or § 3-417(a)).

6) If BONY can shift some or all of the loss to Richmond Bank, can Richmond Bank recover its loss from Massie? § 4-207(a) (or § 3-416(a)).

———————

As the following case reveals, drawers who are victimized by wrongdoers are expanding the circle of potential defendants to include more than just the drawee.

GINA CHIN & ASSOCIATES, INC. v. FIRST UNION BANK
500 S.E.2d 516 (Va. 1998)

LACY, Justice.

Gina Chin & Associates, Inc. (Chin) filed a motion for judgment against First Union Bank alleging that First Union was negligent when it accepted checks drawn on Chin's accounts bearing both forged signatures of the drawer and forged indorsements of the payees. The trial court sustained First Union's demurrer and entered summary judgment. We awarded Chin an appeal, and we will reverse the judgment of the trial court because we conclude that Chin's motion for judgment pled a cause of action pursuant to §§ 8.3A-404 and -405 of the uniform commercial code, code §§ 8.1-101 through 8.11-108 (the UCC).

In reviewing a case decided on a demurrer, we accept as true the facts alleged in the motion for judgment and all reasonable inferences to be drawn therefrom.... Chin, a food wholesaler, maintained checking accounts at Signet Bank and Citizens Bank of Washington, D.C. (the drawee banks). During 1994 and 1995, an employee of Chin, Amie Cheryl Lehman, forged the signature of one of Chin's officers on a number of checks that were payable to Chin's suppliers. Lehman then forged the payees' indorsements and, with the assistance of a First Union teller, deposited the checks in an account which she held at First Union. The drawee banks then paid the checks and debited a total amount of $270,488.72 from Chin's accounts.

First Union asserts that, under the UCC, it is amenable to suit only by the drawee banks based on a breach of warranty of title theory. § 8.4-207.1.[1] Chin's sole cause of action, according to First Union, is against the drawee banks for improperly charging Chin's accounts for the amount of the forged checks. See §§ 8.4-401, -406. Under First Union's interpretation of §§ 8.3A-404 and -405, Chin does not have a cause of action against it pursuant to those sections because they only apply to instances involving a forged indorsement of the payee and not to the circumstances where both the payee's indorsement and the signature of the drawer were forged.

While First Union correctly states that the UCC provides a drawer with a cause of action against a drawee bank that charges a drawer's account based on checks containing a forged signature of the drawer, its conclusion that §§ 8.3A-404 and -405 cannot be utilized by a drawer against the depositary bank in a double forgery situation is erroneous.

Sections 8.3A-404 and -405 were part of the 1992 revisions to the UCC. Revised § 8.3A-404(b) provides that where the payee on a check is fictitious or not the person intended to have an interest in the check by the person determining to whom the check is payable, a forged payee's indorsement on the check is nevertheless effective for one who takes the check in good faith.[2] Similarly, where an employee vested with the responsibility for processing, signing, or indorsing the employer's check makes a fraudulent indorsement of such check, revised § 8.3A-405 continues the prior provision's rule that the indorsement is effective if taken or paid in good faith. However, both revised sections provide that if the person taking the check fails to exercise ordinary care, "the person bearing the loss may recover from the person failing to exercise ordinary care to the extent the failure to exercise ordinary care contributed to the loss." §§ 8.3A-404(d), -405(b).

The revisions to §§ 8.3A-404 and -405 changed the previous law by allowing "the person bearing the loss" to seek recovery for a loss caused by the negligence of any person paying the instrument or taking it for value based on comparative negligence principles. The concept of comparative negligence introduced in the revised sections reflects a determination that all participants in the process have a duty to exercise ordinary care in the drawing and handling of instruments and that the failure to exercise that duty will result in liability to the person sustaining the loss. Nothing in the statutory language indicates that, where the signature of the drawer is forged, the drawer cannot qualify as a "person bearing the loss" or that the drawer is otherwise precluded from seeking recovery from a depositary bank under these sections. In the absence of any specific exclusion, we conclude that the sections are applicable in double forgery situations.

This conclusion is consistent with Comment 2 of the Official Comments to § 8.3A-404, which states that subsection (b) "also applies to forged check cases." Another commentary also concludes that § 8.3A-404 applies to double forgery situations. Remarking that under the previous law, double forgery cases were treated solely as forged drawer's signature cases, allowing the depositary bank to avoid liability, the commentary concludes that the result under the revised section "differs sharply."

---

1. First Union also argued on brief and in oral argument that Chin cannot maintain a cause of action against it for conversion. First Union is correct, see § 8.3A-420; however, Chin is not asserting a cause of action for conversion in this appeal.

2. The person whose intent determines to whom an instrument is payable includes a person who forges the drawer's signature. See § 8.3A-110(a).

In fictitious payee double forgeries under the Revision, some of the ultimate loss will end up on the shoulders of the company that hired the dishonest bookkeeper and failed to supervise the miscreant. The rest will be shouldered by the depositary bank for [its] negligence....

Barkley Clark & Barbara Clark, The Law of Bank Deposits, Collections and Credit Cards ¶12.07[3][b] (rev. ed. 1995).

Accordingly, we hold that Chin was not precluded from asserting a cause of action against First Union pursuant to §§ 8.3A-404 or -405. In light of this conclusion, we next examine Chin's motion for judgment to determine whether it is sufficient to state a cause of action under these sections.

Chin seeks recovery for a loss sustained as a result of the negligent actions of First Union. Chin alleged that its employee, Lehman, forged both its signature and the indorsement of the payees on a number of checks and, with the cooperation of an employee of First Union, deposited the checks into Lehman's account at First Union. The motion for judgment specifically alleged that the acceptance of the forged checks by First Union for payment "was negligent and was in contravention of established banking customs and standards" and "was due to the negligent failure of First Union Bank to supervise its employee." The pleading further asserts that this negligence caused Chin to suffer a loss of over $270,000.

These allegations are sufficient to state a cause of action against First Union pursuant to §§ 8.3A-404 and -405. Accordingly, the trial court erred in sustaining First Union's demurrer. The judgment of the trial court is reversed and the case is remanded for further proceedings.

Reversed and remanded.

Note

Assume that Chin's signature was not forged. Instead, an authorized employee signed checks that were payable to Chin's legitimate suppliers. The checks were intercepted by one of Chin's low-level employees (one without "responsibility" under § 3-405) who forged the suppliers' indorsements and (with the aid of a First Union teller) deposited the checks into the employee's account. Can Chin sue First Union?

5. Duty to Examine Cancelled Items

The drawer has a duty to promptly examine bank statements and cancelled items to determine whether its signature has been forged or any check has been altered, and a duty to timely report any mischief to the drawee. If the drawer fails to perform these duties, who bears the loss? Will it make a difference if the bank is also negligent? § 4-406.

SPACEMAKERS OF AMERICA, INC. v. SUNTRUST BANK
609 S.E.2d 683 (Ga. Ct. App. 2005)

Ellington, Judge.

Spacemakers of America, Inc. sued SunTrust Bank after the bank processed approximately 65 checks that had been forged by the company's bookkeeper. The trial court granted the bank's motion for summary judgment on Spacemakers' claims for negligence, conversion, and unauthorized payment of forged items. Spacemakers appeals, claiming the trial court erred when it misapplied the law, granted summary judgment on its tort claims, and found the bank was not negligent as a matter of law. Because summary judgment was properly granted in this case, we affirm.

In reviewing a grant or denial of summary judgment, this Court conducts a de novo review of the evidence. To prevail at summary judgment ... the moving party must demonstrate that there is no genuine issue of material fact and that the undisputed facts, viewed in the light most favorable to the nonmovant, warrant judgment as a matter of law.... The record in this case shows the following undisputed facts: Jenny Triplett applied with Spacemakers for a bookkeeping position in November 1999. Triplett listed no prior employment on her application, and the application did not inquire about her criminal history. Prior to hiring Triplett, employees of Spacemakers did not ask her about her criminal history or conduct a criminal background check. Had it done so, Spacemakers would have learned that Triplett was on probation from a 1997 conviction for thirteen counts of forgery in the first degree, as well as from convictions for theft by taking and theft by deception in March 1999, just eight months before she applied for the Spacemakers job. All of these convictions were the result of Triplett forging the checks of previous employers.

Spacemakers hired Triplett as a bookkeeper on December 1, 1999, delegating to her the sole responsibility for maintaining the company's checkbook, reconciling it with the monthly bank statements, and preparing financial reports. According to Dennis Rose, Spacemakers' president, Triplett also handled the company's accounts payable and regularly presented him with invoices from vendors and payroll records for employees. Rose stated that he spent several hours reviewing the vendor invoices each month before giving Triplett specific directions about which ones should be paid. After Triplett wrote the checks, she gave them to Rose so he could sign them. No other Spacemakers' employee, however, reviewed the monthly bank statements or looked at the company's checkbook register to ensure that Triplett wrote only authorized checks on the company's account. Further, Rose admitted that no other employee checked the accuracy of Triplett's financial reports and that he simply relied on Triplett's representations regarding how much money was in the bank account at any given time.

On January 3, 2000, just weeks after starting her job at Spacemakers, Triplett forged Rose's signature on a check for $3,000. She made the check payable to her husband's company, "Triple M Entertainment Group," which was not a vendor for Spacemakers. By the end of her first full month of employment, Triplett had forged five more checks totaling $22,320.30, all payable to Triple M. Then, over the next nine months, Triplett forged fifty-nine more checks totaling approximately $475,000. Triplett made all of these checks payable to Triple M. Most of the checks were for amounts between $5,000 and $10,000, and only two of the checks were for an amount over $20,000: a check for $24,500 dated September 1, 2000, and a check for $30,670 dated October 5, 2000. There is no evidence that anyone at Spacemakers other than Triplett reviewed the company's bank statements between January and October 2000 or that Spacemakers ever notified SunTrust that there had been any unauthorized transactions during that period.[1]

---

1. The company's total reliance on Triplett's financial reports, including its failure to look at the monthly bank statements or check the accuracy of the financial reports, is even more remarkable given testimony by Rose and his wife that the company experienced a "precipitous drop" in the company's cash assets during the spring and summer of 2000. During this period, the company barely had enough money to pay its bills and its checks sometimes "bounced," so the Roses opened up a line of credit with SunTrust in order to keep the company in business. Even so, they never investigated Triplett's bookkeeping to see if there had been unauthorized activity within the account.

On October 13, 2000, a SunTrust loss prevention employee visually inspected the $30,670 check. She became suspicious of the signature and immediately contacted Rose. The SunTrust employee faxed Rose a copy of the check, which was made payable to "Triple M." Rose knew that Triple M was not one of the company's vendors and that he had not authorized the check. During the phone conversation, a Spacemakers' employee reminded Rose that Triplett's husband owned Triple M. Rose's wife immediately called the police and Triplett was arrested.

On November 9, 2000, Spacemakers sent a letter to SunTrust demanding that the bank credit $523,106.03 to its account for the forged checks.[2] The bank refused, contending that Spacemakers' failure to provide the bank with timely notice of the forgeries barred its claim under the notice provisions of the account agreement between the bank and Spacemakers, as well as under the notice provisions of the Georgia Commercial Code, specifically OCGA § 11-4-406. The bank also contended that Spacemakers' negligence in hiring and failing to supervise Triplett, a convicted felon, barred the company's claim under OCGA §§ 11-3-406 and 11-4-406. Spacemakers subsequently sued the bank for negligence, conversion, and unauthorized payment of forged items.

In granting summary judgment to the bank, the trial court found that Spacemakers could not recover for the first forged check from January 2000 because it failed to notify the bank of the forgery within 30 days of receiving its bank statement, as required by OCGA § 11-4-406. The trial court also found that, under the same provision, Spacemakers could not recover for the 64 subsequently forged checks because they were all forged by the same person who forged the first check. Further, the court found that there was no evidence that the bank failed to exercise ordinary care in the payment of the checks. Spacemakers appeals.

1. Spacemakers claims the trial court erred in applying OCGA § 11-4-406 to the facts of this case.... [T]his rule imposes upon a bank customer the duty to promptly examine its monthly statements and notify the bank of any unauthorized transaction. If the customer fails to report the first forged item within 30 days, it is precluded from recovering for that transaction *and for any additional items forged by the same wrongdoer.* The underlying justification for this provision is simple: one of the most serious consequences of the failure of a customer to timely examine its statement is that it gives the wrongdoer the opportunity to repeat his misdeeds.... Clearly, the customer "is in the best position to discover and report small forgeries before the [same] wrongdoer is emboldened and attempts a larger misdeed." ...

In this case, the undisputed evidence showed that Spacemakers hired as a bookkeeper a twice-convicted embezzler who was on probation, then delegated the entire responsibility of reviewing and reconciling its bank statements to her while failing to provide any oversight on these essential tasks. The bookkeeper started forging checks within weeks of taking control of the company's checkbook and, by the end of January 2000, had forged six checks totaling $25,320.30. Triplet made all of the checks payable to her husband's company, which had never been a Spacemakers' vendor. There is every reason to believe that, if Spacemakers had simply reviewed its bank statement for January 2000, it would have discovered the forgeries. More importantly, it would have been able to timely notify the bank of its discovery and avoided its subsequent losses of almost $475,000. Clearly, Spacemakers' extensive and unnecessary loss due to forgery is pre-

---

2. Attached to its demand letter was a list of allegedly forged checks. Although Spacemakers included in the list a few suspicious checks that were payable to entities other than Triple M, the company did not include these checks in their suit against the bank.

cisely the scenario that the duties created by OCGA § 11-4-406 were designed to prevent. Accordingly, we find that Spacemakers is precluded as a matter of law from asserting claims based upon the forgeries in this case.... The trial court did not err in granting summary judgment to the bank.

2. Spacemakers also contends the trial court erred in finding that there was no evidence that the bank failed to use ordinary care in processing customers' checks. Specifically, Spacemakers claims a jury issue existed as to whether the bank was negligent because it did "absolutely nothing" to verify signatures on commercial checks written for less than $20,000. Further, Spacemakers argues that if *both* the customer and the bank are negligent, then the loss from the forged checks is allocated between the two parties according to the extent each party's negligence contributed to the loss. See OCGA §§ 11-3-406; 11-4-406(e). Therefore, according to Spacemakers, the bank should be liable for at least part of the company's losses from the forged checks. In order to survive the bank's motion for summary judgment, however, Spacemakers had the burden of presenting some evidence to refute the bank's evidence that it complied with reasonable commercial standards of the banking industry and to show that the bank's negligence contributed to the company's losses. OCGA §§ 11-3-406(c); 11-4-406(e).... As shown below, Spacemakers failed to carry this burden.

Under OCGA § 11-3-103(a)(7),

> "[o]rdinary care" in the case of a person engaged in business means observance of reasonable commercial standards, prevailing in the area in which the person is located, with respect to the business in which the person is engaged. In the case of a bank that takes an instrument for processing for collection or payment by automated means, reasonable commercial standards do not require the bank to examine the instrument if the failure to examine does not violate the bank's prescribed procedures and the bank's procedures do not vary unreasonably from general banking usage.

Ordinary care in this context is comparable to a "professional negligence" standard of care and does not refer to what a "reasonable person" would do under the circumstances....

The bank, in support of its motion for summary judgment, presented a prima facie showing that it exercised ordinary care in this case. According to the affidavit of Jeffrey Dalrymple, a SunTrust Senior Vice-President, the bank's regional operations center handles between 650,000 and 1,200,000 checks per day, and its fraud detection software, ASI/16, is "an industry standard and one of the most sophisticated rules-based fraud detection software systems available." This fraud detection software program reviews every check written for $250 and over[7] and looks for certain suspicious characteristics which may indicate fraud on an account. These characteristics include, but are not limited to, the following: check numbers that are out of sequence; checks that have duplicate, missing, or out-of-range serial numbers; checks for high dollar amounts; checks for an amount greater than average for the account; and checks for an amount which exceeds the largest found in the account's history. If a check meets any of these characteristics, it is "outsorted" and visually inspected by SunTrust employees.[8] Further, commercial checks for

---

7. A SunTrust operations manager deposed that the system "filters" out checks under $250 before screening because it is unlikely that such checks are forged. Notably, none of the forged checks in this case was for an amount less than $250.

8. Checks are also visually inspected for fraud for other reasons not applicable in this case.

$20,000 or greater are automatically reviewed and verified by SunTrust employees. Dalrymple's affidavit also stated that he has personal knowledge of commercial standards in the banking industry in general and in the Atlanta area, as well as SunTrust's policies and procedures regarding the processing of checks. According to Dalrymple, SunTrust's standards with respect to thresholds for sight inspection of checks drawn on commercial accounts not only meet but are in fact more stringent than the standards for sight inspection of such checks among other banks in the Atlanta, Georgia area and are in observance and in fact exceed reasonable commercial standards.

Finally, Dalrymple's affidavit stated that SunTrust followed its standard procedures when it processed checks drawn on Spacemakers' account.

Once the bank presented a prima facie case demonstrating its exercise of ordinary care, the burden shifted to Spacemakers to respond with competent evidence that the bank failed to meet reasonable commercial standards in the banking industry.... The only evidence Spacemakers presented to refute SunTrust's showing was an expert witness, who testified that he had never analyzed fraud detection systems in any national bank in the Atlanta area. He also admitted that he did not know what fraud detection procedures SunTrust actually performs on commercial checks under $20,000. Even so, the witness deposed that, in his opinion, the bank was negligent because it did not visually inspect the signature on every check it processes, regardless of the check's amount. The expert witness later abandoned that position, however, and admitted that he did not think that reasonable commercial standards for national banks in the Atlanta area required banks to visually inspect every check. The witness had no opinion as to how large a check amount would have to be for the bank to be required to visually inspect it for fraud in order to comply with reasonable commercial standards in the Atlanta area. He also deposed that he was not aware of any provision in the Georgia Commercial Code which requires a bank to visually examine every check it processes. Further, although the expert witness claimed SunTrust was negligent for failing to notify its customers of its fraud detection policies and procedures, he admitted that he did not know what SunTrust told its customers, or what other banks in the area tell their customers, regarding their fraud detection program.

Accordingly, we find the record supports the trial court's conclusion that Spacemakers failed to create a jury issue as to whether the bank exercised ordinary care under the circumstances....

3. We also find that, even if OCGA § 11-4-406 did not preclude Spacemakers from recovering from the bank, there was a second basis for granting summary judgment on the company's claims.... The evidence showed that Spacemakers' commercial account with SunTrust was subject to certain terms, which were documented in a booklet entitled "Rules and Regulations [for] Non-Personal Deposit Accounts." The booklet expressly notified commercial customers that the bank does not verify the signatures on every check paid against their account and instructed customers to promptly examine their monthly statements to verify that only authorized checks have been paid. In fact, a second provision specifically detailed the customer's duty with regard to recognizing account discrepancies and its liability to fulfill this duty:

> You should carefully examine the statement and canceled checks (including the face and back), if included in the statement, when you receive the statement. The Bank will not be liable for any unauthorized signature, alteration, misencoding or other error on the face of any item in your statement, or for any incorrect amount or other error on the statement itself ... unless you notify the Bank within thirty (30) calendar days from the date the Bank ... makes your

statement available to you or anyone to whom you request it be sent.... More-over, because you are in the best position to discover an unauthorized signa-ture..., you agree that the Bank will not be liable for paying such items if ... you did not examine the statement and the canceled checks (if included) or you have not reported [the] unauthorized signatures ... to us within the time pe-riod set forth above.

Most importantly, the booklet contained the following provision: "Bookkeepers. In the event you authorize any third person ... to retain possession of or prepare items for [your company], you agree to assume full responsibility for any errors or wrongdoing by such third person ... if the Bank should pay such items." Therefore, under these express provisions, Spacemakers cannot recover from the bank for the payments on the forged checks.

4. Spacemakers claims the trial court erred in finding that the company had failed to notify SunTrust of "any unauthorized signatures" within 30 days, as required by OCGA § 11-4-406.[9] It argues that, after the bank discovered the forged $30,670 check on Octo-ber 13, 2000, the bank had notice of any forgeries that had occurred within the preced-ing 30 days, so the court's finding to the contrary is wrong. Spacemakers claims, there-fore, that it should be able to recover for the 12 forged checks paid by the bank within that period. This issue, however, has already been decided adversely to Spacemakers in Division 1, supra, wherein we held that, under OCGA § 11-4-406(d), a customer's fail-ure to timely report a wrongdoer's first forgery precludes it from recovering for any sub-sequent forgery by the same wrongdoer. This is true even if the subsequent forgery is dis-covered and timely reported to the bank pursuant to OCGA § 11-4-406(c). There was no error.

5. Spacemakers claims the trial court erred in granting summary judgment on its com-mon law claims of negligence, conversion, and breach of statutory duties. We disagree.

Under OCGA § 11-3-420(a)(i), the issuer of a check (in this case, Spacemakers) can-not maintain a claim for conversion against the bank under these circumstances as a mat-ter of law. Further, regardless whether Spacemakers' common law claims can survive in-dependently of the provisions of the Georgia Commercial Code, there is no evidence in the record of this case to support these claims.... Accordingly, summary judgment was appropriate and there was no error.

Judgment affirmed.

ANDREWS, P.J., and MILLER, J., concur.

Notes

1. Courts are enforcing deposit agreements that shorten the one-year bar period of § 4-406(f). See, e.g., American Airlines Employees Federal Credit Union v. Martin, 29 S.W.3d 86 (Tex. 2000) (60 days); Concrete Materials Corp. v. Bank of Danville & Trust Co., 938 S.W.2d 254 (Ky. 1997) (60 days); Stowell v. Cloquet Co-op Credit Union, 557 N.W.2d 567 (Minn. 1997) (20 days); Parent Teacher Ass'n v. Manufacturers Hanover

---

9. Although the trial court's order states that Spacemakers failed to timely notify the bank of "any unauthorized transactions," the court was clearly referring to the lack of notice only as to the first forged check, since it immediately referred to the "sixty-four subsequently forged checks." It is undis-puted that Spacemakers failed to notify the bank of the first forged check within 30 days of receiving the bank statement for January 2000.

Trust Co., 524 N.Y.S.2d 336 (N.Y. Civ. Ct. 1988) (14 days); National Title Ins. Corp. Agency v. First Union National Bank, 559 S.E.2d 668 (Va. 2002) (60 days); Borowski v. Firstar Bank Milwaukee, N.A., 579 N.W.2d 247 (Wis. Ct. App. 1998) (14 days). Some states have adopted a non-uniform amendment to §4-406(f) that shortens the one-year bar period. See, e.g., Ala. Code §7-4-406(f) (180 days), Georgia O.C.G.A. §11-4-406(f) (60 days), Oregon O.R.S. §74.4060(6) (180 days), and Washington R.C.W. §62A.4-406(f) (adopting one-year bar period for any "natural person whose account is primarily for personal, family, or household purposes" and 60-day period for all others).

2. As between the bank and a customer that has breached its examination and notification duties under §4-406(c), the bank bears the loss for checks described on (or returned with) the *initial* periodic statement that reflects payment of a check bearing an alteration or the customer's forged signature unless "the bank also proves that it suffered a loss" as a result of the customer's breach. §4-406(d)(1). One court had the following comments on this nexus requirement:

> The Court believes [the bank] has misinterpreted [4-406(d)(1)], apparently reading it to mean in order to foist liability on a previously-forged check onto its customer, all a bank has to show is that the customer waited too long to notify the bank after receiving the statement which showed the bank had paid on the check. As indicated in [4-406(c)], the statute applies only when the bank has paid on the check before sending the statement to the customer, so the "loss" caused by the customer's delay in reporting the forgery cannot be the bank's prior payment of the check. Instead, the bank must show, for example, that it lost an opportunity to recover from the forger, or probably more likely, from some bank up the line in the check collection process. Other than the fact it had already paid for the checks before [the customer's co-owner] reported the forgeries, [the bank] presented no evidence of any loss it suffered due to [the customer's] delay in reviewing its bank statement. Thus, [4-406(d)(1)] does not enable [the bank] to shift liability to [the customer] on the forged checks it had paid before [the customer's] reporting time had expired.

In re Mid-American Clean Water Systems, Inc., 159 B.R. 941, 947 (Bankr. D. Kan. 1993).

Problem 4-14

```
FNB (drawee)
   3–missing signature
   2–two signatures (one forged)
   3–payee name altered
   2–amount altered
   3–forged indorsements
Walton Tech (drawer)
   CFO (misconduct)
```

Walton Technologies (WT) maintains its corporate checking account with First National Bank (FNB). All checks over $500 require the signature of two WT officers. FNB provides WT with a monthly bank statement. Checks are not returned to customers, but bank statements list the check number, the date paid, and the amount of the check. Under its internal policy, FNB physically reviews all checks for more than $8,000, thirty percent of all checks between $4,000 and $7,999.99, five percent of all checks between $2,000 and $3,999.99, and one percent of all checks not more than $2,000.

Over the course of three months, WT's chief financial officer improperly wrote five checks payable to himself. The CFO signed only his name on three of the checks (#1, #3, and #8 below), and he signed his name and forged another corporate officer's name on two checks (#10 and #13 below). In addition, the CFO intercepted three other checks signed by WT's authorized officers and payable to legitimate creditors. The CFO cashed these three checks (#5, #6, and #12 below) after using chemicals to replace the original payees' names with his own in an expert manner. On yet two other checks (#2 and #9 below) that were authorized by other WT officers and payable to the CFO as expense reimbursements, the CFO used chemicals to alter in an expert manner the amount (both numbers and words) from $135 and $425 to $2,900 and $4,300, respectively, and deposited the checks into his personal account for the altered amounts. Also, the CFO intercepted three outgoing checks (#4, #7, and #11 below) that were payable to legitimate creditors, forged the indorsement of each payee, added his own blank indorsement, and then cashed the checks at his bank.

FNB paid and returned the checks on the following dates:

check #1 (missing signature) for $1,200 paid on June 6 and returned on June 10 (check not among sample of reviewed items);

check #2 (alteration of amount) for $2,900 paid on June 8 and returned on June 10 (check not among sample of reviewed items);

check #3 (missing signature) for $2,600 paid on June 12 and returned on July 10 (check among sample of reviewed items; clerk failed to note noncompliance with dual signature requirement stated on check);

check #4 (forged indorsement) for $3,500 paid on June 15 and returned on July 10 (check among sample of reviewed items; clerk failed to detect forged indorsement);

check #5 (alteration of payee's name) for $1,700 paid on June 16 and returned on July 10 (check not among sample of reviewed items);

check #6 (alteration of payee's name) for $6,200 paid on June 28 and returned on July 10 (check among sample of reviewed items; clerk failed to detect alteration);

check #7 (forged indorsement) for $4,100 paid on July 3 and returned on July 10 (check not among sample of reviewed items);

check #8 (missing signature) for $1,000 paid on July 6 and returned on July 10 (check not among sample of reviewed items);

check #9 (alteration of amount) for $4,300 paid on July 12 and returned on August 10 (check not among sample of reviewed items);

check #10 (one forged signature) for $3,000 paid on July 27 and returned on August 10 (check not among sample of reviewed items);

check #11 (forged indorsement) for $6,700 paid on July 31 and returned on August 10 (check among sample of reviewed items, clerk failed to detect forged indorsement);

check #12 (alteration of payee's name) for $2,200 paid on August 3 and returned on August 10 (check not among sample of reviewed items); and

check #13 (one forged signature) for $11,000 paid on August 8 and returned on August 10 (clerk compared signatures on check to signatures on file and noted some discrepancies with both signatures which clerk did not believe raised forgery concerns).

WT's annual audit in mid-October revealed the CFO's wrongdoing, and WT contacted FNB immediately, insisting that FNB recredit its account for $50,000.

1) Does § 4-406 dictate the loss allocation on all thirteen checks? §§ 4-406(a), (c); 3-403(b).

2) How will any loss covered by § 4-406 be allocated between WT and FNB under § 4-406?

Q: Does the possible loss allocation provide WT's lawyer with an economic incentive to manipulate the facts?

3) Would your loss allocation under § 4-406 change if the CFO's mischief went undetected for eighteen months?

6. Death or Incompetence of Drawer

At common law, death of the principal cancelled the agency relationship, and thereby the authority of the agent to act for the principal. What is the effect of this rule on the authority of a bank to pay a check after the death of a drawer?

Problem 4-15

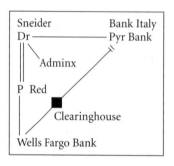

Sneider had an account with Bank of Italy, and on March 13, Sneider drew two checks for $600 each to the order of Red. Red indorsed the checks and deposited them for collection with Wells Fargo Bank. On March 14, the checks were given to Bank of Italy's agent who carried them to the bank. Bank of Italy rejected the checks because the account had insufficient funds. Still later on March 14 someone at Bank of Italy telephoned Wells Fargo Bank and told it to present the checks again. Accordingly on March 15 they were re-presented, but the bank again threatened to reject the checks, because Sneider had died earlier that morning. However, after some controversy the bank did pay them, thereby creating a $361 overdraft in Sneider's account. The administratrix demanded that Bank of Italy recredit Sneider's account and eliminate the overdraft.

1) <u>Review</u>: Can Bank of Italy honor checks that create an overdraft in Sneider's account? §§ 4-401(a), 4-402(a).

2) Can Bank of Italy honor Sneider's checks after learning of his death? § 4-405.

3) Could the administratrix have stopped the payment?

4) Decide the case.

Note

A drawer may file a voluntary bankruptcy petition after issuing one or more checks. Upon the filing of the petition, all of the debtor's assets (including accounts maintained with financial institutions) pass to an estate under Bankruptcy Code § 541. A drawee can continue to honor checks after the petition is filed, without running afoul of Bankruptcy Code provisions that limit the disposition of assets of the estate, if the drawee acts with "neither actual notice nor actual knowledge" of the petition under Bankruptcy Code § 542(c).

7. Stop Payment Orders and Orders to Close Account

A customer may stop payment on any item payable from his account. § 4-403(a). A stop payment order is the converse of an order to pay, and therefore the bank's obligation to honor a stop payment order is consistent with the basic banking principle that a bank may charge its customer's account only where it has followed his order in making payment. But suppose the bank overlooks the stop payment order and pays. Must the bank recredit its customer's account?

ROVELL v. AMERICAN NATIONAL BANK

232 B.R. 381 (N.D. Ill. 1998), aff'd, 194 F.3d 867 (7th Cir. 1999)

Moran, Senior District Judge.

Michael Rovell (Rovell), the Debtor, initiated a voluntary petition for reorganization under Chapter 11 of the Bankruptcy Code in October of 1995. American National Bank and Trust Company of Chicago (Bank) filed a Proof of Claim (claim) for $50,081.25, the amount Rovell admittedly owed on his secured line of credit. Rovell, however, filed an Objection (objection) seeking to reduce ANB's claim by an amount equal to the losses he incurred when the bank paid a check over a stop-payment order. After hearing testimony on March 17, 1997, United States Bankruptcy Judge Robert Ginsberg held that Rovell had failed to overcome the prima facie validity of the bank's claim and allowed it in full (bench order).

Debtor now appeals from both the bench order denying the objection and from Judge Ginsberg's December 22, 1997 order denying Rovell's motion to reconsider (December order). Although we disagree with one of the bankruptcy court's conclusions, we find that the court did not abuse its discretion when it allowed the claim in full. For the reasons stated herein, the decision of the bankruptcy court is affirmed.

BACKGROUND

Most of the facts regarding the stop-payment dispute are uncontested. In September 1994, Michael Rovell, a lawyer, wrote a check for $38,250 to the Pretty Eyes Detective Agency (check #1). After conveying the check to Patricia O'Connor, the owner of Pretty Eyes, Rovell discovered that he had overpaid her firm by more than $10,000. He asked his employee, Lisa Fair (Fair), also a lawyer, to contact the Bank and make sure the check had not cleared. At approximately 1:40 p.m. on September 19, 1994, Fair phoned Linda Williams (Williams), the ANB officer who served as Rovell's account representative, and told her that if the check had not been cashed, Rovell wanted to stop payment and issue a replacement check for the correct amount. Fair informed Williams that she was not sure of the check number or the date of issue, but she did know the account number, the check amount, and the payee.

The parties disagree about what the two women said next. At the evidentiary hearing, Fair testified she told Williams that "there were a number of checks taken from the book as [Rovell was] out of town, and that I thought it was possible that it was in the range of checks beginning with approximately 1084, but that I couldn't even be certain of that." (Fair Testimony (FT) at 17-18). Rovell's checkbook had three checks to a page. Fair further testified that she told Williams that the Pretty Eyes check "could possibly be in a range of approximately six checks, because I knew those had been taken by Mr. Rovell and were in his possession. But I didn't even know if it was in that range of six." (FT at 27-28).

Williams remembered their conversation differently. She testified that although Fair had been unsure of the precise check number, Fair "was 95% sure" that it was check number 1084 or 1086. The first thing Williams did, she recalled, was to key in those two check numbers to see if they had cleared. They hadn't and she told this to Fair.

This brings us to the heart of the dispute. Debtor Rovell contends that the message from Williams was that the "Pretty Eyes check" had not cleared. The Bank, on the other hand, claims that Williams merely informed Fair that checks 1084 and 1086 had not cleared. In fact, the parties would later discover that check number 1105, made payable to "Pretty Eyes," in the amount of $38,250.00, cleared that day.[2]

At this point in their conversation Fair instructed Williams to stop payment on the check. Williams recalls issuing electronic stop-payment orders for checks 1084 and 1086, and a record of this transaction was entered into evidence. Fair maintains she was told by Williams that if she provided the account number, payee, and amount of the check, payment could be stopped without the check number (FT at 18, 31). Williams explicitly denied this in her testimony. (WT at 71 In 17). Both parties, however, remember Williams telling Fair to "wait a couple of days" or "a few days" before issuing a replacement check. (WT at 64 and 80; Appellant's brief at 9). Williams also testified that it was her "routine procedure" to tell "all [her] customers[] that they should wait until they get the check back" (WT at 85-86) and "should check back to make sure if a check has been stopped." (WT at 86). She reportedly asked Fair, "Are these people reputable?" (Williams at 64, 68), referring to the payee.

Working on the assumption that check #1 had not cleared, Rovell's firm issued a second check to Pretty Eyes (check #2) in the amount of $27,284.50 and sent it to the private investigator along with a letter explaining that the new check was intended to replace the original. Rovell does not dispute the Bank's contention that neither Rovell nor Fair called Williams back to confirm that check #1 had not yet cleared. Unfortunately for Rovell, check #2 was also presented and paid, thereby contributing, Rovell contends, to the substantial overdraft on his ANB checking account.

In the meantime, the Bank apparently sent stop-payment confirmation orders to Rovell for checks 1084 and 1086. Fair does not remember receiving the confirmation forms, but acknowledged in her testimony that she found them in the company files while responding to the Bank's discovery request. The forms include the following statement:

> The check(s) appears not to have been paid since the date of your last statement. If the check should be recovered, please promptly advise us in writing, executed by the required number of authorized signers on the account. Please review all information to ensure its accuracy. If any changes are required, call the telephone number listed above. *The primary information required to stop payment on a check is the account number, check number found on the bottom line of the check and exact dollars/cents amount.* (emphasis added).

Neither party disputes Williams' testimony that under the Bank's technology at the time of the stop-payment request, it was not possible to stop a check without the check number (WT at 72-73). Nor do they dispute that Williams did not tell Fair of this impossibility. (WT at 80).

Thus, there are two principal sources of disagreement: first, whether Fair identified checks number 1084 and 1086 as the likely targets for the stop-payment order or indicated, instead, that the check was in a range of about six checks beginning with 1084; and second, whether Williams affirmatively represented to Fair that a check could be stopped despite the absence of a check number. As indicated in the bench order and again

---

2. The Bank represents that the check cleared before the stop-payment order, but the record does not clearly so indicate. It did clear, however, before any stop-payment order could have been effective.

in the December order, the bankruptcy court found both witnesses equally credible. The court suggested that there was "no evidence" tending to show that the recollection of either witness was inaccurate or that either was not telling the truth.

On appeal, Rovell renews his claim that American National Bank breached its agreement to stop payment on check #1. He also claims that ANB was negligent when it informed his representative that the check had not cleared and that payment could be stopped. Ultimately, Rovell argues that he was damaged in the amount of $38,250 when the first check to Pretty Eyes was cashed, or, alternatively, in the amount of $27,284 when he sent the second check to Pretty Eyes "*in reliance on the bank's assurance that the check had not cleared and could be stopped.*" (emphasis added). He asks this court to overturn the judgment of the bankruptcy court and to allow only $11,831.25 or, alternatively, only $22,796.75 of ANB's claim.[5]

DISCUSSION
1. Jurisdiction and Standard of Review

* * *

2. Breach of Contract

Chapter 810 ILCS 5/4-403 codifies the common law right of a depositor to order payment of a check stopped and establishes the requirements in Illinois for an effective stop-payment order. Section 5/4-403(a) provides in relevant part:

> A customer ... may stop payment of any item drawn on the customer's account ... by an order to the bank describing the item ... with reasonable certainty received at a time and in a manner that affords the bank a reasonable opportunity to act on it before any action by the bank with respect to the item described in Section 4-303 [810 ILCS 5/4-303].

Thus, a bank will not be held liable for failing to stop payment on a check that was not "described with reasonable certainty," nor will it be liable if the stop-payment order was untimely. Rovell contends that Fair's request to Williams satisfied both criteria. The burden of establishing the fact and amount of loss resulting from the payment of an item contrary to a stop-payment order is on the customer, 810 ILCS 5/4-403(c), the burden of compliance with a valid stop-payment order is placed squarely on the financial institution. 810 ILCS 5/4-403, Comment 1. This is so "notwithstanding its difficulty, inconvenience, or expense. The inevitable occasional losses through failure to stop should be borne by the banks as a cost of the business of banking." Id. We must determine, therefore, whether Rovell's stop-payment order was a valid one, such that ANB's failure to comply would be a breach of its duty under Illinois law.

(a) Identification

While there is little case law in Illinois detailing what it means for a stop order to describe an item with "reasonable certainty," courts in other jurisdictions interpreting identical provisions have employed one of two distinct approaches. The first assesses the degree to which the customer accurately specified the five identifying features of an individual check: the check number, amount, account number, payee, and date of

---

5. ANB's Proof of Claim was in the amount of $50,081.25. If reduced by the amount of check #1 ($38,250), the remainder would be $11,831.25. If reduced by the amount of check #2 ($27,284.50), the remainder would be $22,796.75.

issue. See, e.g., Sherrill v. Frank Morris Pontiac-Buick-GMC, Inc., 366 So.2d 251 (Ala. 1978) (incorrect identification of the check date and payee constituted insufficient notice to bank, even though depositor accurately provided the check amount); Thomas v. Marine Midland Tinkers Nat'l Bank, 86 Misc.2d 284, 381 N.Y.S.2d 797 (N.Y.City Civ.Ct. 1976) (direction to stop payment correct in all aspects except for single digit mistake on check number provided bank adequate notice and reasonable opportunity to act).

The second, more recent approach considers whether the customer and the bank have satisfied their respective responsibilities in the generation of an effective stop-payment order. Where a bank's system relies exclusively on one or two elements of the description, a number of courts have imposed a duty on the bank to give customers notice of these requirements. See, e.g., Rimberg v. Union Trust Co., 12 UCC Rep.Serv. 527 (D.C. Super. 1973) (bank liable for payment over stop order because teller failed to inform the depositor that the bank's computerized system required the exact amount of the check to effectuate a stop order); Staff Service Associates, Inc. v. Midlantic Nat'l Bank, 207 N.J.Super. 327, 504 A.2d 148 (L.Ct. 1985) ("reasonable opportunity" to act was present where customer only made single digit error in check amount and bank never informed customer that exact amount of check was necessary for computer to pull check); Hughes v. Marine Midland Bank, 127 Misc.2d 209, 484 N.Y.S.2d 1000 (N.Y.City Civ.Ct. 1985) (customer's order correctly stating account number and check amount satisfied requirements of § 4-403 where New York Banks had ample time to design software to meet the Thomas expectation of identification without check number); Parr v. Security National Bank, 680 P.2d 648 (Okla.Ct.App. 1984) (bank was not relieved of liability merely because bank's computers were programmed to stop payment only if reported amount of check was correct); Delano v. Putnam Trust Co., 33 UCC Rep. Serv. 635 (Conn.Super.Ct. 1981) (bank had a duty to inform its customer of the need for precision in reporting the amount before it could rely on customer's error to relieve it of liability).

Here there is no dispute that Fair correctly identified three of the five identifying elements of check #1: the payee, the amount, and the account number. There is also no argument that the bank's system required the check number to guarantee an effective stop payment. At issue is whether Williams informed Fair that the Bank would be unable to stop the Pretty Eyes check without an accurate check number (a factual question) and whether she had a duty to do so (a conclusion of law). As to the latter issue, Rovell relies upon those cases finding an affirmative duty to disclose the computer system requirements and contends that William's alleged omission deems Fair's request sufficient to meet the identification requirement, notwithstanding her inability to provide the exact check number. The Bank relies instead on those cases relieving the bank of liability where individual identifiers were sufficiently inaccurate to conclude that the customer had failed to identify the check with "reasonable certainty."

It is surely reasonable to require banks to inform customers of the requirements for an effective stop-order and to hold them accountable for payment over a stop order where the payment occurred because the customer was unaware the missing information was critical. By codifying 5/4-403 and adopting the accompanying commentary, the Illinois legislature made it clear that depositors expect to be able to stop payment on a check and are entitled to receive this service. This entitlement would be meaningless without guidance from the bank as to the precise information required for processing a stop-payment order. In FJS Electronics, Inc. v. Fidelity Bank, 288 Pa.Super. 138, 431 A.2d 326 (1981), the customer phoned in a stop-payment request correct in all respects except that he misstated the check amount by fifty cents. Because the bank had selected a computer system which relied upon the check amount to identify the item, the customer's error prevented the bank's computer from acting on the stop order. Based on its reading of the official comment to UCC 4-403, the FJS court found that any heightened risk of mistaken payments due to the system's exclusive reliance on an exact check amount should be borne by the bank, and it held the bank liable for the payment over the order. The Oklahoma Court of Appeals in Parr v. Security National Bank subsequently adopted this reasoning, but allowed the bank an affirmative defense if it notified the customer of the required elements at the time the stop order was requested. Parr, 680 P.2d at 651; accord Staff Service Associates, Inc., 504 A.2d at 152. We believe this is the correct approach to assess the identification element of 810 ILCS 5/4-403.

Thus, the court agrees with Rovell that the Bank had a duty to make clear that an exact check number was required to effectuate the stop-payment order, and joins those courts in other jurisdictions which have so held.[8] We are left, however, with the bankruptcy court's assessment regarding the witnesses' credibility. Williams testified that she told Fair that she needed the check number, although she did not inform her that she could only stop checks with an exact check number. According to Williams, Fair told her she was 95% sure that the check was number 1084 or 1086, and Williams stopped payment of those checks. The bankruptcy court was in the best position to evaluate the testimony of both women, and we defer to the court's judgment that Williams' testimony was credible and that, under the standard of proof prescribed by 5/4-403, Rovell failed to establish that the stop order identified the item with "reasonable certainty." In any event, the stop came too late.

(b) Timeliness

The second requirement for a bank to be held liable for payment over a stop-payment order is that the request be received "at a time and in such a manner that the bank has a reasonable opportunity to act." 810 ILCS 5/4-403. Rovell contends that because the bank advised Fair to wait "a couple of days" before issuing a replacement check, ANB must have considered "two days" sufficient time to respond to the stop-payment order, i.e., a "reasonable opportunity to act." The Bank, on the other hand, argues that the bankruptcy court's finding that check #1 was cashed before any computer direction to stop payment would have been effective indicates that the order arrived too late for the bank to stop payment.

A payment in violation of an effective direction to stop payment is an improper payment even though it is made by mistake or inadvertence. 810 ILCS 5/4-403, Comment 7. But while the code places the burden of compliance on the bank, it is not expected to perform miracles. Compare Siniscalchi v. Valley Bank of New York, 79 Misc.2d 64, 66, 359 N.Y.S.2d 173 (N.Y.Dist.Ct. 1974) (bank did not have reasonable time to act upon order where check was cashed Saturday morning and stop order was obtained Monday morning) with Thomas v. Marine Midland Tinkers Nat'l Bank, 86 Misc.2d 284, 287, 381 N.Y.S.2d 797 (N.Y.City Civ.Ct. 1976) (day and one-half was reasonable notice for bank to enforce stop order on check presented at the same branch). The effective time for determining whether a stop order was received too late to affect payment of an item is "receipt plus a reasonable time to act on any of the communications." Siniscalchi, 79 Misc.2d at 66, 359 N.Y.S.2d 173. Further guidance is provided by the reference in 5/4-403 to the ordering of payment responsibilities as set forth in 5/4-303. Under this code

---

8. We leave for another day the question as to whether that duty must be carried out during the customer's initial request or whether the language in the confirmation order would be sufficient to put the depositor on notice.

provision, a stop-payment order comes too late to modify the bank's right or duty to pay a check if it comes after the bank accepts the item or pays the item in cash.... It is undisputed here that any stop-payment order would be effectively programmed into the computer for the opening of business the following day, and by then the check had cleared. Thus, as a matter of law, the order came too late to modify the bank's right or duty to pay the item.

In his reply brief, Rovell argues that under 810 ILCS 5/4-301(a)-(b) and 5/4-104(a)(1) a payor bank has 24 hours to recover or revoke the payment after it is made. "Thus, even if ANB paid the check before the stop-payment got into the system, it *could* have recovered the payment." Rovell reply brief (emphasis added). Perhaps, but the authority given to the bank to revoke a settlement does not change the result that ANB is not liable to Rovell under 5/4-403 for any losses arising out of the payment of check #1105.

ANB initially shared the responsibility to create an effective stop-payment order, but as ANB's customer, Rovell had the burden of establishing the fact and amount of loss resulting from payment over the order. He failed to do so when he could not persuade the bankruptcy court as to his version of events. Moreover, the order came too late to modify ANB's right to pay the check and charge his account for the overdraft.

* * *

CONCLUSION

The court believes it important to make clear that ANB owed a duty to Rovell to clarify any elements of check identification necessary to ensure the generation of an effective stop-payment order. Similarly, we find that ANB was in the business of supplying information to its depositors and thus could have been held liable for a negligent misrepresentation. Ultimately, however, we find that the court correctly placed the liability for Rovell's shortsighted behavior with the Debtor himself. As a matter of law, his stop-payment order came too late to make a difference. As a matter of common sense, and in light of Fair's uncertainty about which check had been written to "Pretty Eyes," Rovell should have postponed sending any replacement check until he was certain the first had been properly identified and had not cleared.

The decision by the bankruptcy court is affirmed and Claim No. 31 as submitted by American National Bank is allowed in its entirety.

Problem 4-16

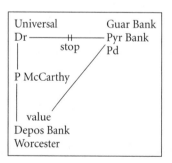

On October 1, Universal issued a check for $10,886, drawn on its account at Guaranty Bank, and payable to the order of McCarthy Motors. The same day McCarthy Motors deposited the check with Worcester Bank for collection only, but in fact the bank allowed McCarthy to draw on the entire balance of its account plus the amount of the check before it cleared. At 9:00 a.m. on October 2, Universal gave Guaranty Bank a stop payment order on the check. Nevertheless when Worcester Bank presented the check to Guaranty Bank at 1:00 p.m. that same day, Guaranty Bank made final payment. Later Guaranty Bank asked Worcester Bank to take back the check, but Worcester Bank refused. Guaranty Bank then debited Universal's account for $10,886. Universal claims this debit was unauthorized.

1) Who will bear the loss? §§ 4-403, 4-407, 4-211, 4-210.

Q: What will lawyers for Guaranty Bank assert during pretrial negotiations with Universal?

2) Was the check properly payable?

3) Has Universal really suffered no loss? § 4-403(c).

Problem 4-17

```
Ned              Par Nat
Dr ———————— Pyr Bank
        stop      Pd
|
P  Bell Mtrs
|
Dep Bank
```

Ned has a checking account with Paradise National Bank (PNB). On March 10, Ned gave a check for $2,050 to Belmont Motors as part of the purchase price of a used car. After driving it off the lot, Ned heard an expensive-sounding noise coming from under the hood. When Ned got home he called PNB and asked it to stop payment on his check. PNB said it would not do that unless Ned came down and signed a stop payment order. Ned went down and signed the order. Ned inserted the correct date, check number, and name of the payee, but in the space where he was required to put the amount of the check he wrote $2,005. When the check came through on March 20, the computer missed it and $2,050 was debited from his account.

1) Must PNB credit Ned's account for $2,050? § 4-403.

Q: Why did the computer miss the check?

Q: What is the issue?

2) Review: Suppose that after stopping payment, Ned had called Belmont Motors, told it of the noise and that he had stopped payment. Belmont then slyly held onto the check for one year before depositing it for collection. When the check arrived, PNB paid it. Who bears the loss? §§ 4-403, 4-404.

3) Review: Suppose that Ned had inserted the correct amount on the form ($2,050), which stated: "Customer agrees that Bank's liability for contrary payment shall not exceed the amount of the item on which the order was placed." Will this clause save the bank? § 4-103(a).

Chapter 5

The Holder's Rights Against the Drawer and Other Parties to Checks and Drafts

We have been considering the relationship between the drawer and drawee. We now shift our focus to the relationship of the payee and depositary bank to the drawer and other parties to the instrument—the drawee or payor and indorsers. This will complete our discussion of the rights and duties of the various parties to checks and drafts.

TEPPER v. CITIZENS FEDERAL SAVINGS & LOAN
38 U.C.C. Rep. Serv. 528 (Fla. Dist. Ct. App. 1984)

FERGUSON, J. The sole question presented is when does the statute of limitations begin to run against a drawer in an action for wrongful dishonor of a check—on the date of issuance of the check or the date of presentment and dishonor?

Rose Tepper (appellant) was adjudicated an incompetent in December, 1982. On examination of her personal effects, a court-appointed guardian discovered a check for the sum of $6,068, dated January 4, 1974. The check was drawn to Rose Tepper by Citizens Federal Savings and Loan Association against its account with Jefferson National Bank.

On December 20, 1982, appellant's representative presented the check to the drawee bank, Jefferson National (not a party to this action), which refused payment. The representative then advised the drawer, Citizens Federal (appellee), of the dishonor. Citizens Federal orally notified appellant's representative that it would neither honor nor refund the instrument. The guardian instituted this action against the drawer on July 12, 1983.

The trial court dismissed the guardian's complaint on appellee's motion, holding that "the statute of limitations began to run on the date of issuance of the check herein sued upon, [so the] action is barred by the applicable five-year statute of limitations." We reverse upon a holding that the statute of limitations begins to run against a drawer of a check on the date of presentment and dishonor.

Although there seems to be a dearth of Florida case law on the issue presented, appellant has found all the law necessary to a correct resolution. The decision here is based upon an application of clear statutes and is supported by several treatises.

A draft is a three-party instrument whereby the drawer orders the drawee to pay money to the payee. See J. White and R. Summers, Uniform Commercial Code § 13-1 (2d ed. 1980). A draft is also called a check when the drawee is a bank and the instrument is payable on demand. § 673.104(2)(b), Fla. Stat. (1983) [R§ 3-104(f)]. A drawee is not liable on the instrument until there has been an acceptance. § 673.409 [R§ 3-408]. The drawee may, by accepting in writing on the instrument, agree to honor it as presented. § 673.410 [R§ 3-

409]. By contrast, a drawee may reject the instrument, as by stamping insufficient funds on a check where the drawer's deposited funds are less than the amount of the instrument. The act of accepting the instrument renders the drawee primarily liable as an acceptor. See §673.414(1) [R§3-413(a)]. Because there are no conditions precedent to its liability, a cause of action accrues against an acceptor in the case of a demand instrument on the date of the instrument or date of issue. §673.122(1)(b) 1 [omitted; see R§3-118 OC 1].

The drawer, on the other hand, is only secondarily liable on the instrument, in that there are conditions precedent to liability. W. Hawkland, Commercial Paper 52 (2d ed. 1979). The normal conditions precedent include presentment to the drawee, dishonor, and notice of dishonor. Id.; see §673.501 [R§3-414(b), R§3-502(b), R§3-501(a)]. Therefore, a cause of action against the drawer of a draft accrues only upon demand following dishonor of the instrument. §673.122(3). Notice of dishonor constitutes a demand. Id. This latter section is clearly dispositive of the issue presented, as a cause of action against the drawer herein, Citizens Federal, thus did not accrue until appellant's representative received notice of dishonor from the drawee, Jefferson National Bank.

Florida case authority for the proposition that the statute of limitations begins to run against an issuing bank on a *cashier's check* at the moment of issuance, Atlantic National Bank of West Palm Beach v. Havens, 45 So. 2d 342 (Fla. 1950), is distinguishable. A cashier's check is a check on which the issuing bank acts as both the drawer and the drawee. Its own act of issuance renders the bank a drawee who has accepted the draft; thus the issuing bank becomes primarily liable as a acceptor. J. White and R. Summers, Uniform Commercial Code §17-5 (2d ed. 1980). Presentment of a negotiable instrument is not necessary in order to establish liability against parties who are primarily liable. In such a case the statute of limitations begins to run on a demand instrument at the moment of issuance. W. Hawkland, Commercial Paper 42–43 (2d ed. 1979). As to parties secondarily liable, however, such as the drawer herein, there is no instant liability and thus no cause of action until demand following presentment and dishonor. H. Bailey, Brady on Bank Checks §4.12 (5th ed. 1979).

The distinction between a cashier's check where the issuing bank is primarily liable and other drafts, where the drawer is secondarily liable, is stated:

> "[U]nder the Code, cause of action against a certifying bank or a bank issuing a cashier's check accrues on the date of the check (or date of issue if the check is undated). This means that the statute of limitations begins to run at that time and suit against the bank will be barred after the statute of limitations has run. But a cause of action against a drawer of a check does not accrue until demand following dishonor. This theoretically means that the time for bringing action against the drawer may be deferred indefinitely if there is no presentment for payment." H. Bailey, Brady on Bank Checks §4.12 (5th ed. 1979).

Under Florida law an action may not be deferred indefinitely in all instances; instead, a drawer will be discharged from its liability if presentment is unreasonably delayed and the drawee bank becomes insolvent during the delay. §673.502(1)(b) [R§3-414(f)]; see also Robinson v. Brunson, 383 So. 2d 964 (Fla. 2d D. Ct. App. 1980).

In that appellee herein was the drawer of the instrument which is the subject of this action, and therefore only secondarily liable, a cause of action did not accrue against it until after demand following presentment and dishonor on December 20, 1982. The action for wrongful dishonor of the instrument was commenced timely.

Reversed and remanded.

Notes

1. What would be the applicable statute of limitations if *Tepper* was decided under the current version of Article 3? § 3-118.

2. Section 3-118 sets out some outside limitation periods, e.g., "10 years after the date of the draft" (§ 3-118(c)), and some limitation periods that begin to run only after a cause of action accrues, thereby drawing a distinction between accrual of a cause of action and the limitation period within which that action must be brought.

The conditions that must be satisfied before an action on an instrument accrues are set out elsewhere in Article 3. For example, with respect to the liability of a drawer of a check the action accrues when the conditions of § 3-414(b) are met. The only express condition is that the check be "dishonored." However, there may be implied conditions, such as presentment and notice of dishonor. In those instances if a check is not presented for payment, it can never be dishonored, and thus a cause of action would never accrue. If a check is dishonored, as a practical matter it probably will not be paid if the holder does not make an additional demand for payment, even though the return of a check legally constitutes notice of dishonor. § 3-503(b). And it is unlikely that an action would be commenced to collect on the check until such steps have been taken.

However, since the only express condition to the drawer's liability is "dishonor," the date of dishonor would no doubt be the date on which the action accrues. It will be noted that the event that triggers the running of the statute of limitations is also "dishonor," i.e., "three years after dishonor of the draft." § 3-118(c). Thus in many instances, it may be found that the action accrues and the statute begins to run simultaneously, even though they are distinguishable events under Article 3. § 3-118 OC 1.

But it is theoretically possible for an action on an instrument to be barred by the running of the statute of limitations before an action ever accrues, e.g., by the passing of ten years from the date of an unaccepted draft that was never presented to the drawee for payment. § 3-118(c).

A. Holder's Rights Against the Drawer

1. Presentment and Dishonor

We begin with the nature of the liability of the drawer. The drawer's liability is conditional and therefore secondary in nature, although the comments indicate that it is "treated" as primary liability. § 3-414 OC 2. If a drawer's liability is conditional, the question naturally arises: what are those conditions? The conditions to a drawer's liability can include presentment (§ 3-501), dishonor (§ 3-502) and notice of dishonor (§ 3-503), depending on the circumstances and the nature of the draft.

The only condition to the liability of a drawer of an *unaccepted* draft, which includes the common check, is dishonor. § 3-414(b). However, in most instances there cannot be a dishonor unless there has been a presentment (see § 3-502(b)), so in that sense presentment is also a condition to the drawer's liability even though it is not mentioned in § 3-414(b). If the draft is accepted rather than dishonored, the acceptance of the draft converts the drawer's liability to that of an indorser, unless the acceptor is a bank, in which case the liability of the drawer (and also the liability of any indorser) will be discharged. §§ 3-414(c) & (d), 3-415(d).

A drawer's liability on an *accepted* draft is conditional upon dishonor and possibly notice of dishonor. §§ 3-414(d), 3-502(d), 3-503(a). An example of such a draft is a draft drawn by a seller on a buyer for the price of goods, payable thirty days after sight or acceptance, assuming the buyer has accepted the draft by writing his signature on it. § 3-409.

The drawee is not liable at all until it accepts the draft, § 3-408, but upon acceptance it becomes primarily liable, § 3-409(a). But what if a draft is never presented to the drawee? Where does that leave the payee-holder? How accurate is it to say that the drawer is primarily liable?

2. Time for Presentment and Dishonor

The major event that triggers the liability of the drawer of an unaccepted draft, which includes the check, is dishonor, and dishonor is the only express condition to the drawer's liability. § 3-414(b). However, in the normal sequence of commercial transactions a draft must be presented for payment or acceptance before the holder will know whether it will be paid, accepted, or dishonored, and therefore presentment is an implied condition to a drawer's liability.

In contrast to former Article 3, revised Article 3 contains no time limits within which presentment must be made to hold a drawer or indorser. For example, F§ 3-503 provided that holders of drafts and checks must present them within a reasonable time after secondary parties become liable thereon. This requirement has been omitted from revised Article 3. This means that the rights of holders against drawers and indorsers normally will not be jeopardized by the lapse of time between receipt of the instrument and presentment for payment (but see § 3-415(e), which discharges an indorser's signature liability if "the check is not presented for payment, or given to a depositary bank for collection, within 30 days after the day the indorsement was made"). However, the time of dishonor does depend upon the time of presentment. For example, if a check is presented for payment "over the counter," it will be dishonored unless the bank pays "on the day of presentment." § 3-502(b)(2). In this instance a failure or refusal of the bank to pay on the day of presentment is a dishonor on the day of presentment.

Problem 5-1

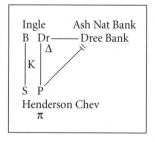

Ingle bought a car from Henderson Chevrolet and gave his note to secure the balance owing, to be paid off in monthly installments of $142. Ingle delivered a check to Henderson Chevrolet in payment of the last installment on November 19, drawn on his account at Asheville National Bank in which he had sufficient funds. On the morning of November 20, Henderson Chevrolet sent its agent, Jake, to Asheville National Bank to collect on the check. When Jake arrived he found there was "a run on the bank." He entered the bank about 10:30 a.m. and remained in line until about 1:00 p.m. and then left before the bank was closed without getting the check cashed. Other customers in line behind Jake did get their checks cashed before the bank closed for the day. The next day when Jake presented the check to the cashier, he was told that all assets and funds on deposit had been exhausted by the end of the previous day. Henderson Chevrolet then demanded payment of the check from Ingle. Ingle refused to pay anything further on the note and Henderson Chevrolet commenced action against him on the check.

1) Decide the case. §§ 3-414(b), 3-501(a), 3-502(b)(2), 1-103(b).

2) Suppose Henderson Chevrolet had deposited the check in its checking account on November 19 and that it had arrived at Asheville National Bank on November 22. How would that affect your decision?

Q: Ignoring the shaky financial position of the bank, how long can Henderson Chevrolet wait before presenting the check without losing its ability to sue Ingle if the check is dishonored? §§ 3-304(a)(2), 4-404, 3-118.

3) Review: Suppose Henderson Chevrolet had deposited the check in its checking account on Friday, November 19, the check had arrived at the payor bank, Asheville National Bank, on Monday, November 22, and the bank did not become insolvent and suspend payments until Thursday, November 25. Bank management now wants to dishonor the check and return it to the depositary bank. Advise the payor bank. §§ 3-502(b)(1), 4-302(a).

4) Review: If you decide Henderson Chevrolet cannot recover on the check, can it now sue Ingle on the note? §§ 3-310(b), 3-603.

3. Presentment for Acceptance and Notice of Dishonor

Problem 5-2

Dunn drew a draft on Ricketts and Company, payable to the order of Sinclair one month after date. Before the month was up Sinclair presented the draft to Ricketts and Company for acceptance, which was refused. Without giving notice of the refusal to anyone, Sinclair negotiated the draft to O'Keefe, who took without notice and for valuable consideration. O'Keefe also presented the draft for acceptance before the month was up, and the drawee again refused to accept it. O'Keefe then gave notice of the nonacceptance to Dunn and demanded payment from him. Dunn refused to pay it on the ground that the failure of Sinclair to give him notice of the nonacceptance discharged him from liability, and that in any event the holder had not yet made presentment for payment.

1) Why would a holder of a draft, payable on a stated date, present it for acceptance before the date of maturity? § 3-409.

2) Is Dunn liable to O'Keefe on the instrument? §§ 3-414(b), (d); 3-502(b)(3), (e); 3-504(a)(iv).

Q: Dunn argues that O'Keefe has not yet presented the draft for payment. How should O'Keefe respond? § 3-504(a)(iv).

3) Did Sinclair's failure to give notice of nonacceptance to Dunn discharge Dunn from liability on the instrument? §§ 3-601(b), 3-414(b).

4) <u>Review</u>: On what theories might O'Keefe sue Sinclair? §§ 3-415(a), (c); 3-416(a).

5) <u>Review</u>: If O'Keefe prevails against Sinclair, could Sinclair then succeed in an action against Dunn? §§ 3-414(b), 3-503 OC 1.

Problem 5-3

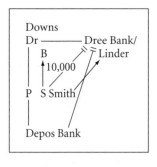

Downs bought a prize bull from Smith and planned to use the bull in the rodeo the following day. Downs gave Smith a check for $10,000 at 3:00 p.m. when it was too late for Smith to have the check certified. The next morning Smith took the check to Downs' bank and asked the bank to certify it. The bank refused. Smith then deposited the check in his account at his own bank. That afternoon at the rodeo his prize bull bucked off last year's world champion bull rider, but then the bull died of a heart attack. In due course Smith received the check marked "NSF."

1) What could Smith have done to avoid this problem? §§ 3-409; 3-104(f), (g), (h); 3-411(b).

2) What are Smith's options now? §§ 3-414(b), 3-502(b)(1), 4-302(a).

3) Determine whether Smith's options differ if Downs had given him a draft for $10,000 drawn on Linder (an all-around cowboy and a solvent friend of Downs), payable in thirty days, but that in the meantime Smith presented the draft to Linder for his acceptance and Linder accepted it. However, when it was presented to Linder for payment at the end of thirty days, Linder refused to pay it. §§ 3-413(a), 3-414(d), 3-502(d)(2), 3-415(c), 3-503(a).

Problem 5-4

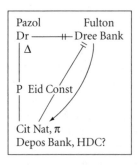

Pazol drew a check for $49,600 on Fulton National Bank (FNB) dated January 4, 2007, payable to the order of Eidson Construction Inc. In fact the check was issued on January 4, 2008. Without indorsing the check, Eidson Construction deposited the check in its account with Citizens Bank, who took it for collection without noticing that it was dated January 4, 2007. Before the check reached FNB, Pazol entered a stop payment order. Without knowledge of the stop payment order Citizens Bank permitted Eidson Construction to withdraw all of the funds represented by the check. FNB refused to pay the check and timely returned it to Citizens Bank on January 13, 2008. Eidson Construction is insolvent. Citizens Bank commences an action against Pazol, who has a good personal defense. Decide the case.

1) What is the broad issue? §§ 3-302, 1-201(b)(21).

2) Pazol argues that Citizens Bank is only an agent for Eidson Construction and therefore subject to defenses good against Eidson Construction. Is he right? §§ 4-201; 3-201; 3-203(b), (c).

3) What about the absence of Eidson Construction's indorsement? § 4-205.

4) What about the date of the check? §§ 3-302(a)(2)(iii), 3-113, 3-304(a). Cf. F§ 3-114(3).

B. Holder's Rights Against the Payor Bank and Collecting Banks

We now shift our focus from the holder's rights against the drawer to consider the holder's rights against the drawee and other parties.

1. Acceptance and Certification

MESSING v. BANK OF AMERICA, N.A.
821 A.2d 22 (Md. Ct. App. 2003)

HARRELL, Judge.

I.

The case *sub judice* involves a bank check. A check is defined as a draft payable on demand and drawn on a bank.... The circumstances which gave rise to the case before us are, in terms of its genesis, reminiscent of those described in the case of *Board of Inland Revenue v. Haddock*.[2] In that case, the protagonist, Mr. Haddock, after some dispute involving uncollected income-taxes owed, elected to test the limits of the law of checks as it existed at British common law at the time. Operating on the proposition that a check was only an order to a bank to pay money to the person in possession of the check or a person named on the check, and observing that there was nothing in statute or custom at the time specifying that a check must be written on paper of certain dimensions, or even paper at all, Haddock elected to tender payment to the tax collector by a check written on the back of a cow. The Collector of Taxes at first attempted to endorse the check, but, we are informed, the check "appeared to resent endorsement and adopted a menacing posture" at which point the Collector abandoned the attempt and refused to accept the check. Mr. Haddock then led the check away and was subsequently arrested in Trafalgar Square for causing an obstruction, upon which he was said to have observed that "it was a nice thing if in the heart of the commercial capital of the world a man could not convey a negotiable instrument down the street without being arrested." He subsequently was summoned by the Board of Inland Revenue for non-payment of income-tax.

The case *sub judice* arises from Petitioner's irritation with the Bank of America's Thumbprint Signature Program. Under the Thumbprint Signature Program, a bank requests non-customer presenters of checks over the counter to place an "inkless" thumbprint or fingerprint on the face of the check as part of the identification process. The program was developed, as the Court of Special Appeals informs us in its opinion in this case, by the American Bankers Association, working with the Federal Deposit Insurance Corporation (FDIC), the Federal Reserve Banks, the Office of the Comptroller of the Currency, the Federal Bureau of Investigation, and other law enforcement officials and banking trade associations across the county in response to rising instances of check

---

2. *Board of Inland Revenue v. Haddock*, known commonly as "The Negotiable Cow" case, is, in fact, a fictitious case which originally appeared in the pages of the British humor magazine *Punch*, and since has been re-printed in A.P. Herbert, Uncommon Law: Being sixty-six Misleading Cases revised and collected in one volume, 201-206 (Dorset Press, 1991) (1935).

fraud.... It is undisputed that the Bank of America's Thumbprint Signature Program uses an inkless fingerprinting device that leaves no ink stains or residue.

II.

At some point in time prior to 3 August 2000, Petitioner, as a holder, came into possession of a check in the amount of Nine Hundred Seventy-Six Dollars ($976.00) (the check) from Toyson J. Burruss, the drawer, doing business as Prestige Auto Detail Center. Instead of depositing the check into his account at his own bank, Petitioner elected to present the check for payment at a branch of Mr. Burruss' bank, Bank of America, the drawee.[3] On 3 August 2000, Petitioner approached a teller at Bank of America's 10 Light Street Banking Center in Baltimore City and asked to cash the check. The teller, by use of a computer, confirmed the availability of funds on deposit, and placed the check into the computer's printer slot. The computer stamped certain data on the back of the check, including the time, date, amount of the check, account number, and teller number. The computer also effected a hold on the amount of $976.00 in the customer's account. The teller gave the check back to the Petitioner, who endorsed it. The teller then asked for Petitioner's identification. Petitioner presented his driver's license and a major credit card. The teller took the endorsed check from Petitioner and manually inscribed the driver's license information and certain credit card information on the back of the check.

At some point during the transaction, the teller counted out $976.00 in cash from her drawer in anticipation of completing the transaction. She asked if the Petitioner was a customer of Bank of America. The Petitioner stated that he was not. The teller returned the check to Petitioner and requested, consistent with bank policy when cashing checks for non-customers, that Petitioner place his thumbprint on the check.[4] Petitioner refused and the teller informed him that she would be unable to complete the transaction without his thumbprint.

Petitioner requested, and was referred to, the branch manager. Petitioner presented the check to the branch manager and demanded that the check be cashed notwithstanding Petitioner's refusal to place his thumbprint on the check. The branch manager examined the check and returned it to the Petitioner, informing him that, because Petitioner was a non-customer, Bank of America would not cash the check without Petitioner's thumbprint on the instrument. After some additional exchanges, Petitioner left the bank with the check in his possession. The branch manager advised the teller that Petitioner had left the bank with his check. In response, the teller released the hold on the customer's funds, voided the transaction in the computer, and placed the cash back in her teller drawer.

Rather than take the check to his own bank and deposit it there, or returning it to Burruss, the drawer, as dishonored and demanding payment, Petitioner, two months later, on 10 October 2000, filed a declaratory judgment action against Bank of America

---

3. Petitioner's choice could be viewed as an attempt at risk shifting. Petitioner, an attorney, may have known that he could have suffered a fee charged by his own bank if he deposited a check into his own account and the bank on which it was drawn returned it for insufficient funds, forged endorsement, alteration, or the like. Petitioner's action, viewed against that backdrop, would operate as a risk shifting strategy, electing to avoid the risk of a returned-check fee by presenting in person the check for acceptance at the drawee bank.

4. The writing surface at each teller station at the branch was posted with a sign relating to the FDIC. Clearly visible in the lower right quadrant of each sign were the following words: "Thumbprint Signature Participating Member. For the protection of our customers, Thumbprint Signatures will be obtained from all non-account holders seeking to cash checks."

(the Bank) in the Circuit Court for Baltimore City. Petitioner claimed that the Bank had violated the Maryland Uniform Commercial Code (UCC) and had violated his personal privacy when the teller asked Petitioner to place an "inkless" thumbprint on the face of the check at issue. Petitioner asked the trial court to declare that: 1) Petitioner had provided "reasonable identification" without his thumbprint; 2) under § 3-501(b)(2), a thumbprint is not reasonable identification; 3) requiring a thumbprint of non-customers to cash a check is illegal, inappropriate, and unnecessary; 4) requiring non-customers to provide a thumbprint is a violation of the personal privacy of non-customers; 5) the Bank be required to cease requiring thumbprints in Maryland; 6) the Bank had "accepted" the check when presented by Petitioner; 7) the Bank "wrongfully dishonored" the check; and 8) the Bank wrongfully converted the check. Petitioner also sought injunctive relief directing Bank of America to cease participation in the Thumbprint Signature Program.

On 15 November 2000, the Bank filed a Motion to Dismiss or, in the alternative, for Summary Judgment. Petitioner opposed the Bank's Motion and filed a "cross" Motion for Summary Judgment. After the Circuit Court heard oral arguments on the pending motions, it denied Petitioner's request for injunctive relief and entered summary judgment in favor of the Bank, dismissing the Complaint with prejudice.

Petitioner appealed on 17 January 2001. The Court of Special Appeals concluded that the Circuit Court's decision in favor of the Bank was legally correct, but remanded the case for entry of a proper declaratory judgment as to the rights of the parties consistent with its opinion....

Petitioner petitioned this Court for a writ of certiorari. On 10 June 2002, we granted the petition....

III.

* * *

IV.

* * *

V.

A. Petitioner's Arguments:

Petitioner argues initially that he properly presented the check to the drawee bank and that the bank accepted the check. In Petitioner's view, the Bank's request for thumbprint identification was unreasonable as it would not aid the Bank in identifying the Petitioner as the proper person to pay at the time payment was made, but would be useful only at some later date, if at all. Petitioner's argument is fairly straight forward, adopting a "follow the bouncing ball" approach to the application of Maryland Code (1957, 2002 Repl.Vol.), Commercial Law Article, Title 3, to the facts of this case.... Petitioner's argument is that § 3-111 instructs that the correct location for him to present the check at issue for payment was at the offices of the bank named on the check as the drawee.... According to § 3-111:

> Except as otherwise provided for items in Title 4 [Bank Deposits and Collections], an instrument is payable at the place of payment stated in the instrument. If no place of payment is stated, an instrument is payable at the address of the drawee or maker stated in the instrument. If no address is stated, the place of payment is the place of business of the drawee or maker. If a drawee or maker

has more than one place of business, the place of payment is any place of business of the drawee or maker chosen by the person entitled to enforce the instrument. If the drawee or maker has no place of business, the place of payment is the residence of the drawee or maker.

In short, Petitioner's position is that, assuming all else is in order, § 3-111 requires Bank of America to pay a check drawn on one of its customer's accounts if presentment is made over the counter at the Bank.[8] Petitioner then argues why his presentment was in order, according to the relevant code provisions, thus, in his view, requiring the Bank to pay the check.

Petitioner cites § 3-501, which states:

(a) "Presentment" means a demand made by or on behalf of a person entitled to enforce an instrument (i) to pay the instrument made to the drawee or a party obliged to pay the instrument or, in the case of a note or accepted draft payable at a bank, to the bank, or (ii) to accept a draft made to the drawee.

(b) The following rules are subject to Title 4, agreement of the parties, and clearinghouse rules and the like:

(1) Presentment may be made at the place of payment of the instrument and must be made at the place of payment if the instrument is payable at a bank in the United States; may be made by any commercially reasonable means, including an oral, written, or electronic communication; is effective when the demand for payment or acceptance is received by the person to whom demand for payment or acceptance is received by the person to whom presentment is made; and is effective if made to any one of two or more makers, acceptors, drawees, or other payors.

(2) Upon demand of the person to whom presentment is made, the person making presentment must (i) exhibit the instrument, (ii) give reasonable identification and, if presentment is made on behalf of another person, reasonable evidence of authority to do so, and (iii) sign a receipt on the instrument for any payment made or surrender the instrument if full payment is made.

(3) Without dishonoring the instrument, the party to whom presentment is made may (i) return the instrument for lack of a necessary indorsement, or (ii) refuse payment or acceptance for failure of the presentment to comply with the terms of the instrument, an agreement of the parties, or other applicable law or rule.

(4) The party to whom presentment is made may treat presentment as occurring on the next business day after the day of presentment if the party to whom presentment is made has established a cutoff hour not earlier than 2 p.m. for the receipt and processing of instruments presented for payment or acceptance and presentment is made after the cutoff hour.

Petitioner argues that he correctly made "presentment" of the check to the Bank pursuant to § 3-111 and § 3-501(a), and demands that, as the person named on the instrument and thus entitled to enforce the check, the drawee Bank pay him. Petitioner

---

8. Petitioner is incorrect. Section 3-111 merely requires the Bank to receive the presentment of a check for payment, return, or dishonor. Put another way, § 3-111 identifies the location where the check ultimately is to be sent so that the drawee Bank may have notice of the order to pay and make a decision with regards to that order. As is discussed infra, § 3-111 does not require the Bank to accept the check (§ 3-409), or to pay the check (§ 3-413 and § 4-215)....

further argues that his presentment was in the proper form set forth in § 3-501(b)(2). Petitioner points out that he exhibited the instrument when he arrived at the counter and that, upon request, he provided reasonable identification in the form of his driver's license and a major credit card, and that he surrendered the check to the teller, who stamped it in her computer. The subsequent request for Petitioner to place his thumbprint on the check was, in Petitioner's view, not "reasonable" and therefore improper under § 3-501(b)(2)(ii). Petitioner argues that the rightness of his view is because the purpose of providing reasonable identification at the time of presentment is so that a bank can assure itself that it is making payment to the proper person at the time payment is made. Petitioner argues that a thumbprint will not provide that information at the time payment is made over the counter, but only at some later date. While we shall address the reasonableness of the thumbprint identification, infra, the issue is not dispositive as to Petitioner's claims against the Bank, and is, in fact, largely collateral.

In a continuation, Petitioner contends that the teller, by placing the check in the slot of her computer, and the computer then printing certain information on the back of the check, accepted the check as defined by § 3-409(a), which states:

> (a) "Acceptance" means the drawee's signed agreement to pay a draft as presented. It must be written on the draft and may consist of the drawee's signature alone. Acceptance may be made at any time and becomes effective when notification pursuant to instructions is given or the accepted draft is delivered for the purpose of giving rights on the acceptance to any person.

Relying on § 3-401(b), Petitioner argues that the act of the Bank's computer printing information on the back of the check constitutes the Bank's signature, and thus effectuates acceptance of the check on the part of the Bank. Section 3-401 states:

> (a) A person is not liable on an instrument unless (i) the person signed the instrument, or (ii) the person is represented by an agent or representative who signed the instrument and the signature is binding on the represented person under § 3-402.

> (b) A Signature may be made (i) manually or by means of a device or machine, and (ii) by the use of any name, including a trade or assumed name, or by a word, mark or symbol executed or adopted by a person with present intention to authenticate a writing.

In support, Petitioner points to part of the Official Comment 2 attached to § 3-409, as follows:

> Subsection (a) states the generally recognized rule that the mere signature of the drawee on the instrument is a sufficient acceptance. Customarily the signature is written vertically across the face of the instrument, but since the drawee has no reason to sign for any other purpose a signature in any other place, even on the back of the instrument, is sufficient. It need not be accompanied by such words as "Accepted," "Certified," or "Good."[9]

Thus, according to Petitioner, because the Bank's computer printed information on the back of the check, under § 3-401(b) the Bank "signed" the check, said "signature" being sufficient to constitute acceptance under § 3-409(a).

---

9. Among other things, Petitioner omits the last sentence of Comment 2, which reads: "The last sentence of subsection (a) states the generally recognized rule that an acceptance written on the draft takes effect when the drawee notifies the holder or gives notice according to instructions."

Petitioner's remaining arguments line up like so many dominos. According to Petitioner, having established that under his reading of § 3-409(a) the Bank accepted the check, Petitioner advances that the Bank is obliged to pay him, pursuant to § 3-413(a) which states:

(a) The acceptor of a draft is obliged to pay the draft (i) according to its terms at the time it was accepted, even though the acceptance states that the draft is payable "as originally drawn" or equivalent terms, (ii) if the acceptance varies the terms of the draft, according to the terms of the draft as varied, or (iii) if the acceptance is of a draft that is an incomplete instrument, according to its terms when completed, to the extent stated in §§ 3-115 and 3-407. The obligation is owed to a person entitled to enforce the draft or to the drawer or an indorser who paid the draft under § 3-414 or § 3-415.

Petitioner continues that because Bank of America accepted the check, but then failed to make payment, by the terms of § 3-502(d)(1) the Bank dishonored the check and became solely liable to Petitioner for payment. Section 3-502(d)(1) states:

(d) Dishonor of an accepted draft is governed by the following rules:

(1) If the draft is payable on demand, the draft is dishonored if presentment for payment is duly made to the acceptor and the draft is not paid on the day of presentment.

Petitioner claims that the drawee Bank of America solely would be liable as the acceptor because, under § 3-414(c), the drawer of the check is discharged upon acceptance by the Bank. Section 3-414(c) states: "If a draft is accepted by a bank, the drawer is discharged, regardless of when or by whom acceptance was obtained."[10]

Petitioner extends his line of reasoning by arguing that the actions of the Bank amounted to a conversion under § 3-420, which states, in allegedly relevant part:

(a) The law applicable to conversion of personal property applies to instruments. An instrument is also converted if it is taken by transfer, other than a negotiation, from a person not entitled to enforce the instrument or a bank makes or obtains payment with respect to the instrument for a person not entitled to enforce the instrument or receive payment. An action for conversion of an instrument may not be brought by (i) the issuer or acceptor of the instrument or (ii) a payee or indorsee who did not receive delivery of the instrument either directly or through delivery to an agent or co-payee.

Based on this, Petitioner argues that because the Bank accepted the check, an act which, according to Petitioner, discharged the drawer, he no longer had enforceable rights in the check and only had a right to the proceeds. Petitioner's position is that the Bank exercised unauthorized dominion and control over the proceeds of the check to the com-

---

10. Petitioner, however, overlooks § 4-601 which states:

(a) The obligation of a party to pay the instrument is discharged as stated in this title or by an act or agreement with the party which would discharge an obligation to pay money under a simple contract.

(b) Discharge of the obligation of a party is not effective against a person acquiring rights of a holder in due course of the instrument [§ 3-302] without notice of the discharge. No one was discharged on the instrument at the time Petitioner acquired rights in it. § 4-102(a) states:

To the extent that items within this title are also within Titles 3 and 8, they are subject to those titles. If there is conflict, this title governs Title 3, but Title 8 [Investment Securities] governs this title.

plete exclusion of the Petitioner after the Bank accepted the check and refused to distribute the proceeds, counted out by the teller, to him.

B. Acceptance under § 3-409(a).

Predictably, Bank of America argues that Petitioner's interpretation of Maryland's U.C.C. is incorrect. Our intermediate appellate court brethren largely agreed with the Bank's point of view. Setting aside for the moment the Bank's arguments as to the reasonableness of requiring a thumbprint, we turn to the Bank's obligations, or lack thereof, with regard to the presentment of a check by someone not its customer. Bank of America argues, correctly, that it had no duty to the Petitioner, a non-customer and a stranger to the Bank, and that nothing in the Code allows Petitioner to force Bank of America to act as a depository bank [§ 4-105] and cash a check for a non-customer. As the Supreme Court pointed out in *Barnhill v. Johnson*, 503 U.S. 393, 398-99, 112 S.Ct. 1386, 118 L.Ed.2d 39 (1992):

> Under the U.C.C., a check is simply an order to the drawee bank to pay the sum stated, signed by the makers and payable on demand. Receipt of a check does not, however, give the recipient a right against the bank. The recipient may present the check, but if the drawee bank refuses to honor it, the recipient has no recourse against the drawee. * * * * * This is because ... receipt of a check gives the recipient no right in the funds held by the bank on the drawer's account.
>
> Absent a special relationship, a non-customer has no claim against a bank for refusing to honor a presented check.... A "transient, non-contractual relationship" is not enough to establish a duty.... It is also well settled that a check does not operate as an assignment of funds on deposit ... and the bank only becomes obligated upon acceptance of the instrument. This is made clear by § 3-408, which states: A check or other draft does not of itself operate as an assignment of funds in the hands of the drawee available for its payment, and the drawee is not liable on the instrument until the drawee accepts it.

Once a bank accepts a check, under § 3-409, it is obliged to pay on the check under § 3-413.[12] Thus, the relevant question in terms of any rights Petitioner had against the Bank turns not on the reasonableness of the thumbprint identification, but rather upon

---

12. These rules of commercial practice are of considerable long standing. In *Moses v. President & Directors of Franklin Bank*, 34 Md. 574, 580-81 (1871), the Court stated:

A check does not, as contended by the appellant, operate as an assignment pro tanto of the fund upon which it is drawn, until it is accepted, or certified to be good, by the bank holding the funds. It is true, a bank, if in funds of the drawer, is ordinarily bound to take up his checks; but it can only be held liable to the holder for its refusal to do so, upon the ground of fraud, whereby he loses the money or some part of it, for which the check is drawn. It is certainly a general rule, that a drawee who refuses to accept a bill of exchange cannot be held liable on the bill itself; nor to the holder for the refusal to accept, except it be upon the ground of fraud and loss to the latter. A bank upon which a check is drawn occupies in this respect a similar position to that of the drawee of a bill of exchange. It is but the agent of the depositor, holding his funds upon an implied contract to honor and take up his checks to the extent of the funds deposited. The obligation to accept and pay is not to the holder of the check, but to the drawer. If, therefore, the depositor should direct that a check should not be paid, the bank would be bound to observe the direction, unless it had previously accepted the check by certifying it to be good, in which case it would be bound to pay; at any rate to a subsequent holder. The bank, therefore, ordinarily, owes no duty to the holder of a check drawn upon it, nor is it bound, except to the depositor, to accept or pay the check, though it may have sufficient funds of the drawer with which to do it.

whether the Bank accepted the check when presented as defined by § 3-409. As will be seen infra, the question of the thumbprint identification is relevant only to the issue of whether the Bank's refusal to pay the instrument constituted dishonor under § 3-502, a determination which has no impact in terms of any duty allegedly owed by the Bank to the Petitioner.

Respondent Bank of America argues that the intermediate appellate court correctly found that it did not "accept" the check as that term is defined in § 3-409(a).... We agree. The mere fact that the teller's computer printed information on the back of the check does not, as Petitioner contends, amount by itself to an acceptance. Section 3-409(a) states:

> (a) "Acceptance" means the drawee's signed agreement to pay a draft as presented. It must be written on the draft and may consist of the drawee's signature alone. Acceptance may be made at any time and becomes effective when notification pursuant to instructions is given or the accepted draft is delivered for the purpose of giving rights on the acceptance to any person.

Petitioner relies on the first two sentences of the statute, while ignoring the balance. The statute clearly states that acceptance becomes effective when the presenter is notified of that fact. The facts demonstrate that at no time did the teller notify Petitioner that the Bank would pay on the check. Rather, the facts show that:

> [T]he check was given back to [Petitioner] by the teller so that he could put his thumbprint signature on it, not to notify or give him rights on the purported acceptance. After appellant declined to put his thumbprint signature on the check, he was informed by both the teller and the branch manager that it was against bank policy to honor the check without a thumbprint signature. Indignant, [Petitioner] walked out of the bank with the check.

143 Md.App. at 19, 792 A.2d at 323. As the intermediate appellate court correctly pointed out, the negotiation of the check is in the nature of a contract, and there can be no agreement until notice of acceptance is received.[13] Id. As a result, there was never acceptance as defined by § 3-409(a), and thus the Bank, pursuant to § 3-408 never was obligated to pay the check under § 3-413(a). Thus, the answer to Petitioner's second question presented is "no."

C. "Conversion" under § 3-420.

* * *

D. "Reasonable Identification" under § 3-501(b)(2)(ii) and "Dishonor" under § 3-502

We now turn to the issue of whether the Bank's refusal to accept the check as presented constituted dishonor under § 3-501 and § 3-502 as Petitioner contends. Petitioner's argument that Bank of America dishonored the check under § 3-502(d) fails because that section applies to dishonor of an accepted draft. We have determined, supra, that Bank of America never accepted the draft. Nevertheless, the question remains as to whether Bank of America dishonored the draft under § 3-502(b), which states:

---

13. Where a check is presented for payment over the counter, it is hard, given general business practices, to imagine where acceptance would be effective before the funds paying the check were handed over to the presenter, except where a certified or cashier's check was involved. *Rezapolvi v. First Nat. Bank of Maryland*, 296 Md. 1, 6, 459 A.2d 183, 186 (1983).

(b) Dishonor of an unaccepted draft other than a documentary draft is governed by the following rules:

(1) If a check is duly presented for payment to the payor bank otherwise than for immediate payment over the counter, the check is dishonored if the payor bank makes timely return of the check or sends timely notice of dishonor or nonpayment under § 4-301 or § 4-302, or becomes accountable for the amount of the check under § 4-302.

(2) If a draft is payable on demand and paragraph (1) does not apply, the draft is dishonored if presentment for payment is duly made to the drawee and the draft is not paid on the day of presentment.

The reason that § 3-502(b)(2) potentially is relevant to the case *sub judice* is because of § 3-501(b)(2) and (3), which state:

(2) Upon demand of the person to whom presentment is made, the person making presentment must (i) exhibit the instrument, (ii) give reasonable identification and, if presentment is made on behalf of another person reasonable evidence of authority to do so, and (iii) sign a receipt on the instrument for any payment made or surrender the instrument if full payment is made.

(3) Without dishonoring the instrument, the party to whom presentment is made may (i) return the instrument for lack of a necessary indorsement, or (ii) refuse payment or acceptance for failure of the presentment to comply with the terms of the instrument, an agreement of the parties, or other applicable law or rule.

The question is whether requiring a thumbprint constitutes a request for "reasonable identification" under § 3-501(b)(2)(ii). If it is "reasonable," then under § 3-501(b)(3)(ii) the refusal of the Bank to accept the check from Petitioner did not constitute dishonor. If, however, requiring a thumbprint is not "reasonable" under § 3-501(b)(2)(ii), then the refusal to accept the check may constitute dishonor under § 3-502(b)(2). The issue of dishonor is arguably relevant because Petitioner has no cause of action against any party, including the drawer, until the check is dishonored....

Respondent Bank of America argues that its relationship with its customer is contractual ... and that in this case, its contract with its customer, the drawer, authorizes the Bank's use of the Thumbprint Signature Program as a reasonable form of identification. The pertinent part of that Deposit Agreement states:

You [customer] agree that we [Bank of America] may impose additional requirements we deem necessary or desirable on a payee or other holder who presents for cashing an item drawn on your account which is otherwise properly payable and if that person fails or refuses to satisfy such requirements, our refusal to cash the item will not be considered wrongful. You [customer] agree that, subject to applicable law, such requirements may include (but are not necessarily limited to) physical ... identification requirements....

According to Respondent, this contractual agreement allowed it to refuse to accept the check, without dishonoring it pursuant to § 3-501(b)(3)(ii), because the Bank's refusal was based upon the presentment failing to comply with "an agreement of the parties." The intermediate appellate court agreed.... We, however, do not.

The reason why the Bank's contract with its customer is not controlling on the issue of the reasonableness of requiring a thumbprint as identification is because the terms of § 3-501 are not modified by the terms of that contract. The terms of § 3-501(b) require an "agreement of the parties." The term "parties" does not refer to the parties of the Deposit Agreement, but rather, according to § 3-103(a)(8), refers to the parties to an instrument. While Petitioner is a party to the instrument, he is not a party to the Deposit Agreement, nor may he be deemed properly a third party beneficiary thereof. To be effective against the Petitioner, Messing, as the party entitled to enforce the instrument, would have to have been a party to the agreement. § 3-117. Thus, while the Deposit Agreement protects the Bank from a suit for wrongful dishonor brought by its customer, the drawer, as a result of the Bank's potential dishonor of the check because the Bank's demand for a thumbprint was not met, [§ 4-402], the contract has no impact on the determination of the "reasonableness" of the requirement for purposes of § 3-501(b), and subsequently whether the instrument was dishonored for purposes of § 3-502(b)(2). In other words, the Bank and its customer cannot through their contract define the meaning of the term "reasonable" and impose it upon parties who are not in privity with that contract. Whether requiring a thumbprint constitutes "reasonable identification" within the meaning of § 3-501(b)(2)(ii) is therefore a broader policy consideration, and not, as argued in this case, simply a matter of contract. We reiterate that the contract does not apply to Petitioner and, similarly, does not give him a cause of action against the Bank for refusing to accept the check.... This also means that the Bank cannot rely on the contract as a defense against the Petitioner, on the facts presented here, to say that it did not dishonor the check.

Petitioner, as noted, argues that requiring a thumbprint violates his privacy,[17] and further argues that a thumbprint is not a reasonable form of identification because it does not prove contemporaneously the identity of an over the counter presenter at the time presentment is made. According to Petitioner, the purpose of requiring "reasonable identification" is to allow the drawee bank to determine that the presenter is the proper person to be paid on the instrument. Because a thumbprint does not provide that information at the time presentment and payment are made, Petitioner argues that a thumbprint cannot be read to fall within the meaning of "reasonable identification" for the purposes of § 3-501(b)(2)(ii).

Bank of America argues that the requirement of a thumbprint has been upheld, in other non-criminal circumstances, not to be an invasion of privacy, and is a reasonable and necessary industry response to the growing problem of check fraud. The intermediate appellate court agreed, pointing out that the form of identification was not defined by the statute, but that the Code itself recognized a thumbprint as a form of signature, § 1-201(39), and observing that requiring thumbprint or fingerprint identification has been found to be reasonable and not to violate privacy rights in a number of non-criminal contexts. Those observations and authorities are set forth in the opinion of that Court and need not be repeated here....

---

17. *Homo Sapiens* possesses a truly opposable thumb. An opposable thumb is a necessary adaptation for a creature whose survival depends on having a firm grasp on the tools and instruments encountered in daily life. In the case *sub judice*, the instrument being grasped was a check. Because when grasping and transferring or receiving a paper, such as a check, one does so normally by holding the paper against the side of the index finger with the assistance of a firmly down pressed thumb, we deduce that on multiple occasions during the passing back and forth of the check while Petitioner attempted to cash it, he inevitably and repeatedly placed his thumbprint upon it. At best, therefore, Petitioner's objection appears not to be to placing his thumbprint on the check, but rather to placing a thumbprint on the check which would be longer lasting and more clearly identifiable over time than would otherwise be the case given normal handling conditions.

More compelling in terms of determining the issue of "reasonableness" is the reasoning of the intermediate appellate court in rejecting Petitioner's argument that § 3-501(b)(2)(ii) implicitly contains a present tense temporal element, stating:

> We agree with [Petitioner] that a thumbprint cannot be used, in most instances, to confirm the identity of a non-account checkholder at the time that the check is presented for cashing, as his or her thumbprint is usually not on file with the drawee at that time. We disagree, however, with [Petitioner's] conclusion that a thumbprint signature is therefore not "reasonable identification" for purposes of C.L. § 3-501(b)(2). Nowhere does the language of C.L. § 3-501(b)(2) suggest that "reasonable identification" is limited to information [Respondent] can authenticate at the time presentment is made. Rather, all that is required is that the "person making presentment must … give reasonable identification." C.L. § 3- 501(b)(2). While providing a thumbprint signature does not necessarily confirm identification of the checkholder at presentment – unless of course the drawee bank has a duplicate thumbprint signature on file – it does assist in the identification of the checkholder should the check later prove to be bad. It therefore serves as a powerful deterrent to those who might otherwise attempt to pass a bad check. That one method provides identification at the time of presentment and the other identification after the check may have been honored, does not prevent the latter from being "reasonable identification" for purposes of C.L. § 3-501(b)(2).

143 Md.App. at 16, 792 A.2d at 321. We agree, and find this conclusion to be compelled, in fact, by our State's Commercial Law Article.

The reason has to do with warranties. The transfer of a check for consideration creates both transfer warranties (§ 3-416(a) and (c)) and presentment warranties (§ 3-417(a) and (e)) which cannot be disclaimed. The warranties include, for example, that the payee is entitled to enforce the instrument and that there are no alterations on the check. The risk to banks is that these contractual warranties may be breached, exposing the accepting bank to a loss because the bank paid over the counter on an item which was not properly payable. See § 4-401…. In such an event, the bank would then incur the expense to find the presenter, to demand repayment, and legal expenses to pursue the presenter for breach of his warranties.

In short, when a bank cashes a check over the counter, it assumes the risk that it may suffer losses for counterfeit documents, forged endorsements, or forged or altered checks. Nothing in the Commercial Law Article forces a bank to assume such risks…. See *Barnhill*, 503 U.S. 393, 398-99, 112 S.Ct. 1386, 118 L.Ed.2d 39 (1992); § 3-408. To the extent that banks are willing to cash checks over the counter, with reasonable identification, such willingness expands and facilitates the commercial activities within the State. In interpreting the Commercial Law Article, we are guided by § 1-102, which states in relevant part:

> (1) Titles 1 through 10 of this article shall be liberally construed and applied to promote its underlying purposes and policies.

> (2) Underlying purposes and policies of Titles 1 through 10 of this article are (a) to simplify, clarify and modernize the law governing commercial transactions; (b) to permit the continued expansion of commercial practices through custom, usage and agreement of the parties; (c) to make uniform the law among the various jurisdictions.

Because the reduction of risk promotes the expansion of commercial practices, we believe that the direction of § 1-102(2)(b) requires that we conclude that a bank's requirement of a thumbprint placed upon a check presented over the counter by a non-customer is reasonable.... As the intermediate appellate court well documented, the Thumbprint Program is part of an industry wide response to the growing threat of check fraud.... Prohibiting banks from taking reasonable steps to protect themselves from losses could result in banks refusing to cash checks of non-customers presented over the counter at all, a result which would be counter to the direction of § 1-102(2)(b).

As a result of this conclusion, Bank of America in the present case did not dishonor the check when it refused to accept it over the counter. Under § 3-501(b)(3)(ii), Bank of America "refused payment or acceptance for failure of the presentment to comply with ... other applicable law or rule." The rule not complied with by the Petitioner–presenter was § 3-502(b)(2)(ii), in that he refused to give what we have determined to be reasonable identification. Therefore, there was no dishonor of the check by Bank of America's refusal to accept it. The answer to Petitioner's third question is therefore "no," as is the answer to Petitioner's first question, though our reasoning differs somewhat from that of the Court of Special Appeals.

E. Declaratory Judgment.

* * *

ELDRIDGE, Judge, concurring in part and dissenting in part.

I agree that the Circuit Court erred in failing to render a declaratory judgment. I cannot agree with the majority's holding that, after the petitioner presented his driver's license and a major credit card, it was "reasonable" to require the petitioner's thumbprint as identification.

Today, honest citizens attempting to cope in this world are constantly being required to show or give drivers' licenses, photo identification cards, social security numbers, the last four digits of social security numbers, mothers' "maiden names," 16 digit account numbers, etc. Now, the majority takes the position that it is "reasonable" for banks and other establishments to require, in addition, thumbprints and fingerprints. Enough is enough. The most reasonable thing in this case was petitioner's "irritation with the Bank of America's Thumbprint Signature Program." (Majority opinion at p. 25.)

Chief Judge Bell has authorized me to state that he joins this concurring and dissenting opinion.

Problem 5-5

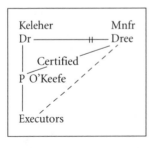

On September 11, 1997, Keleher drew two checks totaling $800 and gave them to O'Keefe in payment of gambling debts. The checks were drawn on Manufacturers' Trust and immediately certified by the bank at the request of O'Keefe. However, O'Keefe did not promptly cash them. He lost or mislaid the checks and eventually died. On November 1, 2008, the executor of O'Keefe's will made a verbal demand on Manufacturers' Trust for payment of the amount of the checks. The executor was unable to produce the checks, and the bank refused to pay. When Keleher learned that the checks had not yet been paid, he went to Manufacturers' Trust and filled out a stop payment form and requested the bank to pay the money to him.

1) What is certification and its legal ramifications? §§ 3-409(d), 3-413, 3-414(d), 3-415(d).

2) Why would the bank hesitate to pay out the money? §§ 4-403, 3-411(b).

3) Who is entitled to the money? § 4-303(a)(1).

4) Would your analysis change if Keleher had certified the checks before giving them to O'Keefe? §§ 3-414(c), 3-415(d).

5) Review: What is the impact of the loss of the instruments on the executor's claim? §§ 3-301, 3-309.

6) What will be the impact of the lapse of time on the executor's claim? § 3-118(d).

2. Conversion

GERBER & GERBER, P.C. v. REGIONS BANK
596 S.E.2d 174 (Ga. App. 2004)

MILLER, Judge.

Over a period of two years, an employee of the Gerber & Gerber, P.C. law firm (G&G) stole from G&G some cashier's checks (endorsed in blank) and some checks payable to G&G (on which she forged G&G's endorsement) and deposited the checks into her personal account at Regions Bank, where G&G also maintained its accounts. Alleging that Regions Bank had acted negligently in accepting the checks for deposit, G&G sued the bank to recover the money lost. The court entered summary judgment in favor of Regions Bank on the cashier's checks but held material issues of fact precluded summary judgment on the forged checks. Both parties appeal the portions of the judgment adverse to their interests. Discerning no error, we affirm.

.... We review the grant of summary judgment de novo, construing the evidence in favor of the nonmovant....

Construed in favor of G&G, the evidence showed that Cynthia Stafford worked for a law firm as a real estate closing secretary. She stole money from that firm through forging the firm's endorsement on checks made payable to the firm (received at the real estate closings) and depositing them into her personal account. When the forgery was discovered, she confessed and worked out an arrangement to continue at the firm at a reduced salary to repay the stolen money. She then stole a second time and the firm closed. The aggregate amount stolen was about $130,000.

Prior to the firm closing, its principal had merger discussions with G&G, during which the principal disclosed some of Stafford's theft and forgery to Sanford Gerber of G&G. Nevertheless, when the merger talks failed, the principal recommended that G&G hire Stafford because of her competency as a real estate closing secretary and because she had rehabilitated. Mr. Gerber interviewed Stafford and felt also that she had reformed. He hired her but warned her that he knew of her prior theft and that if she stole from G&G, he would make sure she went to jail.

Stafford worked as a real estate closing secretary at G&G for over two years. During this time, she stole 29 cashier's checks received by G&G during real estate closings, which checks the payees had endorsed in blank during the closings. She then endorsed these checks herself and deposited them into her personal account at Regions Bank. She also stole ten checks made payable to G&G, which she endorsed in blank on behalf of G&G

(forging Sanford Gerber's signature). She then endorsed the forged checks in her own name and deposited them into her personal account at Regions Bank. Throughout this time, G&G had its escrow and other accounts at Regions Bank and deposited thousands of checks amounting to $150 million to $200 million into those accounts every year. G&G would endorse each deposited check with a rubber stamp for deposit into the G&G account.

The thefts were made possible because G&G did not restrictively stamp the checks immediately at closing but waited until sometime after the closing, during which interim period the checks were kept in an open file left in an area accessible to all G&G employees. Also, at times Stafford was allowed to be the person to stamp and account for the checks. The amount stolen approximated $180,000. Stafford confessed to the thefts, later pleading guilty to criminal charges and receiving a thirty-year sentence (five years to serve). She claimed to have spent the money.

G&G sued Regions Bank to recover the stolen $180,000, alleging counts of conversion and negligence in that the bank improperly accepted the forged checks as well as the true-endorsed cashier's checks into Stafford's personal account. Regions Bank moved for summary judgment, arguing that as a matter of law it had acted appropriately under the Uniform Commercial Code in accepting the checks. The trial court granted the motion insofar as it pertained to the true-endorsed cashier's checks but found that material issues of fact (particularly regarding the parties' comparative negligence) precluded summary judgment as to the forged checks. G&G appealed the partial grant of summary judgment, and Regions Bank cross-appealed the partial denial of summary judgment.

With regard to the blank-endorsed cashier's checks, the court correctly granted summary judgment in favor of the bank. Under the applicable portion of OCGA § 11-3-420(a), a bank converts an instrument if the bank "makes or obtains payment with respect to the instrument for a person not entitled to enforce the instrument or receive payment." The holder of an instrument is a person entitled to enforce the instrument, even though the person is in wrongful possession of the instrument. OCGA § 11-3-301. A person is a holder of a negotiable instrument if that person possesses the instrument and the instrument is payable to bearer. OCGA § 11-1-201(20). An instrument is deemed payable to bearer if it is endorsed in blank (i.e., not specially endorsed). OCGA § 11-3-205(b). "When indorsed in blank, an instrument becomes payable to bearer and may be negotiated by transfer of possession alone until specially indorsed." Id.; see OCGA § 11-3-201(b).

Accordingly, when here the payees of the cashier's checks endorsed the checks in blank, the checks then became bearer paper and could – similar to cash – be transferred by possession alone.... Sanford Gerber even admitted to this well-known fact in his deposition. Thus, Regions Bank quite properly accepted the endorsed-in-blank cashier's checks from the person in possession of them and deposited the checks into that person's account. The court did not err in granting Regions Bank summary judgment on G&G's causes of action arising out of these checks.

More problematic, however, are the forged checks. Although these were also endorsed in blank, the payee's signatures were forgeries and were therefore ineffective as endorsements by the payee. See OCGA § 11-3-403(a). Accordingly, Stafford was not entitled to enforce the instruments or to receive payment thereunder, and Regions Bank converted the instruments when it made or obtained payment on them by allowing them to be deposited into Stafford's personal account. See OCGA § 11-3-420(a).

Regions Bank argues that G&G failed to exercise ordinary care, which substantially contributed to the making of the forged signatures. Regions Bank contends that accordingly G&G was precluded under OCGA § 11-3-406(a) from asserting the forgery against the bank. Indeed, where some evidence shows that the corporate payee acted negligently in failing to prevent the forgery of its endorsement, a jury should decide whether that negligence substantially contributed to the making of the forgery – but only if the defendant bank *in good faith* paid the instrument or took it for value or for collection. See OCGA § 11-3-406(a).... In 1996 the General Assembly amended the applicable definition of "good faith" to mean "honesty in fact and the observance of reasonable commercial standards of fair dealing." ... Thus, even assuming the evidence established as a matter of law that G&G's actions substantially contributed to the making of the forgeries at issue, the question here is whether there is a disputed issue of fact as to Regions Bank's good faith (its honesty in fact and its observance of reasonable commercial standards of fair dealing) in regard to its accepting the forged checks as deposits in Stafford's account.

Regions Bank has presented evidence that it knew nothing of the possible forgery at the time it accepted the checks. The first Regions Bank learned of the forgery was from G&G after the fact. G&G has presented no evidence to contradict this, and thus the undisputed evidence shows Regions Bank's honesty in fact....

However, disputed evidence does exist on the question of whether Regions Bank's actions were in observance of reasonable commercial standards of fair dealing. Significantly, reasonable commercial standards *of fair dealing* are different from reasonable commercial standards of *due care*. "Although fair dealing is a broad term that must be defined in context, it is clear that it is concerned with the fairness of conduct rather than the care with which an act is performed. Failure to exercise ordinary care in conducting a transaction is an entirely different concept than failure to deal fairly in conducting the transaction." UCC § 3-103, Official Comment 4 (2003); see Maine Family Fed. Credit Union v. Sun Life Assurance Co. of Canada, 727 A.2d 335, 342(III)(B)(2) (Me.1999).

Although some older Georgia cases define the reasonable commercial standards of due care..., those addressing the newer language of reasonable commercial standards of fair dealing have not explained it in detail.... The United States Court of Appeals for the Seventh Circuit referred to this standard as the "[a]voidance of advantage-taking." State Bank of the Lakes v. Kansas Bankers Surety Co., 328 F.3d 906, 909 (7th Cir. 2003). The Maine Supreme Court struggled at length with the issue, stating: "The most obvious question arising from the use of the term 'fair' is: fairness to whom? ... If a holder is required to act 'fairly,' regarding all parties, it must engage in an almost impossible balancing of rights and interests." Maine Family, supra, 727 A.2d at 343(III)(B)(2). The Maine court then interpreted a different "fairness" standard of conduct than that required for due care in reaching its result in Maine Family. Id. at 343-344(III)(B)(2). The court noted that a party may be found to act in good faith – even though negligently – if it acts fairly, but may be found to have acted not in good faith, i.e., unfairly, even though it complied with commercial standards of due care. Id. at 343.... The U.S. Fourth Circuit took a similar tact, holding that evidence showing a lack of due care did not show a failure to comply with reasonable commercial standards of fair dealing. Wachovia Bank v. Fed. Reserve Bank of Richmond, 338 F.3d 318, 322-323(II)(A) (4th Cir. 2003). Focusing on the lack of evidence that what the bank did was unfair, the court affirmed summary judgment in favor of the bank. Id. at 323(II)(A). Nevertheless, whether a party's conduct meets this "fairness" standard is ordinarily a question that must be resolved by the factfinder....

In determining whether the conduct of Regions Bank complied as a matter of law with reasonable commercial standards of fair dealing, we note that Henderson, supra, 258 Ga.

at 704(1), 373 S.E.2d 738, upheld a jury verdict finding that a bank did not comply with reasonable commercial standards of due care when it accepted checks payable to a firm, which were endorsed in blank by a firm employee and deposited in his personal account at the bank. The firm had its account at the same bank, and "established practice for the negotiation of checks payable to this account was through the use of a restrictive endorsement stamp." Id. This irregularity should have caused the bank to inquire as to the propriety of the endorsements when the checks being deposited by the firm employee into his personal account were payable to the firm and had been endorsed in blank. Id…."Where endorsements are irregular on their face, and when the draft is offered for deposit into the account of one not the payee, the bank has a duty to inquire to ascertain the authority of the depositor to endorse and deposit the payee's check. [Cit.]" Tifton Bank &c. Co. v. Knight's Furniture Co., 215 Ga.App. 471, 474(1)(b), 452 S.E.2d 219 (1994). The Kansas Court of Appeals even held: "Barring exceptional circumstances, the general rule is that failure of a bank to inquire when an individual cashes a check made payable to a corporate payee and puts the money in his personal account is an unreasonable commercial banking practice *as a matter of law.* [Cits.]" (Emphasis supplied.) 179 Aetna Casualty &c. Co. v. Hepler State Bank, 6 Kan.App.2d 543, 551(III), 630 P.2d 721 (1981).

In light of these cases, we hold that it is at least a fact question whether Regions Bank violated the reasonable commercial standards of fair dealing when it violated known commercial banking practices by accepting checks made payable to G&G into Stafford's personal account. Since Regions Bank also serviced G&G's business accounts and therefore knew that G&G normally placed a restrictive endorsement stamp on checks made payable to G&G, Regions Bank was on heightened notice of the irregularity of the endorsements on the checks deposited by Stafford and therefore could be held to have dealt with G&G unfairly by not making inquiry into the legitimacy of those endorsements. Thus, whether Regions Bank acted in good faith in this matter is a question to be resolved by the jury, which means that its defense under OCGA § 11-3-406(a) cannot be resolved on summary judgment.

Regions Bank also argues that it was a holder in due course under OCGA § 11-3-302 and therefore entitled to summary judgment on the claims asserted in the complaint. For Regions Bank to be a holder in due course, this statute requires that the bank have taken the instruments at issue "[i]n good faith." OCGA § 11-3-302(a)(2)(ii). Since the same definition of good faith discussed above applies to this statute (see OCGA § 11-3-103(a)(4)), the same disputed issues of fact also discussed above preclude Regions Bank on summary judgment from conclusively establishing its status as a holder in due course on the forged checks.

The trial court correctly denied Regions Bank summary judgment on the ten forged checks….

Problem 5-6

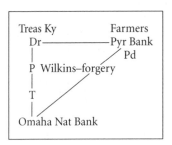

On May 10, the state treasurer of Kentucky issued a veteran's bonus check to Wilkins for $126 drawn on Farmer's Bank. The check was stolen from Wilkins and purported to be indorsed by Wilkins, then by Trapp for deposit into Trapp's account with Omaha National Bank. The check was sent for collection and ultimately paid by Farmer's Bank within a month of its issue. The state treasurer then discovered that Wilkins' signature had been forged by Trapp.

1) <u>Review</u>: The State of Kentucky demands that Farmer's Bank recredit its account because the forged indorsement prevented the check from being properly payable. Which of the following statutes might Farmer's Bank use as a defense against the State of Kentucky? §§ 3-404, 3-405, 3-406, 4-406.

2) <u>Review</u>: Assume Farmer's Bank recredits the account of the State of Kentucky (after which the State of Kentucky issues a second check to Wilkins). On what theory can Farmer's Bank recover its loss, and who are the potential defendants? § 3-417(a) (or § 4-208(a)).

Q: Can Farmer's Bank sue any party for breaching one or more transfer warranties under § 3-416(a) (or § 4-207(a))? § 3-203(a) and OC 1.

3) <u>Review</u>: Assume Farmer's Bank recovers its loss from Omaha National Bank. On what theory can Omaha National Bank recover its loss, and who is the potential defendant? § 3-416(a) (or § 4-207(a)).

4) Ignore the preceding lawsuits. Can Wilkins sue the State of Kentucky on the underlying obligation or the stolen instrument? §§ 3-310(b) and OC 4, 3-414(b), 3-301, 3-309.

5) Ignore the preceding lawsuits. Can Wilkins sue Omaha National Bank and/or Farmer's Bank for conversion? § 3-420.

First test:

Q: Was the movement of the check from Trapp to ONB a "transfer" under § 3-203? What about the movement from ONB to Farmer's Bank?

Q: If the movement was a transfer, was it a non-negotiation under § 3-201?

Q: If the movement was a non-negotiation, was the transferor a PETE under § 3-301?

Second test:

Q: Did Farmer's Bank make or obtain payment? Did ONB make or obtain payment? If so, in each case, to whom?

Q: Was the party to whom payment was made a PETE under § 3-301?

Q: Was the party for whom payment was obtained a PETE under § 3-301?

6) Assume that Wilkins successfully presents its case against ONB and Farmer's Bank for conversion. What additional facts might provide the banks with a good defense to Wilkins' conversion charge? §§ 3-404, 3-405, 3-406.

Note

A defendant in a conversion action may assert § 3-406 as a defense to liability if the perpetrator has made a "forged signature" on the checks. The scope of "forged signature" was at the heart of the case in *John Hancock Financial Services, Inc. v. Old Kent Bank*, 346 F.3d 727 (6th Cir. 2003). A representative of John Hancock Financial Services was authorized to accept investment checks payable to John Hancock. The representative then stamped the checks with an indorsement that read "Sherman and Associates Financial Services." The representative then deposited these indorsed checks into an account bearing the same name at Old Kent Bank. This scheme involved over 70 checks and continued for seven years. After discovering the fraud, John Hancock repaid its clients and sued Old Kent for conversion. The district court granted John Hancock's motion for summary judgment. Old Kent Bank appealed, arguing that the district court erred in concluding that its forgery defense under § 3-406 had no merit. The appellate panel affirmed, addressing the application of § 3-406 as follows.

Old Kent contends that the district court erred in not applying Mich. Comp. Laws § 440.3406 (hereafter referred to as UCC § 3-406) to John Hancock's claims. UCC § 3-406 provides in pertinent part that a party whose negligence "substantially contributes to an alteration of an instrument or to the making of a forged signature on an instrument is precluded from asserting the alteration or the forgery against a person who, in good faith, pays the instrument or takes it for value or for collection." UCC § 3-406(1). As noted above, Sherman indorsed the checks with a stamp that read "Sherman and Associates Financial Services." The district court held that the UCC's preclusion defense did not apply to John Hancock's conversion claim, reasoning that Sherman's indorsement was not a forgery because it "did not appear to be the genuine signature of the payee, John Hancock." Old Kent argues that the district court's definition of "forged signature" is too restrictive.

Because the UCC does not define the term "forged signature," Old Kent looked to Michigan law and the comments to UCC § 3-406 for the meaning of the term. Old Kent cites Pamar Enterprises, Inc. v. Huntington Banks of Michigan, 228 Mich. App. 727, 580 N.W.2d 11, 15 (1998), for the proposition that "[p]ayment of a check with a missing endorsement is the legal equivalent of payment over a forged endorsement." Pamar, however, gives no persuasive reason for this result, and the Michigan Supreme Court has not opined on the issue. Given the lack of a reasoned basis for treating a missing indorsement as the legal equivalent of a forged indorsement, we see no justification to extend Pamar to a case like the present where there is in fact an indorsement quite distinct from the named payee.

In advocating for a broad definition of the term "forged signature," Old Kent also relies on the following official comment to UCC § 3-406:

> An insurance company draws a check to the order of Sarah Smith in payment of a claim for a policy holder, Sarah Smith, who lives in Alabama. The insurance company also has a policyholder with the same name who lives in Illinois. By mistake, the insurance company mails the check to the Illinois Sarah Smith who indorses the check and obtains payment. Because the payee of the check is the Alabama Sarah Smith, the indorsement by the Illinois Sarah Smith is a forged indorsement.

UCC § 3-406 cmt. 3. Old Kent argues that Sherman's indorsements are analogous to those of Illinois Sarah Smith's because they are both indorsements "by someone other than the intended payee." In rejecting this argument, the district court noted that, unlike the hypothetical in Comment 3, Sherman's indorsement was completely different from the payee's. The district court reasoned that the use of a common name in Comment 3 "supports the argument that a forged signature must appear to be the genuine signature of the intended payee." This analysis is consistent with Comment 2 to UCC § 3-406, which suggests that the drafters intended the term "forged signature" to be construed narrowly. Comment 2 provides:

> Section 3-406 refers to "forged signature" rather than "unauthorized signature" that appeared in the former Section 3-406 because it more accurately describes the scope of the provision. Unauthorized signature is a broader concept that includes not only forgery but also the signature of an agent which does not bind the principal under the law of agency. The agency cases

are resolved independently under agency law. Section 3-406 is not necessary in those cases.

UCC § 3-406 cmt. 2.

The district court defined the term "forged signature" within the context of UCC § 3-406 as a signature "substantially similar to the name of the intended signator such that it appears genuine." This definition is consistent with both the common usage of the term "forged" and Comments 2 and 3 above. See also UCC § 3-405 (defining "fraudulent endorsement" as, "in the case of an instrument payable to the employer, a forged endorsement purporting to be that of the employer...."). In sum, we agree with the district court's conclusion that Sherman's indorsements were not "forged signatures." The district court therefore properly declined to apply UCC § 3-406's preclusion defense to John Hancock's conversion claim against Old Kent.

346 F.3d at 730-31.

3. Restrictive Indorsements and Other Instructions

Problem 5-7

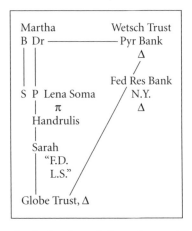

Martha   Wetsch Trust
B Dr ——————— Pyr Bank
                         Δ

                      Fed Res Bank
S P Lena Soma   /   N.Y.
   | π   /   Δ
   Handrulis   /
                  /
   Sarah   /
     "F.D.   /
      L.S."   /
              /
   Globe Trust, Δ

Lena Soma was unable to read or write, and she could barely understand English. She owned some real estate which she sold to Martha Thomas for $10,000. Martha paid with a check drawn on Westchester Trust. Lena had intended to deposit Martha's check in her account at Yonkers Savings, but the sale concluded after banking hours. The realtor involved in the sale, George Handrulis, drove Lena home to Brooklyn, and in the course of doing so persuaded her to entrust the check to him overnight for safekeeping in his safe to avoid the possibility of loss or theft. Instead of returning the check the next morning, however, Handrulis induced Sarah Alkoff to place the following two-line indorsement on the check: for deposit/Lena Soma. Alkoff then deposited the indorsed check into her account with Globe Trust, a member of the Federal Reserve System. Globe Trust indorsed it to the Federal Reserve Bank of New York for collection. That collecting bank presented the check to Westchester Trust, which paid the check. The proceeds were remitted to Globe Trust and deposited into Sarah's account. Sarah then allowed Handrulis to draw checks on her account until the funds were all gone. Handrulis was later convicted of larceny and sent to prison. Lena commenced an action against Globe Trust, the Federal Reserve Bank of New York (FRBNY), and Westchester Trust.

1) How would you describe the two-line indorsement "for deposit/Lena Soma"? § 3-205 OC 2.

2) What is the legal significance of the indorsement "for deposit"? § 3-206(c), (e), (f).

3) Are any of the defendants (Globe, FRBNY, Westchester) a converter under § 3-206(c)?

4) Have any of the defendants converted the check under § 3-420?

Note

Many payees will indorse a check "for deposit only" without adding an account number. A thief that steals a check bearing such an indorsement may deposit the check into its account. Might a depositary bank avoid liability as a converter under § 3-206 by arguing that it complied with the indorsement (i.e., "We followed the indorsement by depositing funds — just not into the account of the indorser. If the indorser expected funds to be deposited into a specific account, it should have supplied an account number.")? Believe it or not, a depositary bank actually made such an argument in State of Qatar v. First American Bank of Virginia, 885 F.Supp. 849 (E. D. Va. 1995). The court was not impressed.

> Thus, a payee who indorses her check in blank runs the risk of having the check stolen and freely negotiated before the check reaches its intended destination. To protect against this vulnerability, the payee can add the restriction "for deposit only" to the indorsement, and the depositary bank is required to handle the check in a manner consistent with that restriction.... And in so adding the restriction, the payee's intent plainly is to direct that the funds be deposited into her own account, not simply that the funds be deposited into some account.... Any other construction of the phrase "for deposit only" is illogical and without commercial justification or utility. Indeed, it is virtually impossible to imagine a scenario in which a payee cared that her check be deposited, but was indifferent with respect to the particular account to which the funds would be credited.

> * * *

> While it is true that the literal command of the bare words "for deposit only" is simply that the check be deposited, such rigid reliance on linguistics in disregard of practical considerations and plain common sense is both unwarranted and imprudent. This is especially so given that the individuals writing and relying upon these restrictive indorsements are not apt to be well versed in the subtleties of negotiable instruments law. As evidenced by numerous authorities ... and common experience, the unqualified phrase "for deposit only" is almost universally taken to mean "for deposit only into the payee's account." To disregard this common understanding in support of an illogical construction is to elevate form over substance.

885 F. Supp. at 852–54.

Problem 5-8

Charles Alcombrack was appointed legal guardian for his son, Chad. Chad was the beneficiary of his grandfather's life insurance policy. When Chad's grandfather passed away, the insurance company issued a check for $30,588.39, payable to the order of the local insurance agent, who indorsed the check over to "Charles Alcombrack, Guardian of the Estate of Chad Stephen Alcombrack a Minor." Charles then indorsed the check as follows:

Charles Alcombrack
Guardian of the Estate of Chad Stephen Alcombrack, a minor

Charles deposited the check into his personal account at Olympic Bank and subsequently depleted all of the trust funds for the personal benefit of himself and his new wife. After Charles depleted his son's estate, J. David Smith was appointed as Chad's new guardian.

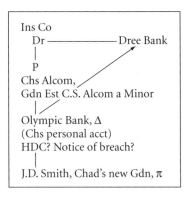

Smith received a judgment against Charles and has sued Olympic Bank for the return of $30,588.39. Olympic Bank argues that it is a holder in due course and is not subject to Smith's claim.

1) Describe Charles Alcombrack's indorsement. §§ 3-205, 3-206(d).

2) At the time of deposit, should Olympic Bank be concerned that Charles may be violating his fiduciary duty? § 3-206(d).

3) At the time of deposit, does Olympic Bank have notice that Charles is breaching his fiduciary duty? § 3-307(a), (b)(1)-(2).

4) Is Olympic Bank a holder in due course? §§ 3-307(b)(1), 3-306, 3-302(a).

Problem 5-9

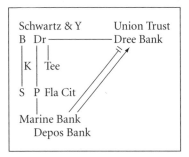

On November 13, Florida Citrus sold a quantity of fruit to Schwartz & Yates, who paid with a check drawn on Union Trust. On November 14, Florida Citrus deposited the check to its account with Marine Bank for collection. Marine Bank gave Florida Citrus provisional credit and forwarded the check to Union Trust for payment. On November 17 Marine Bank received the returned check marked "NSF." Marine Bank promptly notified Schwartz & Yates, who instructed Marine Bank to resubmit the check to Union Trust, which it did the same day, November 17, along with a letter with the instruction to "Return at once if not paid." Union Trust received the check on November 22 but made no settlement. Marine Bank heard nothing further regarding the check until December 6 when Union Trust responded to a tracer (i.e., a letter of inquiry) sent out by Marine Bank. On that day Union Trust returned the check as uncollected. Between November 18 and December 4, the provisional credits to Schwartz & Yates' account exceeded the amount of the check, and during this period some substantial withdrawals were made from the drawer's account exceeding the amount of the check. After December 4, the balances were gradually reduced until December 30, when Schwartz & Yates filed a bankruptcy petition.

1) Is it significant that the provisional balances, between November 18 and December 4, exceed the amount of the Schwartz & Yates check?

2) Who bears the loss: Union Trust, Marine Bank, or Florida Citrus? §§ 4-104(a)(10), (11); 4-215(a), (b); 4-301(a); 4-302(a).

3) Suppose the reason the check was not returned is that the janitor had knocked it out of the "return items" tray and it had fallen under the desk unobserved until a thorough search following receipt of the tracer. Would that affect your analysis? § 4-109, *Blake v. Woodford Bank, supra*.

4) Review: Suppose Marine Bank had allowed Florida Citrus to draw on the funds. What are Marine Bank's options? §§ 4-214(a), 4-302(a).

4. Funds Availability Under Regulation CC

Regulation CC, codified at 12 C.F.R. Pt. 229, "contains rules regarding the duty of banks to make funds deposited into accounts available for withdrawal, including availability schedules." 12 C.F.R. §229.1(b)(2). The following problem explores the contours of the availability schedules.

Problem 5-10

```
Deposits: various kinds, times, places:
Grace ——— TNB
        ——— ATM at TNB
        ——— ATM law schl
```

In each of the following scenarios, Grace makes a deposit on Tuesday, September 18, into her account at the Houston branch of Texas National Bank. Determine the date and hour when Grace may make a cash withdrawal if TNB places the longest hold that it can on her deposit under the general rules of Regulation CC, 12 C.F.R. Pt. 229. See generally §§229.2 (definitions), 229.10 (next-day availability), 229.12 (permanent availability schedule), and 229.19(a), (b) (miscellaneous). Assume that TNB will not invoke any exception under §229.13.

Scenario #1: Grace deposits $400 in cash with a teller at 10:00 a.m.

Scenario #2: Same as #1, except the deposit is made at 1:30 p.m.

Scenario #3: Grace deposits $400 in cash at 10:00 a.m. into an ATM owned and operated by TNB.

Scenario #4: Same as #3, except the deposit is made at 1:30 p.m.

Scenario #5: Same as #3, except Grace uses a generic ATM located in the lobby of her law school.

Scenario #6: Grace deposits, with a teller in the morning, the following checks: $500 federal income tax refund, $500 lottery check, $500 cashier's check drawn on a Florida bank, $500 check drawn on the Dallas branch of TNB, $500 check drawn on the Houston branch of AmeriBank, and $500 check drawn on a California bank.

Scenario #7: Same as #6, except Grace uses an ATM owned and operated by TNB.

C. Payor Bank's Recovery of Money After Final Payment or Settlement

We have now examined the drawer's rights against the drawee bank under the properly payable rule, and we have examined the holder's rights against the drawer, the drawee, and the depositary bank. In several instances we examined situations where the instrument had been dishonored. But suppose the instrument has been honored by mistake, because of forgery or alteration or some other erroneous assumption. What are the payor bank's rights against the other parties to the transaction in these circumstances? If the payor bank pays out wrongfully by mistake, can it get its money back? Or to use the vernacular of the Code, what are the payor bank's rights after final payment and final settlement?

Occasionally a bank will seek to recover funds after final payment or settlement because of a forgery, alteration, or mistake. To what extent is the payment final if it is made on a mistaken assumption? The question has been debated, and settled, for more than two hundred years.

1. Forgery and Payor Bank's Right to Recover After Final Payment

Problem 5-11

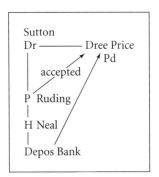

In November 2007, Sutton issued the following draft to Ruding:

> 22 November 2007
>
> To John Price:
>
> Pay $500 to Roger Ruding or order six weeks after date.
>
> *Benjamin Sutton*

Ruding indorsed the draft and then presented it to Price for acceptance. Price wrote on the bill, "Accepted John Price," and returned it to Ruding who then indorsed it to Neal, who took the draft in good faith and for valuable consideration. Price paid the draft to Neal at maturity. Later, Price discovered that the draft had been forged by Lee.

1) Whose signature was forged?

2) Is Price entitled to recover his money back from Neal? § 3-418.

   Q: What part of § 3-418 governs?

   Q: What if Neal had taken the draft under suspicious circumstances?

3) Can Price assert a breach of warranty against either Ruding or Neal? §§ 3-417, 3-301, 3-403.

Problem 5-12

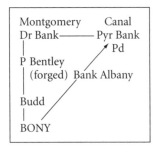

Montgomery Bank drew a draft on Canal Bank payable to the order of Bentley. The indorsements showed that it had been indorsed by Bentley, then by Budd who took in good faith and for value, then by Bank of New York, then by Bank of Albany. Bank of Albany presented the draft to Canal Bank, which timely paid the draft. Later, Canal Bank discovered that Bentley's signature had been forged, and Canal Bank demanded the return of the money from Bank of Albany.

1) Whose signature was forged?

2) Is Canal Bank entitled to recover the money paid out on a mistake theory? § 3-418.

   Q: But will restitution be allowed under Article 3?

3) Is Canal Bank entitled to recover the money paid out on a warranty theory? §4-208 (or §3-417).

Q: Why is Bank of Albany not "a person entitled to enforce," as was Neal in **Problem 5-11**, and what is the rationale for the different results? §3-403.

4) Review: What remedies does Bank of Albany have? §§3-418(d), 3-415, 4-207 (or §3-416).

5) Suppose Bank of Albany had indorsed "without recourse" and "no warranties express or implied." What then? §§3-415(b), 4-208(e) (or §3-417(e)).

6) Review: May the payor bank debit the customer's account? §4-401.

7) Review: What are Bentley's remedies? §§3-420, 3-414, 3-310.

Problem 5-13

Thorp Fin   Peoples
Dr ——————— Payor Bank
| (forged by   ↗ Pd
| Lieding)
|
P Harrison   ╱
| (forged)   ╱
|
Bank Elkhorn
Depos Bank

Lieding, an employee of Thorp Finance, filled out a company check for $5,000 payable to Harrison. Lieding then forged Young's (the manager's) signature on the drawer line. The check was drawn on Peoples Bank. Lieding then forged Harrison's indorsement, indorsed the check with his own name, and deposited it in his account with Bank of Elkhorn. Bank of Elkhorn presented the check for payment to Peoples Bank, which paid the check and charged Thorp Finance's account for $5,000. When Thorp Finance received its statement it discovered the fraud. Who will bear the loss?

1) Review: Allocate the loss between Thorp Finance and Peoples Bank. §§4-401, 3-404, 3-405, 3-406.

2) Can Peoples Bank recover its money from Bank of Elkhorn, in view of the double forgery?

Q: Under the law of restitution? §3-418.

Q: Under breach of warranty? §§4-208 (or §3-417), 3-403, 3-404.

Q: Is Bank of Elkhorn a person entitled to enforce the check? §§3-301, 1-201(b)(21), 3-403, 3-404(b), 4-205.

2. Alteration Before and After Final Payment and Final Settlement

Problem 5-14

On December 1, a stranger made a delivery to Lunt Brothers and received a $25 check payable to the order of Henry Smith (a fictitious person) drawn on Marine National Bank (MNB). The stranger then chemically altered the check by changing the payee's name to Gold Brokers, the amount to $4,079, and the date to December 2. The stranger then used the altered check to purchase gold coins from Gold Brokers. Gold Brokers sent the check for certification. In due course MNB certified and returned the check, and Gold Brokers delivered the gold coins to the stranger. Gold Brokers indorsed the check and deposited

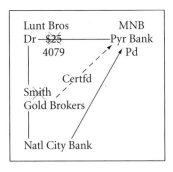

it in its account with National City Bank. The account was overdrawn, but the deposit created a positive balance. The depositary bank sent the check to MNB, which paid the check on the morning of December 3. Later the same day MNB discovered the alterations, notified the depositary bank, and requested repayment. National City Bank refused to repay, having believed the check to be genuine and having credited Gold Broker's account in good faith in payment of the overdraft. Who bears the loss?

1) What was the effect of MNB certifying the check? §§ 3-407, 3-409, 3-414(c), 3-415(d).

Q: What is the obligation of an acceptor of an altered instrument? § 3-413.

2) Is there *any basis* on which MNB might now recover the money paid out? §§ 3-406, 3-418, 4-207 (or 3-416), 4-208 (or 3-417), 3-404.

3) Would it have made a difference if the check had been certified first and then altered? § 3-413.

3. Mistake

Problem 5-15

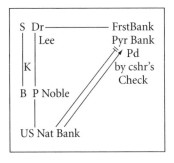

Noble purchased some property from Lee. Later the sale was rescinded and the property was reconveyed to Lee. In return Lee gave his check to Noble for $11,000 drawn on First Bank. Noble indorsed the check in blank and deposited it in U.S. National Bank (USNB) for collection. USNB gave Noble conditional credit for the check with a right of charge back "if not found good." When the check arrived at First Bank, Lee had only $200 in his account, so First Bank dishonored the check, marking it "insufficient funds," and the assistant cashier placed a small symbol in the lower left corner indicating the check was rejected for insufficient funds. First Bank gave timely notice of dishonor to USNB. However, USNB desired final payment of the check and therefore sent the check again by messenger to the Collection and Exchange Department of First Bank, where it was received by Mr. Bohlman, a teller in that department. Mr. Bohlman observed the symbol in the lower left corner and mistook the rejection symbol for payment authorization. Acting on this mistake he drew a cashier's check dated September 24, payable to USNB for $11,000, and stamped the Lee check "paid, etc." The cashier's check was returned to USNB by messenger and credited to Noble's account. On September 25 the cashier's check was presented for collection at 8:45 a.m. at the clearing house and paid. Shortly after 12:00 noon First Bank discovered its mistake and called USNB requesting it to take back the Lee check, arguing that under basic contract law, money paid out on mistake of fact may be recovered. USNB refused.

Is USNB required to return the money to First Bank? §§ 3-418, 3-303, 4-210(a), 4-211.

Problem 5-16

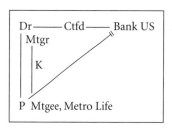

Metropolitan Life Insurance Company held a mortgage on Hotel Martinique Inc. The Hotel drew a check on Bank of U.S. for $11,000, representing an interest payment on the mortgage, and presented it to the bank for certification. At the time the check was presented to the bank for certification the Hotel owed the bank $60,000, with $21,000 on deposit, leaving a difference of $39,000. The Hotel had defaulted on its payments on this debt and the bank exercised its banker's lien or right of setoff against the $21,000 on deposit by putting a "hold" order on the account. But when the check came in for certification, the certification clerk mistakenly overlooked the hold and certified the check. Upon making this discovery the bank immediately notified Metropolitan. Metropolitan presented the check for payment and the bank refused to pay it.

1) Is the bank liable on the check? § 3-409.

2) What is the obligation of an acceptor of an instrument? § 3-413.

D. Cashier's Checks and Teller's Checks

Cashier's checks (§ 3-104(g)) and teller's checks (§ 3-104(h)) are frequently used in two situations. First, upon closing its bank account, a customer may receive from the bank a cashier's check or teller's check for the balance. Second, a party may purchase a cashier's check or teller's check from a bank for the purpose of paying a debt if the obligee refuses to accept the obligor's personal check. (The obligee prefers payment by a cashier's check or teller's check because a bank is less likely to issue a stop payment order on its own check or write its check on rubber paper.)

The following problem explores issues that may arise in transactions involving cashier's checks and teller's checks.

Problem 5-17

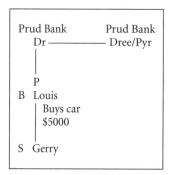

Louis contractually agreed to buy Gerry's car for $5,000. Gerry would not accept a personal check, so Louis purchased a cashier's check from his bank, Prudential Bank (which debited Louis's account for $5,000 when it issued the cashier's check).

1) If Prudential Bank issues the cashier's check payable to Louis, is Louis a PETE while he possesses the check? § 3-301.

2) If Prudential Bank issues the cashier's check payable to Gerry, is Louis a PETE while he possesses the check? § 3-301. What name does Article 3 ascribe to Louis? § 3-103(a)(15).

3) What effect does delivery of the cashier's check to Gerry have on the underlying obligation? § 3-310. Would your answer change if Louis had delivered a personal check?

4) Assume that the cashier's check is payable to Gerry and is dated March 1. Thief steals the check from Louis on March 3. Thief forges Gerry's blank indorsement and deposits the check into his account at Brookwood Bank on March 9. Upon presentment, Prudential Bank pays the check.

  a) If Louis timely completes the necessary paperwork and waits the appropriate period of time, can Louis recover the $5,000 from Prudential Bank? § 3-312. If so, can Prudential Bank recover the $5,000 from Brookwood Bank or Thief?

  b) Instead of pursuing his rights under § 3-312, could Louis recover the $5,000 from Brookwood Bank on a conversion theory?

5) Assume that the cashier's check is payable to Louis and is dated March 1. Louis places his special indorsement on the check and delivers the check to Gerry on March 2. Thief steals the check from Gerry on March 3. Does Gerry have any rights under § 3-312?

6) Assume that the cashier's check is payable to Gerry and is dated March 1. Thief steals the unindorsed check from Gerry on March 3. Thief forges Gerry's blank indorsement and uses the check to purchase a car from Dealer. Dealer deposits the check into its account at Brookwood Bank on March 9. Upon presentment, Prudential Bank pays the check. After Gerry timely completes the necessary paperwork and waits the appropriate period of time, Gerry recovers $5,000 from Prudential Bank, which recovers $5,000 from Brookwood Bank, which debits Dealer's account for $5,000. Can Dealer recover $5,000 from Gerry under § 3-312(c)?

7) Assume that the cashier's check is payable to Gerry and is dated March 1. Thief steals the check on March 3 from Gerry, who had written the following two-line indorsement on the check: for deposit only/Gerry. Thief deposits the check into his account at Brookwood Bank on March 9. Upon presentment, Prudential Bank pays the check. If Gerry timely completes the necessary paperwork and waits the appropriate period of time, can Gerry recover the $5,000 from Prudential Bank? § 3-312.

8) Assume that the cashier's check is payable to Gerry and is dated March 1. Thief steals the check on March 3 from Gerry, who had written the following two-line indorsement on the check: for deposit only/Gerry. Thief waited until June 3 to deposit the check into his account at Brookwood Bank. Upon presentment, Prudential Bank refused to pay the check because it had paid $5,000 to Gerry who had timely completed the necessary paperwork and waited the appropriate period of time under § 3-312. Prudential Bank timely notified Brookwood Bank of its dishonor. To its chagrin, Brookwood Bank discovered that Thief had closed the account and withdrawn the $5,000. Can Brookwood Bank recover the $5,000 from Gerry or Thief? §§ 3-312(c); 3-206(c), (e), (f); 3-302(a); 3-415; 3-416.

Part III

Documentary Transactions

The various documentary transactions we will be discussing in this part have one thing in common—they all arise out of or are connected with a sale of goods, where the buyer and seller are generally located at remote distances from one another. So in one sense, a study of documentary transactions is a mini-course in the sale of goods law, except that the parties are dealing with the documents that represent, symbolize, or determine the right to goods, rather than the goods themselves. We will be interested primarily in the documents used to consummate these transactions—drafts, documents of title, and letters of credit. We will also be interested in the configuration of the various commercial transactions in which these documents are used.

Chapter 6

Documents of Title — Article 7

Documents of title are sometimes referred to as "commodity paper," as distinct from negotiable instruments which are "cash paper." U.C.C. Article 7 contains the law that resolves problems involving commodity paper in intrastate transactions. Article 7 was revised in 2003. Approximately 20-25 states have enacted the revisions.

Article 7 is built upon a combination of the law of contract, bailment, assignment, negotiability, and tort law — areas of the law of which you already have some knowledge. So Article 7 will no doubt look curiously familiar to you. Familiarity with relevant terminology is always a key to understanding, and so we begin with some definitions.

A *document of title* is a "record (i) that in the regular course of business or financing is treated as adequately evidencing that the person in possession or control of the record is entitled to receive, control, hold, and dispose of the record and the goods the record covers and (ii) that purports to be issued by or addressed to a bailee and to cover goods in the bailee's possession which are either identified or are fungible portions of an identified mass. The term includes a bill of lading, transport document, dock warrant, dock receipt, warehouse receipt, and order for delivery of goods." § 1-201(b)(16).

A *bill of lading* is "a document of title evidencing the receipt of goods for shipment issued by a person engaged in the business of directly or indirectly transporting or forwarding goods." § 1-201(b)(6).

A *warehouse receipt* is "a document of title issued by a person engaged in the business of storing goods for hire." § 1-201(b)(42).

A *delivery order* is "a record that contains an order to deliver goods directed to a warehouse, carrier, or other person that in the ordinary course of business issues warehouse receipts or bills of lading." § 7-102(a)(5).

With respect to interstate carriage of goods the rules of Article 7 are pre-empted by the Federal Bills of Lading Act. 49 U.S.C. §§ 81–124. In fact there is a considerable amount of relevant federal legislation and treaties governing interstate and foreign commerce. The Carmack Amendment to the Interstate Commerce Act of 1887 (49 U.S.C. § 20(ll), 1970) is another source of relevant federal law. The Carmack Amendment deals primarily with the liability of interstate carriers with respect to the damage, loss, or destruction of goods during transit, which is an area that Article 7 does not purport to cover. Thus Article 7 is consistent with most of the relevant federal law. Because of this consistency, it is convenient to use Article 7 as a vehicle for studying the law of documents of title, since Article 7 governs not only bills of lading but also warehouse receipts. However, we should be aware of this caveat: Article 7 is subject to any federal treaty or statute or state regulatory statute "to the extent the treaty, statute, or regulatory statute is applicable." § 7-103(a).

A document of title may be either negotiable or nonnegotiable. § 7-104. If the document of title is negotiable, title to the goods is merged in the document. That is, the document of title symbolizes the goods for which it is issued. Possession of a negotiable document of title is equivalent to possessing the goods themselves—so much cotton, iron ore, grain, cattle, refrigerators, etc.

It therefore follows that a negotiable document of title can be used to control the goods it represents without taking physical possession of the goods themselves, because by definition the document evidences "that the person in possession or control of the record is entitled to receive, control, hold, and dispose of the record and the goods the record covers." §1-201(b)(16). This has obvious practical utility in commercial transactions. This means that the mechanics of dealing with goods can be greatly simplified in many instances, because the parties can deal with documents of title rather than the goods themselves.

Although a nonnegotiable document of title does not represent the goods, and therefore transfer of a nonnegotiable document does not have the legal effect of transferring title to the goods, the beneficiary of the nonnegotiable bailment contract, who is usually the bailor, can nevertheless control disposition of the goods. He does so through a combination of assignment plus the cooperation of the bailee. Since the bailee holds the goods at the disposal of the bailor, or a named consignee (possibly a person other than the bailor), the bailor or his consignee can transfer his interest in the goods by communicating this intent to the bailee (often a warehouse or carrier). He does this either by assigning the nonnegotiable document itself to a transferee, followed by the transferee's notification to the bailee of the assignment, or by using a delivery order, or other written instructions, given either to the transferee or directly to the bailee, regarding the consignees's intent to transfer his interest in the bailed goods. Then when the bailee receives notice of transfer, and attorns to or in effect "accepts" the delivery order, the bailee is deemed to hold the goods at the disposal of the transferee. The transferee is now the "person entitled under the document." §§7-403, 7-102(a)(9).

As we go along, we will see examples of why parties may choose a negotiable or nonnegotiable document of title to suit their particular needs.

Using a negotiable document of title may have other consequences that a nonnegotiable document does not. Recall that in negotiable instruments law we learned that if a transferee of a negotiable instrument becomes a holder in due course, he can receive greater rights under the instrument than the transferor had. Similarly, a negotiable document of title has what sometimes is described as "cut-off power." That is, a transferee who has taken a document of title by due negotiation may receive greater rights in the goods it represents than the transferor had.

These bailment and cut-off power aspects of negotiable documents of title will be discussed later. But we might note at this point that if you have taken negotiable instruments law, you already have some transferrable knowledge that will give you considerable insight into the law governing documents of title.

A. Some Comparisons of Documents of Title with Negotiable Instruments

Examine the formal requisites of negotiability for a document of title which are set out in §7-104. Note that they are rather minimal compared to the counterpart rules of negotiability for negotiable instruments found in §3-104.

In discussing negotiable instruments we observed that the rights of the parties arising from the debt created by the underlying contract are merged into the negotiable instrument, and that rights on the underlying contract are suspended until the holder has presented it for payment or until it otherwise comes due. Somewhat analogously, as we have just noted, title to the goods becomes merged in a negotiable document and therefore a holder of the document can control the goods by controlling the document.

In the case of a promissory note, the maker promises to pay money to order or to bearer. Similarly, the issuer of a negotiable document of title, whether warehouse receipt or bill of lading, promises to deliver the goods "to bearer or to the order of a named person." § 7-104(a).

The draft also has its counterpart. The drawer draws upon a drawee to pay money to the order of the payee. Similarly, the bailor of the goods who takes back a nonnegotiable document of title may transfer his title to those goods by drawing a delivery order or other written instructions directing the bailee to deliver the goods to the bailor's transferee, or consignee, as we have described him. Title to the goods does not become merged into a delivery order as in the case of a negotiable document of title, but under a delivery order the bailee becomes legally obligated to comply with this order upon receiving notice of it and to make delivery of the goods to the "person entitled under the document." §§ 7-403, 7-102(a)(9). Of course a bailee is not compelled to accept a delivery order, just as the drawee is not required to accept a draft, but when he does, he becomes obligated to the transferee. "When a delivery order has been accepted by the bailee it is for practical purposes indistinguishable from a warehouse receipt. Prior to such acceptance there is no basis for imposing obligations on the bailee other than the ordinary obligation of contract which the bailee may have assumed to the depositor of the goods." § 7-102 OC 3.

We have observed that basically the person entitled to enforce a negotiable instrument is most frequently the holder or a person with the rights of a holder. § 3-301. The person entitled to enforce a document of title is "the person entitled under the document" as defined by the Code. Unlike the meaning of "person entitled to enforce the instrument" in Article 3, "the person entitled under the document" is defined broadly enough to include not only the holder of a negotiable document of title, but also one who has rights in the goods for which a nonnegotiable document has been issued. § 7-102(a)(9).

The concept of "negotiation" of a negotiable instrument also has its counterpart in the "negotiation" of a document of title. § 7-501. And holder in due course has its counterpart in a transferee of a document of title who has taken the document by "due negotiation." § 7-502.

B. The Parties in a Typical Documentary Transaction

To better understand the nature of a document of title and the role it plays in a documentary transaction, it is necessary to understand something about the commercial context in which documents of title are used. In a typical documentary transaction there are usually two or more of several entities involved—a bailor (who is shipping, storing or selling his goods), a bailee (which will either carry or store the owner's goods), a buyer, and frequently a bank (who discounts, or takes for collection, a draft with a document attached). We begin with a case that illustrates one context in which documents of title are used.

BRANCH BANKING & TRUST CO. v. GILL
237 S.E.2d 21 (N.C. 1977)

[Southeastern Farmers Grain Association (Southeastern) was in the business of buying and selling grain. Southeastern owned a grain storage facility (elevator) which it leased to Farmers Grain Elevator (Elevator), which operated as a public warehouse for the storage of grain. Woodcock, an employee and Secretary-Treasurer of Southeastern, was licensed by the State Warehouse Superintendent, Parham, to act as the local manager of Elevator. To obtain the necessary finances to operate, Southeastern sought a line of credit from Branch Banking & Trust Co. (Bank). The financing plan called for Southeastern to deposit grain with Elevator in return for nonnegotiable warehouse receipts which Southeastern would pledge to Bank for advances or credit. In addition to acknowledging the receipt of a specified number of pounds of grain of the described grade and kind, the receipt form provided: "*The State of North Carolina guarantees the integrity of this receipt*.... Said grain is fully insured by the State Warehouse Superintendent against loss...." Over the course of a year, and after a series of many pledges and cancellations of warehouse receipts, in some instances where there was insufficient grain taken in by Elevator to cover the receipts pledged to Bank, Woodcock, knowing there was not sufficient grain to cover them, issued thirteen warehouse receipts numbered 974–986 to Southeastern. Southeastern then transferred the receipts to Bank as security for loans of over $300,000. However, these thirteen receipts were never properly indorsed by Southeastern. Southeastern's indorsement required the signatures of both its secretary-treasurer and president, but only the name of Southeastern had been stamped on the receipts by Southeastern's bookkeeper. Neither Southeastern nor Bank considered this a proper indorsement. In addition each receipt stated that it represented 112,000 pounds and 20,000 bushels of corn, when in fact 112,000 pounds of corn equals only 2,000 bushels. Nevertheless, with knowledge of Elevator's shortage and the improper issuance of the thirteen warehouse receipts, Bank processed a loan to Southeastern and credited the proceeds to its checking account. Bank then cashed some of Southeastern's checks given to it, exercised its right of set-off against the balance which had been enlarged by the loan, and then closed the account. Southeastern became insolvent. Bank commenced an action against Elevator, Southeastern, the State Representative of Public Warehouses, and others, claiming a right to recover on the thirteen warehouse receipts. Elevator raised certain claims against Southeastern as defenses to the receipts in the hands of Bank. The trial court held in favor of Bank, saying it had taken the receipts by due negotiation. On appeal the North Carolina Supreme Court held against Bank, Gill as custodian of the State Indemnity Fund as surety for the receipts, and others. Gill and others petitioned for a rehearing, which was granted. The court's opinion on the rehearing follows.]

SHARP, CHIEF JUSTICE. In our earlier opinion in this case we held: (1) that the Bank did not take the 13 fraudulent warehouse receipts (Nos. 974–986) by "due negotiation" and thus did not acquire the rights specified in UCC § 7-502; (2) that "nothing else appearing" the Bank was merely a transferee of the negotiable warehouse receipts and thus acquired no greater rights or title than its transferor, Southeastern....

Our prior holding that the Bank did not take the 13 receipts through "due negotiation" is clearly correct.

* * *

By their terms, the grain the 13 warehouse receipts purportedly represented was to be delivered to Southeastern or to its order. These receipts, therefore, were negotiable documents of title. UCC § 1-201(15) [§ 1-201(b)(16)], UCC § 7-102(1)(e), UCC § 7-104(1)(a) [§ 7-104(a)]. These receipts, however, were not indorsed by Southeastern at the time they were delivered to the Bank. Neither Woodcock, the secretary-treasury, nor any other officer of Southeastern ever signed the receipts. Upon Bank's request for its indorsement, Southeastern's bookkeeper, Mrs. Carlton, stamped the name "Southeastern Farmers Grain Association, Inc." on the reverse side of the receipts.

As we said in our former opinion, "[T]he affixing of the payee's (or subsequent holder's) name upon the reverse side of a negotiable document of title by rubber stamp is a valid indorsement, if done by a person authorized to indorse for the payee and with intent thereby to indorse. However, the Superior Court found that Mrs. Carlton, who stamped the name of Southeastern upon the reverse side of these receipts, had neither the authority nor the intent thereby to indorse them in the name of Southeastern. The evidence supports these findings and would support no contrary finding." Since the receipts were not properly indorsed to the Bank, they were not negotiated to it. The Bank, therefore, not having acquired the receipts through "due negotiation," did not acquire the rights provided in UCC § 7-502.

Under UCC § 7-506 the Bank could compel Southeastern to supply the lacking indorsement to the 13 receipts. However, the transfer "becomes a negotiation only as of the time the indorsement is supplied." Since the Bank was specifically informed of the fraud surrounding the issuance of the receipts on the evening of 7 May 1970 any subsequent indorsement by Southeastern would be ineffective to make the Bank "a holder to whom a negotiable document of title [was] duly negotiated." UCC § 7-501(4) [§ 7-501(a)(5)].

Thus, because of the lack of proper negotiation, the Bank became a mere transferee of the 13 warehouse receipts. The status of such a transferee is fixed by UCC § 7-504(1) [§ 7-504(a)] which provides: "A transferee of a document, whether negotiable or nonnegotiable, to whom the document has been delivered but not duly negotiated, acquires the title and rights which his transferor had or had actual authority to convey." Here Southeastern, the Bank's transferor, had no title by way of the fraudulent receipts to any grain held by Elevator, and it had no rights against Elevator. Woodcock, acting for and on behalf of Southeastern, had fraudulently procured the issuance of these receipts to Southeastern without the deposit of any grain. Then, as Southeastern's manager, he had pledged them to Bank in substitution of 16 previously issued receipts purportedly representing corn deposited in Elevator. However, at least six of these represented no grain at the time they were issued, and between the warehouse examiner's inspections of 10 February 1970 and May 1970,—without requiring the surrender of any receipts—Elevator had delivered to or for the account of Southeastern nearly 113,000 bushels of grain more than Southeastern allegedly had in storage there. Thus, Elevator had no obligation to deliver any grain to Southeastern, and it did not become obligated to Bank merely because Southeastern transferred the receipts.

* * *

The purpose of UCC § 7-203 is to protect specified parties to or purchasers of warehouse receipts by imposing liability upon the warehouseman when either he or his agent fraudulently or mistakenly issues receipts (negotiable or nonnegotiable) for misdescribed or nonexistent goods. This section, coupled with the definition of issuer (UCC § 7-102(1)(g) [§ 7-102(a)(8)]), clearly places upon the warehouseman the risk that his agent may fraudulently or mistakenly issue improper receipts. The theory of the law is that the warehouseman, being in the best position to prevent the issuance of mistaken or fraudulent receipts, should be obligated to do so; that such receipts are a risk and cost of the business enterprise which the issuer is best able to absorb.

In the comment to UCC §7-203 it is said: "The issuer is liable on documents issued by an agent, contrary to instructions of his principal, without receiving goods. No disclaimer of the latter liability is permitted." *Issuer* is defined by UCC §7-102 as "a bailee who issues a document.... Issuer includes any person for whom an agent or employee purports to act in issuing a document if the agent or employee has real or apparent authority to issue documents, notwithstanding that the issuer received no goods or that the goods were misdescribed or that in any other respect the agent or employee violated his instructions." Under these provisions Elevator would clearly be liable to the Bank on the 13 fraudulent receipts issued by its agent Woodcock provided the Bank could carry its burden of affirmatively proving that it came within the protection of UCC §7-203.

* * *

We now consider whether the Bank qualifies for this protection. At the outset of our discussion we note that UCC §7-203 contains no requirement that the purchaser take negotiable documents through "due negotiation" before he can recover from the issuer. (Compare this section with the analogous U.C.C. provision covering bills of lading, which provides protection to "a consignee of a nonnegotiable bill who has given value in good faith or a holder to whom a negotiable bill has been duly negotiated relying in either case upon the description...." UCC §7-301(1) [§7-301(a)].) Of course, had the Bank met all the requirements of due negotiation it also would have met the requirements of UCC §7-203.

To be entitled to recover under UCC §7-203 a claimant has the burden of proving that he (1) is a party to or *purchaser* of a *document of title* other than a bill of lading; (2) *gave value* for the document; (3) took the document in *good faith*; (4) *relied* to his detriment upon the description of the goods in the document; and (5) took *without notice* that the goods were misdescribed or were never received by the issuer. Many of these terms are defined in Article 1 of the U.C.C., and those definitions are also made applicable to Article 7.

Under UCC §1-201(33) [§1-201(b)(30)] and UCC §1-201(32) [§1-201(b)(29)] Bank acquired the 13 negotiable warehouse receipts by purchase. Further, when Bank surrendered to Southeastern its old notes and the 16 receipts securing them, taking in return the new notes secured by the 13 receipts, it gave "value." Under UCC §1-201(44) [§1-204] a person, *inter alia*, gives "value" for rights if he acquires them "(b) as security for or in total or partial satisfaction of a pre-existing claim; ... or (d) generally, in return for any consideration sufficient to support a simple contract." It now remains to determine whether Bank, at the time it relinquished the 16 old receipts in return for the 13 receipts, was acting (1) without notice that no goods had been received by the issuer for the 13 receipts, (2) in good faith, and (3) in reliance upon the descriptions in the receipts.

The trial court, after making detailed findings as to facts known to Bank at the time it accepted the 13 receipts, found and concluded the ultimate fact that "the plaintiff Bank did not receive warehouse receipts numbered 974 through 986 in good faith without notice of claims and defenses." This finding, although stated in the negative in order to use the precise language of UCC §7-501(4) [§7-501(a)(5)], is equivalent to a positive finding that Bank took the 13 receipts with notice that they were spurious. On the same findings the judge also concluded that plaintiff did not come into court with "clean hands." This finding likewise is equivalent in import and meaning to a finding that Bank did not take the 13 receipts in good faith.... Upon these findings he held that plaintiff had no cause of action either at law or in equity based on the 13 receipts against either the State Warehouse Superintendent or against the State Treasurer as custodian of the State Indemnity and Guaranty Fund. We must, therefore, determine whether these findings are supported by competent evidence.

Upon our reconsideration of this case we have concluded (1) that the record evidence fully supports the trial judge's findings that Bank did not take the receipts in good faith and without notice that they had been fraudulently issued and (2) that his findings compel his conclusions of law.

[The court then reviewed the evidence regarding Bank's lack of good faith.]

The Code was not designed to permit those dealing in the commercial world to obtain rights by an absence of inquiry under circumstances amounting to an intentional closing of the eyes and mind to defects in or defenses to the transaction. Nor did the General Assembly, when, by G.S. 106-435, it created the State Indemnifying and Guaranty Fund to safeguard the State Warehouse System and to make its receipts acceptable as collateral, intend that it should encourage individuals or financial institutions to engage in transactions from which they would otherwise have recoiled. On the contrary, the fund was created to protect those parties to or purchasers of warehouse receipts who, acting in good faith and without reason to know that the goods described thereon are misdescribed or nonexistent, suffer loss through their acceptance or purchase of the receipt.

The case comes down to this: Plaintiff Bank based its right to recover on the 13 fraudulent warehouse receipts numbered 974–986 for which Elevator received no grain. Its action, if any, was under UCC §7-203. Therefore, if plaintiff could prove it acquired the receipts in good faith and without notice of the fraud, it was entitled to recover, otherwise, not. The trier of facts, upon sufficient evidence, found that plaintiff did not acquire the receipts in good faith and without notice.

The judgment of the trial court is therefore affirmed as to all defendants and our former decision as reported in 286 N.C. 342, 211 S.E.2d 327 (1975) is withdrawn.

Affirmed.

C. The Storage and Carriage Contract: §§ 7-201, 7-302, 7-204, 7-403, 7-309

From the foregoing we see that inherent in a document of title are two contracts: (1) a contract of receipt of the goods by a warehouseman or carrier, and (2) a contract for storage (warehouse receipt) or a contract of carriage (bill of lading).

We now shift our focus to a consideration of the rights and duties of the parties to a document of title under the storage or carriage contract.

1. Scope of Issuer's Responsibility

a. Failure to Deliver

Problem 6-1

Procter & Gamble ("P&G") began selling vegetable oil to Allied Refining. P&G followed the practice of shipping vegetable oil in tank cars to Field Warehousing near the buyer's

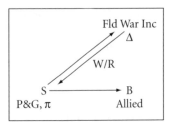

location, where the oil was placed in oil storage tanks until Allied was ready to pay for and take the oil, at which time P&G would give written instructions to Field Warehousing to release the oil to Allied Refining. During March and April, P&G shipped 151 tank loads of oil to the warehouse. The oil had a market value of $1,013,075 on the dates shipped to Field Warehousing, which issued warehouse receipts stating that the oil was "to be delivered to P&G." In June, it was discovered that the oil storage tanks in which the oil was to be stored were empty. Field Warehousing cannot explain how the oil disappeared, but can adduce evidence that it follows reasonably prudent methods in storing all goods. Following discovery of the loss, the market value of vegetable oil dropped by 25% of what it was when the warehouse receipts were issued to P&G. P&G commences an action against Field Warehousing.

1) Did Field Warehousing issue negotiable, or nonnegotiable, receipts to P&G? §§ 7-104, 7-102.

2) What is the responsibility of the warehouse to the holder of the warehouse receipts? §§ 7-403, 7-204.

Q: Who has the burden of proof with respect to the bailee's negligence in the loss or destruction of goods?

Q: Can P&G meet this burden?

Q: In the absence of an explanation of how the oil disappeared, can it be said that the bailee established loss or destruction of the goods for which it is not responsible?

3) Is *res ipsa loquitur* applicable in this type of case? § 7-204.

4) If Field Warehousing is liable, what will be the measure of damages? §§ 7-204, 1-305(a).

Note

See § 7-309 for counterpart provisions for bills of lading. Note the suggestion that federal law may impose strict liability on a carrier in certain cases.

b. Nonreceipt and Misdescription

Problem 6-2

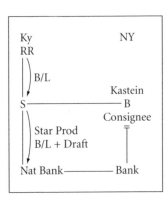

Star Produce of Maysville, Kentucky, raised poultry. Periodically the company shipped poultry to Kastein, a New York customer. On July 6, Chesapeake Railway spotted a car on the produce company's spur track for the purpose of being loaded with poultry. In accordance with prior practice the Railway issued a uniform straight bill of lading to Star Produce for a car of live poultry of the weight of 14,000 pounds with the notation "shipper's load and count" on the bill, consigned to Kastein, the intended buyer. When the Railway issued the bill, only 3,010 pounds of poultry had been loaded. No more poultry was ever loaded onto the car, although the agent was told the loading would be completed that night in time for the car to go out. On July 11, at a time when the Railway knew that the first car had not been completely loaded and was still standing on the spur track, the Railway spotted another car for loading, and issued a straight bill of lading on this second car similar in all respects to the first, except that there was no notation of "shipper's load and count" on the bill, and again covering 14,000 pounds of poultry. No poultry was ever loaded on the second car. On the dates of the two bills of lading, Star Produce drew a draft on the consignee—Kastein—for $10,000 each and discounted the drafts with National Bank. If the cars had been loaded with 14,000 pounds of live poultry, the cargo would have been valued at $10,000 for each car. As a condition to discounting the drafts, the bank required a letter of guarantee of payment of the drafts from the buyer's bank, which in turn guaranteed payment if the cars of live poultry were received in New York within one week from the date of the bill of lading. The drafts, with the respective bills of lading attached, were forwarded for collection, but the consignee refused to pay them and they were returned to the bank. At the time of their return Star Produce had $7,000 on deposit with the bank, which the bank credited against the $20,000 advanced on the two drafts, leaving an unpaid balance of $13,000. The bank had no knowledge that the cars were not loaded. The loading was not completed because Star Produce had become insolvent.

1) Did National Bank take the documents in good faith, relying on the description? §7-301. *Cf.* §7-203 and *Branch Banking & Trust Co. v. Gill*, supra.

2) Who will bear the loss on the first car, the Railway or the Bank? On the second car? §7-301.

Notes

1. A straight bill of lading is a nonnegotiable bill of lading.

2. The Federal Bills of Lading Act (49 U.S.C. §§81 *et seq.*) would apply to this problem because it involves an interstate transaction. Article 7 conforms substantially to the federal act.

D. Impact of Due Negotiation on Equities of Ownership—Cut-Off Power

Problem 6-3

Various owners of cotton hauled their cotton to Gin to be processed and baled. In the absence of the Gin manager, Carr, an employee of Gin, without authorization of the manager, enlisted the aid of Truck Driver to haul a load of cotton to Hodge Warehouse. He then deposited the cotton in the warehouse and requested three warehouse receipts to be issued to the order of three fictitious names. Hodge Warehouse

did so. Carr then drove to a nearby town and sold the receipts to three different buyers—
A, B, and C, indorsing each receipt with the appropriate fictitious name. Although Carr was
an employee and did haul cotton for Gin, he did so only when expressly authorized and was
not to haul except upon specific instructions. When the theft was discovered the owners of
the cotton bales made a demand on Hodge Warehouse for return of the cotton. The in-
dorsees of the warehouse receipts claim the cotton is theirs. Who is entitled to the cotton?

1) Did the holders of the warehouse receipts take by due negotiation? § 7-501. Cf. § 1-
201(b)(9).

2) Assuming they did take by "due negotiation," what did the holders acquire? §§ 7- 502,
7-503, 7-504.

Problem 6-4

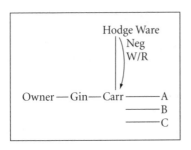

Thief fraudulently represents himself as an agent
of a well-known cotton buyer, Buyer, and thereby
induces Owner to relinquish possession of 100 bales
of cotton to be hauled to Buyer. Instead of hauling
the goods to Buyer, Thief deposits the goods in
Warehouse.

1) Warehouse issues a warehouse receipt to the order
of Thief which Thief indorses to Smith, a cotton
dealer and good-faith purchaser. Who is entitled to
the cotton as between Owner and Smith? §§ 7-501 to 7-504. Cf. §§ 3-404 and 2-403.

2) Warehouse issues Thief a warehouse receipt with the cotton "consigned to Thief." Thief
sells the cotton to Gin, an owner of a cotton gin, for $200 per bale and gives him a de-
livery order on Warehouse for 100 bales of cotton. Owner and Gin claim the cotton. Who
prevails?

Problem 6-5

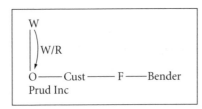

A warehouse receipt covering 200 barrels of wine
was issued to "Prudence Inc. or order" and handed
to Prudence, the president of the company. Shortly
thereafter an agent of Spree Inc. called Prudence
and offered to buy the 200 barrels of wine. Prudence accepted the offer on behalf of Prudence Inc.
and indorsed the warehouse receipt in blank in
anticipation of the arrival of Spree's agent. The agent never arrived, so Prudence put
the receipt in her desk for safe keeping. During the night Custodian took the receipt
from the desk and delivered it to Friend, a friend of his in the liquor business who sold
the receipt to Bender Company for $20,000. Custodian and his friend are no longer
around.

1) Who gets the wine?

2) Would your analysis change if Custodian himself had sold the warehouse receipt to
Bender?

E. Shipments Under Reservation: §§ 2-310, 2-505

Under § 2-310, unless otherwise agreed, delivery and payment are concurrent conditions. But where the parties are located at remote distances from each other the risk that either or both of these obligations will not be performed is greatly increased. Of course the seller is always free to ship the goods and rely upon the buyer's integrity to send the money in payment. On the other hand the buyer is free to send the money in reliance on the seller's promise to ship the goods.

In either case however, there are credit risks and risks of dishonesty. Once a seller is satisfied with the credit and reliability of a customer he is frequently willing to assume such risks. As a result, in domestic transactions shipments pursuant to a straight bill of lading (nonnegotiable) are by far the most common. Until such confidence is established, however, the risks may be minimized by the seller making "shipments under reservation." A diagram of a typical transaction would look something like this:

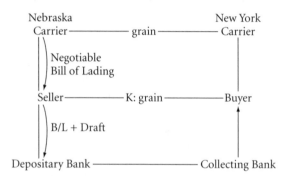

The major components of a shipment under reservation are an order bill of lading issued by a carrier, a draft drawn by the seller on the buyer for the price of the goods, and a bank which will make the documentary collection. Although details of the transaction may vary, the usual practice may be illustrated as follows. Assume we have a sale of a carload of grain by a Nebraska seller to a buyer in New York to whom the grain is to be shipped. The seller fills out an order bill of lading, usually "to the seller's order, notify buyer," and directs the railroad to take possession of the car. In this case the seller is the consignor and the consignee. The seller's instructions to the carrier can take various other forms, such as "to the order of the buyer, notify seller," or "to the order of the buyer, notify buyer." Since the seller determines the risks he is willing to bear, he is free to choose the procedure to be followed by the words he uses in the document.

The seller then either draws a draft on the buyer in the amount of the price or requests his bank to draw the draft, usually at sight, although a 30-, 60- or 90-day trade credit is also common. The seller's bank attaches the bill of lading to the draft and forwards the documents to a bank in the buyer's New York location with instructions not to relinquish the bill of lading to the buyer until he honors the draft pursuant to prior agreement. Thus the buyer is not able to take possession of the goods unless he follows the financing terms of the sales agreement. Conversely the seller may not extract payment until the goods have been shipped. Once the draft has been honored the bill of lading is turned over to the buyer. Upon being notified of the arrival of the grain, the buyer, being "the person entitled under the document," will surrender the bill of lading to the railroad, properly indorsed, and thereby gain access to the car. §§ 7-403, 7-102(a)(9).

Discounting is a common practice in American domestic documentary transactions and in international export traffic. However, in most transactions the bank acts only as a collecting agent, thereby avoiding the risks of nonacceptance or nonpayment by the buyer.

In the course of such documentary transactions there are a number of legal problems that can arise at various stages of the relationships. We have already examined the bailor-bailee relationship to some extent and we consider it further here in the context of a shipment under reservation. We then consider the problems arising out of the relationship between the seller and buyer, and finally we consider the seller and collecting bank relationship.

1. Buyer Defaults—Seller's Rights Against the Bailee

Problem 6-6

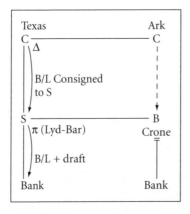

Lydick-Barmann Company of Fort Worth, Texas, sold some roofing materials to Crone Company of Little Rock, Arkansas, for $14,900. An employee of Lydick-Barmann called Ozark Motor Lines and told Ozark that Lydick-Barmann had an "order notify shipment" for Ozark. Ozark furnished a blank bill of lading to Lydick-Barmann. The face of the bill was captioned, "Uniform Motor Carrier Straight Bill of Lading, Nonnegotiable," but it was printed on yellow paper, which is the color reserved by the U.S. Interstate Commerce Commission Act for shipper's order contracts. The bill acknowledged receipt of the freight from Lydick-Barmann and read, "Consigned to Lydick-Barmann Company, destination 616 Street, Louisiana City, Little Rock County, Ark. State. Notify Crone Company." The bill was signed by the agent of the carrier and by the agent of the seller, consignor. Lydick-Barmann then indorsed the bill in blank, attached a draft on Crone Company for the purchase price of the merchandise, and sent both to a Little Rock bank for collection and delivery of the bill of lading. The draft was not paid and both were returned to Lydick-Barmann. When the carrier arrived in Little Rock it was unable to find the destination address of Lydick-Barmann in Little Rock County stated on the bill of lading, and in fact it turned out that Lydick-Barmann had no office or agent at this address. The carrier then took the goods to Crone Company and unloaded. Crone Company has not paid and is insolvent. Under the ICC Act, the word "notify" in bills of lading is required only in shipper's order contracts. Lydick-Barmann sues the carrier for misdelivery.

1) Was this a negotiable or nonnegotiable bill of lading? §§ 7-102, 7-104.

2) What is the legal theory on which Lydick-Barmann will rely? Contract, tort, etc.?

3) Assuming Article 7 controls, who will prevail? §§ 7-102(a)(9), 7-403, 7-404.

   Q: Is "notify Crone" the equivalent of "deliver to Crone"?

4) Will the result be the same whether we treat the document as negotiable or nonnegotiable?

5) The carrier does not wish to encounter the same problems on future transactions. What should the carrier do differently?

2. Buyer Defaults — Seller's Rights Against the Buyer

Problem 6-7

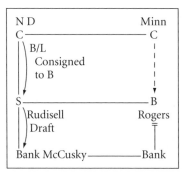

Rudisell, a stock buyer in McClusky, North Dakota, bought thirty-two head of cattle from farmers in the vicinity of McClusky. To obtain funds to pay for them, on November 13, 2008, Rudisell drew a draft on Rogers, Amundson & Flynn Co., cattle dealers in St. Paul, Minnesota, with whom Rudisell had been dealing for some time. He delivered the draft to Bank of McClusky and received unconditional credit for the amount of the draft, with the agreement that the proceeds from the sale of the cattle were thereby assigned to the Bank. Rudisell immediately wrote checks to the farmers from whom he had purchased the cattle and these checks were paid on November 15 and 17. The draft on the St. Paul cattle buyer was as follows:

$32,250. McClusky, N.D., Nov. 13, 2008.

Pay to the order of Bank of McClusky, at the bank, Thirty-two thousand two hundred and fifty dollars. Value received and charge the same to the account of

Signed, R.E. Rudisell

To Rogers, Amundson & Flynn, St. Paul, Minn.
Customer's Draft.

Bank of McClusky then forwarded the draft to a St. Paul bank for collection, along with notice of the assignment of the proceeds of the sale to the bank. On November 18 the draft arrived and it and the notice of assignment were presented to the drawees. They refused to accept the draft, saying that the cattle had not yet arrived and that they were refusing to pay the draft for that reason. The St. Paul bank immediately faxed a notice of nonacceptance to Bank of McClusky. The plan was that Rudisell would not ship the cattle until sufficient time had elapsed to enable the bank to present the draft for acceptance. But the plan went awry because Rudisell shipped the cattle a few hours before the draft was presented for acceptance, and therefore before the seller's bank could know that the draft would not be paid. In the bill of lading the cattle were "consigned to Rogers, Amundson & Flynn," and when the cattle arrived on November 19, Rogers, Amundson & Flynn took possession of them, deducted $30,000 from the total price, claiming Rudisell was indebted to it for that amount, and sent Rudisell a check for the balance. Rudisell is insolvent.

1) How would you describe the bill of lading used by Rudisell? §§ 7-104, 7-102(a)(3), (9).

2) Bank of McClusky consults you. What are its rights? §§ 3-408, 1-103(b), 2-506.

Q: Under the law of equitable assignment does buyer have a right of set-off if he takes possession of the goods after notice that the proceeds of the sale have already been assigned to the bank? That is, does the assignee stand in the shoes of the assignor-seller if seller's potential account debtor is given notice of the assignment before the account arises? Or is buyer estopped from asserting his right of set-off?

Q: If the buyer refused to accept the draft because the cattle had not yet arrived, is there an implied agreement that when the cattle do arrive the buyer will accept the draft?

3) If the bank had consulted you before this transaction, what procedure would you have advised it to follow?

3. Buyer Defaults — Seller's Rights Against Collecting Bank

Problem 6-8

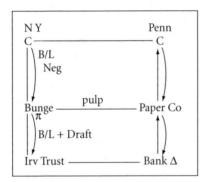

Bunge, a resident of New York, was in the business of selling wood pulp. In September, Bunge agreed to sell a quantity of wood pulp to the Mount Holly Paper Company, Mount Holly Springs, Pennsylvania. The parties agreed that the pulp would be shipped to the purchaser with a sight draft attached to the bill of lading. Accordingly an order bill was completed with the wood pulp "consigned to Bunge or order." Bunge indorsed the bill of lading in blank, and handed it, along with a sight draft in the amount of $30,880 drawn on the paper company, to Irving Trust Company of New York for collection. On October 5, Irving Trust sent the draft, invoices and bill of lading to Bank of Mount Holly Springs with a collection letter with the following instructions,

> "If not paid when due please return notes and clean drafts but hold documentary items informing us immediately of reason for nonpayment. Deliver documents only on payment of draft, unless otherwise instructed by us."

Upon arrival of the documents the Mount Holly Springs bank notified the purchaser and shortly thereafter the purchaser delivered its check drawn on Farmer's Bank in payment of the draft. The bank stamped the draft "Paid," and gave it and the bill of lading to the paper company. The paper company then surrendered the bill of lading to the railroad and took possession of the pulp. Later the same day the paper company notified the bank that it would not accept the pulp and that it did not have sufficient funds in the bank to cover the check. The following day the paper company obtained the bill of lading from the railroad and returned it along with the cancelled draft and invoices to the bank. The bank thereupon returned the check to the paper company, and the bank returned the bill of lading, cancelled draft, and invoices to Irving Trust, and Irving Trust charged Bunge's account for the amount of the draft. Bunge sues Mount Holly Springs bank.

1) You are the judge. Decide the case. §§ 4-201, 4-213, 4-302, 4-203.

2) Would your analysis change if the paper company's check drawn on Farmer's Bank had been certified?

4. Seller Defaults — Buyer's Rights Against Collecting Bank

Problem 6-9

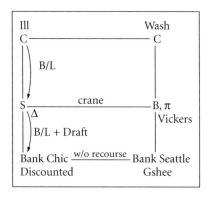

In January, Vickers and Sons Company of Seattle, Washington, purchased a 15-ton crane from Machinery Warehouse Company of Chicago, Illinois, for $88,000, with the machinery company warranting that the crane would pass Seattle inspection. Vickers and Sons advanced $28,000 on the purchase price, with the balance to be paid by sight draft attached to the bill of lading. Upon receipt of the $28,000 the machinery company shipped the crane. The machinery company then drew a draft on the buyer for $60,000 payable to the order of Continental Bank of Chicago, attached an order bill of lading, and discounted the draft at Continental Bank, which in turn credited the machinery company's account with $60,000. Continental Bank then indorsed the draft to Bank of Commerce of Seattle, as follows:

> Pay to the order of Bank of Commerce of Seattle without recourse, either as principal or agent, as to the quantity, quality or delivery of any goods covered by this draft, bill or bills of lading or other documents attached hereto, or herein referred to. Continental Bank. Signed, W.W. Lampert, Cashier.

The draft and other documents were immediately sent on to the Seattle bank for collection. When the crane arrived Vickers and Sons examined it while it was still on the car and found that it would not pass Seattle inspection because of certain defects. Nevertheless the buyer paid the draft (having great need of the crane and thinking it could correct the defects) and took possession of the crane. Vickers and Sons then commenced immediate action against the seller, Machinery Warehouse Company of Chicago, for breach of warranty and obtained a garnishment writ which was served on the Seattle bank, which had not yet remitted the $60,000 to Continental Bank. In due course Vickers and Sons obtained judgment against Machinery Warehouse Company for $40,000 and now seeks to satisfy that judgment from the money frozen in the hands of the Seattle bank by garnishment.

1) Against whom has Vickers and Sons commenced legal proceedings?

2) Is either the Seattle bank or Continental Bank indebted to the seller? §§ 4-210, 4-211.

3) For whom is the Seattle bank holding the $60,000? §§ 4-201, 4-210.

4) Assuming the Washington court has jurisdiction, what should the court hold? §§ 4-201, 4-210.

5) What difference would it make if the machinery company had handed the draft to Continental Bank for collection rather than discounting it?

6) If Vickers and Sons had consulted you while the crane was still on the car, what would you have advised it to do?

5. Seller Defaults—Buyer's Rights Against Depositary Bank

Problem 6-10

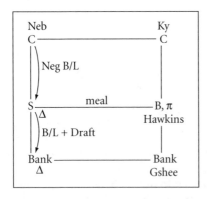

Alfalfa Company of Freemont, Nebraska, sold a carload of meal to Hawkins of Paducah, Kentucky. Pursuant to agreement the sale was by shipment under reservation, with the bill of lading being drawn to the order of Alfalfa Company. Alfalfa drew a draft on Hawkins for $4,000 payable to Freemont Bank, attached the draft to the bill of lading, and discounted the draft to the bank. The draft and bill were sent for collection to Kentucky Bank. Hawkins paid the draft, took possession of the bill of lading, and upon arrival of the car examined the meal for the first time and discovered it was worthless. Hawkins immediately brought suit against Alfalfa Company and Freemont Bank, and attached by garnishment the purchase money which was still in the hands of Kentucky Bank. Hawkins argued that Freemont Bank became liable for breach of the warranty of quality upon purchase of the draft and bill of lading, and that judgment should be satisfied out of the purchase money still being held by Kentucky Bank

1) If Hawkins had been permitted to inspect the goods before payment would he have ended up with the problem he now has?

2) Who is Hawkins suing?

3) You are the judge with complete jurisdiction. Decide Hawkins' case against Freemont Bank and Kentucky Bank. §§ 2-505, 4-201, 4-210, 7-507, 7-508.

4) How does Hawkins' argument differ from the buyer's argument in Problem 6-9?

6. Buyer's Right of Inspection in Domestic and International Transactions

In the absence of agreement to the contrary, there are four basic elements in a contract for the sale of goods: delivery, inspection, acceptance, and payment, not necessarily in that order. § 2-310. Delivery and payment are concurrent obligations. Inspection and acceptance are rights of the buyer, and they are not lost merely because the terms of the contract may require payment before the buyer is permitted to inspect.

Problem 6-11

Capitol Chemical Company of Birmingham, Alabama, sold a carload of naphthalene flakes to Imperial Products Company, West Elizabeth, New Jersey for $26,000. The parties agreed that the goods were to be shipped F.O.B. West Elizabeth for $26,000, but nothing was said about the method of payment. Capitol thereupon obtained an order bill from Pennsylvania Railroad, and shipped the goods f.o.b. buyer's destination. The seller then attached a sight draft for $26,000 drawn on Imperial Products and sent the docu-

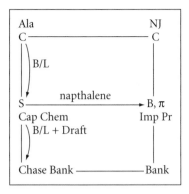

ments to Chase National Bank for collection. In due course the draft was presented to Imperial Products for payment. Imperial Products refused to pay unless it was permitted to inspect the goods. Capitol refused to allow inspection.

1) Is it correct to call this a shipment under reservation?

2) Imperial asks you what it should do. Advise it. §§ 2-310, 2-513, 2-601.

3) Suppose the sales contract had said, "C.O.D., inspection allowed." May buyer inspect? See the small print near the beginning of the Uniform Domestic Order Bill of Lading. It reads as follows:

> "The surrender of the Original Order Bill of Lading properly indorsed shall be required before the delivery of the property. Inspection of property covered by the bill of lading will not be permitted unless provided by law or unless permission is indorsed on the original bill of lading or given in writing by the shipper."

4) What if the contract had provided for "payment against document"? §§ 2-310(c), 2-513(3)(b).

Problem 6-12

Clemens Horst, a hops grower in California, sold a quantity of hops to Biddell Brothers in England. The buyer agreed to pay 90 shillings per 112 lbs., "C.I.F. to London, Liverpool or Hull. Terms net cash." The contract contained no term expressly providing for payment against documents, and no time for delivery of documents either. After the sale, but before shipment, the buyer alleged a right to inspect samples of each bale upon arrival before payment. When the goods were ready for shipment the seller wired to the buyer offering to tender certificates of quality of the Merchants' Exchange along with negotiable bills of lading attached to a draft, and reminding the buyer that it had a right of inspection and rejection after payment against documents if the goods were non-conforming. Buyer, Biddell Brothers, continues to insist on a right to inspect the samples after arrival but before payment.

1) The parties agree that their rights are to be governed by the U.C.C. Biddell Brothers contacts you and asks you for your opinion. What advice would you give? §§ 2-513, 7-305.

2) How can a buyer be sure he will get what he bargains for in a situation like this?

Chapter 7

Letters of Credit

In our consideration of shipments under reservation we observed that a bill of lading accompanied by a draft provides the seller with considerable assurance that he will be paid before the goods are released to the buyer. It also provides the buyer with some assurance that the goods have been shipped. But we have also seen that there remain substantial risks to the seller, buyer, and financing bank under this convention. Most of the problems inherent in shipments under reservation can be eliminated or greatly minimized by using a letter of credit, which is the focus of this chapter.

A letter of credit as a means of financing the sale of goods is very attractive to a remote seller. The key to this appeal is that the known and solid credit of a bank is substituted for the unknown and sometimes shaky credit of the buyer. And because of the usual documentation that tends to verify the condition of the goods shipped—quality and quantity—the letter of credit is also attractive to the buyer.

The letter of credit is of fairly ancient origin and is of several types. But the commercial or bank credit, which is used to finance the sale of goods, is a comparatively modern development. The commercial letter of credit is sometimes referred to as a documentary letter of credit because the obligation of the issuing bank to honor the credit is typically conditioned upon the beneficiary submitting stipulated documents as a condition to the bank's obligation to pay.

Briefly illustrated, a commercial or international letter of credit is used as follows. Buyer in San Francisco desires to import goods from Japan. To reduce the risk of Buyer's nonpayment, Seller insists that Buyer provide a letter of credit. Buyer requests his bank in San Francisco to issue a letter of credit for the benefit of Seller, located in Tokyo. If Buyer's credit warrants the risk, the bank will draw a letter of credit in favor of Seller, thereby committing itself to pay the price upon Seller's compliance with stipulated conditions.

The most important condition requires Seller to tender certain documents, such as a draft drawn on Buyer for the price, clean bills of lading, certificates of quality, consular invoices, marine insurance, weight returns, and other documents that tend to assure Buyer that he is getting what he bargained for and which will be reasonable under the circumstances.

The letter may be sent directly to Seller or, more probably, to a correspondent bank in Tokyo which will advise Seller of the credit. Seller will then deposit the goods with the carrier. The letter of credit now makes it possible for Seller to discount his draft on Buyer with a local bank by virtue of the better-known financial position of the issuing bank, thereby permitting Seller to obtain all or most of the price at the time he ships the goods.

In due course Buyer will obtain the bills of lading from his bank, either by immediate payment of the draft, or under a security agreement traditionally referred to as a trust receipt or bailee receipt. Or Buyer may be granted unsecured credit pursuant to an extensive undertaking, given at the time of application, that the goods and proceeds derived therefrom will be held in trust or stand as security for the debt.

In banking parlance Buyer is the "applicant," and his bank is the "issuer." The correspondent bank may act in a mere advisory capacity (an "adviser"). Alternatively it may act as a "confirmer," in which case it becomes bound to honor the credit in the same way as the issuer. Seller is the "beneficiary." § 5-102.

If the beneficiary satisfies all the conditions stipulated in the letter of credit, the issuing and confirming banks become obligated to pay out on the credit on presentment. § 5-108(a).

Another version of the letter of credit is the "standby" letter of credit. The standby letter of credit is of even more recent origin than the commercial letter of credit and is attributable primarily to the advent of the Uniform Commercial Code. The commercial letter of credit is distinguishable from the standby letter of credit primarily with respect to the conditions that trigger the beneficiary's right to payment. The commercial letter of credit is used to finance the sale of goods, conditioned upon the beneficiary-seller's submission of the stipulated documents. The standby letter of credit is used to assure the beneficiary that the other party to the underlying contract will do something. Thus the beneficiary's right to payment under the standby letter of credit is conditioned upon the customer's failure to perform his obligations on the underlying contract, whether it be to build something, to render a service, or to pay a debt, whereas the beneficiary's right to payment under a commercial letter of credit is conditioned upon his submission of the requisite documents.

The standby letter of credit has become a common mode of guaranteeing payment in nondocumentary transactions. To illustrate the nature of a standby letter of credit, suppose a local school district sells bonds to finance the construction of three new elementary schools. The bonds call for annual payments of principal and interest to the bondholders over a thirty-year period. The bondholders may be concerned that the school district may default on the scheduled payments. To reduce that risk, a bank agrees to issue a standby letter of credit to the bondholders (or to a trustee, who is acting on behalf of all of the bondholders) in which the bank agrees to make the scheduled payments to the bondholders if the school district fails to do so, to be triggered when the bondholders (or the trustee) deliver a written statement of default to the bank.

In these illustrations the standby letter of credit is in effect a guarantee of payment on certain conditions. This conditional obligation of the bank to pay does not arise from the underlying contract between the original parties (the customer and the party with whom the customer contracts—the ultimate beneficiary of the letter of credit), since the bank is not a party to that agreement. This difference distinguishes the bank's obligation under a letter of credit from the bank's obligation as a simple guarantor. The bank's obligation under a letter of credit arises from a separate contract between the bank and the beneficiary of the letter of credit, and therefore the bank is not a simple guarantor of the underlying contract. However, in some cases the courts have looked through form to substance and found that the standby letter of credit was nothing more than a simple guarantee, particularly where the beneficiary was not obligated to tender documents as a prerequisite to the bank's obligation to honor the credit. In most instances it makes no legal difference whether the arrangement is classified as a guarantee or a letter of credit, except where the issuer is a bank. The Federal Reserve Board prohibits banks from guaranteeing the debts of a principal debtor. Thus a standby letter of credit may be used to circumvent this prohibition only if the obligation of the bank to pay arises under the letter of credit and not out of a simple agreement to guarantee payment of a debt.

There is little legislation in most countries purporting to regulate letters of credit. However, in 1929, the International Chamber of Commerce compiled a set of uniform customs known as the Uniform Customs and Practice for Documentary Credits (the

UCP). This document has gone through several revisions. The current revisions became effective on July 1, 2007.[1] Many letters of credit incorporate the UCP by reference (e.g., "This letter of credit is subject to the Uniform Customs and Practice for Documentary Credits (2007 Revision) fixed by the International Chamber of Commerce (I.C.C. Publication No. 600)."). The Uniform Customs are not law, but they take on the force of law because the parties bind themselves to honor them by agreement. It was the uncertainty of whether the UCP should be applied to domestic letters of credit that led to the development of Article 5 of the Uniform Commercial Code, which provides a letter of credit law for domestic transactions within the U.S. Article 5 was revised in 1995 and has been enacted in every state. Unless otherwise noted, citations are to revised Article 5.

Article 5 defines a letter of credit as "a definite undertaking that satisfies the requirements of § 5-104 by an issuer to a beneficiary at the request or for the account of an applicant ... to honor a documentary presentation by payment or delivery of an item of value." § 5-102(a)(10). Under § 5-104, a letter of credit "may be issued in any form that is a record and is authenticated (i) by a signature or (ii) in accordance with the agreement of the parties...."

The opening problem is aimed at introducing some of the basics of letter of credit law. The materials that follow raise issues of material fraud and forgery, wrongful dishonor and subsequent damages, breach of warranty, and strict compliance.

Problem 7-1

Review the following letter of credit and answer the questions that follow.

METROPOLITAN BANK
1300 San Jacinto
Houston, Texas 77002

July 20, 2008

Smith Corporation
1000 Westheimer Avenue
Kennett, Massachusetts 60603

Dear Smith Corporation:

We hereby establish our irrevocable letter of credit no. 2008-127 for eighteen thousand and no/100 U.S. dollars ($18,000.00) to expire October 1, 2008, at 5:00 p.m. (eastern time), in favor of yourselves, available by your draft drawn on us at sight for the account of ABC, Inc., 3525 Dumbarton, Houston, TX 77025.
Your draft must be marked "DRAWN UNDER METROPOLITAN BANK LETTER OF CREDIT NO. 2008-127" and must be accompanied by an original bill of lading, dated no later than September 15, 2008, evidencing your shipment of fifty photocopiers (Solera model no. X-57) to ABC, Inc., 3525 Dumbarton, Houston, TX 77025.
Subject to any contrary statement herein, this letter of credit is subject to the Uniform Customs and Practice for Documentary Credits (2007 Revision), fixed by the International Chamber of Commerce (I.C.C. Pub. No. 600).

---

1. The ICC also has approved the International Standby Practices 1998, a set of rules applicable specifically to standby letters of credit. The ICC publishes "ISP 98" as ICC Publication No. 590.

METROPOLITAN BANK
Albert P. Masterson
Albert P. Masterson, Vice President

1) Identify the applicant, beneficiary, and issuer. § 5-102(a).

Q: Would the letter of credit be governed by U.C.C. Article 5 if it had been issued by a non-bank entity (e.g., an insurance company)?

2) Is the letter of credit a documentary, or standby, letter of credit?

3) Assume that the issuer received no consideration for issuing the letter of credit. May the issuer avoid its obligations under the letter of credit by raising a "no consideration" defense? § 5-105.

4) Assume that the opening paragraph did not include the word "irrevocable." Would the letter of credit be irrevocable, or revocable? § 5-106(a).

5) Assume that the opening paragraph did not state an expiration date. When would the letter of credit expire? § 5-106(c).

6) Assume that Smith Corporation submits the required documents to Metropolitan Bank on the morning of September 20, 2008. How quickly must Metropolitan Bank review the documents? § 5-108(b).

7) Assume that Smith Corporation timely submits documents to Metropolitan Bank. The draft states: "Drawn Under Letter of Credit Number 2008-127 issued by Metropolitan Bank on July 20, 2008." The bill of lading refers to "Salero" models instead of "Solera" models. Should Metropolitan Bank honor or dishonor the presentation? § 5-108(a).

8) Assume that the underlying contract called for Smith Corporation to deliver "model X-57A" photocopiers, rather than "model X-57" photocopiers as stated in the letter of credit. May Metropolitan Bank rightfully dishonor Smith Corporation's timely presentation (which complies with the requirements of the letter of credit) by raising the model discrepancy as a defense? § 5-103(d).

A. Issuer's Duty and Privilege to Honor Letter of Credit

SZTEJN v. J. HENRY SCHRODER BANKING CORP.

31 N.Y.S.2d 631 (N.Y. Sup. Ct. 1941)

SHIENTAG, Justice.

This is a motion by the defendant, the Chartered Bank of India, Australia and China, (hereafter referred to as the Chartered Bank), made pursuant to Rule 106(5) of the Rules of Civil Practice to dismiss the supplemental complaint on the ground that it fails to state facts sufficient to constitute a cause of action against the moving defendant. The plaintiff brings this action to restrain the payment or presentment for payment of drafts under a letter of credit issued to secure the purchase price of certain merchandise, bought by the plaintiff and his coadventurer, one Schwarz, who is a party defendant in this action. The plaintiff also seeks a judgment declaring the letter of credit and drafts thereunder null and void. The complaint alleges that the documents accompanying the drafts are fraudulent in that they do not represent actual merchandise but instead cover boxes fraudulently filled with worthless material by the seller of the goods. The moving defendant urges that the complaint fails to state a cause of action against it because the Chartered Bank is only concerned with the documents and on their face these conform to the requirements of the letter of credit.

On January 7, 1941, the plaintiff and his coadventurer contracted to purchase a quantity of bristles from the defendant Transea Traders, Ltd. (hereafter referred to as Transea) a corporation having its place of business in Lucknow, India. In order to pay for the bristles, the plaintiff and Schwarz contracted with the defendant J. Henry Schroder Banking Corporation (hereafter referred to as Schroder), a domestic corporation, for the issuance of an irrevocable letter of credit to Transea which provided that drafts by the latter for a specified portion of the purchase price of the bristles would be paid by Schroder upon shipment of the described merchandise and presentation of an invoice and a bill of lading covering the shipment, made out to the order of Schroder.

The letter of credit was delivered to Transea by Schroder's correspondent in India. Transea placed fifty cases of material on board a steamship, procured a bill of lading from the steamship company and obtained the customary invoices. These documents describe the bristles called for by the letter of credit. However, the complaint alleges that in fact Transea filled the fifty crates with cowhair, other worthless material and rubbish with intent to simulate genuine merchandise and defraud the plaintiff and Schwarz. The complaint then alleges that Transea drew a draft under the letter of credit to the order of the Chartered Bank and delivered the draft and the fraudulent documents to the "Chartered Bank at Cawnpore, India, for collection for the account of said defendant Transea." The Chartered Bank has presented the draft along with the documents to Schroder for payment. The plaintiff prays for a judgment declaring the letter of credit and draft thereunder void and for injunctive relief to prevent the payment of the draft.

For the purposes of this motion, the allegations of the complaint must be deemed established and "every intendment and fair inference is in favor of the pleading." Madole v. Gavin, 215 App. Div. 299, at page 300, 213 N.Y.S. 529, at page 530; McClare v. Massachusetts Bonding Ins. Co., 266 N.Y. 371, 373, 195 N.E. 15. Therefore, it must be assumed that Transea was engaged in a scheme to defraud the plaintiff and Schwarz, that the merchandise shipped by Transea is worthless rubbish and that the Chartered Bank is not an innocent holder of the draft for value but is merely attempting to procure payment of the draft for Transea's account.

It is well established that a letter of credit is independent of the primary contract of sale between the buyer and the seller. The issuing bank agrees to pay upon presentation of documents, not goods. This rule is necessary to preserve the efficiency of the letter of credit as an instrument for the financing of trade. One of the chief purposes of the letter of credit is to furnish the seller with a ready means of obtaining prompt payment for his merchandise. It would be a most unfortunate interference with business transactions if a bank before honoring drafts drawn upon it was obliged or even allowed to go behind the documents, at the request of the buyer and enter into controversies between the buyer and the seller regarding the quality of the merchandise shipped. If the buyer and the seller intended the bank to do this they could have so provided in the letter of credit itself, and in the absence of such a provision, the court will not demand or even permit the bank to delay paying drafts which are proper in form.... Of course, the application of this doctrine presupposes that the documents accompanying the draft were genuine and conform in terms to the requirements of the letter of credit....

However, I believe that a different situation is presented in the instant action. This is not a controversy between the buyer and seller concerning a mere breach of warranty regarding the quality of the merchandise; on the present motion, it must be assumed that the seller has intentionally failed to ship any goods ordered by the buyer. In such a situation, where the seller's fraud has been called to the bank's attention before the drafts and documents have been presented for payment, the principle of the independence of the bank's obligation under the letter of credit should not be extended to protect the unscrupulous seller. It is true that even though the documents are forged or fraudulent, if the issuing bank has already paid the draft before receiving notice of the seller's fraud, it will be protected if it exercised reasonable diligence before making such payment.... However, in the instant action Schroder has received notice of Transea's active fraud before it accepted or paid the draft. The Chartered Bank, which under the allegations of the complaint stands in no better position than Transea, should not be heard to complain because Schroder is not forced to pay the draft accompanied by documents covering a transaction which it has reason to believe is fraudulent.

Although our courts have used broad language to the effect that a letter of credit is independent of the primary contract between the buyer and seller, that language was used in cases concerning alleged breaches of warranty; no case has been brought to my attention on this point involving an intentional fraud on the part of the seller which was brought to the bank's notice with the request that it withhold payment of the draft on this account. The distinction between a breach of warranty and active fraud on the part of the seller is supported by authority and reason. As one court has stated: "Obviously, when the issuer of a letter of credit knows that a document, although correct in form, is, in point of fact, false or illegal, he cannot be called upon to recognize such a document as complying with the terms of a letter of credit." Old Colony Trust Co. v. Lawyers' Title & Trust Co., 2 Cir., 297 F. 152 at page 158, certiorari denied 265 U.S. 585, 44 S. Ct. 459, 68 L. Ed. 1192....

No hardship will be caused by permitting the bank to refuse payment where fraud is claimed, where the merchandise is not merely inferior in quality but consists of worthless rubbish, where the draft and the accompanying documents are in the hands of one who stands in the same position as the fraudulent seller, where the bank has been given notice of the fraud before being presented with the drafts and documents for payment, and where the bank itself does not wish to pay pending an adjudication of the rights and obligations of the other parties. While the primary factor in the issuance of the letter of credit is the credit standing of the buyer, the security afforded by the merchandise is also taken into account. In fact, the letter of credit requires a bill of lading made out to the order of the bank and not the buyer. Although the bank is not interested in the exact detailed performance of the sales contract, it is vitally interested in assuring itself that there are some goods represented by the documents. Finkelstein, Legal Aspects of Commercial Letters of Credit, p. 238; ... Thayer, Irrevocable Credits in International Commerce, 37 C.L.R. 1326, 1335.

On this motion only the complaint is before me and I am bound by its allegation that the Chartered Bank is not a holder in due course but is a mere agent for collection for the account of the seller charged with fraud. Therefore, the Chartered Bank's motion to dismiss the complaint must be denied. If it had appeared from the face of the complaint that the bank presenting the draft for payment was a holder in due course, its claim against the bank issuing the letter of credit would not be defeated even though the primary transaction was tainted with fraud. This I believe to be the better rule despite some authority to the contrary....

The plaintiff's further claim that the terms of the documents presented with the draft are at substantial variance with the requirements of the letter of credit does not seem to be supported by the documents themselves....

Accordingly, the defendant's motion to dismiss the supplemental complaint is denied.

Note

How would this case be decided under the U.C.C.? §§ 5-108(a), 5-109.

SRS PRODUCTS CO. v. LG ENGINEERING CO., LTD.
994 S.W.2d 380 (Tex. Ct. App. 1999)

KEM THOMPSON FROST, Justice.

This is an accelerated appeal from the trial court's denial of an application for a temporary injunction to enjoin the payment and presentment of a standby letter of credit. Appellant SRS Products Co., Inc. ("SRS") requested a temporary restraining order and a temporary injunction preventing appellee Heritage Bank from paying on a standby letter of credit presented by appellee LG Engineering Co., Ltd. ("LGE"). The trial court granted the temporary restraining order, but denied the temporary injunction. SRS appealed and we granted a temporary injunction preventing payment on the letter of credit during the pendency of this appeal. We affirm the trial court's denial of the temporary injunction and dissolve our temporary injunction.

Factual and Procedural Background

In August 1996, LGE contracted with SRS to purchase a commercial refrigeration unit for use by Thai Plastics Corporation, in Thailand. SRS contracted to design and construct the unit and guaranteed that all materials furnished would conform to LGE's specifications and drawings. SRS also guaranteed that the unit would be fit and sufficient for the purpose for which it was intended, of new and good materials, design and workmanship, and free from defects. LGE agreed to pay in excess of $2.4 million for the unit. SRS agreed to repair or replace free of cost to LGE any part or parts that failed "in the normal use and service and under proper operation, because of faulty design or workmanship or defective materials, within twelve (12) months after being placed in normal operation or within eighteen (18) months from the date of shipment, whichever is sooner, unless otherwise expressly stated in the body of this order." The parties amended the warranty period to make the warranty effective for two years from the date of shipment, or fifteen months after the date of final acceptance.

Originally, the parties' contract called for SRS to issue a performance bond in the amount of ten percent of the contract price to secure its warranty obligations to LGE. At SRS' request, however, LGE agreed to allow SRS to post a standby letter of credit in place of a performance bond, with the only proviso for drawing against it being a written declaration by an executive officer of LGE that SRS had "refused or failed to perform [war-

---

1. The letter of credit provided that Heritage Bank would pay upon LGE's written demand, "plus five (5) banking days any amount claimed ... against [LGE's] written declaration that [SRS] had re-

ranty work] in accordance with the terms and conditions of [LGE's] Purchase Order" for the refrigeration unit. SRS arranged for Heritage Bank to issue a standby letter of credit for $240,147 (10% of the contract price) to cover the cost of potential warranty repairs.[1] After Heritage Bank issued the letter of credit, LGE released a final payment of over $800,000 to SRS.

The refrigeration unit arrived in Thailand in early September 1997. From the outset, LGE experienced numerous and sundry problems with the unit, including misalignment of the gearbox-motor compressor unit, misalignment of shafts and motors, skid bolt openings, severe vibrations in the compressor and other component parts, defective welds on piping, and improper functioning of the controller unit. When LGE called on SRS to make the necessary repairs under the warranty, SRS took the position that the defects occurred in the "delivery and installation phase" and that the warranty covered only defects occurring in the "operational phase." SRS sent repair personnel to Thailand only on condition that LGE pay in advance for their services. Despite repeated efforts to repair and replace the non-working parts, the unit would not function. In December 1997, SRS notified LGE that because LGE (or third parties acting at LGE's direction) had worked on, changed, or modified the unit, the warranty was void.

In May 1998, LGE made a demand on the standby letter of credit, providing Heritage Bank with the written declaration that SRS had failed or refused to perform warranty work on the unit. Under the terms of the letter of credit, Heritage Bank had five days to respond. Before the fifth day, SRS filed suit in the 151st Judicial District Court of Harris County, seeking a temporary restraining order, a temporary injunction and a permanent injunction preventing Heritage Bank from honoring the letter of credit and prohibiting LGE from making demand on it. The ancillary judge granted a temporary restraining order. After a two day hearing in July 1998, at which both sides presented evidence and made arguments, the trial court denied SRS' application for temporary injunction. SRS filed this accelerated appeal and sought injunctive relief from this court during the pendency of the appeal. On August 27, 1998, we granted a temporary injunction blocking payment on the letter of credit pending the decision of this court.

Standard of Review

The denial of a temporary or permanent injunction is within the sound discretion of the trial court. See Walling v. Metcalfe, 863 S.W.2d 56, 58 (Tex. 1993). Our review of the trial court's action is limited to determining whether the action constituted a clear abuse of discretion. See id. A trial court abuses its discretion by (1) acting arbitrarily and unreasonably, without reference to guiding rules or principles, or (2) misapplying the law to the established facts of the case. See Downer v. Aquamarine Operators, Inc., 701 S.W.2d 238, 241–42 (Tex. 1985), cert. denied, 106 S.Ct. 2279 (1986). An abuse of discretion does not exist where the trial court bases its decision on conflicting evidence and evidence appears in the record which reasonably supports the trial court's decision. See Davis v. Huey, 571 S.W.2d 859, 862 (Tex. 1978).

---

fused or failed to perform the warranty obligation under the contract signed by a [sic] executive officer of [LGE]."

The Independence Principle Underlying Letters of Credit

A letter of credit is an engagement by its issuer to honor demands for payment by the beneficiary upon compliance with the conditions specified in the letter. Tex. Bus. & Com.Code Ann. §5.103(a)(1) (Vernon 1994 & Supp. 1998) [R§5-102(a)(10)]. "The purpose of a letter of credit is to assure payment when its own conditions have been met, irrespective of disputes that may arise between the parties concerning performance of other agreements which comprise the underlying transaction." Sun Marine Terminals, Inc. v. Artoc Bank and Trust, Ltd., 797 S.W.2d 7, 10 (Tex. 1990). This principle of independence is the central feature of a letter of credit and is essential to its commercial viability.

Unlike the obligation of a guarantor, which generally does not mature unless the principal debtor has actually defaulted, the facts of the underlying transaction are generally not relevant to the obligation of an issuer of a letter of credit. An issuer's obligation to pay is triggered when the beneficiary presents documents that conform to the terms of the letter of credit. Tex. Bus. & Com. Code Ann. §5.114(a) (Vernon 1994 & Supp. 1998) [R§5-108(a)]. Except in very rare circumstances, courts will not recognize defenses or claims of the account party against the beneficiary as grounds for enjoining presentment or payment on a letter of credit.

The general rule is that an injunction will not issue to block payment of a letter of credit where the beneficiary has presented conforming documents. The Uniform Commercial Code, as adopted in Texas, recognizes only three instances in which a court may enjoin the honoring of an otherwise conforming letter of credit: (i) when documents appear on their face to comply with the terms of a credit, but a required document does not in fact conform; or (ii) when documents appear on their face to comply with the terms of a credit but a required document is in fact forged; or (iii) when there is fraud in the transaction. See Tex. Bus. & Com. Code Ann. §5.114(b) [R§5-109]; AIG Risk Management v. Motel 6 Operating L.P., 960 S.W.2d 301, 305 (Tex.App.–Corpus Christi 1997, no writ). Here, SRS does not claim that the written declaration LGE made to Heritage Bank was nonconforming, nor does SRS otherwise dispute that LGE made the requisite presentation to Heritage Bank to draw on the letter of credit; rather, SRS contends that LGE's declaration was false and, therefore, constitutes fraud that vitiates the entire transaction, entitling it to injunctive relief under section 5.114(b), Texas Business and Commerce Code [R§5-109].

Requisite Showing for "Fraud in the Transaction" Under U.C.C. Section 5.114(b) [R§5-109]

SRS argues that LGE's presentment to Heritage Bank was fraudulent because LGE knew, or should have known, (1) that the problems for which it sought repairs and replacement were not, in fact, warranty obligations because they occurred in the "installation phase of the project and not in normal use and service and under proper operations as required by the warranty;" and (2) that LGE's material modifications to the unit voided the warranty obligations altogether. SRS contends that although LGE made the requisite representation that SRS had defaulted in its warranty obligations, "it was not an honest representation" and therefore, the trial court abused its discretion in refusing to enjoin payment and presentment.

Establishing "fraud in the transaction" under section 5.114(b) [R§5-109] requires more than a showing of untruthful statements in presentment documents. See Philipp Bros. Inc. v. Oil Country Specialists, Ltd., 787 S.W.2d 38, 40–41 (Tex. 1990). The wrongdoing must be so "egregious, intentional, and unscrupulous" that it vitiates the entire transaction such that the legitimate purposes of the independence of the issuer's obligation would no longer be served. GATX Leasing Corp. v. DBM Drilling Corp., 657 S.W.2d 178, 182 (Tex.App.–San Antonio 1983, no writ); see also Paris Sav. & Loan Ass'n v. Walden, 730 S.W.2d 355, 365 (Tex.App.–Dallas 1987, writ dism'd w.o.j.). The exception is applicable only in very limited situations where there has been an intentional perversion of the truth in order to induce another to part with something of value or surrender a legal right. To invoke this narrow exception, there must be evidence of trickery, dishonesty, deception or other wrongdoing that rises to the level of fraud. In most cases finding wrongdoing sufficient to qualify as "fraud in the transaction," the beneficiary of the letter of credit has utterly failed to perform its obligations or has engaged in a deceptive or dishonest scheme. See e.g., Philipp Bros., 787 S.W.2d at 40 (upholding an injunction where substandard condition of goods for which letter of credit had been issued rendered entire inventory virtually worthless, destroying the legitimate purpose of the letter of credit); see also United Bank Ltd. v. Cambridge Sporting Goods Corp., 41 N.Y.2d 254, 392 N.Y.S.2d 265, 360 N.E.2d 943, 946 (1976) (payment on letter of credit enjoined because the beneficiary shipped old and damaged goods instead of the agreed upon goods); Sztejn v. J. Henry Schroder Banking Corp., 177 Misc. 719, 31 N.Y.S.2d 631 (N.Y.Sup.Ct. 1941) (pre-Code case in which payment of a letter of credit was enjoined because the beneficiary had shipped rubbish instead of the goods called for by the agreement).

Typically, the beneficiary of the letter of credit is the seller and the account party is the purchaser. This case presents an interesting variation in that the beneficiary of the letter of credit (LGE) is the purchaser and the account party (SRS) is the seller. LGE paid the entire purchase price for the refrigeration unit, a sum in excess of $2.4 million. At issue is the "reserve" that the parties contracted to set aside via the letter of credit to back SRS' warranty obligations. LGE made demands for warranty work and gave SRS numerous opportunities to perform under the warranty. Despite repeated efforts to remedy the defects and effect the necessary repairs, the unit did not work and SRS refused to honor the warranty. While SRS argues that its warranty obligations were never triggered or, alternatively, that they were voided, and that LGE knew or should have known as much by virtue of its own actions in modifying the equipment, SRS points to no facts which show that the letter of credit was being used as a vehicle for fraud. In fact, the evidence shows that LGE was using the letter of credit exactly as the parties had contemplated at the time it was issued. SRS' steadfast contention that it has no liability on the warranty, even if true, is insufficient to justify enjoining payment on the letter of credit under section 5.114(b) [R§ 5-109]. A dispute over the existence or scope of warranty obligations does not amount to fraud in the transaction, and therefore, does not provide grounds to enjoin payment of a letter of credit issued to secure performance of those obligations. To allow an account party to obtain an injunction based on a mere contractual dispute with the beneficiary would destroy the commercial viability of letters of credit and, in this case, would undermine the rationale for utilizing a letter of credit–to shift leverage back to the purchaser in demanding performance by the seller of the warranty obligations.

The obligation of Heritage Bank (the issuer) to pay LGE (the beneficiary) is entirely independent of any obligation (or lack thereof) of SRS to LGE under the contract between SRS and LGE.[2] Thus, it would fly in the face of Article Five to enjoin payment on the let-

---

2. See Comment 1 to section 5.114, stating that "[t]he letter of credit is essentially a contract between the issuer and the beneficiary and is recognized by this Article as independent of the underlying contract between the customer and the beneficiary."

ter of credit based solely on a dispute between the bank's customer and the beneficiary over underlying contractual obligations.[3] Given that the issuing bank could not defend against the beneficiary by setting up the defenses the bank's customer had against the beneficiary, it would be anomalous if the customer could nonetheless enjoin payment of the letter of credit on the ground that its own obligations to the beneficiary had not been triggered or were in dispute. While there is a clear disagreement between the parties concerning the existence and scope of the warranty's coverage, there is nothing in the record to suggest anything more than a mere contractual dispute. Texas law does not provide for injunctive relief to preclude payment on a letter of credit under such circumstances.

Existence of Conflicting Evidence

At the temporary injunction hearing, the trial judge heard extensive testimony from both sides concerning the nature of the various defects and problems with the refrigeration unit and whether the repair of those defects qualified as warranty work. Even if the evidence SRS presented could somehow be construed as evidence of fraud in the transaction, LGE presented more than enough controverting evidence on this issue to support the trial court's decision. The existence of this conflicting evidence precludes us from saying that the trial court abused its discretion in denying the temporary injunction. See Davis, 571 S.W.2d at 862.

Inadequate Remedy at Law and Irreparable Harm

In addition to meeting the requirements of section 5.114(b) [R§ 5-109], SRS was also required to demonstrate that it had no adequate remedy at law and that absent a temporary injunction, it would suffer irreparable injury. See GATX, 657 S.W.2d at 180–81 (holding that a court may enjoin if the requisites of section 5.114(b) are met and common law requirements for injunctive relief are satisfied.). To prove inadequate remedy at law, SRS was required to show that its damages are incapable of calculation or that LGE is incapable of responding in damages. See Haq v. America's Favorite Chicken Co., 921 S.W.2d 728, 730 (Tex.App.–Corpus Christi 1996, writ dism'd w.o.j.). Similarly, irreparable harm can be demonstrated by showing that damages cannot be measured by any certain pecuniary standard. See id. At the temporary injunction hearing, SRS failed to demonstrate either. The amount in dispute is the amount that LGE sought to draw under the letter of credit, and is clearly calculable. Furthermore, LGE presented uncontroverted testimony that it is financially secure and capable of repaying the full amount of the letter of credit if it were later required to do so.

Inasmuch as SRS failed to demonstrate irreparable harm and inadequate remedy at law, it was not entitled to injunctive relief. For these additional reasons, the trial court did not abuse its discretion in denying SRS' application for temporary injunction.

We affirm the trial court's denial of the temporary injunction and dissolve the injunction entered by this court on August 27, 1998. We direct the clerk of this court to issue the mandate of the court immediately.

---

3. See Texas Business and Commerce Code § 5.114(a), which explicitly provides that the issuer's duty to honor drafts accompanied by documents conforming to the terms of the letter of credit arises *"regardless of whether the goods or documents conform to the underlying contract for sale or to other contracts between the customer and the beneficiary."* (emphasis added).

Problem 7-2

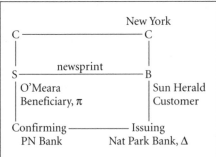

Maurice O'Meara Co., dealers in newsprint and located in New York, sold a quantity of newsprint to Sun-Herald Corporation, also of New York, to be financed by a letter of credit issued at the buyer's request. The letter of credit was in the following form:

The National Park Bank of New York
Our Credit No. 14956
October 28, 2007

Messrs. Maurice O'Meara
49 Chambers Street
New York City, N.Y.

Dear Sirs:

In accordance with instructions received from the Sun-Herald Corporation of this city, we open a confirmed or irrevocable credit in your favor for account of themselves, in amount of $1,349,118, covering the shipment of 1,322 tons of newsprint paper in 72½" and 36½" rolls to test 11–12 points, 32 lbs. at 51 cents per pound weight—delivery to be made in December 2007, and January 2008.

Drafts under this credit are to be drawn at sight on this bank, and are to be accompanied by the following documents of a character which must meet with our approval:

Commercial invoice in triplicate.

Weight returns.

Negotiable dock delivery order actually carrying with it control of the goods.

This is a confirmed or irrevocable credit, and will remain in force to and including February 15, 2008, subject to the conditions mentioned herein.

When drawing drafts under this credit, or referring to it, please quote our number as above.

> Very truly yours,
> *R. Stuart*
> R. Stuart, Assistant Cashier

Accompanying the first draft were the following documents:

1. Commercial invoice from Maurice O'Meara in triplicate, covering three hundred (300) thirty-six and one-half (36½) inch rolls of newsprint paper to test eleven (11), twelve (12), thirty-two (32) pounds.

2. Affidavit of Elwin Walker, verified December 16, 2007, to which were annexed samples of newsprint paper, affirming that the samples were representative of the shipment

covered by the accompanying invoices and to test twelve (12) points, thirty-two (32) pounds.

3. Full weight returns in triplicate.

4. Negotiable dock delivery order on the Swedish American Line, directing delivery to the order of the National Park Bank of three hundred (300) rolls of newsprint paper seventy-two and one-half (72½) inches long and three hundred (300) half rolls of newsprint paper.

The second draft was accompanied by documents similar to the first.

Maurice O'Meara indorsed and discounted the drafts and accompanying documents with Paradise National Bank of New York, which credited O'Meara's account for the face amount of the drafts, and forwarded the drafts and documents to the issuing bank for payment.

When the documents arrived, National Park Bank refused to pay the drafts. Maurice O'Meara commenced an action for damages for loss on the resale of the paper due to a dramatic fall in the market price, and for expenses for lighterage, cartage, storage, and insurance amounting to $6,000.

The bank's answer denied many of the allegations of the complaint and set up the defenses:

1. that Maurice O'Meara was required by the letter of credit to furnish the bank with evidence reasonably satisfactory to the bank that the paper shipped to Sun-Herald was of a bursting or tensile strength of 11 to 12 points at a weight of paper of 32 pounds;

2. that Maurice O'Meara did not furnish such evidence, and that the paper tendered was not in fact of the tensile or bursting strength specified in the letter of credit;

3. that the bank should have been permitted to inspect the paper before payment; and

4. that the bank should have been permitted to test the tensile strength before payment.

1) How should the case be decided under U.C.C. Article 5? §§ 5-102(a)(10); 5-103(d); 5-108(a), (f), (g).

2) What damages can the beneficiary recover for wrongful dishonor? § 5-111.

3) Suppose Elwin Walker's affidavit stated that the paper tested ten (l0) points and thirty-one (31) pounds. Would that change the outcome?

4) Is there any suggestion in the facts as to what might have been the real reason why the bank refused to honor the letter of credit?

COLORADO NATIONAL BANK OF DENVER v. BOARD OF COUNTY COMMISSIONERS OF ROUTT COUNTY, COLORADO

634 P.2d 32 (Colo. 1981)

HODGES, Chief Justice.

We granted certiorari to review the court of appeals' decision affirming a district court's judgment holding the petitioner, the Colorado National Bank of Denver (the Bank), liable for the face amounts of three letters of credit it issued to secure the completion of road improvements by its customer, the Woodmoor Corporation (Woodmoor). We reverse the judgment as to letters of credit No. 1156 and No. 1157, and affirm the judgment as to letter of credit No. 1168.

Woodmoor planned to develop a mountain recreation community in Routt County, Colorado (the County), to be known as Stagecoach. Early in 1973, Woodmoor obtained plat approval from the Routt County Board of County Commissioners (the Commissioners) for several Stagecoach subdivisions. Pursuant to section 30-28-137, C.R.S. 1973 (1977 Repl. Vol. 12), and county subdivision regulations, approval of three of these subdivision plats was conditioned upon Woodmoor's agreement to provide a bond or other undertaking to ensure the completion of roads in accordance with the subdivision design specifications. Accordingly, subdivision improvements agreements were executed between Woodmoor and the county.

At Woodmoor's request, the Bank issued three letters of credit to secure Woodmoor's obligations under the agreements. The first two letters of credit, No. 1156 and No. 1157, were issued January 23, 1973 in the respective amounts of $158,773 and $77,330 bearing expiry dates of December 31, 1975. The third letter of credit No. 1168 was issued March 7, 1973 in the amount of $113,732 bearing an expiry date of December 31, 1976. The face amounts of the letters of credit were identical to the estimated costs of the road and related improvements in the respective subdivision improvements agreements. The County was authorized by each letter of credit to draw directly on the Bank, for the account of Woodmoor, up to the face amount of each letter of credit. Each letter of credit required the County, in order to draw on the letters of credit, to submit fifteen-day sight drafts accompanied by:

> "A duly-signed statement by the Routt County Board of Commissioners that improvements have not been made in compliance with a Subdivision Improvements Agreement between Routt County and the Woodmoor Corporation dated [either January 9, 1973 or March 7, 1973] and covering the [respective subdivisions] at Stagecoach and that payment is therefore demanded hereunder."

Woodmoor never commenced construction of the roads and related improvements. On December 31, 1975, the expiry date of letters of credit No. 1156 and No. 1157, the County presented two demand drafts to the Bank for the face amounts of $158,773 and $77,330. The demand drafts were accompanied by a resolution of the Commissioners stating that Woodmoor had failed to comply with the terms of the subdivision improvements agreements and demanded payment of the face amounts of the letters of credit. On January 5, 1976, within three banking days of the demand, the Bank dishonored the drafts. The Bank did not specifically object to the County's presentation of demand drafts rather than fifteen-day sight drafts as required by the letters of credit.

On December 22, 1976, the County presented the Bank with a demand draft on letter of credit No. 1168 which was accompanied by the required resolution of the Commissioners. The Bank dishonored this draft because of the County's nonconforming demand, viz., that a demand draft was submitted rather than a fifteen-day sight draft. On December 29, 1976, the County presented a fifteen-day sight draft to the Bank. This draft was not accompanied by the resolution of the Commissioners. On December 31, 1976, the Bank dishonored this draft.

The County sued to recover the face amounts of the three letters of credit plus interest from the dates of the demands. The Bank answered the County's complaints alleging several affirmative defenses. The fundamental premise of the Bank's defenses was the assertion that the County would receive a windfall since it had not expended or committed to spend any funds to complete the road improvements specified in the subdivision improvements agreements.

The County filed a motion in limine seeking a determination by the trial court to exclude evidence concerning matters beyond the four corners of the letters of credit and the demands made on the letters of credit. The Bank replied by filing a cross-motion in limine seeking a ruling that it would not be precluded at trial from offering evidence outside the four corners of the letters of credit. The trial court, after extensive briefing by the parties and a hearing, granted the County's motion to limit the admissibility of evidence to the letters of credit, documents and drafts presented thereunder, the demands on the letters of credit, and the Bank's refusals to honor the County's demands for payment.

The remaining issues were whether the County's demands conformed to the letters of credit or, if not, whether the Bank had waived nonconforming demands, and whether interest ought to be awarded. The parties agreed on a stipulated set of facts concerning these remaining issues. The Bank did, however, make an offer of proof as to the rejected affirmative defenses. The Bank would have attempted to prove that the subdivisions in question remained raw, undeveloped mountain property for which there was no viable market and that the County had neither constructed, made commitments to construct, nor planned to construct the roads or other improvements described in the subdivision improvements agreements secured by the letters of credit. These allegations were disputed by the County.

The trial court entered judgment against the Bank for the face amounts of the letters of credit plus accrued interest at the statutory rate from the date of the County's demands. Costs were awarded in favor of the County. The Bank's motion for new trial was denied, and the Bank appealed.

The court of appeals affirmed the judgment of the trial court ruling that standby letters of credit are governed by Article 5 of the Uniform Commercial Code, section 4-5-101 et seq. C.R.S. 1973, and that an issuer must honor a draft or demand for payment which complies with the terms of the relevant credit regardless of whether the goods or documents conform to the underlying contract. The court of appeals affirmed the trial court's refusal to consider any evidence regarding the County's alleged windfall. The court of appeals also held that any defects in the form of the County's demands were waived by the Bank.

I.

We first address the question whether the trial court properly limited the evidence to be presented at trial to the letters of credit, the demands by the County, and the Bank's replies to the demands. The Bank has continually asserted during each stage of this action that it ought to be permitted to show that the County will receive a windfall if the County is permitted to recover against the letters of credit. The Bank requested an opportunity to prove that the County will utilize the funds it would receive in a manner other than that specified in the road improvements agreements. Fundamentally, the Bank seeks to litigate the question of the completion of the purpose of the underlying performance agreements between Woodmoor and the County. This the Bank cannot do.

An overview of the history and law concerning letters of credit is useful in the consideration of this issue. The letter of credit arose to facilitate international commercial transactions involving the sales of goods. Today the commercial utility of the letter of credit in both international and domestic sale of goods transactions is unquestioned and closely guarded. Harfield, *The Increasing Domestic Use of the Letter of Credit*, 4 U.C.C.L.J. 251 (1972); Verkuil, *Bank Solvency and Guaranty Letters of Credit*, 25 Stan.L.Rev. 716 (1973). In recent years, the use of the letter of credit has expanded to include guaranteeing or securing a bank's customer's promised performance to a third party in a variety of situations. This use is referred to as a standby letter of credit. Article five of the Uniform Commercial Code governs both traditional commercial letters of credit and standby letters of credit.

Three contractual relationships exist in a letter of credit transaction. Justice, *Letters of Credit: Expectations and Frustrations*, 94 Banking L. J. 424 (1977); Verkuil, *Bank Solvency and Guaranty Letters of Credit, supra.* Underlying the letter of credit transaction is the contract between the bank's customer and the beneficiary of the letter of credit, which consists of the business agreement between these parties. Then there is the contractual arrangement between the bank and its customer whereby the bank agrees to issue the letter of credit, and the customer agrees to repay the bank for the amounts paid under the letter of credit. See also section 4-5-114(3), C.R.S. 1973 [R§ 5-108(i)]. Finally, there is the contractual relationship between the bank and the beneficiary of the letter of credit created by the letter of credit itself. The bank agrees to honor the beneficiary's drafts or demands for payment which conform to the terms of the letter of credit. See generally sections 4-5-103(1)(a) and 4-5-114(1), C.R.S. 1973 [R§ 5-108(a)]; *White and Summers, Uniform Commercial Code* § 18-6 (2d Ed. 1980).

It is fundamental that the letter of credit is separate and independent from the underlying business transaction between the bank's customer and the beneficiary of the letter of credit. Arnold & Bransilver, *The Standby Letter of Credit-The Controversy Continues*, 10 U.C.C.L.J. 272 (1978); Verkuil, *Bank Solvency and Guaranty Letters of Credit, supra.* "The letter of credit is essentially a contract between the issuer and the beneficiary and is recognized by [article 5 of the Uniform Commercial Code] as independent of the underlying contract between the customer and the beneficiary.... In view of this independent nature of the letter of credit engagement the issuer is under a duty to honor the drafts for payment which in fact conform with the terms of the credit without reference to their compliance with the terms of the underlying contract." Section 4-5-114, Official Comment 1, C.R.S. 1973 [R§ 5-103(d) and OC 1].

The independence of the letter of credit from the underlying contract has been called the key to the commercial vitality of the letter of credit. See, e.g., United States v. Sun Bank of Miami, 609 F.2d 832 (5th Cir. 1980); Pringle-Associate Mortgage Corp. v. Southern National Bank of Hattiesburg, 571 F.2d 871 (5th Cir. 1978). The bank must honor drafts or demands for payment under the letter of credit when the documents required by the letter of credit appear on their face to comply with the terms of the credit. Section 4-5-114(2), C.R.S. 1973 [R§ 5-108(a)]. An exception to the bank's obligation to honor an apparently conforming draft or demand for payment, see Foreign Venture Ltd. Partnership v. Chemical Bank, 59 App.Div.2d 352, 399 N.Y.S.2d 114 (1977), is when a required document is, inter alia, forged or fraudulent, or there is fraud in the transaction. Section 4-5-114(2) [R§ 5-109(a)]. The application of this narrow exception is discussed in detail later in this opinion.

As mentioned above, letters of credit have recently come to be used to secure a bank's customer's performance to a third party. When a letter of credit is used to secure a bank's customer's promised performance to a third party, in whatever capacity that might be, the letter of credit is referred to as a "guaranty letter of credit," see East Bank of Colorado Springs v. Dovenmuehle, supra; Verkuil, *Bank Solvency and Guaranty Letters of Credit, supra*, or a "standby letter of credit," Arnold & Bransilver, *The Standby Letter of Credit— The Controversy Continues, supra*, 12 C.F.R. § 7.1160 (1980). Standby letters of credit are closely akin to a suretyship or guaranty contract. The bank promises to pay when there is a default on any obligation by the bank's customer. "If for any reason performance is not made, or is made defectively, the bank is liable without regard to the underlying rights of the contracting parties." Verkuil, *Bank Solvency and Guaranty Letters of Credit, supra* at 723.

While banks cannot, as a general rule, act as a surety or guarantor of another party's agreed performance, see generally Lord, *The No-Guaranty Rule and the Standby Letter of*

Credit Controversy, 96 Banking L.J. 46 (1979), the legality of standby letters of credit has been uniformly recognized. What distinguishes a standby letter of credit from a suretyship or guaranty contract is that the bank's liability rests upon the letter of credit contract rather than upon the underlying performance contract between the bank customer and the beneficiary of the letter of credit.

The utilization by banks of standby letters of credit is now wide-spread, although some commentators suggest that bankers may not appreciate the legal obligations imposed by the standby letter of credit. Where the bank issues a standby letter of credit, the bank naturally expects that the credit will not be drawn on in the normal course of events, i.e., if the customer of the bank fulfills its agreed-upon performance, then the credit will not be drawn upon. This expectation of the bank must be compared to the bank's expectation with respect to a traditional letter of credit issued as a means of financing a sale of goods. In the latter situation, the bank expects that the credit will always be drawn upon. It has been suggested that bankers may be lax in considering the credit of a customer with respect to issuing a standby letter of credit to secure the integrity of its customer to complete an agreed-upon performance, since it could be easily assumed by the bank that demand for payment would never be made. One solution suggested by many commentators is that the issuing bank treat a standby letter of credit like an unsecured loan. National Banks issuing standby letters of credit are subject to the lending limits of 12 U.S.C. §84 (1976).

We now turn to a discussion of the present case, and why the Bank cannot introduce evidence beyond that directly relating to its contract with the County. As discussed above, the letters of credit, and the Bank's obligations thereunder, are separate and independent from the underlying subdivision improvements agreements between Woodmoor and the County. The fact that the letters of credit issued by the Bank are standby letters of credit does not alter this general rule. The Bank is bound by its own contracts with the County.

Each of the letters of credit prepared and issued by the Bank in this case sets forth specifically the condition for payment, i.e., that Woodmoor failed to make the improvements in conformance with the respective subdivision improvements agreements. Had the Bank desired additional conditions for payment, such as the actual completion of the road improvements prior to payment under the letters of credit, it could have incorporated such a condition in the letters of credit. To demand payment under the letter of credit, the County was only required to submit a "duly-designed statement by the [Commissioners] that improvements have not been made in compliance with [the] Subdivision Improvements Agreement[s]...."

The Bank cannot litigate the performance of the underlying performance contracts. "[P]erformance of the underlying contract is irrelevant to the Bank's obligations under the letter of credit." West Virginia Housing Development Fund v. Sroka, supra at 1114 (W.D.Pa. 1976).... Further a bank cannot challenge the utilization of funds paid under a letter of credit.

The Bank argues that it is entitled to dishonor the County's drafts under section 4-5-114(2), C.R.S. 1973 [R§5-109(a)].... Under this section, the issuer of a letter of credit may in good faith honor a draft or demand for payment notwithstanding notice from its customer that documents are forged, or fraudulent, or there is fraud in the transaction. The issuer may, however, be enjoined from honoring such drafts or demands for payment. Impliedly, the issuer may also refuse to honor such drafts or demands for payment when it has been notified by its customer of these defects. Section 4-5-114, Official Comment 2, C.R.S. 1973; Siderius, Inc. v. Wallace, supra.

In this case, the Bank has not argued, nor can it reasonably assert, that the documents presented by the County are forged or fraudulent. The Bank has not challenged the authenticity of the drafts and demands for payment for the County or the truthfulness of the statements that the requirements of the underlying subdivision improvements agreements have not been fulfilled. The Bank does assert, however, that there has been fraud in the transaction on the basis that the funds the County would receive would be utilized by the County other than to pay for the completion of the road improvements.

Fundamentally, "fraud in the transaction," as referred to in section 4-5-114(2) [R§5-109(a)], must stem from conduct by the beneficiary of the letter of credit as against the customer of the bank. *See generally White and Summers, Uniform Commercial Code* §18-6 (2d ed. 1980). It must be of such an egregious nature as to vitiate the entire underlying transaction so that the legitimate purposes of the independence of the bank's obligation would no longer be served. "[I]t is generally thought to include an element of intentional misrepresentation in order to profit from another...." West Virginia Housing Development Fund. v. Sroka, supra. This fraud is manifested in the documents themselves, and the statements therein, presented under the letter of credit. One court has gone so far as to say that only some defect in these documents would justify a bank's dishonor. O'Grady v. First Union National Bank of North Carolina, 296 N.C. 212, 250 S.E.2d 587 (1978).

In this case, the Bank has not asserted that there is fraud in the transaction between Woodmoor and the County, nor can it reasonably make such an argument. No facts have been pled to establish fraud which vitiated the entire agreement between the County and Woodmoor. No fraud has been asserted by the Bank's offer of proof which would entitle it to dishonor the County's drafts and demands for payment. Thus, the trial court properly granted the County's motion in limine excluding all evidence beyond the four corners of the letters of credit, the demands thereunder, and the Bank's replies.

II.

We next consider whether the drafts and demands for payment by the County complied with the terms of the letters of credit, or if not, whether the Bank waived any nonconforming demands.

* * *

A demand draft is not the same as a fifteen-day sight draft.... Thus, the County's demand did not strictly conform to the terms of the letters of credit....

The Bank did not, however, object to the form of the demands by the County.... In this case, the County did not present its drafts and demands for payment on the letters of credit until the final day of their vitality.... The County could not have cured the defect since the presentment would have then been untimely.... Accordingly, since the County could not have cured its nonconforming demand, we therefore hold that the Bank did not waive its objections to the County's nonconforming demands on letter of credit numbers 1156 and 1157. Therefore the Bank is not liable on these letters of credit....

We reverse the judgment as to letters of credit No. 1156 and No. 1157, and affirm the judgment as to letter of credit No. 1168. This case is returned to the court of appeals for remand to the trial court for the entry of judgment in consonance with the views expressed in this opinion.

MELLON BANK, N.A. v. GENERAL ELECTRIC CREDIT CORP.

724 F.Supp. 360 (W.D. Pa. 1989)

COHILL, Chief Judge.

Plaintiff, Mellon Bank, N.A. ("Mellon"), sues to recover for defendant's allegedly improper draw on a standby letter of credit. The parties have filed cross motions for summary judgment with several briefs and a considerable amount of evidentiary material. The pertinent agreements are before us, and as to most of the issues raised by the parties there are no apparent disputed issues of material fact. Partial summary judgment on these matters is appropriate. However, the parties have failed to address defendant, General Electric Credit Corp.'s ("GECC") defense of anticipatory repudiation, and therefore the cross motions for summary judgment must be denied.

The entity at the eye of this storm is not a party to this litigation. Woodings Consolidated Industries, Inc. ("Woodings") manufactured oil drilling equipment, and over the years Mellon had been Woodings' primary source for financing. By 1986, Woodings owed Mellon more than $5 million.

On April 23, 1985, Woodings entered into a leaseback arrangement with GECC. Under the terms of this agreement Woodings sold GECC a valuable machine (known as a sucker rod machine for reasons we do not care to fathom), and GECC then leased the machine back to Woodings for a specified monthly payment. This contract will be referred to here as the "Lease Agreement."

In conjunction with the Lease Agreement, and to better secure GECC's interest, Woodings and GECC executed a Letter of Credit Agreement. In accord with its terms, Woodings arranged a standby Letter of Credit with Mellon Bank in the amount of $600,000 with GECC as beneficiary. The Letter of Credit issued by Mellon permitted GECC to draw up to $600,000 upon submission of a sight draft by GECC and a typewritten statement that the sum demanded was due and owing.

From 1984 to 1986 Woodings experienced increasing financial losses as a result of a severe downturn in the oil industry. On January 23, 1987 Woodings failed to make its scheduled lease payment to GECC. Defendant also alleges that Woodings failed to present proof of liability insurance for 1987 as required by the Lease Agreement.

Based on these alleged defaults, GECC presented Mellon with a sight draft on the Letter of Credit in the amount of $600,000, and a typewritten statement asserting that Woodings was in default and that the full amount of the draft was due and owing. Mellon paid the full amount to GECC.

Mellon has now sued GECC to recover the $600,000 drawn on the Line of Credit, asserting that Woodings was not in default at the time of the draft, that the $600,000 was not due and owing, and therefore GECC could not properly draw on the Line of Credit. Both sides seek summary judgment, raising a host of intertwined issues which we now attempt to unravel.

I. Default

The Letter of Credit Agreement between Woodings and GECC provides in pertinent part:

> Under the terms hereof, upon the occurrence of any default under the Lease, or upon the filing of a petition by or against Lessee under Title XI of the United States Code or any successor or similar law, GECC shall have the right to present sight draft(s) and a properly-executed statement to the issuer for any amount

not exceeding, in total, the sum of U.S. $600,000.00 and to receive said monies therefrom, at GECC's sole discretion, in lump sum, or in several sums from time to time.

The Letter of Credit issued by Mellon provides in pertinent part:

We [Mellon] undertake to honor from time to time your draft or drafts at sight on us not exceeding in the aggregate U.S. $600,000.00 when accompanied by a signed typewritten statement by GECC stating either (i) that the amount of the accompanying draft is due and owing by Customer to GECC, or (ii) that a petition has been filed by or against Customer under Title XI of the United States Code or a similar or successor law.

On February 11, 1987, GECC presented Mellon with a sight draft for $600,000 and the following typewritten statement:

This is to advise you that Woodings Consolidated Industries, Inc. ("Customer") is in breach of certain agreements with General Electric Credit Corporation ("GECC") and that, accordingly, the amount of SIX HUNDRED THOUSAND AND 00/100 U.S. ($600,000) DOLLARS drawn by GECC under Draft No. 0001 dated February 11, 1987 against Mellon Bank Letter of Credit No. 56540 is due and owing by Customer to GECC.

Mellon honored the draft on the following day.

Mellon describes its claim as a breach of warranty action. Under § 5-111 [R§ 5-110] of the Uniform Commercial Code, a party drawing on a line of credit "warrants to all interested parties that the necessary conditions of the credit have been complied with." ... Thus a beneficiary warrants to the issuing bank the truth of the statements necessary to a draw on the credit....

Mellon contends that GECC was required to make two assertions to effect a draw on the Letter of Credit: 1) that Woodings was in default of the Lease Agreement, and 2) that the amount of the draft was due and owing by Woodings to GECC. In fact, GECC made these assertions in its statement accompanying the sight draft. Mellon argues that both of these assertions were false, that under the terms of the Lease Agreement Woodings was not in default, and the sum of $600,000 was not due and owing at the time of the draw. Therefore Mellon concludes that GECC breached its § 5-111 [R§ 5-110] warranties, and Mellon is entitled to recover the amount of the draw.

The parties have focused most of their time and attention on the question of whether Woodings was in default at the time of the draw. It is admitted that Woodings had failed to make its rental payment for January 1985, and therefore was in breach of its contractual obligation. GECC argues that this is a default, and therefore its assertion in support of the draw is truthful. On the other hand, Mellon contends that the Lease Agreement required a formal declaration of default:

XII. DEFAULT: (a) If Lessee breaches its obligation to pay rent when due and fails to cure said breach within ten (10) days, or if Lessee breaches any of the terms hereof or any of terms or any Schedule hereto ... then in either such case, Lessor may declare this Agreement in default. Such declaration shall be by written notice to Lessee and shall apply to all Schedules hereunder except as specifically excepted by Lessor in such declaration ...

GECC did not make a declaration of default prior to the draw. Thus, Mellon argues, under the terms of the Lease Agreement Woodings was *not* in default at the time of the draw even though it had failed to make a timely payment, and GECC has therefore breached its §5-111 warranty.

The sad part of all of this is that the issue of Woodings' default is utterly irrelevant to analysis of the §5-111 [R§5-110] warranties. Although GECC represented in its statement to Mellon that Woodings was in default at the time of the draw, and though the Letter of Credit Agreement between Woodings and GECC permits a draw only upon a default by Woodings, the Letter of Credit itself *does not require* such an assertion prior to a draw. The Letter of Credit states:

> We [Mellon] undertake to honor from time to time your draft or drafts at sight on us not exceeding in the aggregate U.S. $600,000.00 when accompanied by a signed typewritten statement by GECC stating *either (i) that the amount of the accompanying draft is due and owing by Customer to GECC, or* (ii) that a petition has been filed by or against Customer under Title XI of the United States Code or a similar or successor law.

There simply is no requirement that GECC make any representation of Woodings' status under the contract. Default is irrelevant. The only representation necessary to a draw on the Letter of Credit, in the absence of Woodings' bankruptcy, is that the amount of the draft be due and owing. Thus GECC's assertion that Woodings was in default was merely gratuitous under the Letter of Credit. Though the issue of default may be relevant as between Woodings and GECC under their Letter of Credit Agreement, Mellon was not a party to that agreement, and neither the agreement nor its terms were incorporated in the Letter of Credit issued by Mellon. If no assertion of default is required by the Letter of Credit, no warranties attach to such an assertion. Therefore, even if GECC's statement that Woodings was in default was false, GECC would not be liable for breach of a §5-111 [R§5-110] warranty.

We return then to a consideration of what the Letter of Credit does require. As seen above, absent Woodings' bankruptcy, GECC was required to state that the amount of the draft "is due and owing by [Woodings] to GECC." In fact GECC submitted a draft for $600,000 and stated that this sum was due and owing at the time of the draw. Therefore §5-111 [R§5-110] is applicable, and GECC warranted to Mellon the truth of this assertion.

It is admitted that Woodings was late in making one monthly lease payment of $15,011.40. But GECC has asserted that $600,000 was due and owing, apparently on the basis of provisions of the Lease Agreement for acceleration of payments and stipulated loss.

The pertinent provisions of the Lease Agreement are found in Section XII:

> XII. DEFAULT: (a) If Lessee breaches its obligation to pay rent when due and fails to cure said breach within ten (10) days, or if Lessee breaches any of the terms hereof or any of terms or any Schedule hereto ... then in either such case, *Lessor may declare this Agreement in default.* Such declaration shall be by written notice to Lessee and shall apply to all Schedules hereunder except as specifically excepted by Lessor in such declaration. *Lessee hereby authorizes Lessor at any time after such declaration* to enter, with or without legal process, any premises where any Equipment may be and take possession thereof. *Lessee shall, without further demand, forthwith pay to Lessor, as liquidated damages* for loss of a bargain and not as a penalty, *an amount equal to all rentals and other sums then due hereunder, together with the Stipulated Loss Value of the* Equipment, *calculated as of the date Lessor declared a default hereunder, to-*

gether with interest thereon at the highest rate allowed by law ... (Emphasis added.)

From these provisions it is clear that acceleration of payments and liquidated damages are invoked only after a declaration of default. Indeed accelerated payments and the Stipulated Loss Value are to be calculated "as of the date Lessor declared a default hereunder."

GECC admits that it did not declare a default prior to the draw on the Letter of Credit. Without such a formal declaration, the acceleration of payments and liquidated damages provisions are not applicable. Thus, on the date of GECC's draw on the Line of Credit, Woodings owed GECC the amount of one tardy rental payment. GECC's assertion that $600,000 was due and owing was erroneous, and constitutes a breach of its warranty under § 5-111 [R§ 5-110].

II. Independence Principle

However, GECC objects to Mellon's reliance on the terms of the underlying Lease Agreement. GECC refers to this portion of the Letter of Credit:

We agree that we shall have no duty or right to inquire as to the basis upon which GECC has determined to present to us any draft under this Letter of Credit.

GECC also invokes the doctrine known as the "independence principle," which prohibits reference to underlying contracts to determine the validity of a draft on a letter of credit. Under this principle the issuing bank may only determine whether the appropriate documents have been presented. It may not contest the truth of the assertions in those documents....

Although GECC states the principle accurately, it does not apply it correctly in this case. The independence principle, and the above-quoted portion of the Letter of Credit, speak only to the bank's obligation to honor the sight draft *in the first instance*. They do not preclude subsequent investigation and efforts at recovery....

The purpose of the independence principle, and of the similar provision in Mellon's Letter of Credit, is to provide the beneficiary with an unfettered, immediate remedy upon occurrence of the triggering event on a standby letter of credit. The purpose is not to prevent any subsequent challenge to the validity of the beneficiary's claim, but to ensure that "contractual disputes wend their way towards resolution with money in the beneficiary's pocket rather than in the pocket of the contracting party." ...

Indeed, if interpreted in the manner GECC suggests, the independence principle would make a nullity of § 5-111 [R§ 5-110]. Little purpose would be served if § 5-111 [R§ 5-110] created warranties as to the truth of the conditions necessary to a draw, while the independence principle precluded the bank from contesting the truth of those assertions.

For the reasons stated we conclude that the independence principle and the similar contract provision quoted above are inapplicable to an action for breach of § 5-111 [R§ 5-110] warranties, and do not preclude reference to underlying contractual documents to determine the truth or falsity of the warrantied assertions.

* * *

CONCLUSION

For the reasons stated above, partial summary judgment will be granted in favor of Plaintiff Mellon in the following respects: 1) GECC failed to make a formal declaration of default as required by the Lease Agreement, and as a result acceleration of payments and liquidated damages provisions are inapplicable. 2) Absent anticipatory repudiation, GECC's assertion in support of its draw on the Letter of Credit, that $600,000 was due and owing, was erroneous and in breach of GECC's §5-111 [R§5-110] warranty. 3) The independence principle and the like provision in the Letter of Credit are inapplicable and do not preclude reference to the underlying contractual documents to determine the truth of the warrantied assertions....

B. Issuer's Obligation to the Applicant and the Beneficiary: The Strict Compliance Doctrine

Absent fraud or forgery, an issuer is obligated to honor the beneficiary's demand for payment if presentment "appears on its face strictly to comply with the terms and conditions of the letter of credit." §5-108(a). Occasionally the beneficiary presents documents that fail to strictly comply with the requirements of the letter of credit, placing the issuer in an awkward position. If the issuer refuses to honor the beneficiary's demand for payment, then the beneficiary may bring an action against the issuer for wrongful dishonor. But if the issuer honors the beneficiary's demand for payment, then the applicant may bring an action against the issuer for wrongful payment and avoid honoring its reimbursement obligations to the issuer. Does the doctrine of strict compliance require literal conformity to the terms of the letter of credit, or merely substantial compliance? The contours of the strict compliance doctrine are frequently litigated. The following four cases give you a taste of the litigation.

NEW BRAUNFELS NATIONAL BANK v. ODIORNE
780 S.W.2d 313 (Tex. Ct. App. 1989)

JONES, Justice.

This appeal presents the question of how strictly a beneficiary of a letter of credit must comply with a condition of the credit in order to require payment by the issuer. New Braunfels National Bank (Bank) filed this suit to obtain a judgment declaring that it had properly refused to honor a draft on a $250,000 letter of credit it had issued. Original defendants were (1) P.W. Bates, Superintendent of Insurance, Cayman Islands, British West Indies (Bates), the beneficiary of the letter of credit, and (2) Southern International Insurance Company, Ltd. (Southern), the account party. Bates counterclaimed to recover the amount of the credit from the Bank. Later substituted in place of Southern was State Board of Insurance Liquidator/Receiver James T. Odiorne (Receiver), the court-appointed receiver for Southern. All parties filed motions for summary judgment. The district court granted the Bank's motion, declaring that it had properly dishonored the draft on the letter of credit. Bates appeals from that portion of the judgment pertaining to the Bank's refusal to pay on the credit. We will reverse and render in part, and reverse and remand in part.

The facts are, in large part, undisputed. To the extent they are disputed, we must of course accept as true the version favorable to the non-movant, and we must indulge every reasonable inference and resolve all doubts in favor of the non-movant....

In early 1986 Jerry Goff, Southern's president, acting on behalf of Southern, requested that the Bank issue a $250,000 letter of credit payable to Bates. Southern, an insurance company chartered under the laws of the Cayman Islands, needed the credit to satisfy a regulatory requirement to provide financial security for Southern's policyholders. The Bank finally agreed to issue the credit, but only upon certain conditions, including (1) the execution by Southern of a $250,000 promissory note, (2) assignment to the Bank of a security interest in certain property belonging to Southern, and (3) the deposit in the Bank of "compensating balances" of $250,000 against which the Bank could exercise a right of setoff in the event it ever had to fund the letter of credit. Goff agreed to the conditions.

On April 29, 1986, the Bank issued its irrevocable letter of credit number 86-122-S. The "86" represented the year in which the credit was issued; the "122" represented the numerical sequence of all credits ever issued by the Bank, regardless of the year of issuance; the "S" indicated that the credit was a "standby" letter of credit. The only condition for Bates's drawing on the credit was that any draft be marked as follows: "Drawn under New Braunfels National Bank Irrevocable Letter of Credit Number 86-122-S...." The expiry date of the credit was April 29, 1987.

One year later, on the morning of April 29, 1987, Clive Harris, a representative of Bates, presented to the president of the Bank a letter of introduction and instruction from Bates, a draft signed by Bates, and the original letter of credit. After some study and consultation with its lawyers, the Bank refused to honor the draft because the draft's legend referred to "Irrevocable Letter of Credit No. 86-122-5" instead of "86-122-S." The Bank refused to allow Harris to change the "5" to an "S" without written authorization from Bates. When Bates attempted to wire such authorization, the cable was misdirected and finally arrived–by mail–several days later, after Harris had returned to the Cayman Islands with the original letter of credit. When the error was eventually corrected a week later, the Bank refused to honor the corrected draft on the ground that the credit had expired.

Bates appeals from that portion of the trial court's judgment declaring that the Bank properly dishonored the draft on the letter of credit, complaining that the trial court erred in granting the Bank's motion for summary judgment and in failing to grant his own motion. A letter of credit is an original undertaking by one party to substitute his financial strength for that of another, and involves three separate contracts. The first is between parties to an underlying commercial or other business transaction: an obligor and an obligee; the second contract is between the obligor ("account party") and a bank or other person ("issuer"), whereby the issuer agrees to issue a letter of credit in exchange for the account party's agreement to reimburse the issuer if the credit is drawn on, and often, the payment by the account party of a nonrefundable fee to the issuer; the third contract, represented by the letter of credit itself, is in the nature of an option contract between the issuer and the obligee ("beneficiary"), and provides that the issuer will make payment to the beneficiary upon presentation of a draft and specified documents (a documentary draft) or merely upon presentation of a draft or demand (a clean credit)....

A letter of credit is termed "commercial" when the underlying transaction involves the sale of goods and the credit becomes payable upon the presentation of documents showing that the seller has complied with the sales agreement; a credit is termed "standby" when it functions in a nonsale setting and generally becomes payable upon certification of the obligor's non-compliance with the underlying agreement....

Article 5 of the Uniform Commercial Code provides guiding principles, but not comprehensive rules, for the treatment of credits.... With respect to the issuer's duty to the beneficiary, section 5.114(a) [R§ 5-108(a)] of the Code provides simply that "[a]n issuer must honor a draft or demand for payment which complies with the terms of the relevant credit...," without regard to the facts of the underlying transaction. To enhance the value of credits as a commercial device, and perhaps in recognition of their virtual *sui generis* nature, most courts have required that the beneficiary strictly comply with conditions contained in the credit before an obligation to pay will be imposed on the issuer. Texas follows the strict compliance rule....

None of the parties in the present case pleaded that the credit was ambiguous; accordingly, whether Bates strictly complied with the terms of the credit is a question of law for the court to decide....

Most commentators agree that maintaining the integrity of the strict compliance rule is important to the continued usefulness of letters of credit as a commercial tool.... That does not mean, however, that strict compliance demands an oppressive perfectionism. For example, one noted commentator has recognized a logical distinction between discrepancies that relate to the business of the underlying transaction and those that relate to the banker's own business:

> The strict-compliance rule rests on the judgment that issuers should not be forced into the position of determining whether a documentary discrepancy is significant. The rule assumes that issuers are not in a position to know whether discrepancies matter to the commercial parties. Nothing in that assumption requires courts to absolve issuers from knowing the significance of discrepancies for their own business; while it is consistent with the strict-compliance rule to say that an issuer should not be charged with knowledge of whether an air bill, rather than an ocean bill, covering computer components is a significant defect, it is not consistent with the rule to say that a bank issuer is absolved from knowing whether the abbreviation of the word "number" to "No." in the legend on a draft is a significant defect. Banks presumably know nothing about the shipment of computer components, but they know a great deal about legends on drafts — legends that credits require, usually because the banks insist on them. J. Dolan, The Law of Letters of Credit ¶ 6.03, at S6-4 (Supp.1989) (footnotes omitted).

Two cases exemplify defects in legends, which, as far as we can tell, will always be "noncommercial" defects. In Tosco Corp. v. FDIC, 723 F.2d 1242 (6th Cir. 1983), the credit required that a draft on the credit contain the following legend: "drawn under Bank of Clarksville Letter of Credit Number 105." The bank refused to honor the draft presented by the beneficiary because the legend in the draft (1) added the word "Tennessee" after "Clarksville"; (2) used a lower case "l" in the term "letter of Credit"; and (3) abbreviated "Number" to "No." In First Bank v. Paris Savings & Loan Association, 756 S.W.2d 329 (Tex. App. 1988, writ denied), the credit required that a draft contain the following legend: "Drawn under Paris Savings and Loan Association Letter of Credit No. 1033." The bank refused to honor the draft presented because the legend stated: "Drawn under Paris Savings and Loan Association Letter of Credit No. 1033, dated June 12, 1986, i/a/o $250,000." In both cases, the beneficiary prevailed.

Although Professor Dolan forcefully advocates preserving the integrity of the strict compliance rule, he concludes that the fact situations presented by the Tosco and First Bank cases do not violate the rule:

> The reason for the strict rule is to protect the issuer from having to know the commercial impact of a discrepancy in the documents. Under the strict rule, a bank document examiner does not need to judge whether dried grapes are the same as raisins and does not need to know that "C.R.S." stands for coromandel ground nuts. The legend in [Tosco] and most such legends are for the issuer's benefit. The legends assist the banker in identifying the credit.

* * *

In these cases, it is not asking too much of the document examiner to exercise discretion as a banker, even though it is too much to ask a document examiner to exercise discretion on a commercial matter. Any reasonably prudent document examiner would recognize immediately that the discrepancies in question are de minimis, and courts should not hesitate to hold that they do not violate the strict-compliance standard.

We think the distinction made by Professor Dolan is a sensible and salutary one. Indeed, although Texas courts have not expressly recognized the distinction in those terms, they seem to have done so implicitly. In virtually every recent case in which the defect was a "commercial" one, the issuer has prevailed.... On the other hand, in virtually every recent case in which the defect was a "noncommercial" one, the beneficiary has prevailed....

In the present case, the only defect challenged by the Bank was that the required legend stated it was drawn under New Braunfels National Bank Irrevocable Letter of Credit Number "86-122-5" instead of "86-122-S." By itself, this discrepancy might or might not be of significance. (It was undisputed that none of the reference numbers for credits issued by the Bank ended with a numeral and that Bank officers had no doubt which credit Bates was attempting to draw on.) Here, however, there was more: the draft in question was accompanied by and attached to the original letter of credit, which naturally had the correct credit number prominently displayed. Accompanying documents may be considered in determining whether the presentment made by the beneficiary has strictly complied with the terms of the credit. Temple-Eastex, 672 S.W.2d at 796; see also American Airlines, Inc. v. FDIC, 610 F.Supp. 199 (D. Kan. 1985) (although draft referred to incorrect letter of credit number, cover letter which accompanied draft and which contained correct number established strict compliance). Considering both the draft and the original credit together, it would be obvious to any bank document examiner, prudent or otherwise, that the discrepancy in the present case was merely a typographical or clerical error and of no possible significance.

We therefore sustain Bates's points of error one and three. In so holding, we do not hold that a beneficiary may satisfy noncommercial conditions in a credit by mere "substantial compliance"; we hold only that for such conditions "strict compliance" means something less than absolute, perfect compliance. We make no holding with respect to defects relating to commercial conditions.

* * *

In summary, with respect to Bates's appeal regarding the Bank's refusal to honor the draft on the letter of credit, we hold that the summary judgment evidence shows as a matter of law that Bates's presentment strictly complied with the terms of the letter of credit. Accordingly, we will render judgment in favor of Bates, which is the judgment that the trial court should have rendered....

IN RE CORAL PETROLEUM, INC.
878 F.2d 830 (5th Cir. 1989)

REAVLEY, Circuit Judge:

Tradax Petroleum America, Inc., the beneficiary under an irrevocable standby letter of credit, appeals from the district court's judgment in favor of the issuing bank, French

American Banking Corp. ("FABC"), denying reformation or construction of the letter of credit. We affirm.

I.

In March 1983, Tradax, an oil trading company, contracted to sell to Coral Petroleum, Inc. 31,000 barrels of West Texas Intermediate crude oil for a price of $880,400. The contract imposed upon Coral the obligation of opening a standby letter of credit "in a form and from a bank acceptable" to Tradax. Coral then entered into a contract with FABC under which FABC agreed to issue an irrevocable standby letter of credit in favor of Tradax in the amount of $880,400. Coral specified the documents Tradax would be required to present to draw under the letter of credit and supplied to FABC the precise language to be used. The required documents were (1) a signed statement by an officer of Tradax Petroleum that the West Texas Intermediate was delivered to Coral, (2) an unsigned copy of the shipper's transfer listing indicating transfer to Coral of 31,000 barrels plus or minus 5 percent of "WTNM SO or SR," and (3) a commercial invoice describing the merchandise as 31,000 barrels plus or minus 5 percent of West Texas Intermediate crude oil. FABC issued the letter of credit exactly as requested.

The parties now recognize that Coral made a mistake in designating the type of oil required in the shipper's transfer listing. "WTNM SO or SR" refers to sour oil, while the oil Tradax was to provide, West Texas Intermediate, is a sweet oil. When FABC sent the letter of credit to Tradax for its approval, however, Tradax failed to catch the mistake. Instead, two Tradax employees reviewed the credit for possible errors and determined that it was acceptable as written. In May 1983, Tradax shipped the oil to Coral.

On June 2, 1983, Coral filed for relief under Chapter 11 of the Bankruptcy Code. Thereafter, when Coral failed to pay for the oil that Tradax had delivered, Tradax attempted to draw on the letter of credit. In comparing the documents called for in the letter of credit to those actually presented, FABC found that the shipper's transfer listing which Tradax submitted showed that it had delivered 31,000 barrels of "DOM SWT" to Coral rather than the "WTNM SO or SR" crude specified in the letter of credit. FABC contacted Coral to determine whether it would waive this discrepancy and authorize FABC to pay in spite of it. Coral refused to waive the discrepancy so FABC refused to pay. The letter of credit expired according to its terms on June 30, 1983.

On July 20, 1983, Tradax commenced this adversary proceeding in the bankruptcy court seeking reformation or construction of the letter of credit. On cross-motions for summary judgment, the bankruptcy court concluded that Tradax's presentation did not strictly comply with the letter of credit and accordingly dismissed the proceeding as to FABC. The district court affirmed the judgment of the bankruptcy court. Tradax appeals.

II.

At the outset it is important to note that a letter of credit is not an ordinary contract but instead is a unique device developed to meet the specific needs of the marketplace.... The special law that has developed concerning letters of credit is embodied generally in Article 5 of the Uniform Commercial Code ("UCC") and the Uniform Customs and Practice for Documentary Credits, International Chamber of Commerce Publication No. 400 (1983) ("Uniform Customs")....

The UCC defines a letter of credit as "an engagement by a bank ... made at the request of a customer ... that the issuer will honor drafts or other demands for payment upon compliance with the conditions specified in the credit." U.C.C. § 5-103(1)(a) [R§ 5-102(a)(10)]. As this definition suggests, a letter of credit transaction ordinarily involves three separate contracts: (1) an underlying contract, usually between a buyer of goods, who applies to a bank for the letter of credit, and a seller of goods, who becomes the beneficiary under the credit; (2) a contract between the issuing bank and its customer to issue the letter of credit, and (3) the letter of credit itself, a contract between the issuing bank and the beneficiary.... As a general rule, the obligations and duties created by the contract between the issuer and the beneficiary are completely separate and independent from the underlying transaction between the beneficiary and the bank's customer.... The issuing bank has no obligation to pay unless the beneficiary complies precisely with the documentary requirements spelled out on the face of the letter of credit.... An issuing bank that makes payment upon a presentation that does not conform to the requirements of the credit loses its right to repayment from its customer....

Letters of credit, therefore, are strictly construed. In determining whether payment is warranted in a particular case, the issuing bank has no obligation to go beyond a facial examination of the tendered documents. While the issuer is required to act in good faith and to observe any general banking usage, it is not charged with knowledge of any usage of the trade in which the beneficiary and customer are involved. U.C.C. § 5-109(1)(c) (issuing bank's obligation "does not include liability or responsibility" for "usage of any particular trade") [R§ 5-108(f)(3)]; Uniform Customs (1983 rev.) Arts. 17, 18 ("banks assume no liability or responsibility" for the "description ... of the goods" or for the "interpretation of technical terms"). As the court wrote in Marino Industries Corp. v. Chase Manhattan Bank, N.A., 686 F.2d 112, 115 (2nd Cir. 1982), "[t]he bank's sole function [in a letter of credit transaction] is financing; it is not concerned with or involved in the commercial transaction."

III.

Tradax concedes that the shipper's transfer listing it presented to FABC did not comply strictly with the terms of the letter of credit. It asserts, however, that in order for the doctrine of strict compliance to apply, the letter of credit must be free from ambiguity. In support of its proposition, Tradax cites Marino Industries, in which the Second Circuit wrote that "[t]he corollary to the rule of strict compliance is that the requirements in letters of credit must be explicit, ... and that all ambiguities are construed against the bank." Id. Here, Tradax claims, the letter of credit contained an internal inconsistency which rendered the document ambiguous; therefore, it should have been construed against FABC.

We do not believe that the terms of the letter of credit at issue in this case are ambiguous. Rather, the requirements are quite explicit; the credit unequivocally calls for presentation of a "transfer listing by shipper ... indicating transfer to Coral of 31,000 barrels plus or minus 5 percent of WTNM SO or SR." There is nothing ambiguous about this requirement; therefore, there is nothing to construe.

The terms of the credit are, however, impossible to perform. Tradax could not possibly present documentation indicating that it delivered West Texas Intermediate (sweet oil) and at the same time present documentation indicating the transfer of "WTNM SO or SR" (sour oil). Tradax argues that the district court should have construed the letter of credit to avoid this impossibility. We note that, while there does not appear to be much case law concerning this issue, at least one commentator in the field of letter of credit law has suggested that impossibility does not excuse strict compliance with the terms of a credit:

The strict-compliance rule has the intended salutary effect of requiring the beneficiary to review the credit to be certain that he can comply with it. That inquiry, which permits the beneficiary to verify that the credit complies with the
underlying contract, also permits him to make timely requests for amendments
and to withhold shipment or other performance if the credit does not comply
with the underlying transaction *or is impossible for him to satisfy*. It is more efficient to require the beneficiary to conduct that review of the credit before the
fact of performance than after it, and the beneficiary that performs without see-
ing or examining the credit should pay the piper. J.F. Dolan, The Law of Letters
of Credit, ¶ 6.03 at S6-3 to S6-4 (Supp.1989) (emphasis added).

Similarly, a beneficiary who negligently inspects a letter of credit and thereby fails to
discover that the requirements are impossible for him to satisfy should be required to
"pay the piper" as well. This is especially true in a case such as this one, where the impossibility arises from the use of technical or trade terms and where the bank has performed exactly as requested by its customer. These very facts distinguish the case at bar
from the cases upon which Tradax most heavily relies. In East Girard Sav. Ass'n, the issuing bank drafted a letter of credit on the wrong form; this caused extraneous language
to be included in the credit which in turn created an ambiguity. The court construed the
ambiguity against the bank. 593 F.2d at 602. In Venizelos, the Second Circuit construed
an amended letter of credit against the confirming bank that authored the ambiguous
amendment. 425 F.2d at 466. In neither case were technical or trade terms at issue. Here,
by contrast, the inconsistent terms clearly were technical terms, provided by Coral and
approved by Tradax. As was discussed above, under the general law governing letters of
credit, an issuing bank is expressly exempted from responsibility for knowledge or lack
of knowledge of technical or trade terms.

Tradax does not dispute that, ordinarily, an issuing bank need not know the meanings of technical terms used in trade. It contends, however, that under East Girard Sav.
Ass'n, the bank must know the terms of its own contract with the beneficiary and is required to ensure that the terms of the credit are internally consistent. East Girard Sav.
Ass'n does not support this contention. There, the court simply wrote that "a bank must
use the utmost care in drafting its letters of credit" and that "[b]anks are presumed to be
cognizant of prevailing commercial practices in transacting their business." 593 F.2d at
602–03. In this case, there has been no suggestion that FABC acted carelessly in drafting
the letter of credit. Instead, the letter of credit precisely incorporates the exact terms that
Coral requested. Nor is this a matter involving "prevailing commercial practices" of which
FABC should have been aware. If we were to impose liability on FABC in this case for
failing to ensure that the trade terms listed in the letter of credit were consistent with one
another, we effectively would be circumventing the rule expressly exempting issuing banks
from responsibility for trade terms. This we refuse to do.

Tradax also asserts that it is inequitable to make Tradax assume the risk of nonpayment since Tradax tried to shift that risk by requiring Coral to provide a letter of credit.
We disagree with this assertion for two main reasons. In the first place, we do not agree
that equitable considerations are relevant here. "The right to enforce express terms, without reference to the equities, has long been recognized in letter-of-credit law, and is essential to the proper functioning of the letter-of-credit device." ... Second, we do not believe that a beneficiary under a letter of credit can shift all of the risk to the issuing bank
simply by purporting to enter into a letter of credit transaction. The beneficiary always
assumes the risk that it will not be able to collect from the bank if it does not present
documents in precise compliance with the letter of credit's requirements. This is the very

reason that the beneficiary is given the opportunity to examine and either accept or reject the letter of credit.

In this case, FABC prepared the letter of credit exactly as its customer, Coral, requested. The terms of the letter of credit were explicit. Tradax, after it had a full and fair opportunity to examine the letter of credit, approved it as written. Thereafter, FABC's obligations were controlled solely by the terms of the letter of credit. In attempting to draw on the credit, Tradax failed to present documents which complied precisely with those terms. The district court properly entered judgment in FABC's favor.

IV.

Tradax also argues that the letter of credit should be reformed to obviate the mutual mistake of the parties. As a general rule, a plaintiff seeking reformation must prove (1) a mutual mistake of fact between the parties which (2) renders the contract unreflective of or contrary to the parties' intent, and (3) the existence of extrinsic evidence, generally in the form of an antecedent writing, which does accurately reflect the parties' intent.

We agree with the district court's determination that there was no mutual mistake here. Any mistake made was made by Tradax and Coral only–not by FABC. FABC, without knowledge of the meanings of the technical designations included, prepared the letter of credit precisely in compliance with Coral's request. Tradax then failed to recognize that the letter of credit's terms did not reflect its agreement with Coral. In addition, there is no prior agreement between FABC and Tradax to which this letter of credit could be conformed. Contrary to Tradax's suggestion, neither FABC's internal summary of the transaction nor the underlying agreement between Tradax and Coral is evidence of a prior agreement between FABC and Tradax.

AFFIRMED.

SAMUEL RAPPAPORT FAMILY PARTNERSHIP v. MERIDIAN BANK

657 A.2d 17 (Pa. Super. Ct. 1995)

[Summary of facts: McKlan, Inc., a business entity, agreed to lease a restaurant. To assure performance of its lease obligations, McKlan arranged for Meridian Bank to issue a $100,000 letter of credit for the benefit of the landlord/lessor, who could draw against the letter of credit by providing a certificate of default signed by Marvin Orleans. Subsequently, Marvin Orleans died and the Samuel Rappaport Family Partnership purchased the property from his estate. When McKlan subsequently defaulted, landlord/lessor Samuel Rappaport Family Partnership attempted to draw under the letter of credit. In his draw certificate, Mr. Rappaport indicated that he was the lawful assignee of Marvin Orleans's interest in the lease, that an event of default had occurred under the lease's terms, and that McKlan had failed to cure the default. A bank employee noticed that the default certificate was not signed by Marvin Orleans. McKlan refused to waive this requirement, so the bank refused to honor the draw request. Litigation ensued. One of the issues was whether the bank properly dishonored the draft because the default certificate was not signed by now-dead Marvin Orleans, as required by the terms of the letter of credit.]

HESTER, Judge.

* * *

The death of Mr. Orleans did not render the provisions of the letter of credit ambiguous regarding the continuing necessity of submitting a certificate signed by him in order to obtain payment. Rather, it rendered performance on the requirement impossible. Although appellant characterizes this conclusion as "ludicrous," ... we believe that it conforms with both the nature and purpose of letters of credit. As mentioned previously, the purpose of letters of credit is to assure prompt payment upon the presentation of documents. Moreover, the issuer's payment obligation comes into play only upon the presentation of conforming documents. Finding an ambiguity due to the death of a person mentioned in a letter of credit would have the practical effect of requiring banks and other issuers to go beyond the mere examination of documents to determine whether they facially comply with the terms of the letter of credit. Specifically, issuers would have to determine whether all such people are living and adjust the requirements of the letter of credit accordingly. Such a result would destroy the assurance of prompt payment and lead to uncertainty regarding the requirements necessary to obtain payment. Consequently, it would impair the basic utility of letters of credit.

.... [W]e note that had appellant's agents examined the terms of the letter of credit prior to completing the purchase of the leasehold premises, this entire litigation might have been avoided. Had appellant's agents examined the letter of credit's terms prior to the purchase, appellant could have declined to complete the transaction or made the purchase contingent upon ... McKlan agreeing to modify the requirement at issue. See 13 Pa.C.S. §5106(b) ("Unless otherwise agreed once an irrevocable credit is established as regards the customer it can be modified or revoked only with consent of the customer and once it is established as regards the beneficiary it can be modified or revoked only with his consent."). In the event that appellant chose to exercise neither of those options and completed the purchase, it promptly could have attempted to invoke a lease provision requiring McKlan to take all action necessary to cause the letter of credit to remain in full force and effect during the term of the lease. See Lease §56(b). Appellant's agents, however, did not examine the terms of the letter of credit until after McKlan had declared bankruptcy and defaulted and thus, could not exercise any of the described options. Accordingly, appellant must bear the burden of the impossibility of performance occasioned by Mr. Orleans's death.

As we have concluded that the terms of the letter of credit were not rendered ambiguous by the death of Mr. Orleans, they must be considered to embody the intent of [the parties]. Thus, the premise underlying appellant's challenge to the trial court's grant of judgment n.o.v. to Meridian must fail....

* * *

OLSZEWSKI, Judge, concurring:

We are constrained to concur with the majority that Mr. Rappaport cannot avail himself of the letter of credit. The letter required that Mr. Orleans, as landlord, sign a certificate that his tenants had defaulted on their rent payments. Orleans died and Rappaport bought the property, assuming all of Orleans's rights. When the same tenants defaulted, Rappaport signed the certification of default as landlord, explaining that he was Orleans's lawful assignee under the lease.

While common sense would dictate that Rappaport stood in Orleans's shoes as landlord, the law of letters of credit does not follow the dictates of common sense. Rather, it follows a rule of strict compliance. The letter required Orleans's signature, and once he died, the letter of credit became worthless. It was Rappaport's burden to discover this, and because he did not, he cannot blame the Bank for refusing to honor the letter. Such a departure from reasonable expectations might be unconscionable in the realm of consumer transactions. In the sophisticated area of high finance, it is a valid risk-shifting device.

We therefore concur in the result reached, despite its harsh and counter-intuitive appearance.

KERR-MCGEE CHEMICAL CORP. v. FDIC
872 F.2d 971 (11th Cir. 1989)

Before POWELL, Associate Justice (Retired), United States Supreme Court, RONEY, Chief Judge, and HILL, Circuit Judge.

POWELL, Associate Justice:

The question presented is whether, after initially dishonoring a letter of credit on the basis of specified grounds, a bank may subsequently dishonor the credit on the basis of a different ground. We think that under the Uniform Customs and Practices for Documentary Credits, which are expressly incorporated by the letter of credit at issue here, appellee bank was required to state all of its reasons for dishonoring the credit when it was first presented. Because it failed to do so, we reverse the district court's grant of summary judgment in the bank's favor.

I.

In October 1985, Park Bank issued a $1,002,000 letter of credit on the account of Sabar Chemical Corporation for the benefit of appellant Kerr-McGee Chemical Corporation in connection with a sale of chemicals. The letter of credit explicitly provided that it was to be governed by the Uniform Customs and Practices for Documentary Credits, 1983 Revisions (UCP), a widely used code promulgated by the International Chamber of Commerce. The credit stated that it was available for payment of sight drafts drawn on Park Bank when accompanied by specified documentation, including a "Copy of Commercial Invoice at USD 167.00 per metric ton F.O.B. Vessel. Payment terms net thirty days from invoice date." On the basis of the letter, Kerr-McGee shipped to Sabar 6015.24 metric tons of diammonium phosphate.

Shortly after the sale, Sabar requested a 30-day extension of time to pay in exchange for a one percent increase in price. The letter of credit was amended to require "Commercial invoice at USD 168.87 per metric ton, F.O.B. Vessel. Payment terms net 12/15/85." Despite the change in the unit price, the total amount of the letter of credit remained at $1,002,000. Kerr-McGee presented a sight draft and other documentation to Park Bank for payment on December 23, 1985. The invoice and sight draft reflected a total price of $1,014,590.53 that included the agreed increase. On December 27, Sabar sent a telex to Park Bank asking that it waive the discrepancy between the amount of the invoice and sight draft ($1,014,590.53) and the amount of the letter of credit ($1,002,000).

Park dishonored Kerr-McGee's request for payment on December 30, stating three grounds: (1) Draft exceeds amount of credit. (2) Signatory on notarized notice not listed as officer of Kerr-McGee. (3) Invoice does not show price F.O.B. vessel. Kerr-McGee then submitted additional documentation, including a sight draft for $1,002,000, a statement by the President of Kerr-McGee, and an invoice reflecting the price F.O.B. The total price on the invoice, however, remained $1,014,590.53. On January 2, 1986, two days after the letter of credit expired, Park dishonored the claim, stating two grounds, neither of which had been relied on at the previous dishonor: (1) Amount of invoice exceeds credit (See Article 41(b) of U.C.P.). (2) Draft and invoice amounts are inconsistent with one another (See Article 15 of U.C.P.). Subsequent to the dishonor, Kerr-McGee collected $319,902.88 from Sabar, leaving a balance due and unpaid of $694,687.70.

Kerr-McGee filed this action in the United States District Court for the Middle District of Florida on February 14, 1986. The FDIC assumed control of Park Bank shortly thereafter, and was substituted as defendant. On January 8, 1988, the district court entered summary judgment for the FDIC, rejecting Kerr-McGee's claim that because Park had specified its grounds for the first dishonor, it was estopped from relying on different grounds for the second dishonor.

II.

We begin by recognizing what is not at issue here. The controversy here does not involve the validity of Park's grounds for dishonoring the draft, but rather whether Park was estopped from relying on concededly valid grounds.[1] The parties agree that both the first and second presentments were insufficient under the terms of the credit. Under Florida law, letters of credit are subject to a rule of "strict compliance." Documents presented for payment must precisely meet the requirements set forth in the credit. Any discrepancy entitles the bank to refuse payment, and the bank bases its decision on the documents alone.... If the documents do not on their face meet the requirements of the credit, the fact that a defect is a mere "technicality" does not matter. See, e.g., Beyene v. Irving Trust Co., 762 F.2d 4 (2d Cir. 1985) (misspelling on bill of lading was grounds for dishonor); Courtaulds North American, Inc. v. North Carolina Nat'l Bank, 528 F.2d 802 (4th Cir. 1975) (discrepancy between terms "100% acrylic yarn" and "imported acrylic yarn" grounds for dishonor). As expressed by the Florida Court of Appeals: "Compliance with the terms of a letter of credit is not like pitching horseshoes. No points are awarded for being close." ... In this case, when appellant presented the documents for payment the second time, the amount of the invoice was not consistent with the letter of credit and the sight draft as required by the terms of the credit. As a matter of "strict compliance" alone, this discrepancy would have justified Park's dishonor. But this does not end the matter.

Appellant contends that Park was estopped from relying on this otherwise valid ground for dishonor because it had failed to assert the invoice amount as a ground for dishonor when appellant first presented the documents. We agree. The parties agreed and the letter of credit specifically stated that it was to be governed by the 1983 Revision of the UCP. Article 16 of the UCP provides: If the issuing bank decides to refuse the documents, it must give notice to that effect ... to the beneficiary.... Such notice must state the discrepancies in respect of which the issuing bank refuses the documents.... UCP Art. 16d. The UCP then goes on to state: If the issuing bank fails to act in accordance with the provisions of paragraphs (c) and (d) of this article..., the issuing bank shall be precluded from claiming that the documents are not in accordance with the terms and conditions of the credit. UCP Art. 16e. We think this provision makes plain that a bank will be estopped from subsequent reliance on a ground for dishonor if it did not specify that ground in its initial dishonor. Commentators who have addressed Article 16e are in accord with our view....

---

1. Also not at issue is Park Bank's refusal of Sabar's request to waive the limit of the letter of credit in response to the change in the purchase price. Both parties agree that Park was not bound to honor this request.

Appellee argues that courts have not previously embraced strict estoppel, but have instead found estoppel only on facts showing a complete change of position by the bank. For example, in Barclay's Bank D.C.O. v. Mercantile Nat'l Bank, 481 F.2d 1224 (5th Cir. 1973), the Fifth Circuit found estoppel where a bank affirmatively stated that the documentation was sufficient but dishonored on another ground, and then later in litigation claimed that the documentation had been insufficient.... Appellee and the district court placed major reliance on Philadelphia Gear Corp. v. Central Bank, 717 F.2d 230 (5th Cir. 1983). In Philadelphia Gear, the Fifth Circuit declined to find a bank estopped from raising defects where the bank refused to specify the grounds for its initial dishonor.

Appellee argues that Philadelphia Gear is dispositive here, and that it establishes a bank's right to dishonor any presentment on any valid ground regardless of whether it specified the reasons for its initial dishonor. The flaw in appellee's argument, however, is that none of the cases it cites was decided under the 1983 Revision of the UCP. The 1983 UCP provides that the bank must state its reasons for dishonor, and that failure to state these reasons will preclude a later claim of discrepancy. UCP Art. 16e. It is true that courts have taken varying approaches to the application of estoppel to letter of credit transactions. This fact is not relevant, however, where the parties have explicitly incorporated the 1983 UCP in the letter of credit.

III.

We now apply these principles to the facts. As to the first ground Park stated for the second dishonor, the UCP's strict estoppel rule is plainly dispositive. The amount of the invoice ($1,014,590.53) was inconsistent with the amount of the credit ($1,002,000) at the first presentment. Park's failure to assert this defect at the first presentment precluded it from asserting it at the second. Appellee, however, contends that the district court's judgment in its favor must be affirmed on the basis of the second ground for the dishonor — the discrepancy between the invoice amount and the amount of the draft. Appellee observes that there was no discrepancy between the invoice and the draft at the first presentment, and that Park therefore could not have been required to assert this defect.

We think this argument is meritless, for Park's two objections at the second presentment are in reality only one. Park's default was its failure to object to the amount on the invoice when it was first presented. Appellee's attempt to recharacterize this single defect in the invoice as two separate discrepancies is not persuasive. Appellant could not, of course, have altered the amount of the credit itself, nor could it have allowed the draft amount to remain inconsistent with the credit. Any objection to a discrepancy involving the invoice would therefore have been an announcement to appellant that the invoice amount had to be corrected. The defect in the invoice amount was apparent at the time of the first presentment, but Park elected not to assert this defect as a ground for dishonor. Appellee cannot do so now by describing the fact that the invoice amount necessarily conflicted with the corrected sight draft as a "separate" ground for dishonor.

Because we think Park's failure to allege the defect in the invoice at the first dishonor estopped it from later relying on that ground to avoid payment, we REVERSE the judgment of the district court and REMAND for entry of judgment in favor of appellant.

Note

The court used provisions of the UCP to craft its estoppel argument. A court also could reach the same conclusion under the current version of Article 5. See § 5-108(c).

Problem 7-3

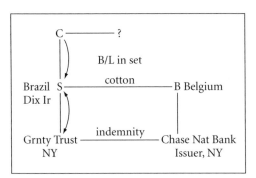

Dixon Irmaos and Company, a Brazilian exporter, contracted to sell cotton to a buyer in Belgium. As a condition to export the seller requested letters of credit. The buyer's bank requested Chase Bank to issue two irrevocable letters of credit for $7,000 and $3,500 to finance the sale. Chase Bank did so and mailed the letters of credit to the seller who received them on May 2. The letters of credit required specific documents, including a "full set of bills of lading," evidencing shipment of the stated quantity and quality of cotton. The seller shipped the cotton in two lots and received a set of bills for each shipment, i.e., two original bills of lading for each shipment. Seller's representative in New York, Guaranty Trust Company, presented the drafts and specified documents to Chase Bank on May 15, but only one of each of the two sets of bills of lading was presented, the mates to these bills having not yet arrived. However, an indemnity agreement guaranteeing against loss from absence of the bills was tendered by Guaranty Trust Company in lieu of the missing bills, in accordance with customary practice. Chase Bank refused to accept the drafts because the full set of bills was not tendered.

1) What is the risk against which the indemnity agreement was given? §§ 7-304(c), 7-403(a).

2) How would the case be decided under the U.C.C.? §§ 5-108(f), 1-303(e).

Part IV

Electronic Fund Transfers and Credit Card Payments

As noted in the introduction to this text, the majority of noncash payments in this country are no longer initiated by check, but rather with a debit or credit card or through an automated clearing house. Almost 37 billion checks were paid in 2003, but over 44 billion electronic payments originated in this country during that year. No doubt that trend – more electronic payments and fewer paper-based payments – has continued.

We divide the materials in this Part IV into three chapters. The focus of Chapter 8 is on consumer electronic fund transfers, with emphasis on the Electronic Fund Transfers Act, enacted by Congress in 1978 and codified at 15 U.S.C. § 1693 et seq., and Regulation E—Electronic Fund Transfers, 12 C.F.R. § 205. Chapter 9 examines commercial electronic fund transfers, which are governed primarily by U.C.C. Article 4A (drafted in 1990 and subsequently enacted in all states) and Regulation J—Funds Transfers Through Fedwire, 12 C.F.R. § 210. Chapter 10 is devoted to selected credit card issues addressed by the Truth in Lending Act, 15 U.S.C. § 1601 et seq.

Chapter 8

Consumer Electronic Fund Transfers

A. The Electronic Fund Transfers Act—
Scope of Coverage

Section 1693a(6) of the Electronic Fund Transfers Act (the "EFTA"), and its legislative history, indicate that the EFTA was designed to govern four common EFT consumer services:

> "[1] automated teller machine transactions, such as cash withdrawals or deposits or transfers between accounts; [2] pay-by-phone services, in which a consumer orders his financial institution to make payments to another; [3] point-of-sale systems, where funds are transferred from a consumer's account to a merchant's through use of a computer terminal at the merchant's place of business; and [4] automated clearing house transactions through which a consumer's account is automatically debited for a recurring payment, like insurance premiums, or is regularly credited with wages, pension benefits, and the like. Each of these EFT transactions is initiated and carried out primarily by electronic means."

S. Rep. No. 915, 95th Cong., 2d Sess. 3 (1978).

The EFTA and Regulation E contain a number of express *exclusions* from their application. For example, an automatic transfer of funds from a consumer's savings account to her checking account as a means of overdraft protection is not covered by the Act. 15 U.S.C. §1693a(6)(D); 12 C.F.R. §205.3(c)(5).

Electronic innovations may lead to the creation or perfection of other transactions that will be governed by the EFTA. One example might be the so-called "smart cards" or "stored value cards," which consist of a microcomputer or memory chip embedded in a plastic card. Other developments are suggested by the recent explosion in the number of cyberspace transactions, such as online banking services now used by approximately 30% of American households.

You will find it helpful to browse through the EFTA and Regulation E before reading the following materials. The EFTA is Title IX of the Consumer Credit Protection Act, §1693 et seq. The EFTA and Regulation E are found in your statutes book.

KASHANCHI v. TEXAS COMMERCE MEDICAL BANK, N.A.
703 F.2d 936 (5th Cir. 1983)

RANDALL, Circuit Judge.

The plaintiff, Morvarid Paydar Kashanchi, appeals from a final judgment of the district court dismissing her complaint for lack of subject matter jurisdiction. The issue on appeal is whether the term "electronic fund transfer" as used in the Electronic Fund Transfer Act ("EFTA" or "the Act"), 15 U.S.C. § 1693 (Supp. V 1981), includes a transfer of funds from a consumer's account, initiated by a telephone conversation between someone other than the owner of the account and an employee of a financial institution, when that transfer is not made pursuant to a prearranged plan or agreement under which periodic transfers are contemplated. For the reasons set forth below, we affirm.

On or about February 9, 1981, the plaintiff and her sister, Firoyeh Paydar, were the sole owners of a savings account at Texas Commerce Medical Bank in Houston, Texas. On or about that date, $4900 was transferred from their account. The transfer was allegedly initiated by a telephone conversation between an employee of the bank and someone other than the plaintiff or her sister. Upon receipt of a March 31, 1981, bank statement showing the $4900 withdrawal, Firoyeh Paydar sent a letter to the bank, dated April 15, 1981, notifying the bank that the withdrawal was unauthorized.

After the bank refused to recredit the account with the amount of the allegedly unauthorized withdrawal, the plaintiff filed this action on December 4, 1981, alleging violations by the bank of the EFTA. The district court granted the defendant's motion to dismiss on the ground that the plaintiff's cause of action was excluded from the coverage of the Act under 15 U.S.C. § 1693a(6)(E). The plaintiff timely appealed.

This is apparently the first case in which we have been called upon to interpret any of the substantive provisions of the EFTA. We begin our inquiry with the language of the statute itself, recognizing that "absent a clearly expressed legislative intent to the contrary, the plain meaning of the language is ordinarily controlling." Johnson v. Department of Treasury, Internal Revenue Service, 700 F.2d 971 (5th Cir. 1983); see also United States v. Martino, 681 F.2d 952, 954 (5th Cir. 1982) (en banc).

The parties agree that the telephonic transfer that allegedly occurred in this case falls within the broad definition of "electronic fund transfers" in the Act:

> [T]he term "electronic fund transfer" means any transfer of funds, other than a transaction originated by check, draft, or similar paper instrument, which is initiated through an electronic terminal, telephonic instrument, or computer or magnetic tape so as to order, instruct, or authorize a financial institution to debit or credit an account. Such term includes, but is not limited to, point-of-sale transfers, automated teller machine transactions, direct deposits or withdrawals of funds, and transfers initiated by telephone.

15 U.S.C. § 1693a(6). Some of what Congress has given, however, it has also taken away. Excluded from the definition of an electronic fund transfer is

> any transfer of funds which is initiated by a telephone conversation between a consumer and an officer or employee of a financial institution which is not pursuant to a prearranged plan and under which periodic or recurring transfers are not contemplated....

15 U.S.C. § 1693a(6)(E). The plaintiff concedes that the unauthorized transfer of her funds was not made "pursuant to any prearranged plan," and that it was made by an employee of the bank. The question in this case is whether the telephone conversation was between the employee and a "consumer."

The Act defines a consumer as "a natural person." 15 U.S.C. § 1693a(5). If we were to apply this definition to the language in the exclusion, we would have to conclude that the withdrawal of the plaintiff's funds was excluded from the coverage of the Act since a natural person, even if the person was neither the plaintiff nor her sister, made the withdrawal. The plaintiff argues, however, that we should read the term "consumer" more narrowly in this portion of the Act; she would have us interpret the provision to exclude only transfers made by the account holder.

The plaintiff maintains that the legislative history of the Act supports her narrow reading of the exclusion. She points out that the House version of the bill used the word "holder," meaning "the individual who is recognized as the owner of the account by the financial institution where the account is held," H.R. 13007, § 903(i), 95th Cong., 2d Sess., 124 Cong. Rec. 25737 (1978), where the Senate version, eventually adopted by Congress as the EFTA, uses the word "consumer." The plaintiff would have us infer that the Senate intended the word "consumer" to be synonymous with "holder." There is no indication in the legislative history, however, that this is what the Senate intended. The only criticism leveled at the definition of consumer concerned the exclusion of corporations, particularly nonprofit corporations, from that definition. See The Electronic Funds Transfer Consumer Protection Act, 1977: Hearings on S. 2065 Before the Subcomm. on Consumer Affairs of the Senate Comm. on Banking, Housing and Urban Affairs, 95th Cong., 1st Sess. 37 (1977) (Statement of Linda Hudak, Legislative Director, Consumer Federation of America).

Secondly, Congress demonstrated in other sections of the EFTA that when it wanted to limit a particular provision of the Act to an account holder, rather than to all natural persons, it was perfectly capable of adding language to do so. For example, the Act defines an "unauthorized electronic fund transfer" as "an electronic fund transfer from a consumer's account initiated by a person other than the consumer without actual authority to initiate such transfer ..." 15 U.S.C. § 1693a(11). It is a well-established principle of statutory construction that "where Congress includes particular language in one section of a statute but omits it in another section of the same Act, it is generally presumed that Congress acts intentionally and purposely in the disparate inclusion or exclusion." United States v. Wong Kim Bo, 472 F.2d 720, 722 (5th Cir. 1972). In addition, reading "consumer" as the equivalent of "holder" would create redundancies in other portions of the Act. See, e.g., 15 U.S.C. § 1693a(8). "[W]ords in statutes should not be discarded as 'meaningless' and 'surplusage' when Congress specifically and expressly included them, particularly where the words are excluded in other sections of the same act." Wong Kim Bo, 472 F.2d at 722; see also Meltzer v. Board of Public Instruction, 548 F.2d 559, 578 n. 38 (5th Cir. 1977), cert. denied, 439 U.S. 1089, 99 S.Ct. 872, 59 L.Ed.2d 56 (1979). In short, the language of the statute would seem to exclude the transfer in this case from the coverage of the Act.

Further, the legislative history of the EFTA is consistent with the plain meaning of the language in the statute and with the presumption arising from Congress's disparate inclusion and exclusion of words of limitation. The plaintiff emphasizes that Congress designed the Act to provide a comprehensive scheme of federal regulation for all electronic transfers of funds. See H.R.Rep. No. 1315, 95th Cong., 2d Sess. 2 (1978); see also Broadman, Electronic Fund Transfer Act: Is the Consumer Protected?, 13 U.S.F.L.Rev. 245 (1979). Congress undoubtedly intended the Act's coverage to be broad; the Act itself provides that its list of electronic fund transfers is not all-inclusive. 15 U.S.C. § 1693a(6). Aware that computer technology was still in a rapid, evolutionary stage of development, Congress was careful to permit coverage of electronic services not yet in existence: "The definition of 'electronic fund transfer' is intended to give the Federal Reserve Board flexibility in determining whether new or developing electronic services should be covered by the act, and, if so, to what extent." S.Rep. No. 915, 95th Cong., 2d Sess. 9 (1978), U.S. Code Cong. & Admin. News 1978, pp. 9273, 9411; see also National Commission on Electronic Fund Transfers, EFT in the United States, 4 (Final Rep. 1977).

Congressional concern about electronic systems not specifically mentioned in the Act was focused, however, on future and as yet undeveloped systems, not on systems that Congress had simply failed to discuss. For example, the report on the House version of the Act explained the need for flexibility in dealing with *future* electronic systems:

> Many aspects of electronic fund transfer systems are undergoing evolutionary changes and, thus, projections about future events necessarily involve a degree of speculation. Consequently, the appropriate approach to those new financial service concepts is, in general, to permit further development in a free market environment and, to the extent possible, in a manner consistent with the nature and purpose of existing law and regulations governing financial services.

H.R.Rep. No. 1315, supra, at 33. The absence of discussion about informal personal phone transfers would seem to indicate an intent not to cover these transfers, or at least an absence of congressional concern about them, in light of the extensive discussion throughout the hearings and reports of the other existing types of electronic transfers. It is highly unlikely that this silence was a result of congressional ignorance of the problem since these informal phone withdrawals presumably had been occurring since shortly after the time of Alexander Graham Bell.

The exclusion of these informal transactions was not in the House version of the EFTA, and presumably it was not in the original version of the Senate bill either, since the minority report criticized the bill's coverage of incidental telephone instructions:

> In an attempt to reach the automatic telephone payments (transfers through a touch-tone telephone and computer network routing instructions to the financial institution) the Committee has also covered incidental telephone instructions by (a) depositor to a teller to make a transfer from a savings account to cover an overdraft or pay a bill.

S.Rep. No. 915, supra, at 24, U.S. Code Cong. & Admin. News 1978, p. 9425. Apparently, this criticism led to the inclusion in the final version of the EFTA of the exemption which is the subject of this suit. Focusing on the Federal Reserve Board's statement that phone transfers made as an "accommodation to the consumer" are not covered by the Act, 46 Fed. Reg. 46880 (1978), and the Senate minority report's discussion of telephone instructions made by a "depositor," the plaintiff would have us conclude that only transactions made as a favor to the actual account holder were excluded from the Act.

These transfers were more probably excluded, however, not because they are made as a favor to the account holder, but because of the personal element in these transfers. On the one hand, as the plaintiff points out, all phone transfers are particularly vulnerable to fraud because there is no written memorandum of the transactions; there is no signature to be authenticated. This lack of a written record was one of the factors that motivated Congress to pass the EFTA. See H.R.Rep. No. 1315, supra, at 2, 4. The other factor, however, was the dependency of electronic fund transfer systems on computers and the resulting absence of any human contact with the transferor. The House report explains: "Consequently, these impersonal transactions are much more vulnerable to fraud, embezzlement, and unauthorized use than the traditional payment methods." Id. at 2. Senator Proxmire opened the hearings on the Senate bill with the warning that "[c]omputer systems are far from infallible, and electronic fund transfers — so totally dependent on computers — will also be error prone." The Electronic Funds Transfer Consumer Protection Act, 1977: Hearings on S. 2065 Before the Subcomm. on Consumer Affairs of the Senate Comm. on Banking, Housing and Urban Affairs, 95th Cong., 1st Sess. 1 (1977); see also 124 Cong.Rec. 25731 (1978) (statement of Rep. Annunzio, bill sponsor). As one commentator explains, telephonic communications were included in the definition of electronic fund transfers in order to extend coverage over computerized pay-by-phone systems; informal non-recurring consumer-initiated transfers were excluded, however, because they are not prone to computer error or institutional abuse since they are handled on a personal basis:

> The final exemption from the purview of the EFT Act is an exclusion for non-recurring transfers of funds that are initiated by an ordinary telephone conversation between a consumer and an officer or employee of the financial institution. In order to extend coverage over computerized "pay-by-phone" systems, the general definition of the term "electronic fund transfer" had to be broad enough to encompass transactions initiated through a telephone. Like automatic debiting of service charges and automatic crediting of interest, however, ordinary nonrecurring transfers informally initiated by a consumer's call to an officer or employee of his neighborhood bank or savings and loan association was not considered to pose a serious threat warranting the coverage and additional costs of the EFT Act. Such requests are handled on a personal basis, so the possibility of computer error or institutional abuse, believed to exist with respect to some other EFT systems, was deemed to be absent.

Brandel & Oliff, The Electronic Fund Transfer Act: A Primer, 40 Ohio St.L.J. 531, 545 (1979). Telephonic transfers made between a natural person and an employee of the financial institution share this element of human contact, regardless of whether the transfer is made by the account holder or someone else.

Finally, we note that the EFTA was passed because "[e]xisting law and regulations in the consumer protection area are not applicable to some aspects of the new financial service concepts." H.R.Rep. No. 1315, supra, at 33. See also 15 U.S.C. § 1693a. The plaintiff suggests in her reply brief that she would have no adequate legal remedy for the wrong she has suffered if she were denied relief under the EFTA. While she conceded at oral argument that she might have an action under state law for conversion or breach of contract (her deposit agreement with the bank), she maintained that a person suffering a loss resulting from the abuse of one of the other electronic fund transfer systems would also have such an action under state law.

The plaintiff ignores the essential difference between electronic fund transfer systems and personal transfers by phone or by check. When the bank employee allegedly agreed to withdraw funds from the plaintiff's account, he or she presumably could have asked some questions to ascertain whether the caller was one of the account holders. The failure to attempt to make a positive identification of the caller might be considered negligence or a breach of the deposit agreement under state law. When someone makes an unauthorized use of an electronic fund transfer system, however, the financial institution often has no way of knowing that the transfer is unauthorized. For example, in order to make a transfer at an automatic teller machine, a person need only possess the machine card and know the correct personal identification number. The computer cannot determine whether the person who has inserted the card and typed in the magic number is authorized to use the system. What might be a withdrawal negligently permitted by the financial institution in one situation might not be a negligent action in the other.

Our analysis of both the language of the EFTA and the legislative history of the Act leads us to conclude that Congress intended to exclude from the Act's coverage any transfer of funds initiated by a phone conversation between any natural person and an officer or employee of a financial institution, which was not made pursuant to a prearranged plan and under which periodic and recurring transfers were not contemplated. Accordingly, we hold that the withdrawal of funds from the plaintiff's account is not covered by the Act even though said withdrawal allegedly was not made by either the plaintiff or his sister. The district court's dismissal of the plaintiff's action for lack of subject matter jurisdiction is AFFIRMED.

Notes

1. Does Kashanchi have any remedy under U.C.C. Articles 3 or 4?

2. What remedies are available to a plaintiff if the EFTA applies? See EFTA § 1693m. See also EFTA § 1693f(e).

3. Meredith buys a new purse at a department store. The clerk asks for a signed check. The clerk enters information from the MICR line, as well as other information, into her terminal and then returns the check to Grace. Grace's checking account will be debited for the purchase in a matter of hours. Is this transaction within the scope of the EFTA? See 15 U.S.C. § 1693a(6) (defining "electronic fund transfer" as "any transfer of funds, *other than a transaction originated by check....*") (emphasis added); Regulation E Commentary (statutes book) at § 205.3(b)(v).

B. Consumer Electronic Fund Transfer Conventions

1. The Automated Teller Machine (ATM)

A popular EFT convention is the automated teller machine (ATM), an electronic terminal which allows a customer (usually with the aid of an access card and a personal identification number) to make a deposit, withdraw money, transfer funds from one account to another, etc. The popularity of ATM transactions is evidenced by a recent American Bankers Association report, indicating that 10.5 billion transactions took place at the nation's 396,000 ATMs in 2005.[1]

ATM systems can be operated either on-line or off-line. If on-line, the bank's computer instantly calculates the running balance of the customer's account. If off-line, the balance is posted periodically through a magnetic tape which records all transactions prior to the pick-up time, e.g., at 2:00 p.m. daily. Because of their advantages, most ATM systems are on-line, although they are more expensive than off-line.

Often the scope of coverage of the EFTA is a threshold issue. For example, in *Curde v. Tri-City Bank & Trust Company*, 826 S.W.2d 911 (Tenn. 1992), the question was whether the EFTA governed the rights of the parties. The plaintiff had attempted to deposit a check through an ATM, but the check was discovered seven months later behind the front cover of the ATM. The court said:

> Therefore, we find that an attempted check deposit to a ATM is an 'electronic fund transfer' covered by the Act. Here, Ms. Curde had a dispute with Tri-City Bank & Trust over whether a deposit had been made to her account. Imposing

---

1. Source: 2006 ABA Issue Summary – ATM Fact Sheet, available at http://www.aba.com/NR/rdonlyres/80468400-4225-11D4-AAE6-00508B95258D/41765/2ATMFacts1.pdf.

a duty on a bank to investigate and report disputed transactions at faceless automated teller machines is precisely the kind of consumer protection the Act is meant to afford. However, because for the purpose of this partial summary judgment motion, Ms. Curde admitted (via stipulation) that she cancelled the attempted deposit (transfer of funds), we hold that the Act does not apply. Once the consumer, by her own action, cancels a transaction, she has prevented the automatic teller transaction from becoming an electronic fund transfer under the Act. In order to come within the Act, the automatic teller transaction must 'order, instruct, or authorize a financial institution to debit or credit an account.' See 15 U.S.C. § 1693a(6) (1988).

826 S.W.2d at 915.

KRUSER v. BANK OF AMERICA NT & SA

230 Cal. App. 3d 741 (Cal. Ct. App. 1991)

STONE (WM.A.), Associate Justice.

In this appeal we interpret the language of a federal banking regulation establishing the respective liabilities of a bank and a consumer for unauthorized electronic transfers of funds from the consumer's account.

THE CASE

Appellants, Lawrence Kruser and Georgene Kruser, filed a complaint against Bank of America NT & SA (Bank) claiming damages for unauthorized electronic withdrawals from their account by someone using Mr. Kruser's "Versatel" card. The trial court entered summary judgment in favor of the Bank because it determined appellants had failed to comply with the notice and reporting requirements of the Electronic Fund Transfer Act (EFTA). (15 U.S.C. §§ 1693–1693r; 12 C.F.R. § 205.6(b)(2).)

THE FACTS

The facts are undisputed:

The Krusers maintained a joint checking account with the Bank, and the Bank issued each of them a "Versatel" card and separate personal identification numbers which would allow access to funds in their account from automatic teller machines. The Krusers also received with their cards a "Disclosure Booklet" which provided to the Krusers a summary of consumer liability, the Bank's business hours, and the address and telephone number by which they could notify the Bank in the event they believed an unauthorized transfer had been made.

The Krusers believed Mr. Kruser's card had been destroyed in September 1986. The December 1986 account statement mailed to the Krusers by the bank reflected a $20 unauthorized withdrawal of funds by someone using Mr. Kruser's card at an automatic teller machine. The Krusers reported this unauthorized transaction to the Bank when they discovered it in August or September 1987.

Mrs. Kruser underwent surgery in late December 1986 or early January 1987. She remained hospitalized for 11 days. She then spent a period of six or seven months recuperating at home. During this time she reviewed the statements she and Mr. Kruser received from the bank.

In September 1987, the Krusers received bank statements for July and August 1987 which reflected 47 unauthorized withdrawals, totaling $9,020, made from an automatic teller machine, again by someone using Mr. Kruser's card. They notified the bank of these withdrawals within a few days of receiving the statement. The Bank refused to credit the Krusers' account with the amount of the unauthorized withdrawals.

DISCUSSION

We summarize briefly the general rules regarding summary judgment.

* * *

The ultimate issue we address is whether, as a matter of law, the failure to report the unauthorized $20 withdrawal which appeared on the December 1986 statement barred appellants from recovery for the losses incurred in July and August 1987. Resolution of the issue requires the interpretation of section 909 of the EFTA (15 U.S.C. § 1693g) and section 205.6 of Regulation E (12 C.F.R. § 205.6), one of the regulations prescribed by the Board of Governors of the Federal Reserve System in order to carry out the purposes of the EFTA. (15 U.S.C. § 1693a(3); 15 U.S.C. 1693b(a).)

In order to show the framework of responsibility for unauthorized transactions, we set out extensive portions of 15 United States Code Annotated section 1693g, with the provisions directly applicable to this case emphasized:

* * *

Notwithstanding the foregoing, reimbursement need not be made to the consumer for losses the financial institution establishes would not have occurred but for the failure of the consumer to report within sixty days of transmittal of the statement (or in extenuating circumstances such as extended travel or hospitalization, within a reasonable time under the circumstances) any unauthorized electronic fund transfer or account error which appears on the periodic statement provided to the consumer under section 1693d of this title.

* * *

Section 205.6 of Regulation E essentially mirrors 15 United States Code section 1693g, and in particular provides:

Limitations on account of liability.

* * *

(2) If the consumer fails to report within 60 days of transmittal of the periodic statement any unauthorized electronic fund transfer that appears on the statement, the consumer's liability shall not exceed the sum of

(i) The lesser of $50 or the amount of unauthorized electronic fund transfers that appear on the periodic statement or that occur during the 60-day period, and

(ii) The amount of unauthorized electronic fund transfers that occur after the close of the 60 days and before notice to the financial institution and that the financial institution establishes would not have occurred but for the failure of the consumer to notify the financial institution within that time.

* * *

(4) If a delay in notifying the financial institution was due to extenuating circumstances, such as extended travel or hospitalization, the time periods specified above shall be extended to a reasonable time.

* * *

The trial court concluded the Bank was entitled to judgment as a matter of law because the unauthorized withdrawals of July and August 1987 occurred more than 60 days after appellants received a statement which reflected an unauthorized transfer in December 1986. The court relied upon section 205.6(b)(2) of Regulation E.

Appellants contend the December withdrawal of $20 was so isolated in time and minimal in amount that it cannot be considered in connection with the July and August withdrawals. They assert the court's interpretation of section 205.6(b)(2) of Regulation E would have absurd results which would be inconsistent with the primary objective of the EFTA—to protect the consumer. (See 15 U.S.C. § 1693.) They argue that if a consumer receives a bank statement which reflects an unauthorized minimal electronic transfer and fails to report the transaction to the bank within 60 days of transmission of the bank statement, unauthorized transfers many years later, perhaps totaling thousands of dollars, would remain the responsibility of the consumer.

The result appellants fear is avoided by the requirement that the bank establish the subsequent unauthorized transfers could have been prevented had the consumer notified the bank of the first unauthorized transfer. (12 C.F.R. § 205.6(b)(2)(ii).) Here, although the unauthorized transfer of $20 occurred approximately seven months before the unauthorized transfers totaling $9,020, it is undisputed that all transfers were made by someone using Mr. Kruser's card which the Krusers believed had been destroyed prior to December 1986. According to the declaration of Yvonne Maloon, the Bank's Versatel risk manager, the Bank could have and would have canceled Mr. Kruser's card had it been timely notified of the December unauthorized transfer. In that event Mr. Kruser's card could not have been used to accomplish the unauthorized transactions in July and August. Although appellants characterize this assertion as speculation, they offer no evidence to the contrary.

In the alternative, appellants contend the facts establish that Mrs. Kruser, who was solely responsible for reconciling the bank statements, was severely ill and was also caring for a terminally ill relative when the December withdrawal occurred. Therefore they claim they were entitled to an extension of time within which to notify the bank. They argue these extenuating circumstances as recognized in both EFTA, 15 United States Code section 1693g(a)(2) and Regulation E, section 205.6(b)(4) present a question of fact about the reasonableness of the time in which they gave notice.

The evidence appellants rely upon indicates in late 1986 or early 1987 Mrs. Kruser underwent surgery and remained in the hospital for 11 days. She left her house infrequently during the first six or seven months of 1987 while she was recuperating. Mrs. Kruser admits, however, she received and reviewed bank statements during her recuperation. Therefore, we need not consider whether Mrs. Kruser's illness created circumstances which might have excused her failure to notice the unauthorized withdrawal pursuant to the applicable sections. She in fact did review the statements in question.

Appellants cite no evidence in support of their contention Mrs. Kruser was also caring for her ill relative during the relevant time period. We need not determine whether that fact might have excused her failure to notice the unauthorized withdrawal.

Moreover, nothing in the record reflects any extenuating circumstances which would have prevented Mr. Kruser from reviewing the bank statements. The understanding he had with Mrs. Kruser that she would review the bank statements did not excuse him from his obligation to notify the bank of any unauthorized electronic transfers.

In Sun 'n Sand, Inc. v. United California Bank (1978) 21 Cal.3d 671, 148 Cal.Rptr. 329, 582 P.2d 920, the Supreme Court held in the case of a dishonest employee who altered her employer's checks to her benefit:

"We made clear in Basch v. Bank of America (1943) supra, 22 Cal.2d 316, 327–328 [139 P.2d 1], that an employer is charged with the knowledge that an honest agent would have gained in the course of a reasonably diligent examination; we explained that 'this rule reasonably imposes upon the depositor the further duty of properly supervising the conduct of his trusted employee …' Sun 'n Sand's failure to discover its mistake within three years of the issuance of the first three checks thus derived from its failure to discharge with reasonable care its duty to supervise its employees." (Id. 21 Cal.3d at p. 702, 148 Cal.Rptr. 329, 582, P.2d 920.)

Although the record is clear Mrs. Kruser did nothing dishonest which led to the failure to report the unauthorized transaction, we see no distinction between the employer's inability to avoid liability by claiming it delegated that duty and Mr. Kruser's inability to avoid liability by claiming he delegated to his wife his duty to discover unauthorized withdrawals on his Versatel card.

Finally, appellants contend evidence of mailing the December bank statement was insufficient to establish "transmittal" as that word is used in section 205.6(b)(2) of Regulation E. They contend actual knowledge is required and rely on the Federal Reserve Board's official staff interpretation of Regulation E relating to the loss or theft provision of section 205.6(b)(1). (See official staff interpretation, 12 C.F.R. part 205, Supp. II (Jan. 1, 1987 ed.) p. 125.)

Section 205.6(b)(1) requires the consumer to notify the bank "within 2 business days after learning of the *loss or theft* of access device …" (Emphasis added.) The question addressed by the staff comment is whether the consumer's receipt of a periodic statement that reflects unauthorized transfers is sufficient to establish knowledge of loss or theft of an access device. The comment provides:

"Receipt of the periodic statement reflecting unauthorized transfers may be considered a factor in determining whether the consumer had knowledge of the loss or theft, but cannot be deemed to represent conclusive evidence that the consumer had such knowledge." (Official staff interpretation, 12 C.F.R. part 205, Supp. II, (Jan. 1, 1987 ed.) 205.6(b), p. 125.)

Here we are not concerned with the loss or theft of an access device. Rather, our question is whether the bank has established the loss of $9,020 in July and August 1987 would not have occurred but for the failure of appellants to report timely the $20 unauthorized transfer which appeared on the December 1986 statement (15 U.S.C. § 1693g(a)(2)).

Appellants cite no authority which supports their claim the consumer must not only receive the statement provided by the bank, but must acquire actual knowledge of an authorized transfer from the statement. Such a construction of the law would reward consumers who choose to remain ignorant of the nature of transactions on their account by purposely failing to review periodic statements. Consumers must play an active and responsible role in protecting against losses which might result from unauthorized transfers. A banking institution cannot know of an unauthorized electronic transfer unless the consumer reports it.

The Bank has established that the losses incurred in July and August 1987 as a result of the unauthorized electronic transfers by someone using Mr. Kruser's Versatel card could have been prevented had appellants reported the unauthorized use of Mr. Kruser's card as reflected on the December 1986 statement. The Bank is entitled to judgment as a matter of law.

DISPOSITION

We affirm the judgment and award costs on appeal to respondent.

Note

Wallace and Helen Johnson contact their attorney with facts almost identical to those in *Kruser*. The attorney is familiar with *Kruser* and the applicable law. What ethical quandary may confront the attorney if the attorney wishes to avoid the same disastrous result?

OGNIBENE v. CITIBANK, N. A.
446 N.Y.S.2d 845 (Civ. Ct. of City of N.Y. 1981)

MARA T. THORPE, Judge.

Plaintiff seeks to recover $400.00 withdrawn from his account at the defendant bank by an unauthorized person using an automated teller machine. The court has concluded that plaintiff was the victim of a scam which defendant has been aware of for some time.

Defendant's witness, an assistant manager of one of its branches, described how the scam works: A customer enters the automated teller machine (ATM) area for the purpose of using a machine for the transaction of business with the bank. At the time that he enters, a person is using the customer service telephone located between the two automated teller machines and appears to be telling customer service that one of the machines is malfunctioning. This person is the perpetrator of the scam and his conversation with customer service is only simulated. He observes the customer press his personal identification code into one of the two machines. Having learned the code, the perpetrator then tells the customer that customer service has advised him to ask the customer to insert his Citicard into the allegedly malfunctioning machine to check whether it will work with a card other than the perpetrator's. When a good samaritan customer accedes to the request, the other machine is activated. The perpetrator then presses a code into the machine, which the customer does not realize is his own code which the perpetrator has just observed. After continuing the simulated conversation on the telephone, the perpetrator advises the customer that customer service has asked if he would try his Citicard in the allegedly malfunctioning machine once more. A second insertion of the cards permits cash to be released by the machine, and if the customer does as requested, the thief has effectuated a cash withdrawal from the unwary customer's account.

Plaintiff testified that on August 16, 1981, he went to the ATM area at one of defendant's branches and activated one of the machines with his Citibank card, pressed in his personal identification code and withdrew $20.00. While he did this a person who was using the telephone between plaintiff's machine and the adjoining machine said into the telephone, "I'll see if his card works in my machine." Thereupon he asked plaintiff if he could use his card to see if the other machine was working. Plaintiff handed it to him and saw him insert it into the adjoining machine at least two times while stating into the telephone, "Yes, it seems to be working."

Defendant's computer records in evidence show that two withdrawals of $200.00 each from plaintiff's account were made on August 16, 1981, on the machine adjoining the one plaintiff used for his $20.00 withdrawal. The two $200.00 withdrawals were made at 5:42 p.m. and 5:43 p.m. respectively; plaintiff's own $20.00 withdrawal was made at 5:41 p.m. At the time, plaintiff was unaware that any withdrawals from his account were being made on the adjoining machine.

The only fair and reasonable inferences to be drawn from all of the evidence are that the person who appeared to be conversing on the telephone observed the plaintiff enter his personal identification code into the machine from which he withdrew $20.00 and that he entered it into the adjoining machine while simulating a conversation with customer service about that machine's malfunctioning. It is conceded in the testimony of defendant's assistant branch manager that it would have been possible for a person who was positioned so as to appear to be speaking on the telephone physically to observe the code being entered into the machine by plaintiff. Although plaintiff is not certain that his card was inserted in the adjoining machine more than twice, the circumstances indicate that it was inserted four times. No issue of fraud by plaintiff or anyone acting in concert with him has been raised by defendant. Having observed plaintiff's demeanor, the court found him to be a credible witness and is of the opinion that no such issues exist in this case.

The basic rights, liabilities and responsibilities of the banks which offer electronic money transfer services and the consumers who use them have been established by the federal legislation contained in 15 U.S.C.A. 1693 et seq., commonly called the Electronic Fund Transfers Act (EFT). Although the EFT Act preempts state law only to the extent of any inconsistency (15 U.S.C.A. 1693q), to date New York State has not enacted legislation which governs the resolution of the issues herein. Therefore, the EFT Act is applicable.

The EFT Act places various limits on a consumer's liability for electronic fund transfers from his account if they are "unauthorized." Insofar as is relevant here, a transfer is "unauthorized" if (1) it is initiated by a person other than the consumer and without actual authority to initiate such transfer, (2) the consumer receives no benefit from it, and (3) the consumer did not furnish such person "with the card, code or other means of access" to his account. 15 U.S.C.A. 1693a(11).

In an action involving a consumer's liability for an electronic fund transfer, such as the one at bar, the burden of going forward to show an "unauthorized" transfer from his account is on the consumer. The EFT Act places upon the bank, however, the burden of proof of any consumer liability for the transfer. 15 U.S.C.A. 1693g(b). To establish full liability on the part of the consumer, the bank must prove that the transfer was authorized. To be entitled to even the limited liability imposed by the statute on the consumer, the bank must prove that certain conditions of consumer liability, set forth in 15 U.S.C.A. 1693g(a) have been met and that certain disclosures mandated by 15 U.S.C.A. 1693c(a)(1) and (2) have been made. Id.

Plaintiff herein met his burden of going forward. He did not initiate the withdrawals in question, did not authorize the person in the ATM area to make them, and did not benefit from them.

However, defendant's position is, in essence, that although plaintiff was duped, the bank's burden of proof on the issue of authorization has been met by plaintiff's testimony that he permitted his card to be used in the adjoining machine by the other person. The court does not agree.

The EFT Act requires that the consumer have furnished to a person initiating the transfer the "card, code, or other means of access" to his account to be ineligible for the limitations on liability afforded by the Act when transfers are "unauthorized." The evidence establishes that in order to obtain access to an account via an automated teller machine, both the card and the personal identification code must be used. Thus, by merely giving his card to the person initiating the transfer, a consumer does not furnish the "means of access" to his account. To do so, he would have to furnish the personal identification code as well. See 12 C.F.R. 205.2(a)(1), the regulation promulgated under the EFT Act which defines "access device" as "a card, code or other means of access to [an] … account *or any combination thereof*" (emphasis added).

The court finds that plaintiff did not furnish his personal identification code to the person initiating the $400.00 transfer within the meaning of the EFT Act. There is no evidence that he deliberately or even negligently did so. On the contrary, the unauthorized person was able to obtain the code because of defendant's own negligence. Since the bank had knowledge of the scam and its operational details (including the central role of the customer service telephone), it was negligent in failing to provide plaintiff-customer with information sufficient to alert him to the danger when he found himself in the position of a potential victim. Although in June, 1981, after the scam came to defendant's attention, it posted signs in its ATM areas containing a red circle approximately 2 _ inches in diameter in which is written "Do Not Let Your Citicard Be Used For Any Transaction But Your Own", the court finds that this printed admonition is not a sufficient security measure since it fails to state the reason why one should not do so. Since a customer of defendant's electronic fund transfer service must employ both the card and the personal identification code in order to withdraw money from his account, the danger of loaning his card briefly for the purpose of checking the functioning of an adjoining automated teller machine would not be immediately apparent to one who has not divulged his personal identification number and who is unaware that it has been revealed merely by virtue of his own transaction with the machine.

Since the bank established the electronic fund transfer service and has the ability to tighten its security characteristics, the responsibility for the fact that plaintiff's code, one of the two necessary components of the "access device" or "means of access" to his account, was observed and utilized as it was must rest with the bank.

For the foregoing reasons and in view of the fact that the primary purpose of the EFT Act and the regulation promulgated thereunder is the protection of individual consumers (12 C.F.R. 205.1(b)), the court concludes that plaintiff did not furnish his code to anyone within the meaning of the Act. Accordingly, since the person who obtained it did not have actual authority to initiate the transfer, the transfer qualifies as an "unauthorized" one under 15 U.S.C.A. 1693a(11) and the bank cannot hold plaintiff fully liable for the $400.00 withdrawal.

To avail itself of the limited liability imposed by the Act upon a consumer in the event of an "unauthorized" transfer, the bank must demonstrate (1) that the means of access utilized for the transfer was "accepted" and (2) that the bank has provided a way which the user of the means of access can be identified as the person authorized to use it. 15 U.S.C.A. 1693g(a) and (b). One definition of "accepted" under the Act is that the consumer has used the means of access. 15 U.S.C.A. 1693a(1). Both of the foregoing conditions of liability have been met here since plaintiff used the means of access to his account to withdraw the $20.00 and had been given a personal identification code.

Additionally, the bank must prove that it disclosed to the consumer his liability for unauthorized electronic fund transfers and certain information pertaining to notification of the bank in the event the consumer believes that an unauthorized transfer has been or may be effected. 15 U.S.C.A. 1693c(a)(1) and (2) and 1693g(b). Defendant did not establish that it made such disclosures to plaintiff. Accordingly, it is not entitled to avail itself of the benefit of the limited liability for unauthorized transfers imposed upon consumers by the Act.

For the foregoing reasons, judgment shall be for plaintiff in the sum of $400.00.

Note

Thieves have been known to deplete a customer's bank account by placing a "skimming device" on an ATM that reads account information (including the customer's PIN) as the customer dips her access card into the ATM and types the PIN. See "*Skimming the cash out of your account,*" at http://www.bankrate.com/brm/news/atm/20021004a.asp. Other technologically-challenged criminals have adopted a "smash and dash" approach by simply attempting to haul away the ATM itself. See "*Thieves finding new ways to break into ATM machines,*" at http://www.alldeaf.com/current-events/34408-thieves-finding-new-ways-break-into-atm-machines.html; "*Robbers hold up, carry off ATMs,*" HOUSTON CHRONICLE at B3 (May 8, 2007).

Problem 8-1

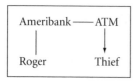

Roger keeps his AmeriBank ATM card (together with his PIN) in his wallet. What is his liability in the following situations? See Regulation E, § 205.6. Assume that AmeriBank's practice is to cancel the validity of any lost or stolen ATM card within 24 hours after it is informed of the loss or theft.

Scenario #1

Thief steals Roger's wallet on Monday and uses the ATM card to withdraw $300. On Tuesday morning, Roger discovers that his wallet has been stolen. That night, Thief withdraws another $300. Roger visits AmeriBank on Wednesday morning and tells the customer account representative that his ATM card has been stolen. On Wednesday afternoon, Thief withdraws $400.

Scenario #2

Thief steals Roger's wallet on Monday and uses the ATM card to withdraw $200. On Tuesday morning, Roger discovers that his wallet has been stolen. That afternoon, Thief withdraws $400. On Wednesday morning, Roger mails a letter to AmeriBank, stating that his ATM card has been stolen. That evening, Thief withdraws $300. On Thursday, Thief withdraws $500. On Friday morning, Thief withdraws $400. AmeriBank receives Roger's letter on Friday afternoon.

Scenario #3

Thief steals Roger's wallet on Monday and uses the ATM card to withdraw $200. On Tuesday morning, Roger discovers that his wallet has been stolen. Thief withdraws $300 on Wednesday, $500 on Thursday, and $300 on Friday morning. On Friday afternoon, Roger mails a letter to AmeriBank stating that his ATM card has been stolen. AmeriBank receives Roger's letter on Saturday morning, three hours before Thief withdraws $400.

Scenario #4

Thief steals Roger's ATM card on Monday (June 1) and withdraws $500 that afternoon and $400 on Thursday. The following Monday, AmeriBank mails to Roger his monthly bank statement for the period of May 7 through June 6. Roger receives the statement the next day. On Wednesday (June 10), Thief withdraws $300. On Thursday, Roger reviews his bank statement, notices several suspicious withdrawals, and concludes that his ATM card has been lost or stolen. On Friday morning Thief withdraws $500. That afternoon, Roger contacts AmeriBank by telephone to report his ATM card has been lost or stolen.

Scenario #5

Thief steals Roger's wallet on Monday (June 1) and withdraws $200 on Tuesday. On Wednesday, Roger discovers that his wallet has been stolen, but he forgets that his ATM card was in the wallet. Thief withdraws $300 on Friday and $500 on Sunday. On Wednesday (June 10), AmeriBank mails to Roger his monthly bank statement for the period of May 10 through June 9. Roger receives the statement one day later but does not review it. Thief withdraws $400 on Monday (June 15).

On Friday (July 10), AmeriBank mails to Roger his monthly bank statement for the period of June 10 through July 9. As before, Roger receives the statement one day later but does not review it.

On Tuesday (August 4), Thief withdraws $400. On Monday (August 10), AmeriBank mails to Roger his monthly bank statement for the period of July 10 through August 9. Roger receives the statement one day later but does not review it. On Saturday (August 15), Thief withdraws $500. On Tuesday (August 18), Thief withdraws $300. On Thursday (August 20), Roger concludes that his ATM card has been stolen and notifies AmeriBank of the theft.

Scenario #6

Same as scenario #5 except (i) Thief steals the ATM card (rather than the wallet), and (ii) Roger does not discover the theft but contacts AmeriBank on August 20 to discuss what look like possible unauthorized transfers on his recent bank statement.

Notes

1. The degree to which a consumer is liable for unauthorized transfers often is dictated by whether the consumer notifies the financial institution within two "business days" after discovering that its access device has been lost or stolen. What is the duration of a "business day"? "A business day includes the entire 24-hour period ending at midnight, and a notice required by the regulation is effective even if given outside normal business hours." 12 C.F.R. pt. 205, App. C, Supp. I, "Official Staff Interpretations" (Section 205.2—Definitions).

2. Can a consumer's negligence increase his liability for unauthorized transfers? No. "Negligence by the consumer cannot be used as the basis for imposing greater liability than is permissible under Regulation E. Thus, consumer behavior that may constitute negligence under state law, such as writing the PIN on a debit card or on a piece of paper kept with the card does not affect the consumer's liability for unauthorized transfers." 12 C.F.R. pt. 205, App. C, Supp. I, "Official Staff Interpretations" (Section 205.6—Liability of Consumer for Unauthorized Transfers).

3. Is a consumer deemed to have knowledge that his access device has been lost or stolen at the moment when the consumer receives a periodic statement that reflects the unauthorized withdrawals? "The fact that a consumer has received a periodic statement that reflects unauthorized transfers may be a factor in determining whether the consumer had knowledge of the loss or theft, but cannot be deemed to represent conclusive evidence that the consumer had such knowledge." 12 C.F.R. pt. 205, App. C, Supp. I, "Official Staff Interpretations" (Section 205.6—Liability of Consumer for Unauthorized Transfers).

2. Point of Sale (POS)

The point of sale (POS) EFT is a convention which provides for the electronic payment for goods at the point of purchase. Typically a customer swipes her plastic *debit* card at a terminal at the point of purchase and with the use of a PIN (personal identification number) the purchaser's bank account is instantly debited. (The customer also may choose to swipe her plastic *credit* card, removing the transaction from the scope of the EFTA because the customer is not directing immediate payment from her account.) POS transactions involving debit cards are very attractive to merchants because the merchants receive immediate credits to their bank accounts — the closest thing to cash payments. For that very reason some customers prefer checks and credit cards to debit cards.

3. ACH Transfers

ACH is the acronym for Automated Clearing House electronic fund transfer systems. An ACH is implemented by a group of banks in a particular region, each connected by their computer systems with the clearing house computer, either through a "dedicated" telephone line or a "dial-up" connection. The clearing house computer is able to debit or credit the Federal Reserve accounts of the banks involved in a given transfer, and these banks in turn debit or credit the accounts of their customers. Consumer transactions typically involve recurring transfers, such as payroll deposits and mortgage payments. In 2005, the ACH network processed a total of almost 10.7 billion transactions worth more than $24 billion.[2]

An important advantage of the ACH system is that it is implemented by preauthorized or prerecorded transfer messages that are received electronically, and the debits and credits of the receiving bank are made automatically. This not only speeds up the transfer process but also eliminates the errors that sometimes arise through manual processing. The customer initiates the transfer by sending the transfer data to his bank, which takes off whatever information affects the accounts of its own customers. The remaining data is forwarded to the ACH, which adjusts the Federal Reserve accounts of the affected banks within its region.

The ACH systems are used not only to make payments (credit transfers, as is done with a check), but also to collect debts (debit transfers, as is done with a draft).

To illustrate the payment process or "credit transfer" function of the ACH system, suppose BizCorp has a large payroll. Rather than paying its employees by check, BizCorp may offer to pay the wages directly into each employee's bank account. If the employees agree to this arrangement, then BizCorp generates a tape or other electronic message with all payroll information on it and sends it to its bank. This bank removes the payroll information for BizCorp employees banking with it and credits their accounts. With respect to BizCorp employees who are banking elsewhere, the tape with the remaining data is sent by BizCorp's bank to the ACH. The ACH will transfer the relevant data to the various receiving banks in its district where BizCorp employees have accounts, which will be credited accordingly.

In addition to facilitating transfers of credits from debtors to their creditors, as illustrated by the payroll example, ACH systems also are being used to facilitate a variety of collections

---

2. Source: http://www.acainternational.org/?cid=8459&printer=yes.

or "debit transfers," as traditionally accomplished with drafts. For example, ElectriCorp provides electricity to most of the residents in its area. Rather than pay their bills by writing checks, licking envelopes, and peeling stamps every month, many customers agree that ElectriCorp may debit their bank accounts for the appropriate charges. Each customer completes the appropriate authorization form (which includes bank account information and often a blank check marked "VOID"), a copy of which is provided to the customer's bank. Every month, ElectriCorp generates a tape or other electronic message with all billing information on it and sends it to its bank. This bank acts on the billing information for ElectriCorp customers banking with it and debits their accounts. For ElectriCorp customers who are banking elsewhere, the tape with the remaining data is sent by ElectriCorp's bank to the ACH. The ACH will transfer the relevant data to the various receiving banks in its district where ElectriCorp customers have accounts, which will be debited accordingly.

The ACH system is under the rule-making authority of NACHA (the National Automated Clearing House Association). NACHA formulates the operating guidelines for the many regional automated clearinghouse associations around the nation. The law governing debit transfers is found in the NACHA Operating Rules. These rules are given the status of federal law through the Federal Reserve Operating Circulars. The NACHA Operating Rules in turn provide that a debit transfer is deemed to be an "item" within U.C.C. Article 4, and Article 4 shall govern debit entries except to the extent Article 4 is inconsistent with the NACHA Operating Rules.

Problem 8-2

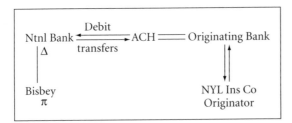

Sandra Bisbey has a checking account with National Bank. She authorized the Bank to debit her account for transfers to New York Life Insurance Company ("NYL") in payment of insurance premiums pursuant to transfer requests submitted monthly by NYL. The September request was not honored because Sandra's account did not have sufficient funds. In October, the September request was resubmitted along with the October payment request. Again there were insufficient funds to pay either premium. However, this time the Bank honored both requests, thereby creating an overdraft in Sandra's account. The Bank then sent two overdraft notices to Sandra, each in the amount of her monthly insurance premium, but it did not charge her any overdraft service fee. By this time Sandra had forgotten that she had not paid the September premium. She notified the Bank that she believed that the Bank had erroneously duplicated the October transfer. At the Bank's request, she sent a letter of confirmation one week later. About ten days after Sandra called in her complaint a bank officer telephoned Sandra and explained that there had been no improper duplication of her premium payments because the facts were as stated above. Nevertheless Sandra was not satisfied with this explanation and shortly thereafter notified the Bank of her dissatisfaction. She then filed suit under the EFTA requesting damages, costs, and attorney's fees.

1) Is this a debit or credit transfer? EFTA §§ 1693e, 1693a(9).

2) Is the Bank obligated to investigate the complaint? EFTA § 1693f.

3) What response is the Bank required to give Sandra? EFTA § 1693f.

4) Will Sandra succeed in her action for damages, costs, and attorney's fees? EFTA § 1693m(a).

Problem 8-3

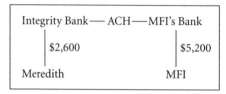

Integrity Bank — ACH — MFI's Bank

$2,600 $5,200

Meredith   MFI

Meredith maintains her personal account with Integrity Bank. Last year she financed the purchase of a new home with funds borrowed from Mortgage Finance Inc. ("MFI"). After writing mortgage payment checks for several months, Meredith authorized MFI to withdraw $2,600 on the 10th of each month from her personal account with Integrity Bank (which received a copy of all necessary paperwork).

Meredith received her June statement from Integrity Bank on July 6. She reviewed the statement that night, noting that it erroneously reflected two $2,600 withdrawals by MFI (one posted on June 10 and the other posted on June 24). Distracted by a family emergency, Meredith did not contact Integrity Bank and explain the problem until July 13. Meredith insists that Integrity Bank recredit her account for MFI's unauthorized withdrawal of $2,600 on June 24.

If both parties can satisfy their respective burdens of proof, how will the $2,600 loss be allocated between Meredith and Integrity Bank? Regulation E, § 205.6.

Chapter 9

Commercial Electronic Fund Transfers

In this chapter we turn our attention more particularly to the application of U.C.C. Article 4A to commercial electronic fund transfers. In Chapter 8 we noted that consumer EFTs are governed primarily by the EFTA and Regulation E. Commercial EFTs are governed primarily by U.C.C. Article 4A and Regulation J, 12 C.F.R. pt. 210, subpart B. Observe that if any part of an EFT is governed by the EFTA, Article 4A will not apply. §4A-108. That is, the EFTA, a federal statute that governs consumer transfers, preempts Article 4A where there is an overlap. Thus Article 4A can apply only if the EFTA does not govern the transaction. Because of the broad definition of "electronic fund transfer" in the EFTA, see 15 U.S.C. §1693a(6), there would be no room for the application of Article 4A to EFTs were it not for the scope of coverage limitations and express exclusions stated in the EFTA. As we have seen, the EFTA is intended primarily for "the protection of individual consumers engaging in electronic fund transfers." 12 C.F.R. §205.1(b). Further, because of the express exclusion from the EFTA of consumer transfers over Fedwire and certain other consumer transfers (see 15 U.S.C. §1693a(6)(B) and 12 C.F.R. §205.3(c)(3)), there remains a considerable scope of coverage for Article 4A.

Commercial transfers (often referred to as "wholesale transfers") differ from consumer transfers primarily in the dollar value of a single transfer. For example, each wholesale transfer averages well over $1 million. Consumer transfers (sometimes described as "retail transfers") are much more frequent in number, but their average dollar value is vastly lower by comparison.

A. Wholesale Wire Transfers and Article 4A

Wire transfers that are exclusively commercial or wholesale in nature are governed by Article 4A, if they otherwise meet the conditions of Article 4A. However, if any part of the transfer is consumer in nature, the entire transfer is excluded from Article 4A and is governed by the EFTA and other laws. An exception to this consumer exclusion applies if the consumer utilizes Fedwire (or CHIPS) to transfer funds, in which case Article 4A applies because the transfer is excluded from the scope of the EFTA by 15 U.S.C. §1693a(6)(B).

The two most instructive definitions in Article 4A are the definitions for "funds transfer" and "payment order." A "funds transfer" is defined as "the series of transactions, beginning with the originator's payment order, made for the purpose of making payment to the beneficiary of the order. The term includes any payment order issued by the originator's bank or an intermediary bank intended to carry out the originator's payment order. A funds transfer is completed by acceptance by the beneficiary's bank of a payment order for the benefit of the beneficiary of the originator's payment order." § 4A-104(a).

A "payment order," which is the other basic definition in Article 4A, is defined as "an instruction of a sender to a receiving bank, transmitted orally, electronically, or in writing, to pay, or to cause another bank to pay, a fixed or determinable amount of money to a beneficiary if: (i) the instruction does not state a condition to payment to the beneficiary other than time of payment, (ii) the receiving bank is to be reimbursed by debiting an account of, or otherwise receiving payment from, the sender, and (iii) the instruction is transmitted by the sender directly to the receiving bank or to an agent, funds-transfer system, or communication system for transmittal to the receiving bank." § 4A-103(a)(1). Thus by definition, Article 4A governs only credit transfers.

Because of the large sums involved in a typical wholesale EFT, the risk of loss to banks at some stage of the payment process can be great. These risks can arise in various ways, such as by one or more banks granting credit in connection with a transfer for even a short period of time, or from a bank failing to execute a payment order as ordered by its customer, or from executing an order too late, or from errors in the payment order. Risks of loss also arise from the possibility of unauthorized payment orders or duplicate payment orders. As a result, a major policy underlying the development of Article 4A relates to the appropriate allocation of risks of loss in these and other circumstances.

Although it is convenient to discuss consumer and commercial EFTs separately, the wire networks over which these transfers are made are not so exclusive. That is, a given wire transfer system may be used to execute a commercial transfer in one instance and a consumer transfer in another. A discussion of two popular wire networks – Fedwire and CHIPS – follows.

B. Fedwire

Fedwire is an EFTS owned by the United States and operated by the Federal Reserve System throughout the nation. Fedwire, or the "wire transfer system" as it is sometimes referred to, does not include the automated clearing house (ACH) system. Regulation J, § 210.26(e).

The Fedwire system is divided into twelve regions. Member banks of the Federal Reserve System will generally have a "dedicated" telephone line for their Fedwire system which keeps them in contact at all times with their host bank—the Federal Reserve Bank for their region. A dedicated line of this sort is rather expensive compared to the "dial-up" system sometimes used to implement the ACH system. Smaller banks that are not members of the Federal Reserve System can use Fedwire by working through a correspondent bank that is a member.

Fedwire is generally the swiftest funds transfer method, depending on the type of transfer being made, because very little implementation or lead time is required between the request to make the transfer and the time when the transfer itself is made. The payment message to the receiving bank and the transfer payment by the sending bank are usually sent simultaneously with no intervening time, as is required by some systems. But Fedwire is not always the most practical or economical method of making EFTs.

Selected Fedwire statistics for calendar year 2005 follow:[1]

Number of transfers originated	132,437,838
Value of transfers originated (in millions)	$518,546,592
Average value per transfer (in millions)	$3.92
Average daily value of transfers (in millions)	$2,065,923

C. CHIPS

In the larger financial centers such as New York City, some of the bigger banks have established their own ACH systems, such as CHIPS (the New York Clearing House Inter-Bank Payments System), which is a private association whose participants are financial institutions that maintain a presence in New York City. CHIPS is governed by its own transfer rules. Although CHIPS makes some domestic transfers, most of its transfers are to overseas beneficiaries.

As we have noted, in the case of a funds transfer over Fedwire the transfer message and the funds transfer are made simultaneously. However CHIPS rules provide for a time gap to intervene between the payment message sent to the receiving bank and the actual funds transfer. Typically the message that a transfer is to be made will be sent in the morning, but the funds transfer will not be made until the end of the banking day.

Selected CHIPS statistics for calendar year 2006 follow:[2]

Number of transfers originated	77,876,444
Value of transfers originated (in millions)	$394,567,305
Average value per transfer (in millions)	$4.89
Average daily value of transfers (in millions)	$1,571,981

The European wire network with which CHIPS interfaces is SWIFT (the Society for Worldwide Interbank Financial Telecommunication). SWIFT is a cooperative organized under Belgian law in 1973. It is owned and controlled by its member banks and financial institutions. SWIFT supplies secure messaging services and interface software to over 8,000 financial institutions in 206 countries and territories. In calendar year 2006, SWIFT carried over 2.8 billion messages, and its average daily value of payment messages is estimated at more than $6 trillion.[3]

D. Terminology and Basic Concepts

The following materials introduce you to the terminology and basic concepts of U.C.C. Article 4A. Before proceeding, you may find it helpful to review the "Prefatory Note" to Article 4A (particularly the sections entitled "Description of transaction covered by Ar-

---

1. Source: http://www.federalreserve.gov/paymentsystems/fedwire/fedwirefundstrfann.htm.
2. Source: http://www.chips.org/docs/000652.XLS. For a self-described diagram that illustrates "how CHIPS works," visit http://www.chips.org/about/pages/000702.php.
3. Source: http://www.swift.com.

ticle 4A," "Concept of acceptance and effect of acceptance by the beneficiary's bank," and "Acceptance by a bank other than the beneficiary's bank"), as well as §§ 4A-103, 4A-104, 4A-209, 4A-211, 4A-301, 4A-402, 4A-404, and 4A-406.

BANQUE WORMS v. BANKAMERICA INTERNATIONAL
570 N.E.2d 189 (N.Y. Ct. App. 1991)

ALEXANDER, J. On April 10, 1989, Security Pacific International Bank (Security Pacific), a federally-chartered banking corporation with offices in New York City, mistakenly wired $1,974,267.97 on behalf of Spedley Securities (Spedley), an Australian corporation, into the account of Banque Worms, a French Bank, maintained with BankAmerica International (BankAmerica), another federally-chartered bank with New York offices. Initially intending to make payment on its debt to Banque Worms under a revolving credit agreement, Spedley instructed Security Pacific, which routinely effected wire transfers for Spedley, to electronically transfer funds from Security Pacific to Banque Worms' account at BankAmerica.

A few hours after directing this wire transfer, Spedley, by a second telex, directed Security Pacific to stop payment to Banque Worms and to make payment instead to National Westminster Bank USA (Natwest USA) for the same amount. At the time Security Pacific received the telexes, Spedley had a credit balance of only $84,500 in its account at Security Pacific, but later that morning, Security Pacific received additional funds sufficient to cover the transaction and then began to execute the transaction. However, in mistaken disregard of Spedley's second telex cancelling the wire transfer to Banque Worms, Security Pacific transferred the funds into Banque Worms' account at BankAmerica. The funds were credited to the account after Banque Worms was notified through the Clearing House Interbank Payment System (CHIPS) that the funds had been received. That afternoon, Security Pacific executed Spedley's second payment order and transferred $1,974,267.97 to NatWest USA. Spedley's account at Security Pacific was debited twice to record both wire transfers thus producing an overdraft.

Meanwhile, at Security Pacific's request made prior to the transfer to Natwest USA, BankAmerica agreed to return the funds mistakenly transferred, provided Security Pacific furnished a United States Council on International Banking, Inc. (CIB) indemnity. The indemnity was furnished and the funds returned to Security Pacific on the following day. Banque Worms, however, refused BankAmerica's request that it consent to its account being debited to reflect the return of the funds. Consequently BankAmerica called upon Security Pacific to perform pursuant to the CIB indemnity and return the funds. Security Pacific's attempt to obtain funds from Spedley to cover this indemnity was unavailing because by that time, Spedley had entered into involuntarily liquidation.

Banque Worms brought suit against BankAmerica in the United States District Court for the Southern District of New York seeking to compel BankAmerica to re-credit $1,974,267.97 to Banque Worms' account. BankAmerica instituted a third-party action against Security Pacific for return of the funds, and Security Pacific counterclaimed against Banque Worms seeking a declaration that neither Banque Worms nor BankAmerica were entitled to the $1,974,267.97. Eventually, for reasons not here pertinent, Security Pacific returned the funds to BankAmerica, BankAmerica re-credited Banque Worms' account and was voluntarily dismissed from the case leaving only Banque Worms and Security Pacific as the sole contestants seeking entitlement to the $1,974,267.97.

On their respective motion and cross-motion for summary judgment, the District Court, applying the discharge for value rule, granted judgment for Banque Worms.... Security Pacific appealed to the United States Court of Appeals for the Second Circuit, arguing that New York neither recognized nor applied the discharge for value rule in situations such as this; that the controlling rule under New York law was the "mistake of fact" rule pursuant to which, in order to be entitled to retain the mistakenly transferred funds, Banque Worms was required to demonstrate detrimental reliance. The case is before us upon a certified question from the Second Circuit (see, Section 500.17 of the Court of Appeals Rules of Practice) inquiring "[w]hether in this case, where a concededly mistaken wire transfer by [Security Pacific] was made to [Banque Worms], a creditor of Spedley, New York would apply the 'Discharge for Value' rule as set forth at Section 14 of the Restatement of Restitution or, in the alternative, whether in this case New York would apply the rule that holds that money paid under a mistake may be recovered, unless the payment has caused such a change in the position of the receiving party that it would be unjust to require the party to refund."

For the reasons that follow, we conclude that, under the circumstances of this case, the discharge for value rule should be applied, thus entitling Banque Worms to retain the funds mistakenly transferred without the necessity of demonstrating detrimental reliance.

I

A

In the area of restitution, New York has long recognized the rule that "if A pays money to B upon the erroneous assumption of the former that he is indebted to the latter, an action may be maintained for its recovery. The reason for the rule is obvious. Since A was mistaken in the assumption that he was indebted to B, the latter is not entitled to retain the money acquired by the mistake of the former, even though the mistake is the result of negligence" (Ball v. Shepard, 202 N.Y. 247, 253).... Where, however, the receiving party has changed its position to its detriment in reliance upon the mistake so that requiring that it refund the money paid would be "unfair," recovery has been denied....

This rule has evolved into the "mistake of fact" doctrine, in which detrimental reliance is a requisite factor, and which provides that money paid under a mistake of fact may be recovered back, however negligent the party paying may have been in making the mistake, unless the payment has caused such a change in the position of the other party that it would be unjust to require him to refund" (National Bank of Commerce v. National Mechanics' Banking Association, 55 N.Y. 211, 213; see also, Hathaway v. County of Delaware, 185 N.Y. 368; Mayer v. Mayor, 63 N.Y. 455, 457 ["general rule that money paid under a mistake of material fact may be recovered back ... is subject to the qualification that the payment cannot be recalled when the position of the party receiving it has been changed in consequence of the payment, and it would be inequitable to allow a recovery"]).

The Restatement of Restitution (Second), on the other hand, has established the "Discharge for Value" rule which provides that "a creditor of another or one having a lien on another's property who has received from a third person any benefit in discharge of the debt or lien, is under no duty to make restitution therefor, although the discharge was given by mistake of the transferor as to his interests or duties, if the transferee made no misrepresentation and did not have notice of the transferor's mistake" (Restatement of Restitution [Second] § 14[1]).

The question as to which of these divergent rules New York will apply to electronic fund transfers divides the parties and prompts the certified question from the Second

Circuit. Security Pacific argues that New York has rejected the "discharge for value" rule and has required that detrimental reliance under the "mistake of fact" rule be demonstrated in all cases other than where the mistake was induced by fraud. Banque Worms, on the other hand, invokes the discharge for value rule, arguing that because it is a creditor of Spedley and had no knowledge that the wire transfer was erroneous, it is entitled to keep the funds. It points out that, as indicated by the official comment to section 14(1) of the Restatement of Restitution, the discharge for value rule is simply a "specific application of the underlying principle of bona fide purchase" set forth in section 13 of the Restatement (Restatement of Restitution [Second], §14 [comment a]).

* * *

B

Electronic funds transfers have become the preferred method utilized by businesses and financial institutions to effect payments and transfers of a substantial volume of funds. These transfers, commonly referred to as wholesale wire transfers, differ from other payment methods in a number of significant respects, a fact which accounts in large measure for their popularity. Funds are moved faster and more efficiently than by traditional payment instruments, such as checks. The transfers are completed at a relatively low cost, which does not vary widely depending on the amount of the transfer, because the price charged reflects primarily the cost of the mechanical aspects of the funds transfer (Prefatory Note to Official Comment to Article 4A). Most transfers are completed within one day and can cost as little as ten dollars to carry out a multi-million dollar transaction.... The popularity of wholesale wire transfers is evidenced by the fact that nearly $1 trillion in transactions occur each day, averaging $5 million per transfer and on peak days, this figure often approaches $2 trillion....

Wholesale wire transfers are generally made over the two principal wire payment systems: the Federal Reserve Wire Transfer Network (Fed Wire) and the Clearing House Interbank Payment System (CHIPS). The CHIPS network handles ninety-five percent of the international transfers made in dollars, transferring an average of $750 billion per day.... These funds are transferred through participating banks located in New York because all of the banks belonging to the CHIPS network must maintain a regulated presence in New York. As a result, this state is considered the national and international center for wholesale wire transfers.

The low cost of electronic funds transfers is an important factor in the system's popularity and this is so even though banks executing wire transfers often risk significant liability as a result of losses occasioned by mistakes and errors, the most common of which involve the payment of funds to the wrong beneficiary or in an incorrect amount.... Thus, a major policy issue facing the drafters of the UCC Article 4A was determining how the risk of loss might best be allocated, while preserving a unique price structure. In order to prevent or minimize losses, the industry had adopted and employed various security procedures designed to prevent losses such as the use of codes, identifying words or numbers, call-back procedures and limits on payment amounts or beneficiaries that may be paid.

As indicated above, it was the consensus among various commentators that existing rules of law did not adequately address the problems presented by these wholesale electronic funds transfers. Thus, the National Conference of Commissioners on Uniform State Laws (NCCUSL) and the American Law Institute (ALI) undertook to develop a body of unique principles of law that would address every aspect of the electronic funds transfer process and define the rights and liabilities of all parties involved in such transfers (Prefatory Note to Official Comment, supra). After extensive investigation and debate and through a number of drafts, in 1989, both the NCCUSL and the ALI approved a new Article 4A of the Uniform Commercial Code.... In 1990, the New York State Legislature adopted the new Article 4A and incorporated it into the New York Uniform Commercial Code. Although the new statute, which became effective January 1, 1991, may not be applied retroactively to resolve the issues presented by this litigation, the statute's legislative history and the history of Article 4A of the Uniform Commercial Code from which it is derived and the policy considerations addressed by this legislation, can appropriately inform our decision and serve as persuasive authority in aid of the resolution of the issue presented in this case....

II

Both the NCCUSL and ALI drafters of Article 4A and the New York Legislature sought to achieve a number of important policy goals through enactment of this Article. National uniformity in the treatment of electronic funds transfers is an important goal, as are speed, efficiency, certainty (i.e. to enable participants in fund transfers to have better understanding of their rights and liabilities), and finality. Establishing finality in electronic fund wire transactions was considered a singularly important policy goal.... Payments made by electronic funds transfers in compliance with the provisions of Article 4A are to be the equivalent of cash payments, irrevocable except to the extent provided for in Article 4A....

This concern for finality in business transactions has long been a significant policy consideration in this State. In a different but pertinent context, we observed in Hatch v. National Bank (147 N.Y. 184) that "to permit in every case of the payment of a debt an inquiry as to the source from which the debtor derived the money, and a recovery if shown to have been dishonestly acquired, would disorganize all business operations and entail an amount of risk and uncertainty which no enterprise could bear" (id. at 192).

This concern for finality in business transactions has led to the adoption of a rule which precludes recovery from a third person, who as the result of the mistake of one or both of the parties to an original transaction receives payment by one of them in good faith in the ordinary course of business and for a valuable consideration.... This rule is grounded in "considerations of public policy and convenience for the protection and encouragement of trade and commerce by guarding the security and certainty of business transactions, since to hold otherwise would obviously introduce confusion and danger into all commercial dealings" (22 NY Jur. Payment § 107; see also, Southwick v. First National Bank, 84 N.Y. 420). We have previously held that from these considerations, "the law wisely ... adjudges that the possession of money vests the title in the holder as to third persons dealing with him and receiving it in due course of business and in good faith upon a valid consideration" (Stephen v. Board of Education 79 N.Y. 183, 188).

The discharge for value rule is consistent with and furthers the policy goal of finality in business transactions and may appropriately be applied in respect to electronic funds transfers. When a beneficiary receives money to which it is entitled and has no knowledge that the money was erroneously wired, the beneficiary should not have to wonder whether it may retain the funds; rather, such a beneficiary should be able to consider the transfer of funds as a final and complete transaction, not subject to revocation.

We believe such an application accords with the legislative intent and furthers the policy considerations underlying Article 4A of the New York Uniform Commercial Code. Although no provision of Article 4A calls, in express terms, for the application of the discharge for value rule, the statutory scheme and the language of various pertinent sections, as amplified by the official comments to the UCC, support our conclusion that the discharge for value rule should be applied in the circumstances here presented.

Subject to certain exceptions not here relevant, NYUCC §4-A-209(2) provides that a beneficiary's bank accepts a payment order when the bank pays the beneficiary by crediting the beneficiary's account and notifying the beneficiary of the right to withdraw the credit (see, §§4-A-209[2][a]; 4-A-405[1][i]). When a payment order has been accepted by the beneficiary's bank, cancellation or amendment of that payment order is not effective unless, for example, the order was issued because of a mistake of the sender resulting in a duplicate payment order or an order that directs payment to a beneficiary not entitled to receive the funds (see, §4-A-211[3][b][i][ii]). Where a duplicate payment order is erroneously executed or the payment order is issued to a beneficiary different from the beneficiary intended by the sender, the receiving bank in either case is entitled to recover the erroneously paid amount from the beneficiary "to the extent allowed by the law governing mistake and restitution" (see, §4-A-303[1] and [3]).

More specifically, §4A-303(3) instructs that "[i]f a receiving bank executes the payment order of the sender by issuing a payment order to a beneficiary different from the beneficiary of the sender's order and the funds transfer is completed on the basis of that error, the sender ... [is] not obliged to pay the payment order [ ]. The issuer of the erroneous order is entitled to recover from the beneficiary ... to the extent allowed by the law governing mistake and restitution." The official comment to UCC 4A-303 from which the identical New York statute is derived, explains that although section 4A-402(3) obligates the sender to pay the transfer order to the beneficiary's bank if that bank has accepted the payment order, section 4A-303 takes precedence and "states the liability of the sender and the rights of the receiving bank in various cases of erroneous execution" (see, Official Comment to UCC §4A-303, Comment 1).

Thus, as in the example discussed in Comment 2, where the originator's bank mistakenly directs payment of $2,000,000 to the beneficiary's bank but payment of only $1,000,000 was directed by the originator, the originator's bank is obligated to pay the $2,000,000 if the beneficiary's bank has accepted the payment, although the originator need only pay its bank the $1,000,000 ordered. The originator's bank ordinarily would be entitled to recover the excess payment from the beneficiary, the comment points out, however, that "if Originator owed $2,000,000 to Beneficiary and Beneficiary received the extra $1,000,000 in good faith in discharge of the debt, Beneficiary may be allowed to keep it. In this case Originator's bank has paid an obligation of Originator and under the law of restitution ... Originator's bank would be subrogated to Beneficiary's rights against Originator on the obligation paid by Originator's Bank" (see, Official Comment to UCC §4A-303, Comment 2).

A further example discussed in Comment 3 of the Official Comment is of a duplicate payment order erroneously made, which transfers a second $1,000,000 payment to beneficiary's bank and beneficiary's bank accepts the payment. Although the originator's bank is only entitled to receive $1,000,000 from the originator, it must pay $2,000,000 to beneficiary's bank and would be relegated to a remedy the same as "that of a receiving bank that executes by issuing an order in an amount greater than the sender's order. It may recover the overpayment from Beneficiary to the extent allowed by the law governing mistake and restitution and in a proper case ... may have subrogation rights if it is not entitled to recover from Beneficiary" (Official Comment to UCC 4A-303, supra, Comment 3).

Although it seems clear from these provisions of Article 4A and the official comments that the drafters of UCC Article 4A contemplated that the discharge for value rule could appropriately be applied in respect to electronic fund transfers, Security Pacific argues that to do so would undermine the low cost structure of wholesale electronic fund transfers and impose extraordinary risks upon banks implementing these enormously large transactions. This argument is unpersuasive. Article 4A contemplates, in the first instance, that a mistake such as occurred here can be effectively held to a minimum through the utilization of "commercially reasonable" security procedures in effecting wire transfers. These security procedures are for the purpose of verifying the authenticity of the order or detecting error in the transmission or content of the payment order or other communication (see, e.g., NYUCC § 4-A-201).

For example, under NYUCC § 4-A-202(2), if a bank accepts a payment order that purports to be that of its customer after verifying its authenticity through an agreed upon security procedure, the customer is bound to pay the order even if the payment order was not authorized. The customer will be liable, however, only if the court finds that the security procedure was a "commercially reasonable" method of providing security against unauthorized payment orders (id.). If the bank accepts an unauthorized payment order without verifying it in compliance with a security procedure, the loss will fall on the bank.

Other mechanisms for preventing loss are also provided for in the statute. A bank may avoid a loss resulting from the insolvency of a sending bank by accepting the payment order on the condition that it first receives payment from the sending bank (see, NYUCC §§ 4-A-209[2][a][ii]; 4-A-209[2][c]; 4-A-403[1][a] and [b]; see also, American Law Institute Approves UCC Article Governing Wire Transfers, 52 Banking Report [BNA], p. 1150 [June 5, 1989], supra; Prefatory Note of Official Comment of Article 4A [a receiving bank can always avoid this risk by accepting a payment order after the bank has received payment]). Risk of loss can also be minimized by the institution keeping track of all transactions with a particular bank so that overall debits and credits can be netted.

Application of the discharge for value rule to the circumstances presented here is particularly appropriate. The undisputed facts demonstrate that Security Pacific executed Spedley's initial order directing payment to Banque Worms notwithstanding having already received a cancellation of that order. The District Court also found that the second transfer to NatWest USA was executed despite the fact that Spedley's account did not have sufficient funds to cover this second transfer. Moreover, it appears that, as a creditor of Spedley, Banque Worms was a beneficiary entitled to the funds who made no "misrepresentation and did not have notice of the transferor's mistake."

Accordingly, we conclude, in answer to the certified question, that the "discharge for value" rule as set forth at Section 14 of the Restatement of Restitution, should be applied in the circumstances in this case.

Notes

1. Does Article 4A expressly adopt the "discharge for value" rule?

2. What is the legal significance under Article 4A of BankAmerica's notification to Banque Worms?

3. The *Banque Worms* opinion and the discharge-for-value rule featured prominently in *Credit Lyonnais v. Koval*, 745 So.2d 837 (Miss. 1999). Koval had approximately $87,000 on deposit in a Luxemburg branch of Bank of Credit and Commerce International ("BCCI") when the bank failed. Koval was insured against loss by DPS (a foreign equivalent to the FDIC) for $14,450.45. DPS directed its bank to wire that amount (less minor wire service charges) to an account maintained by Koval at Hancock Bank in the United

States. DPS's bank instructed its U.S. correspondent bank, Credit Lyonnais, to wire the funds. Credit Lyonnais did so—twice, once on July 12, 1993, and again the next day by mistake. Koval, arguing that he had a valid claim against BCCI for his uninsured balance, refused to return the funds from the second wire, so Credit Lyonnais sued Koval. A jury returned a verdict, and judgment was entered, in favor of Koval. The initial appellate court affirmed, but a subsequent appellate court reversed, concluding that Koval was told by the BCCI liquidator that he would receive one wire transfer, so Koval should have known that the second wire transfer was a mistake not intended for him. Koval appealed.

In a 5-4 decision, the Mississippi Supreme Court reversed the second appellate court and reinstated the decision of the initial appellate court (effectively affirming the jury verdict in favor of Koval). After reviewing *Banque Worms* ("the preeminent case on erroneous wire transfers") and discussing the discharge-for-value rule and its underlying policy, the majority of the Mississippi Supreme Court ruled that Koval did not have knowledge of the mistake and therefore was entitled to keep the funds from the second wire transfer under the rule.

¶ 28. Here, the record supports the jury's finding that Koval made no misrepresentations which induced the duplicate payment and that Koval did not have notice of Credit Lyonnais's mistake. The fact that Koval knew that DPS was to pay him around $13,000 as an insurer of his deposit, is not necessarily determinative, where a jury could reasonably find that such knowledge did not amount to notice of Credit Lyonnais's mistake. And the record facts reasonably support just such a finding.

¶ 29. Koval testified that it was his understanding that he would receive money from DPS and from the BCCI liquidators. He knew approximately how much DPS would be paying; but, he did not know how much he would get from the liquidators. Prior to being informed by Credit Lyonnais of the erroneous deposit, Koval discovered that he had additional funds in his account. Upon his discovery, Koval testified that he was not aware of the source of the funds, but assumed that it was associated with BCCI. Koval also stated that the only way to determine who deposited the funds was to speak to a someone in customer service, which he did not do. Also, Koval's bank statement does not show the originator of the two deposits; the statement merely designates them as deposits. It appears that the funds were wired directly into Koval's account. Koval did not know the funds were there until sometime later. It was not until some months later, according to his testimony, that Credit Lyonnais asserted an error had been made. Under the circumstances the jury cannot be faulted for concluding that Koval did not have notice of the mistake.

Id. at 842-43.

The dissenting justices disagreed, concluding that Koval was aware of the mistake and could not invoke the discharge-for-value rule.

¶ 36. The discharge for value rule of restitution does not apply to Koval's case for two reasons. First, Koval was not entitled to receive from the originator (DPS) the funds in the erroneous, duplicate wire transfer. BCCI owed Koval $86,986.46, the amount of money which Koval had on deposit at BCCI at the time BCCI was liquidated. DPS only owed Koval $14,403.54, which was the amount of money to which Koval was entitled under the Luxemburg deposit protection program. Even Koval admitted that DPS only owed him $14,403.54. The $14,403.54 debt owed by DPS to Koval was satisfied by the first wire transfer. The sender/originator of the second wire transfer was DPS, not BCCI, and the funds in the second wire transfer belonged to Credit Lyonnais, not to BCCI; thus, Koval was not entitled to receive from DPS the funds transmitted by the second wire transfer.

¶ 37. Second and most importantly, Koval knew or should have known the second wire transfer was a mistake. Koval testified at trial that he was told that DPS would send him one payment of $14,500 less wire charges but that he received one payment of $14,500 less wire charges on one day and a second payment of $14,500 less wire charges on the next day. Koval claimed at trial that he did not know who wired the funds. The advice on the second wire transfer clearly shows that the funds were wired at the direction of DPS. Without question, Koval was on notice that the second wire was not intended for him since the debt owed by DPS to Koval had been paid in full by the first wire transfer. Koval cannot claim that he had no knowledge that the second wire was a mistake.

Id. at 844.

Do you agree with the majority or the dissent?

Problem 9-1

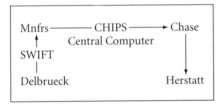

Delbrueck & Co., a German banking, brokerage, and investment bank, was involved in the purchase and sale of large amounts of foreign currency. Delbrueck had an account with Manufacturers Bank who in turn had an account with Chase Bank for the purpose of making transfers to Herstatt. On June 14, Delbrueck entered two foreign currency exchange contracts with Manufacturers for the transfer of funds to the account of Herstatt on June 26, one for the transfer of $10 million, and the other for the transfer of $2.5 million. Delbrueck also had another contract requiring Manufacturers to transfer $10 million to Herstatt on June 27. On June 25, Delbrueck sent a telex payment order to Manufacturers directing it to transfer $12.5 million to Herstatt's account at Chase on June 26. Early on June 26, Delbrueck sent to Manufacturers another telex payment order directing transfer of $10 million to Herstatt's account at Chase on June 27. Later on June 26, at 11:30 a.m., Delbrueck telexed Manufacturers instructing it not to pay Chase the $10 million due Herstatt on June 27. Manufacturers complied. At 11:36 a.m. on June 26, Manufacturers commenced the transfer of $10 million to Chase through the CHIPS terminal at Manufacturers and at 11:37 a.m. another $2.5 million pursuant to Delbrueck's instructions of June 25. Accordingly, the CHIPS operator at Manufacturers directed the CHIPS central computer to debit the account of Manufacturers and to credit the account of Chase, and also instructed Chase to credit the account of Herstatt. After verification, CHIPS executed the order by notifying Chase, and at that moment Manufacturers became bound to Chase under CHIPS rules. At noon on June 26, 45 minutes after Delbrueck learned that Herstatt had closed because of financial failure, Delbrueck telephoned Manufacturers directing it to stop transfer to Chase of the $12.5 million which had just been transferred to Chase pursuant to the instructions of June 25. That afternoon, Manufacturers made several telephone calls to Chase requesting it to cancel the payment order. Chase refused to do so, and at 9:00 p.m. on June 26, Chase credited the Herstatt account with $12.5 million.

1) Who bears the loss of the $12.5 million under Article 4A?

Q: When did Manufacturers "accept" Delbrueck's $12.5 million payment order? §4A-209(a).

Q: When did Manufacturers "execute" Delbrueck's $12.5 million payment order? §4A-301(a).

Q: What obligations did Manufacturers incur upon accepting Delbrueck's $12.5 million payment order? §4A-302.

Q: What was the effect of Delbrueck's telephone call at noon on June 26, directing Manufacturers to cancel that day's transfer of $12.5 million to Chase? §4A-211(a)-(c).

Q: What was the effect of Manufacturers' afternoon telephone calls to Chase requesting it to cancel the payment order of $12.5 million? §§4A-211(a)-(c); 4A-209(b); 4A-405(a)(iii); 4A-403(a)(1), (b), and OC 4; 4A-404(a). Would your analysis change if Manufacturers had made the transfer via Fedwire? §4A-209(b) and OC 6 (first paragraph) and 8 (first paragraph).

2) Was Manufacturers legally obligated to comply with Delbrueck's telex order on June 26 to cancel the $10 million *payment order for June 27*? §§4A-211(a), (b), (e), and OC 3; 4A-209(a).

Note

In the case upon which **Problem 9-1** is based, *Delbrueck & Co. v. Manufacturers Hanover Trust Co.*, 464 F.Supp. 989 (S.D.N.Y.), aff'd, 609 F.2d 1047 (2d Cir. 1979), the court describes the mechanics of making an interbank payment under the CHIPS system. Of particular interest is the description of the verification or security procedures taken in a typical transfer, as follows:

> The New York Clearing House Association ("Clearing House") maintains computer facilities and implements techniques for the transfer of funds among its member banks. In June, 1974 the Clearing House was using the Clearing House Interbank Payments System ("CHIPS"), a computerized interbank system for the transfer of funds involving international customers of Clearing House member banks. Manufacturers and Chase were member banks of the Clearing House and participants in CHIPS.
>
> The CHIPS system eliminates checks for interbank transfers. Under it, funds are transferred electronically through a central computer located at the Clearing House with connecting terminals located at the member and associate member banks.[FOOTNOTE 5]
>
> [FOOTNOTE 5] The mechanics of effecting an interbank payment under the CHIPS systems are as follows: When the paying or sending bank (Manufacturers) receives a telex from one of its customers (Delbrueck) instructing it to make a payment to a receiving bank (Chase), another member of the CHIPS system, for the account of one of the receiving bank's customers (Herstatt), the paying bank (Manufacturers) first tests and verifies the telex. Thereafter, the tested and verified telex is sent to one of the CHIPS computer terminal operators and the payment order contained in the telex is programmed into the terminal by typing into the computer the relevant information—i.e., the identifying codes for the party originating the transfer (Delbrueck), the receiving bank (Chase), the party for whom the receiving bank is receiving the transfer (Herstatt) and the amount of the transfer ($10 million and $2.5 million). This information is then

transmitted to the central computer located at the Clearing House, which, based upon the identifying codes searches out all the necessary clerical information, stores the message and causes a sending form to be automatically typed at the sending bank. In this case, this step was effected on June 25, 1974.

Once the programming of the computer has been completed, the send form is sent to the appropriate area at the sending bank for approval. When a determination is made at the sending bank (Manufacturers) to make the payment, the form is returned to one of the computer terminal operators, reinserted in the computer and the release key is depressed. At that moment, the central computer at the Clearing House causes a credit ticket to be printed automatically at the terminal of the receiving bank (Chase) and a debit ticket to be printed at the terminal of the sending bank (Manufacturers).

Further, the central computer automatically makes a permanent record of the transaction and debits the Clearing House account of the sending bank and credits the Clearing House account of the receiving bank. In this case, this step was effected at 11:36 and 11:37 for the $10 million and $2.5 million payment, respectively, from Manufacturers for Delbrueck to Chase for Herstatt.

The funds received by a receiving bank (e.g., Chase) for the account of one of its customers (e.g., Herstatt) via the receipt of a CHIPS credit message are made available to the customer and can be drawn upon by the customer in the discharge of its obligations that same day, as soon as the receiving bank is aware of the fact that the funds have been received. This running tabulation by the receiving bank is generally referred to as a "shadow balance."

At the end of the day, the central computer correlates all of the day's transactions, nets out the debits and credits, and prints out reports showing which banks owe money and which have money due them. That information is delivered to the New York Federal Reserve Bank the next business day and adjustments are made on the appropriate books of account.

464 F.Supp. at 992.

Prior to 1981, as indicated in the above quote, settlement between banks was done the day following the funds transfer. However, in October of 1981, the rules were changed to require same-day settlement, so that all banks were required to settle between 5:30 p.m. and 5:45 p.m. on the basis of the CHIPS computer report for that day. See also § 4A-403 OC 4.

E. Erroneous Submission or Execution

The following problem examines the legal ramifications of a payment order that has been erroneously submitted or executed by one of the parties.

Problem 9-2

Wallace Enterprises owes $50,000 to Dumbarton Corporation. Wallace decides to pay its bill by wire transfer from its account with First Bank into Dumbarton's account with Second Bank. Wallace directs First Bank to pay $50,000 into "Account #14723 at Second Bank f/a/o Dumbarton Corporation."

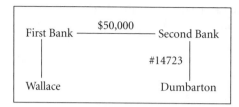

Scenario #1: First Bank forwards the message to Second Bank, which credits Account #14723 for $50,000. Assume that Dumbarton Corporation is not the customer on that account. Who bears the loss? §4A-207. Would your analysis change if the owner of Account #14723 is Vanguard Steel, a major supplier for Wallace Enterprises and a past-due creditor for $85,000?

Scenario #2: First Bank forwards the message to Second Bank after erroneously typing "Account #14732." Second Bank credits Account #14732 for $50,000. Who bears the loss? §§4A-301(a), 4A-402(b)-(c), 4A-303.

Scenario #3: First Bank forwards the message to Second Bank after erroneously typing "$60,000." Second Bank credits Account #14723 for $60,000. Who bears the loss? §§4A-301(a), 4A-402(b)-(c), 4A-303.

Scenario #4: On November 1, Wallace directs First Bank to pay $50,000 on November 10 into "Account #14723 at Second Bank f/a/o Dumbarton Corporation." First Bank jumps the gun, sending a payment order on November 2 to Second Bank, which credits Dumbarton's account for $50,000. On November 5, Wallace's chief financial officer discovers an accounting error and realizes that Wallace owed only $35,000 to Dumbarton. On November 6, Wallace telephones First Bank to cancel the $50,000 payment order. What result? §§4A-209(a), (d); 4A-301(b); 4A-402(c); 4A-211(a), (b), (e).

F. Unauthorized Transfers

Sometimes the criminal element is introduced into a funds transfer, resulting in an unauthorized transfer. The following materials examine the loss allocation rules which apply in these situations.

REGATOS v. NORTH FORK BANK
804 N.Y.S.2d 713 (N.Y. App. 2005)

ROSENBLATT, J.

The United States Court of Appeals for the Second Circuit, by certified questions, asks us whether a commercial bank customer can recover funds that the bank improperly transferred out of his account, even though he did not notify the bank of the unauthorized transfer until well after the time limit stated in his account agreement. This issue requires us to decide whether the one-year period of repose in our Uniform Commercial Code §4-A-505 may be modified by agreement. We also resolve whether UCC 4-A-204(1) requires the bank actually to send the customer notice of an unauthorized transfer in order to trigger the running of a "reasonable time" within the meaning of that section, or whether a private agreement to hold a customer's mail can allow constructive notice to start that period. These are questions of first impression in this Court, and apparently in every other court of last resort in states that have adopted the relevant statutes.

In accord with the United States District Court for the Southern District of New York, we hold for the customer on both questions. The one-year period of repose in UCC 4-

A-505, governing the customer's time in which to notify the bank of the unauthorized transfer, may not be modified by contract. Furthermore, both the one-year statute of repose and the "reasonable time" referred to in section 4-A-204(1), which determines the customer's ability to recover interest on the misallocated money, begin to run when the customer receives actual notice of the improper transfer.

I.

Tomáz Mendes Regatos held a commercial account with Commercial Bank of New York, the predecessor to North Fork Bank. His agreement with the bank required him to notify the bank of any irregularity regarding his account within 15 days after the bank statement and items were first mailed or made available to him.[1] The agreement did not provide for notice to him of electronic funds transfers, except to the extent those transfers appeared on his monthly statements. The bank adopted a practice of holding Regatos's bank statements rather than mailing them to him, and expected him to request the statements when he wanted to see them.

On March 23, 2001, the bank received a funds transfer order from someone it believed to be Regatos, but failed to follow agreed security procedures[2] to confirm the order. Without authorization, the bank then transferred $450,000 out of his account. On April 6, 2001, the bank received another transfer order, again failed to follow its security procedures and without authorization transferred an additional $150,000 out of his account. Together, these transfers represented most of the value of the account.

Regatos did not learn of the unauthorized transfers until he checked his accumulated account statements on August 9, 2001. The transfers were reflected on statements issued on March 23, 2001 and April 25, 2001, but the bank held these statements until he asked for them, following its standard practice in relation to him. He informed the bank of the unauthorized transfers on the day he learned of them, August 9, 2001.

When the bank refused to reimburse Regatos for the lost funds, he sued in the United States District Court for the Southern District of New York. In a comprehensive, well-reasoned opinion, District Judge Shira Scheindlin denied the bank's motion for summary judgment and held that the one-year statute of repose may not be shortened by agreement. The court ruled that, in any event, the 15-day notice period set by the account agreement was unreasonable and invalid. The Federal District Court further held that the UCC 4-A-505 period to notify the bank began to run when Regatos received actual notice of the error on August 9, 2001 (Regatos v. North Fork Bank, 257 F.Supp.2d 632 [S.D.N.Y.2003]).

---

1. The relevant part of the account agreement stated that "[t]he depositor will exercise reasonable care and promptness in examining such statement and items to discover any irregularity including, but not limited to, any unauthorized signature or alteration and will notify the Bank promptly in writing of any such discovery, and in no event more than fifteen (15) calendar days subsequent to the time that such statement and items were first mailed or available to the depositor. In those situations in which the depositor has authorized the Bank to hold his correspondence, this section shall apply as if the depositor received such statement on the date shown on the statement."

2. The security procedures here involved nothing more than checking Regatos's signature against the signature on the faxed transfer order and calling him to confirm (cf. UCC 4-A-201 ["Comparison of a signature on a payment order or communication with an authorized specimen signature of the customer is not by itself a security procedure"]). Apparently, the bank did not require any password, even for large sums. Here, the bank compared the signature on the fax to its signature on file, but did not realize that the fax signature had been forged. The jury found that the bank did not telephone Regatos to confirm that the order was legitimate.

A federal jury found in favor of Regatos. Following UCC 4-A-204, the court awarded him both the principal ($600,000) and the interest from the date the bank improperly transferred the funds.

The bank appealed, and the United States Court of Appeals for the Second Circuit determined that the legal issues necessary to dispose of the case were novel, important questions of New York law. The Second Circuit certified to this Court, and we accepted, the following questions:

"[1] Can the one-year statute of repose established by New York U.C.C. [ ] 4-A-505 be varied by agreement? If so, are there any minimum limits on the variation thereof (such as 'reasonable time') that estop [the bank] from denying Regatos recovery in this case? …

"[2] In the absence of agreement, does New York U.C.C. Article 4-A require actual notice, rather than merely constructive notice? If so, can this requirement be altered by agreement of the parties and was such achieved here?" (Regatos v. North Fork Bank, 396 F.3d 493, 498-499 [2005] [Wesley, J.].)

We answer the first part of the first question "no," rendering the second part academic. We answer the first part of the second question "yes" and the second part of the second question "no."

II.

UCC 4-A-204 establishes a bank's basic obligation to make good on unauthorized and ineffective[4] transfers and, with one exception, forbids any variation of that obligation by agreement. UCC 4-A-204 reads as follows:

"(1) If a receiving bank accepts a payment order issued in the name of its customer as sender which is (a) not authorized and not effective as the order of the customer under Section 4-A-202, … the bank shall refund any payment of the payment order received from the customer to the extent the bank is not entitled to enforce payment and shall pay interest on the refundable amount calculated from the date the bank received payment to the date of the refund. However, the customer is not entitled to interest from the bank on the amount to be refunded if the customer fails to exercise ordinary care to determine that the order was not authorized by the customer and to notify the bank of the relevant facts within a reasonable time not exceeding ninety days after the date the customer received notification from the bank that the order was accepted or that the customer's account was debited with respect to the order. The bank is not entitled to any recovery from the customer on account of a failure by the customer to give notification as stated in this section.

"(2) Reasonable time under subsection (1) may be fixed by agreement as stated in subsection (1) of Section 1-204, but the obligation of a receiving bank to refund payment as stated in subsection (1) may not otherwise be varied by agreement."

Furthermore, UCC 4-A-505 provides that

"[i]f a receiving bank has received payment from its customer with respect to a payment order issued in the name of the customer as sender and accepted by

---

4. Ineffective transfers are those in which the bank has not properly executed security procedures (UCC 4-A-202).

the bank, and the customer received notification reasonably identifying the order, the customer is precluded from asserting that the bank is not entitled to retain the payment unless the customer notifies the bank of the customer's objection to the payment within one year after the notification was received by the customer." (UCC 4-A-505.)

Regatos argues that the one-year statutory period is an integral part of the bank's "obligation ... to refund payment" under UCC 4-A-204(1) and so, pursuant to UCC 4-A-204(2), "may not ... be varied by agreement." The bank and its supporting amici point out that the notice provision is in section 4-A-505, not section 4-A-204(1), and rely on UCC 4-A-501(1), which declares that "[e]xcept as otherwise provided ... the rights and obligations of a party to a funds transfer may be varied by agreement of the affected party."[5] The bank maintains that the customer's duty to notify the bank of the error before recovering misallocated funds is an "obligation" separate from that created by section 4-A-204(1) and therefore modifiable.

We agree with Regatos's reading of the statutes. In context, the policy behind article 4-A encourages banks to adopt appropriate security procedures. Only when a commercially reasonable security procedure is in place (or has been offered to the customer) may the bank disclaim its liability for unauthorized transfers (UCC 4-A-202). Permitting banks to vary the notice period by agreement would reduce the effectiveness of the statute's one-year period of repose as an incentive for banks to create and follow security procedures.

While the issue is close, we cannot accept the bank's argument that the customer's responsibility to notify the bank of its error is modifiable. UCC 4-A-204(1) states that "[t]he bank is not entitled to any recovery from the customer on account of a failure by the customer to give notification as stated in this section."[6] Accordingly, a bank has an obligation to refund the principal regardless of notice, provided such notice is given within one year in accordance with UCC 4-A-505.... Moreover, as the District Court pointed out, section 4-A-505 (the one-year notice period) appears in the "Miscellaneous Provisions" part of the article, not the parts touching upon substantive rights and obligations (Regatos, 257 F.Supp.2d 632, 644 n. 19 [2003]). The period of repose in section 4-A-505 is essentially a jurisdictional attribute of the "rights and obligations" contained in UCC 4-A-204(1). To vary the period of repose would, in effect, impair the customer's section 4-A-204(1) right to a refund, a modification that section 4-A-204(2) forbids.

Article 4-A was intended, in significant part, to promote finality of banking operations and to give the bank relief from unknown liabilities of potentially indefinite duration.... This legislative purpose does not suggest that those interests alter (or should alter)

5. In support of this position, the amici urge that article 4-A is not a consumer protection statute, especially considering that it applies solely to presumably sophisticated commercial parties. While this is true to some extent, the provision in section 4-A-204 refusing to allow parties to modify the bank's basic obligation to refund unauthorized transfer funds contradicts the amici's argument because the provision clearly protects consumers, even commercial consumers, from bearing the burden of this type of bank error.

6. "A customer that acts promptly is entitled to interest from the time the customer's account was debited or the customer otherwise made payment.... But the bank is not entitled to any recovery from the customer based on negligence for failure to inform the bank. Loss of interest is in the nature of a penalty on the customer designed to provide an incentive for the customer to police its account. There is no intention to impose a duty on the customer that might result in shifting loss from the unauthorized order to the customer" (UCC 4-A-204, Comment 2, reprinted in McKinney's Cons Laws of NY, Book 62 1/2 , UCC 4-A-204, at 622).

the statute's fine-tuned balance between the customer and the bank as to who should bear the burden of unauthorized transfers.

Therefore, we hold that the one-year repose period in section 4-A-505 cannot be modified by agreement. By notifying the bank on August 9, 2001, the day he received actual notice, and four or five months after the statements were available, Regatos acted either way within the year-long period of repose. This clearly satisfied the statutory requirement and he is entitled to recover at least his $600,000 principal.

III.

The Second Circuit next asks whether actual notice is required under article 4-A (or whether mere constructive notice will do) and, consequently, whether Regatos is also entitled to recover interest on the misdirected funds.

The bank made Regatos's monthly account statements available for his review, but waited for him to request them rather than send them to him. According to its agreed security procedures, the bank was to reach him by telephone immediately after it received a funds transfer order, to confirm that he had actually authorized the transfer. Other than that call, which the jury found was never made, the only notice available to him would come from his own perusal of the account statements.

In his earlier dealings with the bank, Regatos tended to check his statements regularly. By 2001, however, he reviewed the bank's statements only intermittently. In that year, he asked to see his statements some time before the unauthorized transfer on March 23, 2001 and did not ask again until August 9, 2001, after the bank had generated statements on March 23, 2001 and April 25, 2001. These two statements revealed the unauthorized transfers, but the bank continued to hold the statements until Regatos asked for them. As discussed, he immediately notified the bank of its error when he discovered it on August 9, 2001.

The bank argues that Regatos obtained constructive notice of the transfers on March 23, 2001 and April 25, 2001, when the statements disclosing them were first generated. UCC 4-A-204 requires a customer seeking to recover interest on funds lost due to an unauthorized transfer "to notify the bank of the relevant facts within a reasonable time not exceeding ninety days after the date the customer received notification from the bank that the order was accepted." We agree with Regatos that this requirement may not be waived.

Under the bank's reading of the statute, an agreed 15-day notice period could run before a bank statement was even available for the customer's review. If the burden of checking whether the bank has wrongfully transferred funds out of the customer's account were to fall on the customer, as it would under a constructive notice interpretation, the customer's duty to check would presumably arise as soon as the data became available for review. In electronic funds transfers, the bank would be able to inform an inquiring customer of the transfer well before the formal monthly statement is compiled. Conceivably, the crucial information could be sitting in the bank's possession for weeks, awaiting discovery by the customer. If the customer did not inquire, and the agreement's 15-day period ran, the customer would lose the transferred funds even though the error was entirely the bank's. This seems to us both the logical consequence of a constructive notice system and an unreasonable view of actual banking relationships. Because interpretation of the UCC is always conducted with an eye toward business realities and the predictable consequences of legal rules, we reject a statutory interpretation that conflicts with reasonable business practices.

Policy arguments support an actual notice requirement. An invariable statutory rule provides a bright line for banks and their customers, bringing reliability and certainty to these dealings. Constructive notice is far less exact, leaving too much room for varying interpretation and disorder. If the bank had complied with its security procedures, it would have called Regatos the same day it received each purported transfer order, thereby providing him with actual notice of the events.

Even where customers enter "hold mail" agreements with their banks, the actual notice rule still applies. Just as the one-year notice limitation is an inherent aspect of the customer's right to recover unauthorized payments, the actual notice requirement provides the bedrock for the exercise of that right. Permitting banks to enforce "agreements" to accept constructive notice would defeat article 4-A's guarantee of recovery for unauthorized payments.

In response to the second certified question, we answer that article 4-A requires actual notice, and that this requirement cannot be varied by a "hold mail" agreement, neither to begin the statute of repose, nor to begin "reasonable time" under the account agreement. Regatos notified the bank of his loss within an indisputably reasonable time after receiving actual notice, and is therefore entitled to recover the interest on his lost principal (UCC 4-A-204).

Accordingly, the first part of certified question 1 should be answered in the negative and the second part not answered as unnecessary, and the first part of certified question 2 should be answered in the affirmative and the second part in the negative.

Chief Judge KAYE and Judges G.B. SMITH, CIPARICK, GRAFFEO, READ and R.S. SMITH concur.

(Post-certification opinion by federal appellate court)
431 F.3d 394 (2nd Cir. 2005)

WESLEY, Circuit Judge.

Familiarity with the facts of this case, as set forth in our prior opinion, see Regatos v. North Fork Bank, 396 F.3d 493 (2d Cir. 2005), is assumed. The Commercial Bank of New York and its successor-in-interest, North Fork Bank (together, "CBNY"), appeal from a judgment of the United States District Court for the Southern District of New York (Scheindlin, J.). The District Court denied CBNY's motion for summary judgment, holding that the one-year statute of repose created by UCC §4A-505 cannot be varied by agreement of the parties and accordingly rejected CBNY's argument that Regatos failed to protest the bank account transfers at issue in a timely manner, as required by his account agreement. We found that the appeal raised important, unsettled questions of New York law and certified two questions to the New York Court of Appeals:

> (1) Can the one-year statute of repose established by New York U.C.C. Article 4-A-505 be varied by agreement? If so, are there any minimum limits on the variation thereof (such as "reasonable time") that estop CBNY from denying Regatos recovery in this case?

> (2) In the absence of agreement, does New York U.C.C. Article 4-A require actual notice, rather than merely constructive notice? If so, can this requirement be altered by agreement of the parties and was such achieved here?

Id. at 498, 499.

The New York Court of Appeals accepted certification and answered both questions.... The Court of Appeals answered the first part of the first question in the negative, thereby rendering the second part moot. Embracing to a large extent Judge Scheindlin's reasoning in the district court opinion, the Court of Appeals characterized the period of repose in §4-A-505 as "essentially a jurisdictional attribute of the 'rights and obligations' contained in UCC 4-A-204(1)." ... As such, the court reasoned, any modification of the period of repose is prohibited by section 4-A-204(2).... The Court of Appeals then answered the first part of the second question in the affirmative and the second part in the negative. It considered a constructive notice requirement in conflict with both reasonable business practices and with public policy and refused to find that the actual notice requirement can be varied by agreement....

The Court of Appeals's answers to the certified questions are dispositive of this appeal.

Accordingly, the District Court's order of September 3, 2003, awarding plaintiff Regatos $731,005.48 in principal and prejudgment interest pursuant to a jury verdict is hereby AFFIRMED WITH COSTS.

Problem 9-3

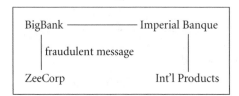

BigBank has agreed to execute wire transfers on behalf of its customer ZeeCorp if ZeeCorp's instructions are encrypted and include a 20-character alphanumeric code. Part of the code is fixed and unique to ZeeCorp. Another part of the code varies with the amount to be wired. A third part of the code varies with the date of the message. The correctness of the two variable parts of the code are tested by an algorithm run by BigBank on receipt of the instruction.

On February 1, 2008, BigBank receives an encrypted instruction to transfer $1.25 million to an account maintained by "International Products, Inc." at Imperial Banque in the Bahamas. BigBank timely complies with the instruction, which includes the correct code.

Timmy Zee, ZeeCorp's chief financial officer, discovers this unauthorized wire transfer when he reviews ZeeCorp's bank statement in March 2008. The account maintained by the perpetrator in the name of "International Products, Inc.," has a balance of less than $100, but the perpetrator is tracked down, confesses, and repays $650,000 before beginning a lengthy prison sentence.

1) Who bears the remaining loss of $600,000 for the unauthorized wire transfer if the perpetrator is Willy Beekaut, chief technology officer for ZeeCorp, who initiated the unauthorized wire transfer after discovering the code through sophisticated computer sleuthing? §§4A-201, 4A-202, 4A-203.

2) Who bears the remaining loss of $600,000 for the unauthorized wire transfer if the perpetrator is Imogene Yuss, a brilliant computer technician, who initiated the unauthorized wire transfer after hacking into ZeeCorp's computer system, accessing the encryption software, and obtaining the code through sophisticated spyware and keystroke monitoring? Does your answer turn on whether Imogene sent the message from ZeeCorp's computer or Imogene's personal computer? Does your answer turn on the presence or absence of ZeeCorp's computer safeguards? §§4A-201, 4A-202, 4A-203.

3) Who bears the remaining loss of $600,000 for the unauthorized wire transfer if the perpetrator is M. Bezzler, a senior employee who has worked for several years in BigBank's wire transfers department? §§4A-201, 4A-202, 4A-203.

4) Would your preceding analysis change if ZeeCorp and BigBank had agreed that Big-Bank would not act on any messages directing payment (i) in excess of $1.2 million or (ii) to a beneficiary (such as "International Products, Inc.") not listed on a pre-approved list? §4A-202(b).

5) Would your preceding analysis change if ZeeCorp and BigBank had contractually agreed that BigBank's loss from any unauthorized payment order "shall not exceed the lesser of (i) $250,000 and (ii) 10% of the amount of the payment order"? §4A-202.

6) Assume that the unauthorized wire transfer is reflected on ZeeCorp's bank statement, which ZeeCorp receives on March 15. Would your previous loss allocation be affected if ZeeCorp did not discover and report the unauthorized wire transfer until (i) May 1, (ii) August 15, or (iii) fourteen months later? §§4A-204; 4A-402(d), (f); 4A-505; 4A-506.

Chapter 10

Credit Cards

A. The Nature and Operation of the Credit Card Payment System

Credit cards. Most of us have at least one. For many of us, the credit card is our most common form of payment device. We love the convenience, the rewards (points, miles, cash back, etc.), the buyer protections, the written monthly summaries, and other advantages associated with credit card use. Consider the following statistics:[1]

- 1.3 billion credit cards were in circulation in the United States in 2004, with 76% of Americans holding at least one credit card (the average graduate student had six);

- the credit card industry mailed over 6 billion credit card offers in 2005 (six offers per household per month);

- fee income from late payments, over-limits, and balance transfers was $43 billion in 2004;

- late fee penalties exceeded $11 billion in 2005;

- general purpose credit cards represented 23.6% of the overall consumer spending volume in 2005 (cash at 13.7%);

- average household credit card debt increased 167% between 1990 and 2004;

- American households charged $412 billion on credit cards in 2004;

- the average interest rate paid on credit cards in 2005 was 14.54%; and

- the average credit card balance in 2005 would require more than 13 years to pay in full if the customer made only minimum payments of 4% at an interest rate of 14%.

Basically there are three types of credit cards—bank cards, such as Mastercard and Visa, travel and entertainment cards, such as American Express and Diners Club, and two-party merchant cards such as Texaco and Sears. We will focus primarily on bank cards.

Typical bank card systems, such as Mastercard and Visa, consist of a group of member banks who issue credit cards to customers for the payment of debts created by their use. Bank card systems also provide clearing house services within various regions of the country through which card receipts are paid. A diagram of a typical bank card system would look something like this:

---

1. These statistics were viewed in May 2007 at a web site hosted by CreditCards.com (specific link: http://creditcards.com/statistics/statistics.php). Used with permission.

A bank becomes a member of a bank card system by entering into an agreement with the host organization, such as Mastercard Inc. Under the agreement member banks agree to be bound by the by-laws and regulations of the system. Pursuant to the agreement member banks agree to issue Mastercards to their customers and to provide clearing house services. These banks are referred to as "issuing banks."

Member banks also promote the system by soliciting merchants to accept their bank cards. In this capacity these banks are known as "acquiring banks" or merchant banks because in due course they will acquire and give credit for the sales slips that are generated by cardholders who make purchases from participating merchants. The soliciting or merchant bank may be the issuing bank or it may be another member bank in the system.

In return for member banks entering the system, Mastercard Inc. agrees to indemnify member banks against nonpayment or other expenses incurred if other member banks fail to pay sales slips pursuant to their agreement and Mastercard by-laws.

When a cardholder presents his card in payment, the merchant will contact the issuing bank electronically or by phone to confirm that the customer is entitled to credit on the card. If the issuing bank authorizes the credit it will also provide a transaction code to be printed on the sales slip.

The sales slips or receipts are collected through a private clearing house system organized under the regulations of Mastercard Inc. This system is separate and distinct from the Federal Reserve collection system for checks.

On a daily basis (unless the parties have provided for electronic authorization and crediting on an individual basis) the receipts will be bundled and deposited with the merchant's bank, which may be the soliciting bank or a local bank that has agreed to accept them on behalf of the soliciting bank. Then the bank will give the merchant credit with right of withdrawal according to the terms of their agreement, which could be immediately or within two or three banking days. The slips then are forwarded to a bankcard association for processing. The association then sends the relevant information to Mastercard Inc., who presents the information to the respective issuing banks for payment. The processing route can vary from one network to another, and to some extent, according to the circumstances.

In most instances the receipts themselves will be held by the acquiring bank and only the requisite information on the slips will be presented electronically to the issuing bank. In this respect the collection process is comparable to the truncated collection system for checks. The issuing bank will then debit the cardholder's account and pay the receipt.

The issuing bank has a right of chargeback in some instances, that is, when the terms of the agreement so provide. For example, if the cardholder returns the merchandise and the merchant accepts it, something the merchant is not obligated to do unless it has so agreed, the merchant then will notify its bank that the cardholder is to be reimbursed, and this information is relayed back to the issuing bank, which then credits the customer's account.

If the credit card is used for a consumer credit transaction, it is subject to the Truth in Lending Regulations—Regulation Z (12 C.F.R. Pt. 226), promulgated to implement the Consumer Credit Protection Act, 15 U.S.C. § 1601 et seq. The primary policy of this law is to "promote the informed use of consumer credit by requiring disclosures about its terms and costs." 12 C.F.R. § 226.1(b).

The following cases will illustrate further the nature and operation of the credit card payment system, some of the legal problems generated by credit card use, and relevant legislation. We divide the material into three discrete topics: liability for unauthorized use, resolution of billing errors, and assertion of claims and defenses against the card issuer.

B. Unauthorized Use

The following three cases address liability for unauthorized use of a credit card. Review CCPA §§ 1602(j), (k), (l), (m), (n), (o), and 1643.

TELCO COMMUNICATIONS GROUP, INC. v. RACE ROCK OF ORLANDO, L.L.C.

57 F.Supp.2d 340 (E.D. Va. 1999)

BRINKEMA, District Judge.

Before the Court is defendant's Motion to Dismiss this breach of contract action between a long-distance phone company and its customer. Plaintiff Telco Communications Group, Inc., ("Telco") is a Virginia corporation that provides long distance phone services. Defendant Race Rock of Orlando, L.L.C., ("Race Rock") is a Florida entity which uses plaintiff's long-distance services. The amount in controversy exceeds $75,000.

On May 20, 1997, Race Rock entered into a Service Order Form with Telco in which Race Rock ordered five telephone calling cards. According to Race Rock, upon receipt of Telco's January 1, 1999, invoice, Race Rock's Director of Finance and Administration, Larry Cate, realized that card # 9863959246BC had been stolen. The invoice included charges for over $92,000 in telephone calls to Iraq, Mexico, Pakistan, Vietnam and numerous places in Central and South America. Race Rock contends that no employee of Race Rock placed the calls or authorized anyone else to place those calls. The physical calling card was in the possession of Race Rock at all times and was destroyed after Race Rock received the invoice.

Upon receipt of the invoice, Cate informed Race Rock's long-distance broker, Mike McNally of TMA, Inc., who reported the unauthorized use to Telco. Cate and McNally had numerous conversations with Telco employees in January, February and March 1999, and Telco allegedly informed Cate that it was aware of fraudulent activity and that Telco understood that Race Rock employees did not make the calls. In March, Cate received a statement from Jeff Renner of Telco indicating that a balance was past due. Cate corresponded with Telco officials and was under the impression that Telco would not hold Race Rock liable for the unauthorized calls. However, on May 25, 1999, Telco informed Race Rock that the invoice was being turned over to an attorney for collection.

On June 22, 1999, Race Rock was served with Telco's Motion for Judgment, in which Telco claimed $92,721.29 arising out of "a contractual relationship to have Plaintiff Telco supply long distance services." Motion for Judgment at ¶ 3. On June 24, 1999, defendant removed the Motion for Judgment to this Court.

Telco alleges that the agreement and relevant federal tariffs provide for liability for unpaid amounts, a 1.5% finance charge for late payments, and attorneys' fees.

Analysis

Defendant Race Rock's Motion to Dismiss presents the novel question of whether a telephone calling card is covered by Regulation Z, the federal regulation that implements the Truth in Lending Act. Within this regulation is a provision that caps liability for unauthorized use of credit cards at $50. See 12 C.F.R. §226.12(b) (1999). Plaintiff maintains that Regulation Z does not govern the instant case because the telephone calling card provided to defendant is not a credit card and, moreover, the parties' relationship is governed by contract and applicable tariffs.

Regulation Z promulgates liability caps for the unauthorized use of credit cards. Section 226.12 provides:

> (b) Liability of a cardholder for unauthorized use–(1) Limitation on amount. The liability of a cardholder for unauthorized use of a credit card shall not exceed the lesser of $50 or the amount of money, property, labor or services obtained by the unauthorized use before notification to the card issuer under paragraph (b)(3) of this section.

"Public utility credit" is normally exempt from the protections of Regulation Z, see §226.3(c), and plaintiff argues that if a telephone calling card is deemed "public utility credit" it would not be covered by Regulation Z's liability caps for unauthorized use. Telephone credit would clearly qualify as public utility credit, which is defined in §226.30 of Regulation Z as:

> An extension of credit that involves public utility services provided through pipe, wire, other connected facilities, or radio or similar transmission (including extensions of such facilities), if the charges for service, delayed payment, or any discounts for prompt payment are filed with or regulated by any government unit.

However, the Federal Reserve Board amended §226.3 to extend the protections of Regulation Z to any credit card, even that which extends public utility credit:

> The provisions of §226.12(a) and (b) governing the issuance of credit cards and the liability for their unauthorized use apply to all credit cards, even if the credit cards are issued for use in connection with extensions of credit that otherwise are exempt from this section.

§226.3 n. 4. Thus, if a telephone calling card involves "an extension of credit," it would be covered by Regulation Z, and the Motion to Dismiss would have to be granted.

I. Does a telephone calling card extend credit?

Defendant relies on several sources of authority for its argument that telephone calling cards involve extensions of credit. First, the Federal Reserve Board clearly recognizes telephone calling cards as credit cards. The Final Rule amending 12 C.F.R. §226.3 explains that "[t]he vast majority of credit cards that are affected by this amendment are telephone calling cards." Truth in Lending; Credit Cards; Issuance and Liability, 49 Fed.Reg. 46,989, 46,990 (1984). Moreover, as the Board of Governors of the Federal Reserve wrote in amending Regulation Z:

> The questions regarding the applicability of the credit card amendments to telephone cards take on particular importance because of the millions of telephone

credit cards that have been issued in recent years ... [U]nless the credit card protections in Truth in Lending apply to these cards, it is unknown what policies
will be set by these companies in the future. It is possible that the companies
will reverse their past policies and seek to impose liability on the cardholder
whose card is used for unauthorized calls.

Id. We view this language as strong evidence of the Federal Reserve's intent to bring telephone calling cards within the protections of Regulation Z.[3]

Plaintiff admits that it provided defendant with five wallet-sized cards that resemble
credit cards. However, plaintiff argues that the calling card number printed on the card,
coupled with a Personal Identification Number (PIN), merely provides a method for ac-
cessing its public utility function from alternate sites and have no independent or potential credit function. Plaintiff relies on Swift v. First USA Bank, et al., No. 98 C 8238,
1999 WL 350847 (N.D.Ill. May 21, 1999), which involved a telephone calling card with
the ability to become a credit card after a single activation call. Such a card is sometimes
referred to as a "dual purpose" card. Under the Truth in Lending Act, companies may
not send unsolicited credit cards, but they may send unsolicited calling cards. See 15
U.S.C.A. § 1642 (1998). Swift sued First USA Bank, the marketing company, and the long
distance company on the theory that they had sent an unsolicited credit card. The court
granted the long-distance company's motion to dismiss, ruling that the long-distance
provider did not extend consumer credit and was therefore not governed by the Truth in
Lending Act. See Swift, 1999 WL 350847 at *4. Plaintiff argues that the Telco card is even
less like a credit card than the card in Swift because the Telco card can never be used to
access credit and has no magnetized strip.

Defendant distinguishes Swift by arguing that the court only granted the long-distance company's motion to dismiss because, under the specific credit arrangement at
issue, only First USA was extending credit. The court noted that the plaintiff did not allege that either the telephone company or the marketing company "extends ... consumer
credit or is 'the person to whom the debt ... is initially payable.'" Swift, 1999 WL 350847
at *4. Because the telephone company was not in the position of extending credit, and
specifically because the customer did not write checks to the telephone company (but
rather to the credit card company), the Swift court distinguished between a "credit" card
and the calling card. However, in the instant case, Race Rock paid Telco directly, and
Telco was the entity that was "extending credit." We agree with defendant that the facts
of our case render Swift inapplicable.

Plaintiff contends that its card is more akin to a membership card because it allows
a user to consolidate all phone charges on a single invoice, no matter the calling location. The card can only be used to purchase telephone time, not other items normally
bought with consumer credit. Further, the card exhibits no characteristics of a normal
credit: there are no extended payment terms, partial payments, credit limits, or restrictions from certain merchants. Furthermore, according to Telco officials, the entire bill
is due and payable in full upon receipt of each monthly invoice. Finally, plaintiff argues
that the actual product is a telephone authorization code; therefore, the physical card is
insignificant.

---

3. Race Rock also argues that it cannot be held liable even for $50 because Telco did not comply
with 12 C.F.R. § 226.12(b)(2), which requires that the credit card issuer notify the user that his or
her liability will not exceed $50 (or any lessor amount) for unauthorized use. According to Race Rock,
Telco did not provide such notice, and, therefore, Race Rock cannot be liable for the $50. We agree
that Telco has not complied with this regulation.

We find plaintiff's arguments unpersuasive. Regulation Z broadly defines "credit" as "the right to defer payment of debt or to incur debt and defer its payment." § 226.2(a)(14). A "credit card" is defined as "any card, plate, coupon book, or other single credit device that may be used from time to time to obtain credit." Id. at § 226.2(a)(15). The Federal Reserve Board has provided a list of examples of credit cards. See 12 C.F.R. pt. 226, Supp. 1 § 226.2(a)(15). Plaintiff correctly notes that a telephone calling card is not specifically listed. We find, however, that the list does include "an identification card that permits the customer to defer payment on a purchase." Id. The telephone calling card at issue precisely meets this definition because the Telco card permitted Race Rock to defer payment on the purchase of telephone time until the invoice was due and payable. We agree with defendant's view of the regulation and conclude that because a telephone calling card allows the holder to obtain services and delay the payment for those services, it is covered by the protections of Regulation Z.

Plaintiff further tries to distinguish its card from a credit card by conceding that its telephone calling card may in fact be a "charge card," which the regulation defines as a "card" used "in connection with an account on which outstanding balances cannot be carried from one billing cycle to another and are payable when a periodic statement is received." 12 C.F.R. pt. 226 Supp. I § 2(a)(15) ¶ 3 (1999). This argument, however, does not save plaintiff's case. Although the regulations recognize a distinction between credit and charge cards in relation to applications and solicitations, disclosure requirements, changes in account insurance, and the effect of state laws, see, e.g., §§ 226.5a, 226.9(e), 226.9(f), and 226.28(d), and appendices G-10 through G-13, the regulations are notably silent as to any distinction between credit and charge cards for the purposes of the applicability of § 226.12(b), the provision governing unauthorized use. Thus, even if the Telco card were deemed a charge card, we find that it is still governed by the protections of Regulation Z.

II. May a party limit the scope of Regulation Z protections through its tariffs?

* * *

We agree with defendant that to find in plaintiff's favor on this issue would allow utility companies to contract around important consumer protections simply by filing tariffs. This result would create confusion and uncertainty among potential customers who would have to investigate each long distance company's FCC tariffs to determine their liability under various calling plans. For these reasons, we find that Telco's filing of a tariff does not exempt its telephone calling cards from the protections of Regulation Z.

CONCLUSION

We conclude that the most persuasive legal argument is defendant's reliance on the Final Rule amending 12 C.F.R. § 226.3, in which the Federal Reserve notes that "[t]he vast majority of credit cards that are affected by this amendment are telephone calling cards." Truth in Lending; Credit Cards; Issuance and Liability, 49 Fed.Reg. 46,989, 46,990 (1984). From that statement, coupled with the broad definitions of credit in the regulations, we are satisfied that it was the clear intention of the Federal Reserve to include telephone calling cards within the protections of Regulation Z's liability cap. Moreover, this conclusion is fully consistent with the consumer protection concerns addressed in Regulation Z. Credit cards are subject to the $50 cap, presumably, because they can be easily stolen and massive bills can be amassed in a very short time. Both of those vulnerabilities are equally present with telephone calling cards. Because the purpose of §226.12(b) is to protect consumers, it makes little difference if the entire telephone bill is due and payable at the end of the month, or if the customer chooses to pay a finance fee. The distinctions between credit cards and charge cards–and credit cards and telephone calling cards, for that matter–are irrelevant to the ultimate goal of protecting the consumer from being liable for unauthorized use. Finally, imposing a $50 cap may provide an incentive to telephone calling card companies to make their accounts more secure, which would cut down on unauthorized use and improve the overall profitability of the enterprise.

For the reasons stated above, defendant's Motion to Dismiss will be GRANTED.

The Clerk is directed to forward copies of this Memorandum Opinion to counsel of record.

MARTIN v. AMERICAN EXPRESS, INC.

361 So.2d 597 (Ala. Civ. App. 1978)

BRADLEY, Judge.

In the summer of 1972 appellant (Robert A. Martin) applied for and was issued an American Express credit card. Approximately three years later, in April of 1975, Martin gave his credit card to a business associate named E. L. McBride. The reason for this action by Martin was apparently to enable McBride to use the card for the purpose of a joint business venture into which the two men had entered. Martin claimed that he orally authorized McBride to charge up to $500 on the credit card. However, in June of 1975 Martin received a statement from American Express which indicated that the amount owed on his credit card account was approximately $5,300. Martin denied that he had signed the credit card invoices which demonstrate that an amount has been charged to the cardholder's account. Upon learning of Martin's refusal to pay the charges incurred through the use of his credit card, American Express filed suit against Martin to obtain the money which it claimed Martin owed.

As the suit proceeded, American Express deposed Martin. In his deposition Martin admitted that he had given his credit card to McBride for use in a joint venture. Martin further stated that he did not know McBride very well, but that he (Martin) was not concerned about that fact because he told McBride not to charge more than $500 to his (Martin's) credit card account. Martin was also relying on a letter which he had sent to American Express prior to giving his card to McBride. Martin testified that in this letter he asked American Express not to allow the total charges on his account to exceed $1,000. Moreover, in his deposition Martin indicated that McBride subsequently returned the credit card to him (Martin) and shortly thereafter disappeared.

On the basis of this deposition American Express moved for summary judgment. The trial court granted this motion and Martin filed an appeal to this court. We affirm.

Despite the various arguments presented by the attorneys in this case, we perceive only one issue before us on this appeal. That issue is whether the use of a credit card by a person who has received the card and permission to utilize it from the cardholder constitutes "unauthorized use" under the Truth in Lending Act, 15 U.S.C.A. §1602(o) and §1643(a). We hold that in instances where a cardholder, who is under no compulsion by fraud, duress or otherwise, voluntarily permits the use of his (or her) credit card by another person, the cardholder has authorized the use of that card and is thereby responsible for any charges as a result of that use.

Section 1643(a)[1], which is of principal concern in this case, limits a cardholder's liability to $50 for the "unauthorized use of a credit card." However, the statutory limitation on liability comes into play only where there is an "unauthorized use" of a credit card.... And § 1602(o) defines "unauthorized use" as the "use of a credit card by a person other than the cardholder (a) who does not have actual, implied, or apparent authority for such use, and (b) from which the cardholder receives no benefit."

American Express argues that the actions of Martin in giving McBride the credit card clearly demonstrated that Martin was not entitled to rely on the $50 limitation for unauthorized use of a credit card. Conversely, Martin relies on the familiar principle of agency law that a principal has the right to presume that his agent will act only within the sphere of his authority, and that in the absence of circumstances sufficient to place him on notice, a principal will not be held liable for his failure to ascertain that his agent is acting beyond the scope of his authority.... Thus, Martin submits that he cannot be held liable for the acts of his agent in that the latter was authorized to charge only $500 to Martin's American Express account, yet exceeded his authority by charging in excess of that amount.

We fail to see the applicability of common law principles regarding agents and the scope of their authority to the statutory provisions in question. The Truth in Lending Act is to be liberally construed in favor of the consumer.... And its terms are to be strictly enforced. However, it is a well-settled rule of statutory construction that the plain language of a statute offers the primary guidance to its meaning.... Accordingly, where the language found in the statute is clear and unambiguous and the words used therein plainly and distinctly demonstrate the intent of the framers of the statute, there is no occasion to resort to any other means of interpretation or to interject common law principles into the statutory provisions in question.

We believe Congress clearly indicated that "unauthorized use" of a card would occur only where there was no "actual, implied or apparent authority" for such use by the cardholder. In the present case Martin maintains that the actual, implied or apparent authority given by him to McBride was limited to the $500 amount which Martin told McBride not to exceed. Thus, Martin says he gave no authority for McBride to charge the large sum which eventually resulted in this suit. Furthermore, Martin asserts that prior to giving the card to McBride, he (Martin) wrote American Express and requested that its employees not allow the amounts charged to his credit card account to exceed $1,000. And since no such action was taken, Martin argues that any sum charged in excess of $1,000 constituted an "unauthorized" charge on his credit card.

We cannot accept either of the above contentions. McBride was actually authorized by Martin to use the latter's card. Martin admitted this fact. And the authority to use it, if not actual, remained apparent even after McBride ignored Martin's directions by charging over $500 to Martin's credit card account. Consequently, Martin was not entitled to rely on the provisions contained in § 1643(a) and he must be held responsible for any purchases made through the use of his card.

Nor are we aware of any requirement, either by statute, contract or trade usage, which would compel a credit card issuer to undertake a policy whereby the issuer would see to

---

1. "A cardholder shall be liable for the unauthorized use of a credit card only if the card is an accepted credit card, the liability is not in excess of $50..., and the unauthorized use occurs before the cardholder has notified the card issuer that an unauthorized use of the credit card has occurred or may occur as a result of loss, theft, or otherwise."

it that charges on a cardholder's account do not exceed a specified amount. Such a policy would place a difficult and potentially disastrous burden on the issuer. We know of no authority which requires a card issuer to perform services of this nature and Martin has provided us with none.

The express intent of Congress in enacting the Truth in Lending Act was to protect the consumer or cardholder against charges for the unauthorized use of his or her credit card and to limit his or her liability for such unauthorized use to a maximum of $50 providing, however, that the conditions set forth in the statute are complied with.... We believe that § 1643(a) clearly indicates that such protection is warranted where the card is obtained from the cardholder as a result of loss, theft or wrongdoing.[2] However, we are not persuaded that § 1643(a) is applicable where a cardholder voluntarily and knowingly allows another to use his card and that person subsequently misuses the card.

Were we to adopt any other view, we would provide the unscrupulous and dishonest cardholder with the means to defraud the card issuer by allowing his or her friends to use the card, run up hundreds of dollars in charges and then limit his or her liability to $50 by notifying the card issuer.[3] We do not believe such a result was either intended or sanctioned by Congress when it enacted § 1643(a).

Based on the pleadings and deposition before it, the trial court concluded that there was no genuine issue as to any material fact and that the moving party (American Express) was entitled to a judgment as a matter of law. The court did not err in reaching such a conclusion. Accordingly, the judgment of the trial court granting American Express's motion for summary judgment is affirmed.

MINSKOFF v. AMERICAN EXPRESS TRAVEL RELATED SERVICES CO.
98 F.3d 703 (2d Cir. 1996)

MAHONEY, Circuit Judge:

Plaintiffs-appellants Edward J. Minskoff and Edward J. Minskoff Equities, Inc. ("Equities") appeal from a final judgment entered September 15, 1995, in the United States District Court for the Southern District of New York ... that granted the motion of defendant-appellee American Express Travel Related Services Company, Inc. ("American Express") for summary judgment dismissing plaintiffs-appellants' complaint. The complaint asserted claims under 15 U.S.C. § 1643, a provision of the Truth in Lending Act, 15 U.S.C. § 1601 et seq. (the "TILA"), and New York General Business Law § 512 for recovery of $276,334.06 paid to American Express through checks forged by an Equities employee to cover charges incurred by that employee on American Express credit cards that were fraudulently obtained and used by the employee.... The complaint also sought a declaratory judgment that plaintiffs-appellants were not liable for the balance of the unpaid charges outstanding on those credit cards, but the district court granted Ameri-

---

2. This construction is supported by two of the conditions for limitation of liability in unauthorized use situations under § 1643(a). Those conditions are: (1) that the card issuer has provided the cardholder with a self-addressed, pre-stamped notification to be mailed by the cardholder in the event of loss or theft of the credit card; and (2) that the unauthorized use occurs before the cardholder has notified the card issuer that an unauthorized use of the credit card has occurred or may occur as the result of loss, theft or otherwise.

3. By this statement we do not mean to imply that Martin acted dishonestly or deceitfully in this matter. Indeed, he appears merely to be the victim of his own generosity.

can Express summary judgment in the amount of $51,657.71 on its counterclaim for that balance....

We vacate the judgment of the district court and remand for further proceedings.

Background

Minskoff is the president and chief executive officer of Equities, a real estate holding and management firm. In 1988, Equities opened an American Express corporate card account (the "Corporate Account") for which one charge card was issued in Minskoff's name. Minskoff also maintained a personal American Express account, which was established in 1963.

In October 1991, Equities hired Susan Schrader Blumenfeld to serve as its assistant to the president/office manager. Blumenfeld was responsible for both the personal and business affairs of Minskoff, and her duties included screening Minskoff's mail, reviewing vendor invoices and credit card statements (including statements for the Corporate Account), and forwarding such invoices and statements to Equities' bookkeepers for payment. Prior to Blumenfeld's employment with Equities, Minskoff personally reviewed all Corporate Account statements; after hiring Blumenfeld, he no longer reviewed any of these statements.

In March 1992, defendant-appellee American Express received an application for an additional credit card to issue from the Corporate Account in Blumenfeld's name. The application had been pre-addressed by American Express and mailed to Minskoff at his business address. It had been completed and submitted by Blumenfeld without the knowledge or acquiescence of Equities or Minskoff. American Express issued the supplemental card and mailed it to Equities' business address. From April 1992 to March 1993, Blumenfeld charged a total of $28,213.88 on that card.

During this period, American Express sent twelve monthly billing statements for the Corporate Account to Equities' business address. Each statement listed both Blumenfeld and Minskoff as cardholders on the Corporate Account, and separately itemized Corporate Account charges for Minskoff and Blumenfeld. These twelve statements show a total of $28,213.88 in charges attributed to Blumenfeld and $23,099.37 in charges attributed to Minskoff, for a total of $51,313.25. Between April 1992 and March 1993, American Express received twelve checks, drawn on accounts maintained by Minskoff or Equities at Manufacturers Hanover Trust ("MHT"), in payment of these charges, with each check made payable to American Express and bearing Equities' Corporate Account number. Minskoff did not review any statements or cancelled checks received during 1992 and 1993 from either his personal account with MHT or the Equities account with MHT.

In July 1992, American Express sent Minskoff an unsolicited invitation to apply for a platinum card. Blumenfeld accepted the invitation on behalf of Minskoff, again without the knowledge or acquiescence of either Minskoff or Equities.[3] Blumenfeld also submitted a request for a supplemental card to issue from this new account (the "Platinum Account") in her name. When platinum cards arrived in both Minskoff's and Blumenfeld's names, Blumenfeld gave Minskoff his card, claiming that it was an unsolicited upgrade of his American Express card privileges. Minskoff proceeded to use his platinum card for occasional purchases, and Blumenfeld charged approximately $300,000 to the Platinum Account between July 1992 and November 1993.

---

3. It is not clear from the record whether the invitation to receive a platinum American Express card was directed to Minskoff in his individual capacity or in his official position as president of Equities. The solicitation was preprinted with Minskoff's home address, and the record does not reveal how it ended up in Blumenfeld's hands at the Equities office.

Between August 1992 and November 1993, American Express mailed sixteen Platinum Account monthly billing statements to Equities' business address. Each statement named Blumenfeld and Minskoff as cardholders and itemized charges for each separately. These statements attributed a total of $250,394.44 in charges to Blumenfeld and $10,497.31 to Minskoff, for a total of $260,891.75. These bills were paid in full with checks drawn on the MHT accounts, made payable to American Express, and bearing the Platinum Account number.

In November 1993, Equities' controller, Steven Marks, informed Minskoff that MHT had called to inquire about a check made payable to American Express for approximately $41,000 that had been written on Equities' MHT account. Minskoff stopped payment on the check, initiated an internal investigation of Equities' accounts that revealed the full extent of Blumenfeld's fraudulent activities, and gave notice to American Express of Blumenfeld's unauthorized charges to the Platinum and Corporate Accounts. Blumenfeld subsequently stated in an affidavit that she had forged approximately sixty checks drawn on Equities' MHT account and Minskoff's personal MHT account, including at least twenty payments to American Express for charges to the Platinum and Corporate Accounts. Although some of these checks were used to pay legitimate obligations of plaintiffs-appellants, an accounting analysis attributed losses totalling $412,684.06 to Blumenfeld's theft. In January 1994, Blumenfeld agreed to repay $250,000 to Minskoff and Equities in return for their promise not to institute legal action against her.

Plaintiffs-appellants initiated this action in the United States District Court for the Southern District of New York on February 15, 1994. As previously noted, they sought (1) to recover $276,334.06 that had been paid to American Express in satisfaction of unauthorized charges by Blumenfeld, and (2) a declaration that they were not liable for the outstanding balances on the Platinum Account. The district court, however, dismissed their complaint and awarded American Express $51,657.71 on its counterclaim for that balance.... The district court reasoned that the $50 limit on a cardholder's liability for the unauthorized use of the cardholder's credit card specified in 15 U.S.C. § 1643(a)(1)(B), see supra note 1, did not apply to plaintiffs-appellants because their negligence in failing to examine credit card statements that would have revealed Blumenfeld's fraudulent charges "resulted in an appearance of authority [to use the cards] in Blumenfeld." ...

This appeal followed.

Discussion

We review de novo the district court's grant of summary judgment.... In determining whether a grant of summary judgment is appropriate, the district court must "draw all factual inferences in favor of, and take all factual assertions in the light most favorable to, the party opposing summary judgment." Rule v. Brine, Inc., 85 F.3d 1002, 1011 (2d Cir. 1996). A grant of summary judgment should be affirmed only where "there is no genuine issue as to any material fact and ... the moving party is entitled to a judgment as a matter of law." Fed.R.Civ.P. 56(c).

Plaintiffs-appellants contend that because Blumenfeld obtained the platinum and corporate credit cards through forgery and fraud, her use of the cards is per se unauthorized under section 1643, see supra note 1, and plaintiffs-appellants' liability is therefore limited to $50 by section 1643(a)(1)(B). Section 1643 applies, however, only in the case of an "unauthorized use" of a credit card. See § 1643(a)(1), (d). The term "unauthorized use" is defined as "a use of a credit card by a person other than the cardholder who does not have actual, implied, or apparent authority for such use and from which the cardholder receives no benefit." 15 U.S.C. § 1602(o). In determining whether a use is unauthorized, "Congress apparently contemplated, and courts have accepted, primary reliance on background principles of agency law in determining the liability of cardholders for charges incurred by third-party card bearers." Towers World Airways v. PHH Aviation Systems, 933 F.2d 174, 176–77 (2d Cir.), cert. denied, 112 S.Ct. 87 (1991).

Under general principles of agency, the authority of an agent "is the power of the agent to do an act or to conduct a transaction on account of the principal which, with respect to the principal, he is privileged to do because of the principal's manifestations to him." Restatement (Second) of Agency (the "Restatement") § 7 cmt. a (1958). Such authority may be express or implied, but in either case it exists only where the agent may reasonably infer from the words or conduct of the principal that the principal has consented to the agent's performance of a particular act.

Apparent authority is "entirely distinct from authority, either express or implied," and arises from the "written or spoken words or any other conduct of the principal which, reasonably interpreted, causes [a] third person to believe that the principal consents to have [an] act done on his behalf by the person purporting to act for him." ... Apparent authority, then, is normally created through the words and conduct of the principal as they are interpreted by a third party, and cannot be established by the actions or representations of the agent....

The existence of apparent authority is normally a question of fact, and therefore inappropriate for resolution on a motion for summary judgment.... However, a principal may be estopped from denying apparent authority if (1) the principal's intentional or negligent acts, including acts of omission, created an appearance of authority in the agent, (2) on which a third party reasonably and in good faith relied, and (3) such reliance resulted in a detrimental change in position on the part of the third party....

Viewing the facts in the light most favorable to plaintiffs-appellants, it is clear that Blumenfeld acted without actual or implied authority when she forged the platinum card acceptance form and supplemental card applications. Accordingly, plaintiff-appellants cannot be held accountable for Blumenfeld's initial possession of corporate and platinum cards. As we stated in Towers:

> Though a cardholder's [voluntary] relinquishment of possession may create in another the appearance of authority to use the card, [15 U.S.C. §§ 1602(o) and 1643] clearly preclude[ ] a finding of apparent authority where the transfer of the card was without the cardholder's consent, as in cases involving theft, loss, or fraud. However elastic the principle of apparent authority may be in theory, the language of the 1970 Amendments [to the TILA] demonstrates Congress's intent that the category of cases involving charges incurred as a result of involuntary card transfers are to be regarded as unauthorized under sections 1602(o) and 1643.

Towers, 933 F.2d at 177.

This result is consistent with the underlying policy of the TILA to protect credit card holders against losses due to theft or fraudulent use of credit cards on the theory that the card issuer is in the better position to prevent such losses. See Walker Bank & Trust Co. v. Jones, 672 P.2d 73, 77 (Utah 1983) (Durham, J., dissenting).... We accordingly disagree with the decision of the district court insofar as it imposed upon plaintiffs-appellants the entire burden of the unauthorized charges made by Blumenfeld to the Corporate and Platinum Accounts....

However, while we accept the proposition that the acquisition of a credit card through fraud or theft cannot be said to occur under the apparent authority of the cardholder, our statement in Towers should not be interpreted to preclude a finding of apparent authority for the subsequent use of a credit card so obtained. Under the rule urged by plaintiffs-appellants, a cardholder could disregard both credit card and bank statements indefinitely, or even fail to act upon a discovery that an employee had fraudulently obtained and was fraudulently using a credit card, and still limit his liability for an employee's fraudulent purchases to $50. Cf. Transamerica Ins. Co. v. Standard Oil Co., 325 N.W.2d 210, 215 (N.D. 1982) ("[A]n unscrupulous cardholder could allow another to charge hundreds of dollars in goods and services and then attempt to limit his liability to 50 dollars."). Nothing in the TILA suggests that Congress intended to sanction intentional or negligent conduct by the cardholder that furthers the fraud or theft of an unauthorized card user. We therefore agree with the district court to the extent that it decided that the negligent acts or omissions of a cardholder may create apparent authority to use the card in a person who obtained the card through theft or fraud.... Apparent authority created through the cardholder's negligence does not, however, retroactively authorize charges incurred prior to the negligent acts that created the apparent authority of the user.

Applying these principles to the case at hand, we address the district court's conclusion that plaintiffs-appellants' failure to examine credit card and bank statements amounts to negligence which created an appearance of authority in Blumenfeld to use the card.... Under New York law, consumers are obligated to "exercise reasonable care and promptness to examine [bank] statement[s] ... to discover [any] unauthorized signature or any alteration." N.Y.U.C.C. §4-406(1).... This provision is derived from a common law obligation to examine bank statements and report forgeries or alterations, and it is based upon a determination that "the depositor [is] in the better position to discover an alteration of the check or forgery of his or her own signature." Woods v. MONY Legacy Life Ins. Co., 641 N.E.2d 1070, 1071 (1994) (extending application of N.Y.U.C.C. §4-406 to brokerage accounts).

This policy is no less applicable to credit card holders than it is to bank depositors. Once a cardholder has established a credit card account, and provided that the card issuer is in compliance with the billing statement disclosure requirements of 15 U.S.C. §1637, the cardholder is in a superior position to determine whether the charges reflected on his regular billing statements are legitimate. A cardholder's failure to examine credit card statements that would reveal fraudulent use of the card constitutes a negligent omission that creates apparent authority for charges that would otherwise be considered unauthorized under the TILA....

It is undisputed that between April 1992 and November 1993, American Express mailed to Equities' business address at least twenty-eight monthly billing statements documenting charges made to the Platinum and Corporate Accounts. Each of those statements clearly lists Blumenfeld as a cardholder, and each specifically itemizes those charges attributable to her credit card. During that same period, MHT mailed to Equities' business address numerous bank statements showing that checks made payable to American Express had been drawn on Equities' business account and Minskoff's personal account to pay these American Express charges. Minskoff concedes that he failed to examine any of these statements until November 1993, and no other employee or agent of Equities (other than Blumenfeld) became aware of the disputed monthly payments to American Express prior to the inquiry by Bankers Trust in November 1993. These omissions on the part of plaintiffs-appellants created apparent authority for Blumenfeld's continuing use of the cards, especially because it enabled Blumenfeld to pay all of the American Express statements with forged checks, thereby fortifying American Express' continuing impression that nothing was amiss with the Corporate and Platinum Accounts.

Plaintiffs-appellants argue that summary judgment is inappropriate because they exercised reasonable care in the hiring and supervision of Blumenfeld and in the implementation and administration of internal accounting procedures designed to detect and prevent fraud. In this case, however, while American Express concedes that Equities employed bookkeepers who were responsible, *inter alia*, for reviewing credit card statements and arranging for their payment, as well as reviewing bank statements and cancelled checks, the inadequate manner in which these procedures were performed from April 1992 to November 1993 enabled Blumenfeld to acquire unauthorized American Express credit cards, run up more than $300,000 in invalid American Express charges, and pay for them with approximately twenty forged checks drawn on Equities' MHT account and Minskoff's personal MHT account, without detection.

A cursory review of any of the American Express statements would have disclosed charges by Blumenfeld made with an unauthorized credit card. A review of any MHT statement would have disclosed one or more payments to American Express (or, if the cancelled checks had previously been removed by Blumenfeld, charges that could not be matched to cancelled checks) generally in amounts far exceeding Minskoff's habitual American Express charges. We are not dealing in this case with an occasional transgression buried in a welter of financial detail. In our view, once a cardholder receives a statement that reasonably puts him on notice that one or more fraudulent charges have been made, he cannot thereafter claim lack of knowledge. The district court was justified in determining that no reasonable jury could conclude that this standard had been satisfied as to plaintiffs-appellants on the record presented in this case, warranting summary judgment in favor of American Express to the extent that we have previously indicated.

In our view, the appropriate resolution in this case is provided by adapting the ruling in Transamerica to provide that

> [American Express] is liable for [Blumenfeld's] fraudulent purchases [as to each credit card] from the time the credit card was issued until [plaintiffs-appellants] received the first statement from [American Express] containing [Blumenfeld's] fraudulent charges plus a reasonable time to examine that statement. After that time, [plaintiffs-appellants are] liable for the remaining fraudulent charges.

325 N.W.2d at 216. We accordingly vacate the judgment of the district court and remand for further proceedings to make this determination. We leave it to the district court in the first instance to ascertain whether, as the record is developed on remand, any issues require submission to a jury. The judgment of the district court is vacated and the case is remanded for further proceedings. The parties shall bear their own costs.

DBI ARCHITECTS, P.C. v. AMERICAN EXPRESS TRAVEL-RELATED SERVICES CO.

388 F.3d 886 (D.C. Cir. 2004)

Rogers, Circuit Judge:

The Truth in Lending Act ("TILA"), 15 U.S.C. § 1601, et seq. (2000), limits the liability of a cardholder for "unauthorized use of a credit card," id. § 1643(a)(1), which is defined as use without "actual, implied, or apparent authority" that does not benefit the cardholder, id. § 1602(o). The principal issue on appeal is what creates apparent authority to limit cardholder protection under § 1643. The district court, in granting summary judgment to American Express Travel-Related Services Co. ("AMEX"), ruled that DBI Architects, P.C. ("DBI") clothed its accounting manager with apparent authority to use its corporate AMEX account by failing to examine monthly billing statements that identified all cardholders and their charges. We hold that, while DBI did not clothe its accounting manager with apparent authority by failing to inspect its monthly billing statements, DBI did clothe its accounting manager with apparent authority by repeatedly paying after notice all charges made by the accounting manager on its corporate AMEX account, thereby misleading AMEX reasonably to believe that the accounting manager had authority to use the account. We remand DBI's § 1643 claim to the district court to determine precisely how many payments created apparent authority and thus limited DBI's protection under TILA. Otherwise, we affirm the grant of summary judgment.

I.

DBI is a corporation with its principal place of business in the District of Columbia. It had an AMEX corporate credit card account, which it authorized certain employees to use. On March 14, 2001, DBI appointed Kathy Moore as the Accounting Manager for its District of Columbia and Virginia offices. In that position, Moore was in charge of both approval and payment functions in the cash disbursement system: she controlled accounts receivable, accounts payable, corporate checking, corporate credit cards, and all other financial aspects of DBI's business. She had authority to issue DBI corporate checks to pay bills and invoices from vendors, was "entrusted with the duty of affixing authorized signatures and approvals to checks and other documents," and was responsible for the receipt, review, and payment of DBI's AMEX invoices....

On or about August 10, 2001, AMEX added Moore as a cardholder on DBI's corporate account at Moore's request and without DBI's knowledge or approval. On August 22, 2001, AMEX sent DBI an account statement identifying Moore as a corporate cardholder and itemizing her annual membership fee. From August 2001 to May 2002, Moore charged a total of $134,810.40 to DBI's corporate AMEX card, including $1,555.51 in authorized corporate charges and $133,254.79 in unauthorized charges for clothing, travel, jewelry, and other personal items. During this period, AMEX sent DBI ten monthly billing statements, each listing Moore as a corporate cardholder and itemizing her charges. Between August 2001 and June 2002, Moore paid for these charges with thirteen DBI checks made payable to AMEX. In addition, between July 2001 and March 2002, Moore paid for $162,139.04 in charges on her personal AMEX card with fourteen DBI checks made payable to AMEX. Most of these checks were signed or stamped in the name of Alan L. Storm, the president of DBI; none were signed in Moore's own name.

On May 31, 2002, DBI notified AMEX of Moore's fraudulent charges and requested a refund of $133,254.79 for the corporate account and $162,139.04 for the personal account. AMEX denied the request. DBI sued AMEX in the Superior Court for the District of Columbia, alleging, in Count One of the complaint, that AMEX had violated TILA, 15 U.S.C. § 1643, by refusing to repay DBI for the $133,254.79 in fraudulent charges made by Moore on DBI's corporate AMEX card. Count Two of the complaint alleged that AMEX was liable for conversion for using DBI's corporate funds to credit the $162,139.04 in charges on Moore's personal AMEX card. Following AMEX's removal of the case to the United States District Court for the District of Columbia, AMEX moved for summary judgment, and DBI moved for partial summary judgment on the issue of liability. The district court granted AMEX's motion for summary judgment, denying DBI recovery except for two months of charges on the corporate account, and DBI appeals. Our review of the grant of summary judgment is de novo....

II.

Congress enacted the credit card provisions of the Truth in Lending Act "in large measure to protect credit cardholders from unauthorized use perpetrated by those able to obtain possession of a card from its original owner." *Towers World Airways Inc. v. PHH Aviation Sys. Inc.*, 933 F.2d 174, 176 (2d Cir.1991).... Responding to concerns about the abuse of uninformed cardholders by a growing credit card industry ... Congress strictly limited the cardholder's liability for "unauthorized" charges, see 15 U.S.C. § 1643(a)(1), placed the burden of establishing cardholder liability on the card issuer, see id. § 1643(b), and imposed criminal sanctions for the fraudulent use of credit cards, see id. § 1644. Specifically, § 1643 provides that a cardholder is not liable for the unauthorized use of a card unless the issuer previously provided the cardholder with information about potential liability, a means of reporting a lost or stolen card, and a means of identifying the authorized user. Id. § 1643(a)(1)(c), (D), (F). Even then, the cardholder's maximum liability is $50, id. at § 1643(a)(1)(B), and in any event, the cardholder is not liable for unauthorized charges incurred after the cardholder notifies the issuer of the fraud. Id. § 1643(a)(1)(E).

The protections under § 1643, however, apply only to "unauthorized use," which Congress defined as "a use of a credit card by a person other than the cardholder who does not have actual, implied, or apparent authority for such use and from which the cardholder receives no benefit." Id. § 1602(o); see Regulation Z, 12 C.F.R. § 226.12(b)(1) n. 22. Because the parties agree that Moore had neither actual nor implied authority to use DBI's corporate AMEX card, the question is whether Moore's charges were "authorized" as a result of her apparent authority to use the card and thus fall outside the protections available to DBI under § 1643....

The Federal Reserve Board's official staff interpretation of Regulation Z, 12 C.F.R. § 226.12(b)(1), states that "whether [apparent] authority exists must be determined under state or other applicable law." 12 C.F.R. pt. 226, Supp. I, at 418. The Second Circuit observed in *Towers World Airways*, 933 F.2d at 176-77, that "[b]y defining 'unauthorized use' as that lacking in 'actual, implied, or apparent authority,' Congress apparently contemplated, and courts have accepted, primary reliance on background principles of agency law in determining the liability of cardholders for charges incurred by third-party card bearers." The common law rule provides that apparent authority arises from the "written or spoken words or any other conduct of the principal which, reasonably interpreted, causes [a] third person to believe that the principal consents to have [an] act done on his behalf by the person purporting to act for him." Restatement (Second) of Agency § 27, at 103 (1958). The District of Columbia has adopted a similar definition: "apparent authority of an agent arises when the principal places the agent in such a position as to *mislead* third persons into believing that the agent is clothed with authority which in fact he does not possess." ... The existence of apparent authority is a question of fact that should normally be left to the jury.... However, a principal may be estopped from denying apparent authority if the principal intentionally or negligently created an appearance of authority in the agent, on which a third party relied in changing its position.... We need not decide whether District of Columbia law or the common law of agency provides the rule of decision, as we discern no difference between them for the purposes of this case.

The district court ruled that Moore did not have apparent authority to become a cardholder on DBI's corporate AMEX account. But distinguishing between the acquisition and use of a credit card, the court ruled that DBI's negligent failure to examine its monthly billing statements from AMEX created apparent authority for Moore's use of the corporate card. The court relied on an analogy to District of Columbia banking law, under which depositors are required to "exercise reasonable promptness in examining the statement ... to determine whether any payment was not authorized," D.C.Code § 28:4-406(c), and embraced the analysis of the Second Circuit in *Minskoff v. American Express Travel Related Services Co.*, 98 F.3d 703 (2d Cir.1996), which involved a nearly identical fact situation. There, as here, an employee of a corporation fraudulently acquired a corporate credit card from AMEX, charged personal expenses to the card, and paid for the charges with corporate checks. AMEX sent monthly statements listing the employee as a cardholder and itemizing the employee's charges, but the corporation failed to review the statements, continued to make payments, and demanded a refund upon discovering the fraud....

The Second Circuit held in *Minskoff* that TILA "clearly preclude[s] a finding of apparent authority where the transfer of the card was without the cardholder's consent, as in cases involving theft, loss, or fraud." ... Regarding the employee's use of the card, however, the court drew an analogy from New York banking law, under which depositors are obligated to "exercise reasonable care and promptness" in examining their bank statements and reporting unauthorized charges, id. at 709 (quoting N.Y. U.C.C. §4-406(1)), and held that a "cardholder's failure to examine credit card statements that would reveal fraudulent use of the card constitutes a negligent omission that creates apparent authority for charges that would otherwise be considered unauthorized under the TILA." ... The court noted that the corporation's negligence "enabled [the employee] to pay all of the American Express statements with forged checks, thereby fortifying American Express' continuing impression that nothing was amiss." ... The court reasoned that, as a policy matter, cardholders are in a better position than card issuers to discover fraudulent charges, and that "[n]othing in the TILA suggests that Congress intended to sanction intentional or negligent conduct by the cardholder that furthers the fraud or theft of an unauthorized card user." ... Accordingly, the court concluded that AMEX was liable only for the fraudulent charges incurred before the corporation had a reasonable opportunity to examine its first billing statement, and remanded the case for the district court to make this determination, including whether, as the record developed on remand, any issues required submission to the jury....

On appeal, DBI contends that the district court erred in following *Minskoff*. Because TILA and Regulation Z oblige the card issuer to protect the cardholder from fraud, DBI maintains that the district court erred in imposing on the cardholder a "novel duty ... derived from a rough analogy to D.C. banking law" to inspect monthly billing statements and to notify the card issuer of fraud.... AMEX responds that, by continuing to pay without objection all charges on its corporate account, DBI vested Moore with apparent authority to use its corporate credit card. We conclude that both parties are correct. DBI is correct that its failure to inspect its monthly billing statements did not clothe Moore with apparent authority to use its corporate AMEX account. AMEX is correct that DBI clothed Moore with apparent authority to use its corporate AMEX account by repeatedly paying without protest all of Moore's charges on the account after receiving notice of them from AMEX.

Nothing in the law of agency supports the district court's conclusion that DBI's mere failure to review its monthly billing statements created apparent authority for Moore to use its corporate AMEX account. DBI's silence without payment would be insufficient to lead AMEX reasonably to believe that Moore had authority to use DBI's corporate account, as such silence would be equally consistent with DBI's never having received the statements.... Indeed, in *Crestar Bank, N.A. v. Cheevers*, 744 A.2d 1043 (D.C.2000), the District of Columbia Court of Appeals held that a cardholder's "failure to object to the [disputed] charges within a reasonable time ... [did not] constitut[e] ratification and acceptance of those charges." ... The court distinguished *Minskoff* as involving more than mere silence: whereas in *Crestar Bank* there was no relationship between the cardholder and the third party who made the fraudulent charges, and the cardholder neither received notice of the charges nor paid them, in *Minskoff* the cardholder's employee made the fraudulent charges, and the cardholder both received notice of the charges and paid them in full for sixteen consecutive months....

Further, the view that mere silence does not confer apparent authority is consistent with the text and purpose of § 1643 and Regulation Z. The plain language of § 1643 does not require a cardholder to inspect monthly billing statements in order to invoke its protections. The text sets no preconditions to its protections, such as an exhaustion requirement, and makes no reference to other remedies, such as those under the Fair Credit Billing Act, 15 U.S.C. § 1666 (2000), which permits – but does not require – a cardholder to seek correction of billing errors by reporting them to the card issuer in writing. Rather, § 1643 places the risk of fraud primarily on the card issuer. Designed to remedy the problem that "if a consumer does not immediately discover and report a card loss, he can be liable for thousands of dollars in unauthorized purchases made by a fast working thief," S.Rep. No. 91-737, at 5, § 1643 requires the card issuer to demonstrate that it has taken certain measures to protect the cardholder from fraud before it can hold a cardholder liable for any unauthorized charges. 15 U.S.C. § 1643(a)(1), (b). The text of § 1643 thus indicates that Congress intended for the card issuer to protect the cardholder from fraud, not the other way around. Explaining the rationale underlying Congress's "policy decision that it is preferable for the issuer to bear fraud losses from credit card use," one commentator has suggested that Congress understood that "[a] system of issuer liability is preferable because it stimulates more efficient precautions against losses," with cardholder liability incurred "only [to] the degree ... necessary to ensure proper control of his card and prompt notice of loss to the issuer." ...

Regulation Z likewise reflects the remedial purpose of § 1643. Filling in the gap between TILA and the Fair Credit Billing Act, the Federal Reserve Board explains in Regulation Z that a cardholder need not contest charges under § 1666 in order to pursue remedies under § 1643.... Specifically, the Board's official staff interpretation of 12 C.F.R. § 226.12(b)(3) states that "[t]he liability protections afforded to cardholders in § 226.12 [under § 1643] do not depend upon the cardholder's following the error resolution procedures in § 226.13 [under § 1666]." Although § 1666 and § 226.13 apply only to "consumer credit" and not to corporate credit, see §§ 1666(a), 1602(h), they nevertheless support the general proposition that a cardholder's failure to report fraudulent charges does not create apparent authority for such charges. Congress instructed the Federal Reserve Board to promulgate regulations to carry out the purposes of TILA, see 15 U.S.C. § 1604(a), and the Supreme Court has held that courts owe deference to the Board's regulations and its interpretation of its regulations under TILA.... Because the Board's interpretation is consistent with § 1643 and § 1666, deference to Regulation Z is due.... Indeed, in *Crestar Bank*, 744 A.2d at 1048, the District of Columbia Court of Appeals deferred to Regulation Z and rejected an interpretation that "reads into § 1643 a presumption that if the cardholder fails to notify the [card issuer] that the disputed charges are not his, they will be deemed to have been authorized by the cardholder."

Thus, there is no need for a court to look to banking laws to resolve the risk allocation and public policy issues regarding credit card fraud. While the district court duly noted that DBI had paid Moore's charges in full for ten months, cf. *Minskoff*, 98 F.3d at 710, the court ultimately relied on an analogy to District of Columbia banking law in concluding that DBI's negligent failure to examine its monthly billing statements created apparent authority for Moore to use its corporate AMEX account. In so doing, the district court gave insufficient weight to the fact that § 1643 places the risk of fraud primarily on the card issuer. Under the district court's approach, once a card issuer sends a billing statement to the cardholder, the statutory burden shifts to the cardholder to prove that it fulfilled its duty to review the statement and to report fraudulent charges. As DBI suggests, the effect is to make § 1666 a fraud shield for AMEX. This interpretation hardly seems consistent with the courts' liberal construction of TILA in light of its remedial purposes. Congress's plan for addressing credit card fraud places the burden on the card issuer to prove that it has taken certain measures to protect the cardholder from fraud before it can hold the cardholder liable for any unauthorized charges, see 15 U.S.C. § 1643(a)(1), (b), and even then, limits the cardholder's liability to $50, see id. § 1643(a)(1)(B), (d). In other words, the consequence of the cardholder's failure to examine its billing statements is that it may not be able to take advantage of the opportunity Congress provided under § 1666 to correct a billing error, not that it forfeits protections against liability for unauthorized use under § 1643.... The district court thus erred in imposing a duty on DBI to inspect its monthly billing statements because such a duty effectively creates an exhaustion requirement that neither § 1643 nor Regulation Z contemplates.

Consequently, AMEX cannot meet its burden to show that it is entitled to judgment as a matter of law ... based solely on DBI's failure to examine its monthly billing statements. Indeed, AMEX makes no such attempt. AMEX contends, and we hold, that DBI cannot avoid liability for Moore's fraudulent charges because its repeated payments in full after notice led AMEX reasonably to believe that Moore had the authority to use DBI's corporate credit card. Imposing liability based on the cardholder's payment after notice is not inconsistent with Congress's plan for allocating loss from credit card fraud. By identifying apparent authority as a limit on the cardholder's protection under § 1643, Congress recognized that a cardholder has certain obligations to prevent fraudulent use of its card. DBI's troubles stemmed from its failure to separate the approval and payment functions within its cash disbursement process. Moore had actual authority both to receive the billing statements and to issue DBI checks for payment to AMEX. While DBI did not voluntarily relinquish its corporate card to Moore, it did mislead AMEX into reasonably believing that Moore had authority to use the corporate card by paying her charges on the corporate account after receiving AMEX's monthly statements identifying her as a cardholder and itemizing her charges. While payment may not always create apparent authority, this is not a case involving "an occasional transgression buried in a welter of financial detail." *Minskoff*, 98 F.3d at 710. Nor is this a case involving payment without notice, as might occur when a cardholder authorizes its bank to pay its credit card bills automatically each month. Where, as here, the cardholder repeatedly paid thousands of dollars in fraudulent charges for almost a year after monthly billing statements identifying the fraudulent user and itemizing the fraudulent charges were sent to its corporate address, no reasonable juror could disagree that at some point the cardholder led the card issuer reasonably to believe that the fraudulent user had authority to use its card.

DBI's remaining contentions have no merit. DBI's reliance on the provision limiting a cardholder's liability to charges made on an "accepted" credit card, see 15 U.S.C. § 1643(a)(1)(A), is misplaced, for Moore's charges were not "unauthorized" because DBI's payments created apparent authority for Moore to make them. DBI's insistence that it derived no benefit from Moore's purchase of jewelry, shoes, and clothing is irrelevant because the use of a card is "unauthorized" only if the cardholder derives no benefit from it *and* it lacks actual, implied, or apparent authority. See id. § 1602(o). Because DBI's payments created apparent authority, the use was not "unauthorized."

Accordingly, we hold that DBI is estopped from avoiding liability to AMEX for the charges Moore incurred on the corporate account after her apparent authority arose. The question remains when Moore's apparent authority arose. The district court held, consistent with AMEX's alternative prayer for relief, that DBI could recover payment for the first two months of Moore's charges following her unauthorized acquisition of the card on DBI's corporate account. But no relevant statute sets a time period that is controlling. Both § 1666 and Regulation Z allow the cardholder 60 days from the date of the credit card statement to notify the card issuer of a billing error, see 15 U.S.C. § 1666(a); 12 C.F.R. § 226.13(b)(1), and District of Columbia banking law, on which the district court may have relied, allows the customer a "reasonable period of time, not exceeding 30 days," to examine a bank statement and to notify the bank of any fraudulent charges. D.C.Code § 28:4-406(d)(2); cf. *Minskoff*, 98 F.3d at 709-10. Because the question of precisely when apparent authority arose cannot be resolved as a matter of law, we remand DBI's § 1643 claim to the district court to determine, or as appropriate to allow a jury to determine, at what point DBI's payment created apparent authority and thereby terminated DBI's protection under the statute. AMEX did not cross-appeal, and therefore the district court's award of $21,748.87 for the first two months of use sets a floor for DBI's recovery....

* * *

Accordingly, we affirm in part the grant of summary judgment to AMEX on DBI's § 1643 claim and we remand in part....

C. Billing Errors

Sooner or later, almost everyone has a billing dispute with a credit card company. The following cases discuss billing dispute resolution procedures and the penalties for noncompliance. Review CCPA §§ 1640(a)(1)-(3), 1666, and 1666a.

GRAY v. AMERICAN EXPRESS COMPANY
743 F.2d 10 (D.C.Cir. 1984)

MIKVA, Circuit Judge.

We are called upon to determine what rights, if any, appellant Oscar Gray has against American Express arising from the circumstances under which it cancelled his American Express credit card. The District Court granted summary judgment to American Express; we vacate that judgment and remand for further proceedings.

I. BACKGROUND

Gray had been a cardholder since 1964. In 1981, following some complicated billings arising out of deferred travel charges incurred by Gray, disputes arose about the amount due American Express. After considerable correspondence, the pertinence and timeliness of which we will detail below, American Express decided to cancel Gray's card. No notification of this cancellation was communicated to Gray until the night of April 8, 1982, when he offered his American Express card to pay for a wedding anniversary dinner he and his wife already had consumed in a Washington restaurant. The restaurant informed Gray that American Express had refused to accept the charges for the meal and had instructed the restaurant to confiscate and destroy his card. Gray spoke to the American Express employee on the telephone at the restaurant who informed him, "Your account is cancelled as of now."

The cancellation prompted Gray to file a lengthy complaint in District Court, stating claims under both diversity and federal question jurisdiction.... He alleged that the actions of American Express violated the contract between them, known as the "Cardmember Agreement," as well as the Fair Credit Billing Act (the "Act"), 15 U.S.C. §§ 1666–1666j (1974). The District Court granted summary judgment for American Express and dismissed the complaint.

The surge in the use of credit cards, the "plastic money" of our society, has been so quick that the law has had difficulty keeping pace. It was not until 1974 that Congress passed the Act, first making a serious effort to regulate the relationship between a credit cardholder and the issuing company. We hold that the District Court was too swift to conclude that the Act offers no protection to Gray and further hold that longstanding principles of contract law afford Gray substantial rights. We thus vacate the District Court's judgment and remand.

II. DISCUSSION
A. The Statutory Claim

The Fair Credit Billing Act seeks to prescribe an orderly procedure for identifying and resolving disputes between a cardholder and a card issuer as to the amount due at any given time. The Supreme Court, in American Express Co. v. Koerner, 101 S.Ct. 2281 (1981), succinctly described the mechanics of the Act as follows:

> If the [cardholder] believes that the statement contains a billing error [as defined in 15 U.S.C. § 1666(b)], he then may send the creditor a written notice setting forth that belief, indicating the amount of the error and the reasons supporting his belief that it is an error. If the creditor receives this notice within 60 days of transmitting the statement of account, [§ 1666(a)] imposes two separate obligations upon the creditor. Within 30 days, it must send a written acknowledgment that it has received the notice. And, within 90 days or two complete billing cycles, whichever is shorter, the creditor must investigate the matter and either make appropriate corrections in the [cardholder's] account or send a written explanation of its belief that the original statement sent to the [cardholder] was correct. The creditor must send its explanation before making any attempt to collect the disputed amount. A creditor that fails to comply with [§ 1666(a)] forfeits its right to collect the first $50 of the disputed amount including finance charges. [15 U.S.C. § 1666(e)]. In addition, [§ 1666(d)] provides that, pursuant to regulations of the Federal Reserve Board, a creditor operating an "open end consumer credit plan" may not restrict or close an account due to a [cardholder's]

failure to pay a disputed amount until the creditor has sent the written explanation required by [§ 1666(a)] (footnote omitted).

Other obligations also attach. First, if "appropriate corrections" are made, the card issuer also must credit any finance charge on accounts erroneously billed. 15 U.S.C. § 1666(a)(B)(i). Second, the card issuer must notify the cardholder on subsequent statements of account that he need not pay the amount in dispute until the card issuer has complied with § 1666. 15 U.S.C. § 1666(c)(2). Third, the card issuer may not report, or threaten to report, adversely on the cardholder's credit before the card issuer has discharged its obligations under § 1666, 15 U.S.C. § 1666a(a), and, if the cardholder continues to dispute the bill in timely fashion, the card issuer may report the delinquency only if it also reports that the amount is in dispute and tells the cardholder to whom it has released this information. 15 U.S.C. § 1666a(b). The card issuer is further obliged to report any eventual resolution of the delinquency to the same third parties with whom it earlier had communicated. 15 U.S.C. § 1666a(c). Finally, a card issuer that fails to comply with any requirements of the Act is liable to the cardholder for actual damages, twice the amount of any finance charge, and costs of the action and attorney's fees. 15 U.S.C. § 1640(a).

American Express is, of course, a creditor for purposes of the Act....

1. The Billing Error

The billing dispute in issue arose after Gray used his credit card to purchase airline tickets costing $9312. American Express agreed that Gray could pay for the tickets in 12 equal installments over 12 months. In January and February of 1981, Gray made substantial prepayments of $3500 and $1156 respectively. He so advised American Express by letter of February 8, 1981. There is no dispute about these payments, nor about Gray's handling of them. At this point the numbers become confusing because American Express, apparently in error, converted the deferred payment plan to a current charge on the March bill. American Express thereafter began to show Gray as delinquent, due at least in part to the dispute as to how and why the deferred billing had been converted to a current charge.

The District Court held that Gray failed to trigger the protection of the Act because he neglected to notify American Express in writing within 60 days after he first received an erroneous billing. Gray insists that his first letter to American Express on April 22, 1981, well within the 60 day period set forth in the statute, identified the dispute as it first appeared in the March, 1981 billing. According to Gray's complaint, the dispute continued to simmer for over a year because American Express never fulfilled its investigative and other obligations under the Act.

The District Court made no mention of the April 22, 1981 letter, deeming instead a September, 1981 letter as the first notification from Gray as to the existence of a dispute. We conclude that the District Court erred in overlooking the April letter.

Gray's April 22, 1981 letter complained specifically about the March bill and the miscrediting of the prepayments. Whatever the import and impact of other correspondence and actions of the parties, we hold that, through this earlier letter, Gray triggered the procedural protections of the Act. The letter enabled the card issuer to identify the name and account number, indicated that the cardholder believed that an error existed in a particular amount and set forth the cardholder's reasons why he believed an error had been made. 15 U.S.C. § 1666(a).... The later correspondence and activities may be treated as evidentiary in nature–sufficient perhaps to show that American Express fulfilled all of its obligations under the Act, but not pertinent to the question of whether the Act was triggered in the first place....

2. Reporting and Collection Efforts

Gray alleged in count III that, notwithstanding his having given notice of dispute under § 1666 through his letters, American Express nevertheless turned over his account for collection to a bill collection agency. The District Judge dismissed this count by concluding that it failed to state a claim for relief. The District Court erred. See 15 U.S.C. §§ 1640(a), 1666a. We think that count III states an independent cause of action under § 1666a because Gray's April 22, 1981 correspondence brought the dispute within the Act's coverage. The question of American Express' compliance with the reporting and collection requirements of the Act also warrants consideration on remand.

3. The Act and the Cardmember Agreement

As we have indicated above, the District Court summarily resolved Gray's statutory claims by wrongly concluding that the Act did not apply. On appeal, American Express also urges that, even if the Act is otherwise pertinent, Gray was bound by the terms of the Cardmember Agreement which empowered American Express to cancel the credit card without notice and without cause. The contract between Gray and American Express provides:

> [W]e can revoke your right to use [the card] at any time. We can do this with or without cause and without giving you notice.

American Express concludes from this language that the cancellation was not of the kind prohibited by the Act, even though the Act regulates other aspects of the relationship between the cardholder and the card issuer.

Section 1666(d) of the Act states that, during the pendency of a disputed billing, the card issuer, until it fulfills its other obligations under § 1666(a)(B)(ii), shall not cause the cardholder's account to be restricted or closed because of the failure of the obligor to pay the amount in dispute.... American Express seems to argue that, despite that provision, it can exercise its right to cancellation for cause unrelated to the disputed amount, or for no cause, thus bringing itself out from under the statute. At the very least, the argument is audacious. American Express would restrict the efficacy of the statute to those situations where the parties had not agreed to a "without cause, without notice" cancellation clause, or to those cases where the cardholder can prove that the sole reason for cancellation was the amount in dispute. We doubt that Congress painted with such a faint brush.

The effect of American Express's argument is to allow the equivalent of a "waiver" of coverage of the Act simply by allowing the parties to contract it away. Congress usually is not so tepid in its approach to consumer problems. See 118 Cong. Rec. 14,835 (1972) (remarks by Sen. Proxmire, principal proponent of the Act, concerning a technical amendment to a predecessor bill later carried over into the Act; its purpose was to prevent "possible evasion" by precluding the creditor from including a pre-dispute waiver provision in the card agreement); ... Koerner v. American Express Co., 444 F. Supp. 334, 341 (E.D. La. 1977) (Koerner trial court's recitation of Act's legislative history reflecting congressional concern about card issuers' "high-handed tactics" in handling of consumer billing disputes).

Moreover, the consumer-oriented statutes that Congress has enacted in recent years belie the unrestrained reading that American Express gives to the Act in light of its contract. Waiver of statutory rights, particularly by a contract of adhesion, is hardly consistent with the legislature's purpose. The rationale of consumer protection legislation is to even out the inequalities that consumers normally bring to the bargain. To allow such protection to be waived by boiler plate language of the contract puts the legislative process to a foolish and unproductive task. A court ought not impute such nonsense to a Congress intent on correcting abuses in the market place.

Finally, American Express also contends that, even if the Act is not waived totally, its cancellation was proper because it was for reasons other than those prohibited by the statute. A showing of whatever limited grounds for cancellation remain available under § 1666(d) while a dispute is pending calls for substantial evidentiary proceedings, however. If American Express seeks to avail itself of these grounds, a more substantial factual predicate than that established through summary judgment is necessary....

Thus we hold that the Act's notice provision was met by Gray's April 22, 1981 letter and remand the case to the District Court for trial of Gray's statutory cause of action. American Express will be obliged to justify its conduct in this case as fully satisfying its obligations under the Act.

B. The Contract Claim

Gray stated a second cause of action in diversity, a contract claim, in which he alleged that American Express violated the Cardmember Agreement by wrongfully cancelling it. Notably, in Koerner, supra, the Supreme Court on very similar facts observed that a cardholder could state, in addition to, and separate from, his federal claim under the Act, a claim under state law for cancellation arising out of a credit card billing dispute.... Although a state law claim was raised, and addressed, in this case, neither the parties nor the District Court considered the preliminary question of choice of law. The parties failed again to address it on appeal. As a court sitting in diversity, we are obliged, however, to examine that issue.

1. Choice of Law

* * *

2. Notice

We are asked to interpret the "without notice" provision in the Cardmember Agreement. Gray challenges the card issuer's extreme and, in our view, unreasonable interpretation of this language. The District Court concluded that the notice provision was enforceable. We disagree.

It is certainly true that, from the common law immemorial, parties have been free to include whatever conditions and limitations that they may desire in a contract. Absent a statutory prohibition or some public policy impediment, the very essence of freedom of contract is the right of the parties to strike good bargains and bad bargains.... However traditional "cancellation for cause" and "with notice" provisions are to a contract, parties sometimes agree to give them up. Appellant thus would not be the first nor the last cardholder to have surrendered substantial rights. Nor does the fact that Gray paid $35.00 per year for his cardholding privileges automatically entitle him to receive notice or to insist on some showing of cause before his card is cancelled. Indeed, American Express generously provides for a pro-rata refund of the annual charge in the event of cancellation.

The problem, then, is not, as Gray would suggest, the unconscionable nature per se of this clause. Nor is it that this clause contradicts in any actionable way the advertising and puffing that he claims American Express used to entice him into the relationship. (E.g., "When you're out of cash, you're not out of luck."; " ... flexibility to travel and entertain when and where you want, virtually without interruption.") The problem stems from the card issuer's attempt to interpret the "without notice" provision so as to give the creditor's internal cancellation decision effect as against irreversible transactions that already have been completed.

Commonly understood, the function of notice is to provide forewarning of an event. Similarly, in the context of contractual relations, notice allows the party notified to contemplate, and to prepare for, an action that will occur.... By contrast, and reasonably interpreted, a contract that is cancellable without notice implies that it can be terminated without forewarning. Such a contract provision ordinarily does not suggest, however, that the cancellation is effective retrospectively to events that transpired prior to notification of the decision to cancel.... Indeed, counsel for American Express made this point for us indirectly at oral argument. When he was asked whether, based on his client's interpretation of the "without notice" clause, American Express was empowered to cancel the agreement "retroactively," he answered "yes," but was quick to add that his client would never take such action against a cardholder. We see little, if any, principled distinction, however, between admittedly "retroactive" cancellation and cancellation effective against irreversible obligations incurred after cancellation but before the cardholder learns his card has been cancelled.

The importance of effective notice of contract termination has not escaped the attention of the New York courts and legislature, particularly where an individual could suffer substantial harm if a contract to which he is a party is cancelled without his ever knowing. The most obvious examples come from the field of insurance law where New York, by statute, requires an insurer to give notice of its decision to cancel a policy. The obvious, and salutary, purpose behind this policy is not to allow the insured to contest the decision, but to enable him to take steps to avoid a lapse in protection—a risk not wholly unlike that which a cardholder who intends to use his card to pay for a completed and irreversible transaction expects to avoid.

The parallel between New York insurance law and credit card law carries into contract interpretation, too. The New York case law instructs us to interpret credit card agreements by using the "rules for construction of insurance contracts." ... Like the insurance contract, the Cardmember Agreement was not negotiated, but was prepared exclusively by the card issuer; consequently, it should be construed narrowly against the creditor.... This rule blends two independent canons of construction: first, that a contract is interpreted against its drafter and second, that a contract of adhesion should be strictly construed.

These authorities confirm our conclusion, as a court sitting in diversity, that the interpretation American Express proffers would not find favor in the New York courts. There can be no dispute that American Express drew the language for a broad application. But if American Express were correct in its interpretation, it even could refuse to honor past charges long since incurred—an outcome that must be rejected even in application of *strictum jus*. The right to cancel "without giving you notice" means that the decision to cancel can be entirely unilateral and instantaneous. It cannot, however, be an internalized decision which is never communicated to the cardholder. Such a reading defies any reasonable expectation that the parties could have had about their contractual relationship.... Thus, we think that the "without notice" provision is given full weight by allowing the cancellation to be unilateral and to be given contemporaneous effect upon communication. To say that "without notice" also means that it never need be communicated to the cardholder extends the clause, and the waiver it contains, "to circumstances not covered."....

Indeed, the interpretation of the language urged by American Express would subsume the entire contract and make the underlying contractual relationship illusory. See Niagara Mohawk Power Corp. v. Graver Tank & Mfg. Co., 470 F. Supp. 1308, 1316 (N.D.N.Y. 1979) (applying New York law; presence of notice requirement in otherwise broad termination provision prevents promise from being illusory); Restatement (Second) of Contracts § 77 comment a (illusory promises); 1A Corbin on Contracts § 163 at p. 76 (1963) ("If a promisor reserves the power to cancel at any time without notice, his promise seems to be unenforceable,...."); 1 Williston, supra, § 105 at p. 418 ("An agreement wherein one party reserves the right to cancel at his pleasure cannot create a contract.") (footnote omitted). We therefore hold that, even as a contract of adhesion, the language quoted above has limitations. The card can be revoked without cause and without any waiting period, but it cannot be revoked for transactions that already have occurred.

American Express suggests that if the clauses are not upheld in the manner it urges, there will be a great risk thrown on the credit card business. We think they protest too much. Within the limits of state and federal statutes, credit cards can still be cancelled without cause and without notice. But the cancellation can affect only transactions which have not occurred before the cancellation is communicated to the cardholder. In practical terms American Express will have to make an effort to communicate its cancellation decision to the cardholder. The effort may be as informal as a phone call or a telegram. We leave to future cases the question of what constitutes a good faith effort to communicate the cancellation decision to the cardholder.

Nor need we decide what fact situations would allow the communication of the cancellation to take place through the merchant involved in the transaction. If a cardholder seeks to use his American Express card to buy a car, for example, we think that a communication, through the car dealer, that the card has been cancelled prior to title passing to the cardholder may effect notice in reasonable fashion. But where the meal has been consumed, or the hotel room has been slept in, or the service rendered, the communication through the merchant comes too late to void the credit for that transaction.

Even contracts of adhesion are contracts. To allow cancellation without any communication of the decision is to turn the contract into a snare and deceit. It may well be that an offeree has less expectation of performance and that the terms and conditions of withdrawal of the offer can be, as American Express argues, much more absolute and ex parte. But contracts, as opposed to offers, are made of sterner doctrine; to interpret this contract so as to sanction the conduct of American Express in this case would empty the agreement of all meaning.

* * *

We therefore hold that the cancellation without notice provision, as interpreted by American Express, is unenforceable. We remand the case to the District Court to resolve Gray's claims under the contract.

* * *

STRANGE v. MONOGRAM CREDIT CARD BANK OF GEORGIA
129 F.3d 943 (7th Cir. 1997)

DIANE P. WOOD, Circuit Judge.

It can be annoying, difficult, and ultimately expensive for a consumer to straighten out errors in a credit card statement, as Jeffrey Strange found out when he purchased a window at Home Depot, Inc., for $346.21. He charged the purchase to his Home Depot credit card, which had been issued by the Monogram Credit Card Bank ("Monogram"). Strange soon discovered that the size of the window had been mislabeled and that he therefore could not use it. He returned it to the Home Depot store from which he had obtained it, and, he thought, received a credit for the return. Wrong he was. When his monthly credit card statement arrived in November 1994, he discovered that his account had not been credited for the return. Following the instructions on the bill, Strange wrote to the address listed requesting that his account be corrected. Neither Home Depot nor Monogram responded to his letter. When his next monthly statement again did not reflect any credit for the returned window, Strange wrote a second letter, again asking that the billing error be corrected. Once again, his efforts were to no avail: neither company responded, and subsequent monthly billing statements continued to reflect the billing error of $346.21.

Strange ultimately filed suit against both Home Depot and Monogram for violations of the Truth in Lending Act (TILA), 15 U.S.C. § 1601 et seq. He alleged that both companies were liable for failing promptly to credit the purchase price of the returned window to his account in violation of § 1666(c) and (d) (Count I), and that they were also liable for not acknowledging receipt of the billing error notices within 30 days of receiving them, for failing to investigate and resolve the billing error dispute within two complete billing cycles or 90 days, and for continuing to attempt collection of the amount in dispute and to impose finance charges on the disputed balance, all in violation of § 1666 (Count II). Each count requested recovery "for each and every violation of the Act." The complaint also requested that the court "[a]ward statutory damages in the amount of twice the finance charge not to exceed $1000 in accordance with 15 U.S.C. § 1640(a)(2)" and that it award costs and reasonable attorneys' fees under § 1640.

Both Strange and Home Depot moved for summary judgment. The district court denied Strange's motion with respect to Home Depot but granted it with respect to Monogram, which the court found had violated the TILA by failing to send Strange a written explanation of the billing error. The court granted Home Depot's summary judgment motion because it was not a "creditor" under the terms of the statute. It ordered damages for Strange in the amount of $1,000, the statutory maximum under § 1640.

Not satisfied, Strange (through another lawyer in the office) filed a petition requesting $21,743.75 in attorneys' fees for his lawyers, Jeffrey Strange & Associates. Monogram opposed the petition, claiming that it was excessive and that the proper award for the credit dispute under the TILA was $100—an amount that made Strange's fee request some two hundred times the amount in controversy. In keeping with this argument, Monogram also filed a Motion for Reconsideration of Statutory Damages Award, requesting that the statutory penalty be reduced to $100. In response to that motion, the court reduced the award for Strange to $54.72, twice the erroneously billed finance charge of $27.36.

The district court rejected Strange's request for the full $21,743.75 in attorneys' fees, explaining its decision as follows:

> I granted Mr. Strange summary judgment on his claim against Monogram, but awarded Mr. Strange a judgment of only $54.72. Had he properly researched the issues in this lawsuit when he first filed his complaint, Mr. Strange would have known that this amount would be all he was awarded. Even if there were some question as to whether he was entitled to multiple recoveries for multiple violations, Mr. Strange pled only six violations of the TILA. Thus at most Mr. Strange would only be entitled to $328.32. It was not reasonable for Mr. Strange to incur over $21,000 in attorney's fees to prosecute a claim worth, at most, $328.32.... Here I find that it was absurd for Mr. Strange to spend 123 hours to establish a $54 (or even $328) claim ... The problem with Mr. Strange's fee re-

quest, however, is not that his attorney's billing rate of $175/hr is too high, but that the amount of time he spent on this case was excessive. I therefore grant his fee request only for the reduced amount of $3,000....

Strange argues now that the court erred both in reducing his award to $54.72 and in cutting his attorneys' fees so substantially.

District courts have wide latitude in determining attorneys' fee awards, and our review of these decisions is "a highly deferential abuse of discretion standard." ... Recognizing the problems this poses for him, Strange argues that the court did not use the proper analysis in determining the award, and in that way abused its discretion. It failed, he believes, to follow the method the Supreme Court established in Hensley v. Eckerhart, 103 S.Ct. 1933 (1983), under which the court begins with "the number of hours reasonably expended on the litigation multiplied by a reasonable hourly rate." Id. at 1939.... The Hensley Court went on to say that the district court "should exclude from this initial fee calculation hours that were not 'reasonably expended.'... Cases may be overstaffed, and the skill and experience of lawyers vary widely. Counsel for the prevailing party should make a good faith effort to exclude from a fee request hours that are excessive, redundant, or otherwise unnecessary...." Id. at 1939–40.

Hensley reflects the fact that attorneys' fees are normally determined using the "lodestar" method.... The fee claimant bears the burden of substantiating the hours worked and the rate claimed.... Once he has done so and submitted a lodestar, the district court may increase or decrease the amount in light of the Hensley factors, which include the time and labor required, skill needed, amount involved and results obtained, time limitations imposed by the case, experience, and reputation and ability of the lawyers.... A "concise but clear explanation" should accompany any modification by the court of the submitted lodestar.... The court may not cut down the requested fees by an arbitrary amount just because they seem excessive....

In this case, the district court considered both the hourly rate charged and the number of hours expended. Judge Bucklo explained why she found the number of hours requested to be unreasonable, in light of the stakes involved in the litigation and the time and labor that reasonably should have been expended. She also took into account both the results Strange actually obtained and the maximum amount he could have hoped for, given his demands and the statutory framework. This approach to a fee award was expressly approved by the Supreme Court in Farrar v. Hobby, 113 S.Ct. 566, 574 (1992). While it was brief, her explanation for the reduction she ordered was the kind of "concise but clear" statement Estate of Borst required; it was not an unfounded, arbitrary reduction based on the court's subjective view of what might be excessive. We therefore find no abuse of discretion in either the analytical framework the court used or her ultimate decision on the amount of fees Strange was to receive.

Strange also challenges the court's conclusion that he was entitled only to twice the amount of the finance charge assessed by Monogram, rather than the minimum award of $100 he claims the TILA requires. We review this decision de novo, as it deals with a question of statutory interpretation.... Section 1640 provides the measure of damages for violations of the TILA's requirements for credit transactions. It specifies that:

(a) Except as otherwise provided in this section, any creditor who fails to comply with any requirement imposed under this part, including any requirement under section 1635 of this title, or part D or E of this subchapter with respect to any person is liable to such person in an amount equal to the sum of—

(1) any actual damage sustained by such person as a result of the failure;

(2)(A)(i) in the case of an individual action twice the amount of any finance charge in connection with the transaction, (ii) in the case of an individual action relating to a consumer lease under part E of this subchapter, 25 per centum of the total amount of monthly payments under the lease, except that the liability under this subparagraph shall not be less than $100 nor greater than $1,000, or (iii) in the case of an individual action relating to a credit transaction not under an open end credit plan that is secured by real property or a dwelling, not less than $200 or greater than $2,000....

15 U.S.C. § 1640 (1996). The district court found that Monogram had failed to send Strange a written explanation regarding the billing error. Monogram's action violated § 1666, which governs such errors. Because § 1666 is found in part D of the relevant subchapter, the language quoted above governs the award of damages here.

Monogram concedes that, under § 1640(a)(2)(A)(i), Strange is entitled to the minimum award of $100. In its Motion for Reconsideration of Statutory Damages Award it challenged only the district court's decision to award the maximum award of $1,000. It never argued that the award should be only twice the amount of the finance charges assessed against Strange, and before this court it again conceded that the court erred in awarding Strange less than the $100 statutory minimum. Even though Monogram chose not to fight the point, it is notable that the district court interpreted the statute otherwise. Because this is a pure question of law on a matter of considerable commercial interest, we think it best to decide now which is the proper interpretation of the statute. As the statute now reads, § 1640(a)(2)(A)(ii) states that "the liability under this subparagraph shall not be less than $100 nor greater than $1,000;" subsection (A)(i) is silent on the question, and subsection (A)(iii) establishes a floor of $200 and a ceiling of $2,000. One could argue that § 1640(a)(2)(A)(i) and (ii) are separate "subparagraphs," and that "liability under this subparagraph" means only liability under § 1640(a)(2)(A)(ii). Although that reading has a certain appeal given the fact that subsection (ii) is the only one of the three subparts to mention the $100/$1,000 amounts, the history of this part of the statute suggests that such a reading has its own problems. Until 1995, § 1640(a)(2)(A) had only two subsections, the present (i) and (ii). Courts uniformly interpreted the final clause, which established the $100 minimum and the $1,000 maximum, as applying to both (A)(i) and (A)(ii). See, e.g., Mars v. Spartanburg Chrysler Plymouth, Inc., 713 F.2d 65, 67 (4th Cir. 1983) (plaintiff's recovery under § 1640(a)(2)(A)(i) capped at statutory limit of $1,000 where doubled finance charges totaled $2,348.70); Pendleton v. American Title Brokers, Inc., 754 F.Supp. 860, 864 (S.D. Ala. 1991) (plaintiff's recovery under § 1640(a)(2)(A)(i) boosted to statutory minimum of $100 where doubled finance charges were less than that amount). It was the 1995 addition of sub-subsection (A)(iii) that introduced the ambiguity with which we are now confronted. In our view, the 1995 amendment was designed simply to establish a more generous minimum and maximum for certain secured transactions, without changing the general rule on minimum and maximum damage awards for the other two parts of § 1640(a)(2)(A). We therefore conclude that the "subparagraph" mentioned in § 1640(a)(2)(A)(ii) continues to encompass what is now codified as subparts (A)(i) and (A)(ii), not just subpart (A)(ii). Strange was therefore entitled to receive the $100 minimum for the billing error in his case, as Monogram now concedes.

We accordingly AFFIRM the district court's award of attorneys' fees, and we REVERSE its award of $54.72 and REMAND for entry of judgment for Strange in the amount of $100. Each side is to bear its own costs on appeal.

Note

Can a credit card issuer successfully argue that its customer bears the loss for unauthorized (and unpaid) charges under CCPA § 1643 if the customer fails to timely alert the issuer of the charges under CCPA § 1666? The issuer made that argument in Crestar Bank, N.A. v. Cheevers, 744 A.2d 1043 (D.C. Ct. App. 2000), when the customer did not notify the issuer until January 1996 of unauthorized charges in October and November 1994 for which the issuer sought payment from the customer. The trial court rejected the issuer's argument, as did the appellate court.

> We turn first to Crestar's argument that: "In its simplest form, 15 U.S.C. § 1666 (1998) requires cardholders to inform card issuers of any errors on their statements, in writing, within sixty (60) days of the receipt of the statement." Crestar seeks to impose a notification requirement on Mr. Cheevers that does not exist either under the plain words of § 1666 or its legislative history. Rather, § 1666 requires the bank or a creditor to take certain action after the cardholder notifies it of a billing error.... Thus, § 1666 recognizes that a cardholder may inform the bank of a billing error, but does not mandate such notification.... In addition, § 1666 imposes on the card issuer or the bank an obligation to acknowledge and investigate the alleged billing error....

> This reading of the statute is consistent with the legislative history of § 1666 which reveals Congress' intent to protect the consumer against the creditor's unfair and inaccurate billing practices. Moreover, it is consistent with Federal Reserve Board staff interpretation of the unauthorized use provision of § 1643 and the billing error provision of § 1666 of Regulation Z, 12 C.F.R. pts. 226.12 and 226.13, regulations promulgated by the Board of Governors of the Federal Reserve System to implement TILA. In interpreting the notice to card issuer provision, the staff of the Board stated:

>> Notice of loss, theft, or possible unauthorized use need not be initiated by the cardholder.... The liability protections afforded to cardholders in § 226.12 do not depend upon the cardholder's following the error resolution procedures in § 226.13. For example, the written notification and time limit requirements of § 226.13 do not affect the § 226.12 protections.

> 12 C.F.R. pt. 226, Supp. I, at 354. Courts must give deference to agency interpretations of TILA and its implementing regulations.... Consequently, we conclude that § 1666 imposed no requirement on Mr. Cheevers to notify Crestar of a billing error before he could invoke the protections of § 1643. We turn now to § 1643.

> Crestar maintains that Mr. Cheevers' "failure to object to the [disputed] charges within a reasonable time, even if not his, constituted ratification and acceptance of those charges," and that under contractual and common law, "if the cardholder fails to notify the bank of any dispute within a reasonable period, he is deemed to have admitted the authenticity of the charges." In essence, Crestar reads into § 1643 a presumption that if the cardholder fails to notify the bank that the disputed charges are not his, they will be deemed to have been authorized by the cardholder. This presumption is at odds with the plain words of § 1643 which impose on the bank the burden to show authorized use of the card, or liability of the cardholder for unauthorized use. As the trial court concluded, nothing in the record demonstrated that Mr. Cheevers authorized the charges on his credit card in November and December 1994.[FN4]....

FN4. This case differs from Minskoff v. American Express Travel Servs., 98 F.3d 703 (2d Cir.1996) on which Crestar relies. In that case, the corporate assistant to the president of the corporation that the bank sued made the fraudulent charges, and the court determined that the president was liable for charges made after the bank sent a statement showing the initial unauthorized charges. In addition, sums reflected in the monthly billing statements, including the disputed charges, were paid in full for sixteen consecutive months prior to notification that the charges were unauthorized. In contrast, in the case before us, there is no showing that Mr. Cheevers had any relationship with the person who charged the Amtrak tickets to his credit card, and Mr. Cheevers never paid the disputed charges....

744 A.2d at 1047–48.

Problem 10-1

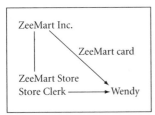

Wendy received her ZeeMart credit card statement on June 1. The postmark indicated that the statement had been mailed on May 26. In reviewing the charges, Wendy noticed that she had been billed twice for the same purchase (a problem she thought the clerk had fixed at the store).

1) Wendy wants ZeeMart to delete the duplicate charge. Should she contact ZeeMart by telephone or in writing? What information should she give to ZeeMart? How soon should she contact ZeeMart?

2) What action, if any, must ZeeMart take after learning of the error?

3) Time passes, and ZeeMart is about to send the next month's statement to Wendy. ZeeMart has not yet resolved Wendy's problem. Can ZeeMart continue to reflect the disputed charge on the statement? Can the statement reflect accrued finance charges on the disputed charge? Can ZeeMart deduct the disputed charge in calculating Wendy's unused credit line? Can ZeeMart cancel Wendy's card during the dispute resolution process?

4) Assume that Wendy has been charged only once for the purchase, a new exterior door for her home. While installing the door, Wendy notices a crack in one of the glass panes. Wendy genuinely believes that the glass must have been cracked prior to her purchase. Does the product defect provide Wendy with a reason to assert a "billing error" when she receives her statement on which this charge is reflected?

D. Asserting Claims and Defenses Against the Issuer

Occasionally a consumer may use a bank credit card to purchase from a merchant what turns out to be a defective product. May the consumer refuse to pay the charge by asserting, against the card issuer, the claim or defense that it has against the merchant? The following materials explore this issue. Review CCPA § 1666i.

IZRAELEWITZ v. MANUFACTURERS HANOVER TRUST COMPANY

465 N.Y.S.2d 486 (N.Y. Civ. Ct. 1983)

IRA B. HARKAVY, Judge.

As the texture of the American economy evolves from paper to plastic, the disgruntled customer is spewing its wrath upon the purveyor of the plastic rather than upon the merchant.

Plaintiff George Izraelewitz commenced this action to compel the Defendant bank Manufacturers Hanover Trust Company to credit his Mastercharge account in the amount of $290.00 plus finance charges. The disputed charge, posted to Plaintiff's account on July 16, 1981, is for electronic diagrams purchased by Plaintiff via telephone from Don Britton Enterprises, a Hawaii-based mail order business.

On September 9, 1981 Plaintiff advised Defendant bank, Manufacturers Hanover Trust Company (Trust Company), that the diagrams had been unsuitable for his needs and provided Defendant with a UPS receipt indicating that the purchased merchandise had been returned to Don Britton. Defendant's Customer Service Department credited Plaintiff's account and waived finance charges on the item. Trust Company subsequently proceeded to charge back the item to the merchant. The merchant refused the charge back through The 1st Hawaii Bank, and advised Defendant bank of their strict "No Refund" policy. Don Britton also indicated that Plaintiff, during the course of conversation, had admitted that he was aware of this policy. On April 1, 1982 Defendant advised Plaintiff that his account would be redebited for the full amount. At two later dates, Plaintiff advised Trust Company of said dispute, denied knowledge of the "No Refund" policy and stated that the goods had been returned. The Trust Company once again credited Plaintiff's account and attempted to collect from Don Britton. The charge back was again refused and Plaintiff's account was subsequently redebited.

Bank credit agreements generally provide that a cardholder is obligated to pay the bank regardless of any dispute which may exist respecting the merchandise. An exception to this rule arises under a provision in the Truth in Lending Law which allows claimants whose transactions exceed $50.00 and who have made a good faith attempt to obtain satisfactory resolution of the problem, to assert claims and defenses arising out of the credit card transaction, if the place of the initial transaction is in the same state or within 100 miles of the cardholder. Consumer Credit Protection Act, 15 U.S.C.A. § 1666i.

It would appear that Plaintiff is precluded from asserting any claims or defenses since Britton's location exceeds the geographical limitation. This assumption is deceiving. Under Truth in Lending the question of where the transaction occurred (e.g. as in mail order cases) is to be determined under state or other applicable law. Truth in Lending, 12 CFR, § 226.12(c). Furthermore, any state law permitting customers to assert claims and defenses against the card issuer would not be preempted, regardless of whether the place of the transaction was at issue. In effect, these federal laws are viewed as bare minimal standards.

In Lincoln First Bank, N.A. v. Carlson, 103 Misc.2d 467, 426 N.Y.S.2d 433 (1980), the court found that:

> "(T)he statement that a card issuer is subject to all defenses if a transaction occurred less than 100 miles from the cardholder's address, does not automatically

presume a cardholder to give up all his defenses should the transaction take place at a distance of greater than 100 miles from the mailing address." Id. at 436.

The facts at bar do not warrant a similar finding. Whereas in Lincoln, supra, the cardholder's defense arose due to an alleged failure of the card issuer itself to comply with statutory rules, the Defendant herein is blameless. The geographical limitation serves to protect banks from consumers who may expose them to unlimited liability through dealings with merchants in faraway states where it is difficult to monitor a merchant's behavior. These circumstances do not lend the persuasion needed to cast-off this benefit.

Considering, arguendo, that under the Truth in Lending Act, Plaintiff was able to assert claims and defenses from the original transaction, any claims or defenses he chose to assert would only be as good as and no better than his claim against the merchant. Accordingly, Plaintiff's claim against the merchant must be scrutinized to ascertain whether it is of good faith and substantial merit. A consumer cannot assert every minuscule dispute he may have with a merchant as an excuse not to pay an issuer who has already paid the merchant.

The crux of Plaintiff's claim, apparently, is that he returned the diagrams purportedly unaware of merchant's "No Refund" policy. The merchant contends that Plaintiff admitted that he knew of the policy and nonetheless used deceptive means to return the plans; in that they were sent without a name so they would be accepted; were not delivered to an employee of the company; were not in the original box; and showed evidence of having been xeroxed.

"No Refund" policies, per se, are not unconscionable or offensive to the public policy in any manner. Truth in Lending Law "(n)either requires refunds for returns nor does it prohibit refunds in kind." Truth in Lending Regulations, 12 CFR, § 226.12(e). Bank-merchant agreements, however, usually do contain a requirement that the merchant establish a fair policy for exchange and return of merchandise.

To establish the fairness in Don Britton's policy, the strength of the reasons behind the policy and the measures taken to inform the consumer of it must necessarily be considered. Don Britton's rationale for its policy is compelling. It contends that printing is a very small part of its business, which is selling original designs, and "once a customer has seen the designs he possesses what we have to sell." Britton's policy is clearly written in its catalog directly on the page which explains how to order merchandise. To compensate for not having a refund policy, which would be impractical considering the nature of the product, Britton offers well-advertised backup plans with free engineering assistance and an exchange procedure, as well, if original plans are beyond the customer's capabilities. The Plaintiff could have availed himself of any of these alternatives which are all presumably still open to him.

On the instant facts, as between Plaintiff and the Defendant bank, Plaintiff remains liable for the disputed debt, as he has not shown adequate cause to hold otherwise.

Judgment for Defendant dismissing the complaint.

PLUTCHOK v. EUROPEAN AMERICAN BANK
540 N.Y.S.2d 135 (N.Y. Dist. Ct. 1989)

MARVIN E. SEGAL, Judge.

This is an action by plaintiff Plutchok against the defendant European American Bank to recover the sum of $249.00 representing the sum paid for membership in a travel club.

After the trial held on the 6th day of December, 1988, the Court has made the following findings of fact:

The plaintiff received a postcard from Holiday Magic Travel Club, Inc. ("Holiday") of Miami, Florida, stating that he had been selected to receive a pre-paid luxury cruise plus hotel accommodations. The plaintiff called "Holiday" on December 19, 1986 and received details of the vacation offer and "Holiday's" money back guarantee, as well as assurances of the company's good standing, including bank references.

The plaintiff obtained membership in "Holiday's" discount travel club via telephone by giving the number of his European American Bank ("EAB") mastercard to a representative of "Holiday." He paid $249.00 by credit card. "Holiday" thereafter sent membership materials to the plaintiff, who decided that he did not want to obtain membership in the club. The plaintiff requested a refund from "Holiday," but received no reply. Apparently, plaintiff was lured into a scam, and recovery of the $249.00 from "Holiday" appears to be impossible since "Holiday" cannot be located.

Plaintiff had purchased the membership over the telephone on December 19, 1986. The defendant claims that plaintiff received a statement reflecting his purchase on January 3, 1987. The plaintiff contends that the credit statements received on January 3, 1987 and April 3, 1987, did not contain the $249.00 purchase. Plaintiff concedes that he did not notify the defendant of the requested billing correction until April 25, 1987. The Court notes that neither the plaintiff nor defendant submitted into evidence a copy of the EAB credit statements sent to plaintiff on January 3, 1987 and on April 3, 1987.

The credit card transactions between the credit card issuer and the credit card holder are governed by the Truth in Lending Law codified in the Consumer Credit Protection Act, 15 U.S.C.A. § 1666. Section 1666 of the Consumer Credit Protection Act requires the credit card holder to notify the credit card issuer of any "billing error" within sixty (60) days from the receipt of a credit statement of the credit card holder's account sent by the card issuer. A "billing error" includes "a reflection on a statement of goods or services not accepted by the obligor [credit card holder] or his designee ..." 15 U.S.C.A. § 1666(b)(3). Any claims asserted by a credit card holder against a card issuer pursuant to 15 U.S.C.A. § 1666i require the card holder to comply with the sixty (60) day notice provision of 15 U.S.C.A. § 1666(a)....

In the instant case, the plaintiff has the burden of proving that he gave the sixty (60) days notice, from the date of receipt of the credit statement, of the "billing error" to EAB. The "billing error" constituted the travel membership cancelled by the plaintiff. Plaintiff contends that the sixty (60) day notification was given within sixty (60) days from receipt of the April 3, 1987 statement, which did not, but should have, reflected the charge of $249.00 to plaintiff's account. Defendant claims that the January 3, 1987 statement sent to plaintiff reflected the $249.00 charge to plaintiff's account, and therefore, the sixty (60) day period started to accrue from January 3, 1987. Defendant concludes that plaintiff's notice to EAB on April 25, 1987, was too late.

Plaintiff has failed to introduce into evidence a copy of plaintiff's EAB credit account statements received on January 3, 1987 and April 3, 1987 to support plaintiff's contention that the $249.00 charge never appeared on the credit card statements. Accordingly, plaintiff has failed to prove that the sixty (60) day notice required by 15 U.S.C.A. § 1666(a) was ever given to defendant.

Even if plaintiff did provide defendant with the sixty (60) days notice pursuant to 15 U.S.C.A. § 1666(a), plaintiff would still not be able to assert a claim against defendant pursuant to 15 U.S.C.A. § 1666i to recover the $249.00. Section 1666i(a) provides that a card issuer "shall be subject to all claims and defenses arising out of any transaction in which the credit card is used as a method of payment or extension of credit ... the place where the initial transaction occurred was within 100 miles from [the card holder's] address." The question of where the transaction occurred is to be determined by State law. 12 C.F.R. §226.12(c); see Izraelewitz v. Manufacturers Hanover Trust Co., 465 N.Y.S.2d 486 (1983). Under New York State law, a contract is transacted in the State where there is an acceptance and completion of a contract, and completion of a contract may be made by telephone....

In the instant case, the plaintiff, a resident of New York State, received a mail solicitation from "Holiday," a Miami corporation. "Holiday's" mail solicitation was an invitation for plaintiff to make an offer of membership for $249.00. The solicitation, through advertising, constitutes a request for offers, and once the offers are tendered, the seller has the option to accept or reject any or all of them.... Plaintiff's telephone conversation, where he purchased membership by giving his credit card number, constituted an offer which was accepted by "Holiday." ... Consequently, the transaction occurred in Florida and outside the 100 mile requirement of 15 U.S.C.A. §1666i since the transaction was complete when "Holiday" accepted plaintiff's membership offer.

Accordingly, based upon the above findings of law and fact, the Court renders judgment in favor of the defendant.

Notes

1. Not all courts agree with the *Plutchok* court's conclusion that "[a]ny claims asserted by a credit card holder against a card issuer pursuant to 15 U.S.C.A. §1666i require the card holder to comply with the sixty (60) day notice provision of 15 U.S.C.A. §1666(a)." In *CitiBank (South Dakota), N.A. v. Mincks*, 135 S.W.3d 545 (Mo. Ct. App. 2004), Mincks faxed an order from Missouri to an Ohio merchant for several high-definition, high-color postcards priced at $7,600. The order form provided a Citibank credit card as the form of payment. The merchant later ceased operations without ever delivering the postcards. Mincks sought to avoid payment of the charge by invoking his rights under §1666i. The trial court agreed that Mincks could do so. Citibank appealed, contending that non-delivery created a "billing error" under §1666. Because Mincks failed to timely invoke the billing error provisions, Citibank argued that Mincks could not assert any rights under §1666i. After construing the merchant's solicitation as an "offer" and Mincks's fax as an "acceptance," the appellate court ruled that the transaction occurred in Missouri, allowing Mincks to comply with the technical requirements of §1666i. The court then turned its attention to the interplay between §1666 and §1666i, offering the following analysis in part:

> Thus, §1666 only affects the amount of the debt in the event of a creditor's noncompliance with the statute. When this occurs, however, the creditor may still sue on the debt if there is a remaining balance due after subtracting the $50 forfeiture sum. If we were to accept Citibank's argument, it would mean that a consumer who failed to utilize this billing error statute – through ignorance, inadvertence, or purposeful action – would completely forfeit his right to contest the debt owed in a collection lawsuit. The creditor, on the other hand, could knowingly and willfully ignore its responsibilities under this statute and only be penalized a maximum of $50. In our view, this interpretation of the statute leads to an absurd result and turns topsy-turvy our duty to liberally construe the Truth-in-Lending-Act in a consumer's favor. Again, we decline to do so.
>
> Our construction of how the billing error rule operates also is supported by the Official Staff Interpretations of Regulation Z.... In this very specialized area of law

governing commerce in credit, we believe the Federal Reserve Board's interpretation of the Truth-in-Lending-Act and its implementing regulations are entitled to substantial deference as we analyze the issues presented in Citibank's appeal.

The regulation dealing with a consumer's right to correct billing errors is 12 C.F.R. § 226.13. The regulation dealing with a consumer's right to assert claims and defenses is 12 C.F.R. § 226.12. The Official Staff Commentary for 12 C.F.R. § 226.12 states, in pertinent part:

12(c) Right of cardholder to assert claims or defenses against card issuer.

1. Relationship to § 226.13. The § 226.12(c) credit card "holder in due course" provision deals with the consumer's right to assert against the card issuer a claim or defense concerning property or services purchased with a credit card, if the merchant has been unwilling to resolve the dispute. Even though certain merchandise disputes, such as non-delivery of goods, may also constitute "billing errors" under § 226.13, that section operates independently of § 226.12(c). The cardholder whose asserted billing error involves undelivered goods may institute the error resolution procedures of § 266.13; but whether or not the cardholder has done so, the cardholder may assert claims or defenses under § 226.12(c). Conversely, the consumer may pay a disputed balance and thus have no further right to assert claims and defenses, but still may assert a billing error if notice of that billing error is given in the proper time and manner. An assertion that a particular transaction resulted from unauthorized use of the card could also be both a "defense" and a billing error.

See Pt. 226, Supp. I p. 419. Thus, the Federal Reserve Board recognizes that the claims and defenses rule operates independently of the billing error rule. As the Board's analysis of the proper relationship between these two different rules and their respective remedies is not demonstrably irrational, we accept it as dispositive here.

For all of the foregoing reasons, we reject Citibank's argument that a consumer's failure to give a creditor timely notice of a billing error precludes the consumer from later invoking the claim and defense provisions of 15 U.S.C. § 1666i and 12 C.F.R. § 226.12(c) if the creditor sues on the debt. Citibank's second point is denied.

Id. at 559-60.

2. In *In re Standard Financial Management Corp.*, 94 B.R. 231 (Bankr. D. Mass. 1988), a bankrupt merchant sold rare coins through its store and over the telephone. Some customers used credit cards to make purchases. During the bankruptcy proceedings, the court addressed where telephonic sales took place for purposes of the 100-mile limitation of 15 U.S.C. § 1666i. The following is the court's analysis:

Social policy favors finding that the transaction took place in the customer's home. TILA, it is true, intended to limit the liability of merchants to far away customers who might fraudulently chargeback a purchase, secure in the knowledge that the company will not sue because the sum is usually too minor. In this case, however, the seller came into the customer's house by calling the customer. The seller, by soliciting the sale in distant regions, implicitly states that doing business in those areas is not too minor for the seller to take whatever action it needs to protect its rights. Conversely, the customer who is solicited at home has a reasonable expectation that future contacts can likewise be adjusted at or near his home. The Court finds the transaction took place at the customer's home and, therefore, does not find under the facts of this case that the 100 mile limitation applies.

94 B.R. at 239.

3. The legislative history of CCPA § 1666i explains the policy behind the geographic limitation.

> The purpose of this geographic limitation is to avoid the possibility of impairing the nationwide acceptability of third-party credit cards. During the hearings, it was argued that a merchant may be reluctant to honor an out-of-state bank credit card if the card holder has the legal right to withhold payment from the bank and the bank, in turn, has the legal right to charge the disputed item back to the merchant as banks now have under the terms of bank credit card plans. Under these circumstances, it was argued that the merchant would have difficulty in collecting from a recalcitrant card holder who refused to pay a legitimate debt and who might live thousands of miles from the merchant's place of business. Because of these potential difficulties, it was argued that some merchants would refuse to honor out-of-state credit cards issued by banks or other third parties, if the issuer were subject to all card holder claims and defenses. In order to prevent this possibility, the Committee recommends the aforementioned geographic restrictions on the ability of card holders to assert claims or defense against card issuers.

Sen. Rep. No. 278, 93rd Cong., 1st Sess. 11 (1973).

Query whether the absence of any geographic limitation would prompt a mass rejection of credit cards held by out-of-state consumers. Perhaps in some instances the consumer would offer an alternative form of payment (e.g., a check), but in many transactions the consumer might very well decide not to make the purchase, resulting in a lost sale for the merchant. Also consider the difficulty of applying the geographic limitation to the "online" transaction that occurs with increasing popularity every year. Where does a sale take place when the consumer uses a credit card to purchase an item over the Internet?

Problem 10-2

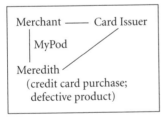

Last month, Meredith bought an 80-gigabyte MyPod (a portable device that stores music, videos, photos, and other information) at an electronics store not too far from her home in Boston, Massachusetts. She charged the $350 purchase price to her bank credit card. The MyPod never seemed to work properly, despite numerous telephone conversations with store personnel and two return visits to the store for repairs. The merchant refused to refund the purchase price or offer an exchange, erroneously believing that Meredith had damaged the MyPod by engaging in illegal downloading.

1) Can Meredith avoid paying her bank the purchase price of the MyPod by asserting its defective quality?

2) Would your answer change if Meredith purchased the MyPod while visiting a friend in: (i) Springfield, Massachusetts (more than 100 miles from her billing address), (ii) Providence, Rhode Island (within 100 miles of her billing address), or (iii) Hartford,

Connecticut (more than 100 miles from her billing address, but within 100 miles of the Massachusetts–Connecticut state line)?

3) Would your answer change if the dispute concerned an allegedly defective set of headphones, priced at $45? What if Meredith purchased a $350 MyPod and a $45 set of headphones in a single transaction, and only the headphones were defective?

4) Would any of your answers change if Meredith purchased the items at GigaLand with her GigaLand credit card?

5) Assume that Meredith charged the $350 purchase price of the MyPod to her bank credit card. During her discussions with the merchant, she receives and pays part of her credit card bill. As a result of her payment, the outstanding charge for the MyPod is reduced to $120. If Meredith asserts her rights under CCPA § 1666i after partially paying her bill, can she not only avoid paying the $120 balance but also receive a $230 credit from the bank?

Table of Cases

References are to page numbers. Principal cases appear in bold.

Table of Statutes

References are to page numbers.

U.C.C.

U.C.C. *continued*

U.C.C. *continued*

U.C.C. *continued*

U.C.C. *continued*

7-103(a): 193
7-104: 193, 194, 200, 206
7-104(a): 195
7-203: 201
7-204: 200
7-301: 201
7-304(c): 245
7-305: 209
7-309: 200
7-403: 194, 195, 200, 204, 205
7-403(a): 245

7-404: 205
7-501: 195, 202
7-502: 195, 202
7-503: 202
7-504: 202
7-507: 208
7-508: 208

Article 9

9-322(a): 59

Federal Statutes and Regulations

11 U.S.C. §541: 148
11 U.S.C. §542(c): 148
12 U.S.C. §4001 et seq.: 106
15 U.S.C. §1601 et seq.: 247, 291
15 U.S.C. §1602(j): 291
15 U.S.C. §1602(k): 291
15 U.S.C. §1602(l): 291
15 U.S.C. §1602(m): 291
15 U.S.C. §1602(n): 291
15 U.S.C. §1602(o): 291
15 U.S.C. §1640(a): 308
15 U.S.C. §1643: 291, 318
15 U.S.C. §1666: 308, 318, 323
15 U.S.C. §1666a: 308
15 U.S.C. §1666i: 319, 323, 324, 325, 326
15 U.S.C. §1693 et seq.: 247, 249
15 U.S.C. §1693a(6): 249, 254, 267
15 U.S.C. §1693a(9): 265
15 U.S.C. §1693e: 265
15 U.S.C. §1693f: 254, 265
15 U.S.C. §1693m: 254, 266
15 U.S.C. §§5001-5018 (Check 21): 104
49 U.S.C. §20: 193
49 U.S.C. §81 et seq.: 193, 201

12 C.F.R. Part 205 (Regulation E): 247
12 C.F.R. §205.1: 267
12 C.F.R. §205.3: 249, 267
12 C.F.R. §205.6: 262, 266
12 C.F.R. Part 210 (Regulation J): 106, 247, 267
12 C.F.R. §210.1: 106
12 C.F.R. §210.5(a): 60
12 C.F.R. §210.6(b): 60
12 C.F.R. §210.26(e): 268
12 C.F.R. Part 226 (Regulation Z): 290
12 C.F.R. §226.1: 291
12 C.F.R. Part 229 (Regulation CC): 106, 184
12 C.F.R. §229.1: 184
12 C.F.R. §229.2: 184
12 C.F.R. §229.10: 184
12 C.F.R. §229.12: 184
12 C.F.R. §229.13: 184
12 C.F.R. §229.19: 184
12 C.F.R. §229.34: 60
16 C.F.R. §444.2: 30
16 C.F.R. Part 433 (FTC HDC Regulation): 92
16 C.F.R. §433.2: 86

Misc.

International Standby Practices (ISP) 1998: 213
P.E.B. Commentary #11: 49
Restatement (Third), Suretyship and Guaranty §1: 46

Tex. Civ. Prac. & Rem. Code §17.001: 52
Tex. R. Civ. Pro. 31: 52
Uniform Customs and Practice for Documentary Credits (UCP): 212, 213

Index